the *CRUSH* SAT with GROWTH MINDSET

A Complete Program to Overcome Challenges, Unleash Potential and Achieve Higher Test Scores

Paul Koontz & Stephen Tarsitano

 Ulysses Press

Published in the United States by:
Ulysses Press
P.O. Box 3440
Berkeley, CA 94703
www.ulyssespress.com

ISBN: 978-1-61243-844-3
Library of Congress Control Number 2018944080

Printed in Canada by Marquis Book Printing
10 9 8 7 6 5 4 3 2 1

Acquisitions editor: Casie Vogel
Managing editor: Claire Chun
Editor: Shayna Keyles
Proofreader: Jessica Benner
Front cover/interior design and layout: what!design @ whatweb.com
Production: Jake Flaherty, Claire Sielaff
Cover art: © Tancha/shutterstock.com

Distributed by Publishers Group West

To all of our former students,
who showed us that there is no limit to what a person can achieve.

Contents

Chapter 3

Chapter 4

Chapter 5

Chapter 6

Chapter 7

Chapter 8

Chapter 9

Chapter 10

Chapter 11

Chapter 12

Chapter 13

Chapter 14

Chapter 15

Chapter **16**

Chapter **17**

Chapter **18**

Chapter **19**

Chapter **20**

Introduction

Successful people come from all different backgrounds and attain success in all different ways. While their journeys and skill sets might be different, though, they all share one common denominator: growth mindset. Growth mindset is the secret ingredient to success of any kind. It is the belief that through hard work, perseverance, and learning from failures, we can grow our abilities, IQ, and talents.

While working with countless teenagers over the past 13 years, we have learned that your potential can be reached only by taking control of your thoughts and feelings, and by adopting the correct mindset. To attain higher test scores, you must first believe you can attain them. Mindset matters, and once you convince yourself of what is possible, learning our unique and proven strategies will make success on the SAT inevitable.

Crush the SAT with Growth Mindset delivers these educational principles, practices, and mindset trainings in a simple, easy-to-follow program. At the core of this book are the steps to shift your mindset from fixed to growth. Having a growth mindset will transform the way you learn and unlock your true potential. It's our mission to not only prepare you for the SAT so that you earn your dream score, but also change the way you view your own intelligence and abilities.

As you progress through this text, you will undergo great changes that will help you become a more confident, resilient, and intelligent person. Simply by reading and practicing the SAT concepts and mindset training throughout the book, you will build positive habits and adopt the mental outlook necessary for success in all aspects of life.

Who Will Benefit from This Book

This book was written so that *any* student can benefit from it. This is not just for the A+ students, nor is it only for the below-average students. *Crush the SAT with Growth Mindset* is for everyone. If you have fallen behind because you didn't do well in math or English or didn't learn the basic skills in those classes, do not worry. This book will fill in the gaps and rebuild your foundations in both math and English.

This book is structured in such a way that each chapter builds upon the previous chapter. With this format, all students will get the scaffolding they need to develop or affirm their confidence in their SAT ability. Each strategy provided in this book is simple enough for you to use without ever having seen the SAT. As you use them with more frequency and learn how they relate to each other, you will develop new layers of skill that help you exponentially accelerate your growth as a test taker.

In sum, for those who are willing to begin this journey, this book will transform you into a great test taker, capable of accomplishing any goal you set your mind to. Success on the SAT, or any other standardized test, isn't as hard as it seems. *Any* student can score high on the SAT.

How Should I Use This Book?

Crush the SAT with Growth Mindset is structured around three different components. These components are integral to your eventual success on the test, and each chapter will feature each of the three components.

The first component is growth mindset and its transformative power in all aspects of test taking and the SAT. As you work through the book, we will teach you how to develop the correct mindset for success through re-visioning, stress-relieving exercises, visualization, goal setting, and mindfulness training.

The second component is strategy. We will show you how simple SAT prep can be by arming you with our unique, proven strategies for conquering both the English and math sections of the test.

The third component is regular, tiered practice, which will build your confidence, perseverance, and testing stamina, while also rewiring your brain to become accustomed to welcoming challenge.

This structure will allow you to practice incrementally. You'll learn about a mindset strategy, develop skills, see examples, and practice regularly to keep building on what you've learned. Think of your practice as a snowball gaining size and momentum as it rolls down a mountain.

The Layout of the SAT

Although it might seem a bit intimidating right now, over the course of this book, you will learn strategies for conquering both the SAT questions that lay ahead and the mental anxiety that tends to accompany them. The SAT consists of two English, two math, and one optional essay section. The test takes approximately 3 hours, or 4 if you tackle the essay. Below, we've laid out the order and structure of the SAT. Take note of the duration of each section, when it appears, and the important considerations for each category.

Section 1: Reading Test

TIME: 65 minutes

NUMBER OF QUESTIONS: 52

SECTION STRUCTURE: Reading passages with accompanying questions that test critical reading ability.

THINGS TO CONSIDER: This section is not divided up into separate parts, so you must complete it all in one sitting. Building reading stamina and concentration through practice is key.

Section 2: Writing and Language Test

TIME: 35 minutes

NUMBER OF QUESTIONS: 44

SECTION STRUCTURE: Passages with accompanying grammar- or expression-based questions that require you to correct the underlined portion.

THINGS TO CONSIDER: This section tests you on both grammar and content (how the author expresses ideas).

Section 3: Math: No Calculator

TIME: 25 minutes

NUMBER OF QUESTIONS: 20

SECTION STRUCTURE: This section contains 15 multiple-choice questions followed by five grid-in questions.

THINGS TO CONSIDER: Do not worry about not being able to use a calculator, as these questions will not require one. You may be asked to complete some arithmetic, so make sure to practice adding, subtracting, multiplying, and dividing without a calculator. Questions in this section may be about Heart of Algebra, Passport to Advanced Math, or Additional Topics, including geometry.

Section 4: Math: Calculator

TIME: 55 minutes

NUMBER OF QUESTIONS: 38

SECTION STRUCTURE: This section will have 30 multiple-choice questions and 8 grid-in questions.

THINGS TO CONSIDER: While a calculator is not necessary to solve many of these questions, you should use it for most calculations. This will save you time and help you avoid careless mistakes. Questions in this section may be about Heart of Algebra, Data and Analysis, Passport to Advanced Math, or Additional Topics, including geometry.

Section 5: Essay (Optional)

TIME: 50 minutes

NUMBER OF QUESTIONS: 1

SECTION STRUCTURE: Passage with an accompanying essay prompt requiring you to analyze how the author builds his argument.

THINGS TO CONSIDER: This essay is optional, so you have to decide whether you want to do it, which we will cover in Chapter 18. This essay does not ask for your opinion, so do not give it.

Scoring

The SAT is scored on a scale of 400–1600. Your English score is out of 800 and is a combination of your Reading Test and Writing and Language Test, and your math score, also out of 800, is a combination of your No Calculator and Calculator sections. To get your total score, simply add the English and Math scores together to get a score out of 1600. Your essay score is a separate score and does not factor in to your score out of 1600.

What You Will Need for This Book

To complement the practice questions found in this book, we have included College Board Practice at the end of each English and Math section. You will be directed to complete actual SAT questions produced by the creators of the test that correspond to the topic you just learned. You will also be prompted to complete some timed practice, in which you will complete sections under test conditions by timing yourself. These questions and practice tests can be found in *The Official SAT Study Guide,* or online at the College Board website, collegeboard.org. We have provided a link to this website and some additional information on our websites at ZenTestPrep. org and GrowthMindsetU.com. You will also need a calculator, some scrap paper, and a box of pencils.

Warning

Students who complete this book will experience the following side effects:

- Positive attitude

- Improved confidence

- Sense of purpose

- Healthier self-image

- Increased focus

- Greater self-discipline

- Better time-management skills

- Enthusiasm for learning

In some cases, students have experienced a desire to write a paper or work on math problems. A few rare cases have resulted in a love for fractions.

And so it begins, time to embark on the journey. Remember, each day is a step on the path to a new and better you. Good luck!

Chapter **1**

The Great Test Taker

Odds are that you know someone who is really good at taking tests. This student never gets stressed out, is always prepared, and never gets a bad grade. He or she didn't hire a tutor or take a prep class, and yet somehow managed to get an easy 1350 on the SAT. Students like this make it look so simple. Are they born with this ability?

The truth is they are not. No one is born a great test taker. Test-taking savvy is something that you develop over time.

Let's repeat that—there is no great test-taking gene, no special talent that some have and others do not. Sure, some people appear to be inherently great test takers, but that's only because they have developed a positive self-image early in life that gives them confidence in their own intelligence and abilities. These positive attributes help students handle stress and master the skills needed on the test. In reality, though, anyone can work to achieve these traits, and so, anyone can become a great test taker.

This realization about learning is called **growth mindset**. When you have a growth mindset, you believe in your own ability to improve through strategic practice and effort, as well as perseverance in the face of challenges. This belief propels you to achieve whatever goal you set. Learning new topics becomes easier and your skills always improve.

Fixed mindset is the opposite of growth mindset. When you have a fixed mindset, you believe your intelligence and abilities are set in stone. As a result, you give up when challenges pile up or obstacles seem too daunting, blaming yourself and your "low IQ." You believe you are set up for failure.

The good news is that you can change your fixed mindset. Developing a growth mindset and becoming a great test taker are actually quite simple and it all begins with believing in your ability to grow and learn.

What Is Growth Mindset and Why Is It Necessary Today?

We live in a culture obsessed with naming, identifying, measuring, and categorizing. Upper class, middle class, blue collar, white collar, nerd, jock, etc.

In school, it's even worse. From the moment you enter kindergarten until the day you graduate college, you are being assessed, measured, and quantified. You can be in Gifted and Talented or in Remedial English; on Varsity or Junior varsity. You get a GPA, a class rank, grades, standardized test scores, and an IQ. All these titles, categories, and measurements have an effect on us—they change the way we view ourselves, convincing us that we are *born* a certain way, with a certain ability level and intelligence. For most students, this society-perpetuated view of themselves falls far short of their true abilities.

The truth, however, despite what the media says and what our culture dictates, is that inborn ability has very little to do with success. As we stated above, no one is born a great test taker, and no one is born destined for success. Success takes effort and practice.

A growth-mindset approach to learning has the power to make ordinary people extraordinary. Rather than having a fixed mindset, or belief that you are what you are and there is no changing it, you can develop a growth mindset. Here are the core principles of growth mindset:

- You can learn and accomplish anything through effort and practice.

- Embrace challenges and failures as catalysts for growth.

- True transformation is possible through passion and perseverance.

In the upcoming chapters, we will give you the tools to develop a growth mindset and show you how to use it to greatly improve your self-confidence, determination, and overall test-taking ability.

> **"*It takes the most effort to appear effortless.*"**
> —Ben Mitchell

Reading Test: Overview

The SAT rewards you for paying attention in high school. Your British literature, biology, AP environmental, and US history classes will all help you navigate the reading passages, many of which were taken from high-school level sources. The SAT also rewards independent readers by including articles from *The New York Times*, *The Washington Post*, *Scientific American*, *Psychology Today*, and other such publications. It is important to remember that the reading section of the SAT is not an IQ test; in fact, because it rewards independent reading and employs sources from high school reading, adopting a growth mindset and challenging yourself to keep learning and keep reading will greatly benefit you. If you begin to think of each primary source you read in history class, each classic novel in British literature, and each science text in biology as an opportunity to grow your reading ability for the SAT and familiarize yourself with the test content, you will be capitalizing on growth mindset.

The SAT reading passages will either be **long** (one passage with one author or set of authors) or **paired** (two passages with two separate authors discussing the same topic). Most students who have already taken a Preliminary SAT (PSAT) know of the dreaded paired passages. Try to change the way you think of paired passages. Rather than being intimidated by them, see them as challenges that will reward effort and hone your reading skills twice as fast.

The topics on the SAT reading passages may include the following:

- History, typically older historical passages on government, civil rights, or women's suffrage.

- Natural sciences. These will include graphs, technical jargon, and detailed science material. Be ready to read about sea otters, honey bees, DNA, ecosystems, and the like.

- Social sciences, including writing on economics, sociology, psychology, or technology. These passages are typically contemporary (meaning they were published in the last 10 years) and are about on how we interact with our world.

- Eighteenth- to twentieth-century United States or British literature. These tend to be filled with lengthy sentences and archaic vocabulary, and often discuss social class and customs.

- Contemporary world literature. These are excerpts of fiction from countries around the world and typically feature the unique cultures and traditions of those countries.

In this chapter, we will discuss the elements that are most important in the construction of the passage and will be most important for your analyses. By underlining these elements when you encounter them, you will highlight the most important information in the passage—information that deals with the main idea and purpose, which will undoubtedly be asked about in the questions.

Contrast

The SAT reading passages will essentially fall into two major categories: informational or argumentative passages (nonfiction) and literary passages (fiction). Both types of writing are centered on contrast, or the use of opposing viewpoints and character conflict to convey the main idea and theme.

Contrast in Informational and Argumentative Writing

Informational or argumentative passages, which include the natural science passage, history passage, and social sciences passage, are typically structured in a point/counterpoint fashion. This is when an author will quote or paraphrase the viewpoint of another theorist/writer or provide the reader with a commonly held belief, only to refute it and then assert his or her own viewpoint.

This method is highly effective because it is based on the principles of argument. When we argue, we typically argue in point/counterpoint fashion. In this type of argument, we acknowledge the other person's side before making our own groundbreaking point. This takes the power away from an opposing viewpoint by anticipating and poking holes in possible counterarguments.

For example, if your mom forbids you from going to the big party on Saturday night, you don't argue by saying, "You should let me go. Let me go! Please!" Instead, you should first acknowledge your mom's point and the risks about which your mother is mostly concerned. You might say, "Mom, I know you are worried that there will be kids drinking there, and I'm not going to lie to you, there will be. But you know me, and I promise that I won't associate myself with that crowd. I won't drink. And I'll be back by curfew." This is a much better strategy because it anticipates and weakens your mom's counterargument by addressing each of its points. Moreover, it is the structure of almost all informational and argumentative passages on the SAT, so it is crucial to understand.

Look out for this structure on the SAT. To help you find it, underline contrast words, such as *but*, *yet*, *although*, and *however*, and whatever follows them, because these words most likely will precede the author's main point.

Here is an example from the *Appeal for a Sixteenth Amendment* by Elizabeth Cady Stanton, Matilda Joslyn Gage, and Susan B. Anthony:

> "Having petitioned to our law-makers, State and National, for years, many from weariness and despair have vowed to appeal no more; for our petitions, say they, by the tens of thousands, are piled up mid the National archives unheeded and ignored. Yet, it is possible to roll up such a mammoth petition, borne into Congress on the shoulders of stalwart men, that we can no longer be neglected or forgotten. Statesmen and politicians, alike, are conquered by majorities. We urge the women of this country to make now the same united effort for their own rights, that they did for the slaves at the south, when the 13th amendment was pending. Then a petition of over 300,000 was rolled up by the leaders of the suffrage movement and presented in the Senate by the Hon. Charles Sumner. But the leading statesmen who welcomed woman's untiring efforts to secure the black man's freedom, frowned down the same demands when made for herself. Is not liberty as sweet to her as to him? Are not the political disabilities of Sex as grievous as those of color? Is not a civil rights bill that shall open to woman the college doors, the trades and professions—that shall secure her personal and property rights, as necessary for her protection, as for that of the colored man?"

Stanton, Gage, and Anthony use contrast to set up and underscore their two important points: that it is indeed possible to win the right to vote through overwhelming majority, and that it is hypocrisy to secure the "black man's freedom" and deny that same freedom to women. By underlining "yet" in the third sentence and what follows, and "but" toward the end of the passage and what follows, you are clued into these two points. It is much more persuasive and rhetorically effective for Stanton, Gage, and Anthony to first acknowledge what most women are probably thinking so as to not seem out of touch with the reality of the situation. It also primes the audience for their counterpoint, which is that there is still hope for change if *everyone* joins the cause. Later, by highlighting the inconsistency in lawmakers' logic, Stanton, Gage, and Anthony again add power to their argument that women should also be granted the right to vote.

Contrast in Narrative Writing and Fiction

Narratives taken from literature are also fundamentally centered upon contrast. This is because our lives are centered upon contrast, and literature and storytelling are representations of our lives. Contrast in narrative writing comes in the form of conflicts that the character must overcome, and changes or differences in the character's beliefs or thinking.

In fiction, we are introduced to a character and soon discover conflict, contrast, or opposition. We see an obstacle that he or she must overcome, and how that character changes because of it. Remember, most journeys and conflicts are not so much about the actual journey or conflict, but about the change within the character. This change in the character is the vehicle by which many stories typically teach their morals. Because of this, when we read fiction, we should look for words or actions that signify a change of thinking or epiphany in the protagonist (the main character of the story).

Here are some examples discussing scenes from literature:

Example One: In Shakespeare's *Macbeth*, the previously boastful, proud, and tyrannical Macbeth, in his newly stolen kingship, relates his famous soliloquy about the meaninglessness of life. This soliloquy signifies an epiphany and major change within our tragic hero; we see a significant contrast between early Macbeth and later Macbeth. It illuminates one of the most important themes of the play: appearance versus reality. Macbeth's ambition and ultimate usurpation of the throne appear to give his life meaning, but they actually are the cause of his demise, and lead to his proclamation that life is meaningless. His soliloquy also illustrates the irony of Macbeth's actions, with the tragic hero showing remorse for his actions after it is too late to reverse them.

Example Two: In *Pride and Prejudice*, Elizabeth reads a letter from Darcy, a character to whom she is initially in opposition. In this letter, though, Elizabeth learns of Darcy's generosity in helping her sister and the cause for many of his actions. This produces a change in Elizabeth; we see a contrast between what Elizabeth once believed and what she is starting to believe, and through this, we are exposed to an important theme: prejudice and cursory, snap judgment as obstacles to love.

Example Three: In *Lord of the Flies*, Ralph initially finds Piggy, his portly bespectacled friend, to be annoying, dorky, and extremely uncool, but eventually Ralph changes his thinking. He begins to respect Piggy for his intelligence and comes to see him as a true friend. This contrast between Ralph's original thinking and his new thinking illuminates a major theme within the work: that true humanity is born of civilization and learned behaviors.

Takeaway

On the SAT, it's important to know how to look for contrast, as it almost always reveals an important point.

- Contrast words usually precede an important point by the author. Underline them and what immediately follows.

- When you are reading a passage from a work of fiction, underline the parts of the passage that signify a conflict in the story or a change in the protagonist.

- Look for contrast words like *but, despite, although, however, yet.*

PRACTICE

Read the following excerpt from Barack Obama's 2013 inaugural address and underline the contrast words and the sentence that follows. Then write the central point that you think is illuminated through the contrast word.

"… Through it all, we have never relinquished our skepticism of central authority, nor have we succumbed to the fiction that all society's ills can be cured through government alone. Our celebration of initiative and enterprise, our insistence on hard work and personal responsibility, these are constants in our character.

"But we have always understood that when times change, so must we; that fidelity to our founding principles requires new responses to new challenges; that preserving our individual freedoms ultimately requires collective action. For the American people can no more meet the demands of today's world by acting alone than American soldiers could have met the forces of fascism or communism with muskets and militias. No single person can train all the math and science teachers we'll need to equip our children for the future, or build the roads and networks and research labs that will bring new jobs and businesses to our shores. Now, more than ever, we must do these things together, as one nation and one people…"

CENTRAL POINT:

_____

_____

_____

Check Your Work

"… Through it all, we have never relinquished our skepticism of central authority, nor have we succumbed to the fiction that all society's ills can be cured through government alone. Our celebration of initiative and enterprise, our insistence on hard work and personal responsibility, these are constants in our character.

"But we have always understood that when times change, so must we; that fidelity to our founding principles requires new responses to new challenges; that preserving our individual freedoms ultimately requires collective action. For the American people can no more meet the demands of today's world by acting alone than American soldiers could have met the forces of fascism or communism with muskets and militias. No single person can train all the math and science teachers we'll need to equip our children for the future, or build the roads and networks and research labs that will bring new jobs and businesses to our shores. Now, more than ever, we must do these things together, as one nation and one people…"

Through the use of contrast, Obama illuminates his central point: that despite the consistency of character and admirable values of the American people, Americans must also change in response to society and bond together to preserve individual liberty.

Repetition

In almost all writing, readers can identify what is important to the author by noticing what is repeated. Repetition is often underestimated due to its simplicity, but it is nonetheless one of the easiest ways of identifying the author's theme or main idea. Just underline the words, phrases, or ideas that repeat in any passage. This applies to both fiction and nonfiction.

Again, you can look to life to explain why this is an important reading strategy. Take a moment and see what you repeat frequently, in speech, writing, or actions. When you have jotted down these repetitions, you might find a theme in your life, a belief system of your own, or a personal ideology. Pattern recognition is one of the most effective tools for deducing and predicting meaning, and it is one of the most straightforward in its application to the SAT.

Excerpted from Barack Obama's 2013 inaugural address:

"Together, we determined that a modern economy requires railroads and highways to speed travel and commerce, schools and colleges to train our workers.

Together, we discovered that a free market only thrives when there are rules to ensure competition and fair play.

Together, we resolved that a great nation must care for the vulnerable, and protect its people from life's worst hazards and misfortune."

Through his repetition of "Together, we," Obama emphasizes the importance of cooperation and American unity.

Takeaway

- Underline repeated words, images, or ideas and try to find patterns by categorizing what you underline under different headings.

- In fiction, determining why elements repeat will give you the theme. In informational texts, determining why elements repeat will give you the main idea or author's purpose.

PRACTICE

Roger slumped against the sagging shed. His eyes drooped and landed on a small ant struggling beneath a burden far too large for its body. The weak winter sun cast barely visible shadows, making the landscape seem blurry and out of focus.

What do you notice repeats? What words, images, ideas? By analyzing what repeats, you can figure out the tone. The tone is the attitude of the narrator toward the subject matter, and can sometimes be connected to the overall mood, or feeling, of a passage.

Now come up with a tone and a prediction about the character.

Tone: _____

Prediction: _____

Check Your Work

Roger <u>slumped</u> against the <u>sagging</u> shed. His eyes <u>drooped</u> and landed on a <u>small ant struggling</u> beneath a <u>burden far too large for its body</u>. The <u>weak</u> winter sun cast <u>barely visible</u> shadows, making the landscape seem <u>blurry</u> and <u>out of focus</u>.

Hopefully, you picked up on the tone of exhaustion, resignation, and defeat. Perhaps Roger has had enough with life, perhaps he feels overwhelmed, defeated. Here we might say he is surrendering, throwing in the towel.

Mindset Tip

Did you underline the same content as in the section above? Do not get upset or frustrated if you didn't. Comparing the differences between what you underlined and what is underlined above is actually a better opportunity for growth. So, examine the differences, take note of them, and move on with new learning.

Beginnings, Endings, and Topic Sentences

Beginnings and endings are important places in any form of writing. In literature, a beginning sets the tone for the story about to unfold, and the ending can provide resolution, and perhaps a final shift, change, or moral. By comparing the beginning and ending of a literary passage on the SAT, you will be able to identify theme and main idea much more easily. Additionally, in informational passages, beginnings and endings are crucial. Think about how you start and end your essays, your research papers, and any academic writing—you give a thesis in the beginning and restate it in the conclusion. SAT passages are no different. If we search the beginnings and endings of the passages for key points (those ideas that are repeated or given extra emphasis), we will most likely find the author's important ideas.

> "It is a truth universally acknowledged, that a single man in possession of a good fortune, must be in want of a wife. However little known the feelings or views of such a man may be on his first entering a neighbourhood, this truth is so well fixed in the minds of the surrounding families, that he is considered the rightful property of some one or other of their daughters."

In the very first line of the very first chapter of *Pride and Prejudice,* shown above, Austen reveals the main focal point of the novel, marriage. As you can see, beginnings are very important places in literature and often introduce a theme or idea that will carry on throughout the work.

Takeaway

- When answering a question about the author's purpose or main idea, always reread the beginning and ending, as it will enlighten you to the passage's central meaning.

- If rereading the beginning and ending does not provide enough information, reread the topic sentence of each paragraph and see what ideas or points continue throughout the passage.

Extreme Language

Extreme words or phrases are important both because of their rarity and their connection to the theme or author's purpose.

EXTREME IN TONE. When we speak or write, typically the words we exclaim or give a significant tone to are the ones we emphasize the most. If you were to yell, "He's the absolute *worst*!" you are clearly emphasizing that idea. Even without an exclamation ("I *despise* his existence"), we can assume the message is important due to its extreme tone. SAT passages are mostly neutral or slightly positive or negative in tone and, as a result, when we see these extreme tonal statements like *loves* or *hates*, we should underline them because they are both rare and important to the passage's meaning.

EXTREME IN DEGREE. When we generalize, make ultimatums, or group many ideas or people into one statement, we are trying to create emphasis by extending our point so that it seems to encompass much more. Some words that typically mark an extreme ultimatum or generalization are *totally, all, always, never, completely, absolutely, every, entire,* etc. For instance, if you are reading a passage and the author says, "This event changed my entire world," you should probably underline it. If you see a statement in which the author claims, "No one will ever visit his house again," you should underline it. These types of statements are extreme in degree and thus important to the passage's meaning.

"… It is in vain, sir, to extenuate the matter. Gentlemen may cry, Peace, Peace but there is no peace. The war is actually begun! The next gale that sweeps from the north will bring to our ears the clash of resounding arms! Our brethren are already in the field! Why stand we here idle? What is it that gentlemen wish? What would they have? Is life so dear, or peace so sweet, as to be purchased at the price of chains and slavery? Forbid it, Almighty God! I know not what course others may take; <u>but as for me, give me liberty or give me death!</u>"

This speech, Patrick Henry's *Give Me Liberty or Give Me Death,* is exceptional in its rhetoric. Take a look at what we underlined as important. Henry makes use of a great deal of extreme language associated with slavery and imprisonment to communicate his point. He also uses rhetorical questions, exclamations, and contrast to underscore the only action left for the colonies to take. His final line of "give me liberty or give me death!" sums up this rhetorical strategy of contrast to emphasize his point.

Colorful Language

Colorful language is also rare and can tell you a lot about the intent of a passage. This can consist of imagery or metaphorical language that conveys a powerful feeling, such as "awe-inspiring avalanche," or "her eyes glimmered like two sapphires." Both these statements have charged language, language that is not technically "extreme" but that conveys a colorful or powerful emotion or idea. Thus, we would underline this language as well, since it will most likely be important to the passage's meaning.

"… Before this ugly edifice, and between it and the wheel-track of the street, was a grass-plot, much overgrown with burdock, pig-weed, apple-peru, and such unsightly vegetation, which evidently found something congenial in the soil that had so early borne the black flower of civilised society, a prison. But on one side of the portal, and rooted almost at the threshold, was a wild rose-bush, covered, in this month of June, with its delicate gems, which might be imagined to offer their fragrance and fragile beauty to the prisoner as he went in, and to the condemned criminal as he came forth to his doom, in token that the deep heart of Nature could pity and be kind to him."

In this excerpt from Nathaniel Hawthorne's *The Scarlet Letter,* we see important colorful diction, with the prison described as a flourishing "black flower," having "found something congenial in the soil." It is as if the prison grows naturally out of the ground, watered by the fears, hatred, and sins of the community. In direct contrast to this is the "wild rose bush," with its "delicate gems," an important contrast that further highlights the darkness of the town.

Takeaway

- Because of its rarity in academic writing and its significance to character and plot in fiction, extreme or colorful language is always integral to meaning.

- Underline any extreme or colorful language and predict what it might mean for theme, tone, or author's purpose.

Opinion Words and Telling Details

These types of words or phrases are important because they convey the author's opinion and motivation for writing, or the character's opinion and motivation for carrying out certain actions. When we see phrases like "I think," or "I believe," in a passage, we should underline them because they reveal the opinion of the author/narrator or character. Less obvious are words like "should," or "must," which again reveal what the author or character believes.

Telling details are words or short phrases that "tell" something about a character's or author's beliefs, disposition, purpose, or inner conflict. They are important primarily because in a few simple words, a great deal can be revealed about the author's point of view, the theme or moral of a story, and character development. To spot them, ask yourself, *What does this detail reveal?* A clock that is an hour behind in the foyer of a house might not mean much, but several broken clocks in the home an elderly man is telling. This could hint at several possible themes: fear of death, trying to stop the inexorable march of time, or a refusal to acknowledge reality.

> "One day I discovered to my amazement that the popular view grounded in superstition, and not the medical one, comes nearer to the truth about dreams. I arrived at new conclusions about dreams by the use of a new method of psychological investigation, one which had rendered me good service in the investigation of phobias, obsessions, illusions, and the like, and which, under the name "psycho-analysis," had found acceptance by a whole school of investigators."

In the excerpt above, Sigmund Freud explains how "[he] discovered" something new about dreams and that he has "arrived at new conclusions." Both phrases are important because they show a new development in Freud's thinking and lead to a central idea of his paper on the psychology of dreams.

> "4 May.—I found that my landlord had got a letter from the Count, directing him to secure the best place on the coach for me; but on making inquiries as to details he seemed somewhat reticent, and pretended that he could not understand my German. This could not be true, because up to then he had understood it perfectly…"

In this excerpt from Bram Stoker's *Dracula,* the character Jonathan Harker, who is on a journey to meet Dracula for the first time to deal in certain business matters, is asking the landlord of his inn about the letter just sent by the Count. We have underlined the telling details that show the reticence (or inclination to remain silent) of the landlord. We have also underlined the line that shows that the landlord pretended to not know German, even though he understood it perfectly just before. These details are telling and foreshadow something ominous regarding "the Count."

Takeaway

Whenever you see "I think," "I believe," "should," "must," or telling details about the character, make sure you underline them.

PRACTICE

In the passage below, underline opinion words/telling details, repetition, extreme or colorful language, and contrast words and what follows immediately after.

She seemed oblivious to his curious eye. As Thomas, mohawk carefully spiked, looked on from two desks behind her, Eva took notes, and notes, and notes. Her head never came up. The sound of the pencil pressing down hard as she wrote grated on Thomas' ears. But, what about all those tattoos? What about the lip ring, and the middle finger she casually rolled out for the cops who patrolled the school parking lot? Thomas felt his chest tighten. Had he been going about it all wrong? He ever so slightly adjusted his perfect slouch, sitting straighter, paused, and then took out his pencil.

Check Your Work

In this passage we will <u>underline opinion words/telling details</u>, *italicize repetition and extreme or colorful language*, and **bold contrast words and what follows immediately after**.

She seemed oblivious to his curious eye. As Thomas, <u>mohawk carefully spiked</u>, looked on from two desks behind her, Eva took *notes, and notes, and notes*. Her head never came up. The sound of the pencil pressing down hard as she wrote <u>grated on Thomas' ears</u>. **But, what about all those tattoos**? What about the lip ring, and the middle finger she casually rolled out for the cops who patrolled the school parking lot? <u>Thomas felt his chest tighten</u>. **Had he been going about it all wrong**? He ever so slightly adjusted his *perfect slouch*, sitting straighter, paused, and then <u>took out his pencil</u>.

Based on our annotations, if we were to sum up this passage or give its central idea, we would say it is about a character who recognizes a misconception in his judgment and undergoes a dramatic change in perspective upon observing another character. Thomas thought he knew the image he should put forth to gain Eva's attention, but after observing Eva's studiousness, despite her bad-girl façade, realizes he was wrong, feels the discomfort of a perspective shift, and changes.

Mindset Tip

Most students believe that their reading level and reading speed is set for life. This is fixed-mindset thinking. In reality, by following a couple of simple steps, we can grow our reading level. Reading level and speed are made up of two factors: short-term memory and vocabulary. To improve short-term memory, you must consistently practice reading fluidly and actively (we will review active reading in the next chapter). And to improve vocabulary, you must study key vocabulary words in small chunks. At the end of each chapter, learn the vocabulary listed and you will notice your reading level grow.

Vocabulary Words 1–15

On the SAT, vocabulary is tested solely in context and so, to prepare, you must familiarize yourself with the types of words that will appear in the different contexts the SAT provides. With that in mind, we will focus on the following types of vocabulary:

- Literature vocabulary, with a concentration on seventeenth- through early-twentieth-century language

- Natural sciences vocabulary, with a concentration on ecosystems, chemistry, and biology

- History vocabulary, with a concentration on language found in primary sources and relating to abolition, women's suffrage, and the role of government and its relationship to man

- Social sciences vocabulary, focused primarily on sociology and economics

We will combine the study of vocabulary with the study of Latin and Greek roots to develop your ability to break down foreign words and deduce their meaning.

As you study the vocab and make flashcards, try to run the vocabulary through other channels in your brain and through your muscles. What does this mean? Act word outs, create hand gestures, use mnemonic reminders, color code the words, or find images or people that you associate with the words. Do anything that helps you learn!

1) **disposition** (n). a) emotional outlook, attitude, or personality: *A person with a pleasant disposition is good company;* b) an inclination or preference: *Joe has a disposition to gamble.*

2) **distress** (n). a) great pain or sorrow; b) a state of hardship or misfortune: *Bobby was in a state of great distress after he found out his car had been towed.*

3) **vex** (v). to annoy: *Roy was vexed by the seagull that kept hovering around him as he ate his chips on the beach.*

4) **indulgent** (adj). characteristically lenient and likely to permit certain behaviors: *Charles was an indulgent parent, giving in to his child's every whim.*

5) **governess** (n). a woman who is hired to care for and educate children: *Mary Poppins was a governess to a British family.*

6) **peculiar** (adj). a) odd: *Roger wore a peculiar hat that drew much attention and staring;* b) distinct from others; particular; c) belonging characteristically to: *Camouflage is not peculiar to any one species of animal, but rather an attribute of many.*

7) **bear** (v). a) to support; b) to tolerate or withstand: *Peter could not bear the thought of three more hours of pre-season conditioning workouts;* c) to produce, bring about: *The experiment bore many positive results.* d) to go in a certain direction: *The ship was taken along the coast by a south-bearing wind.*

8) **solitude** (n). the state of being alone or secluded: *Superman constructed a fortress of solitude in Antarctica where he could be alone with his thoughts.*

9) **constitution** (n). a) the fundamental principles by which a nation or state is governed: *The Constitution of the United States is the document by which our country is governed;* b) the state of health; the quality of one's immune system: *The boy had a strong constitution and thus never got sick.*

10) **amiable** (adj). friendly: *Puppies are amiable little creatures.*

11) **despondent** (adj). depressed; without hope: *Phillip was feeling despondent after his cat died.*

12) **want** (v). a) to desire; b) lacking: *Jonathan did not lose the student council election for want of friends; he was quite popular.*

13) **gluttony** (n). eating or drinking in excess: *Henry was known for his gluttony; he often ate five burritos in one sitting.*

14) **venture** (v). a) to undertake, carry out, or embark on: *George ventured into the cold wilderness of Alaska;* b) to attempt something that involves risk and uncertainty of the outcome: *It was a risky venture, but the businessman decided to continue with the merger nonetheless.*

15) **analogy** (n). a) a similarity or comparison: *People often make the analogy of dating to fishing, claiming that there are many fish in the sea.*

Latin and Greek Roots 1–6

Another skill that might appear inborn or innate is language ability, but this is again untrue. With a growth mindset, you can develop a formidable understanding of languages. How? Simple: by learning Latin and Greek root words. Root words are the building blocks of words, and while it may seem like your bilingual friend has a much better vocabulary and language ability than you, it is just the work of root words. These root words can be found in Latin, Greek, Spanish, French, Italian, and many other languages. As a result, when we study them, we develop the ability to decode words. Vocabulary begins to make sense. So, after the vocabulary at the end of each English section, learn your roots and watch your language ability grow.

1) A: without (atheist, atypical, anonymous, apathy, amorphous, anomaly)

2) AB: off, away from, apart (abduct, abhor, abolish, abstract, abnormal)

3) AC/ACR: sharp, bitter (acid, acute, acerbic, exacerbate, acrid, acrimonious, acumen)

4) AD: toward, near (adjacent, addict, admire, adhere, advocate)

5) AL/ALI/ALTER: other, another (alternative, alias, alibi, alien, allegory)

6) AM/EM: love (amorous, enamored, amiable, amicable, empathy, emulate)

Math Test: Heart of Algebra Building Blocks

> *"Math has a way of bringing out the resourceful problem-solver in all of us. Creativity, passion, focus, and optimism can all be developed from even the most basic math problems."*

Math on the SAT is a little bit different from math in school. More than anything else, it requires keen problem solving. If you want to be a great test taker, then you need to become a great problem solver.

From Sherlock Holmes to Albert Einstein, Steve Jobs to Katherine Johnson, great problem solvers have certain things in common. Their traits were all developed over time. Just like great test takers, great problem solvers are made, not born. They all approached problem solving with resourcefulness, creativity, and curiosity, and possessed an extensive skill set.

Heart of Algebra is one of the four math areas that the SAT will test you on, and it will be the foundation for your skill set. You will be tested on:

1) Solving linear equations and linear inequalities

2) Solving systems of linear equations

3) Writing linear equations, inequalities, functions, and systems

4) Interpreting the meaning of parts of linear equations and functions

5) Graphing linear equations, inequalities, and systems of equations

While the questions relating to Heart of Algebra will vary, they will all relate to linear equations and functions. Heart of Algebra questions make up about a third of the test, so this is a great opportunity to quickly improve your score while ingraining the habits of a great problem solver.

You will progress through each of these topics as you work through the book, with more advanced concepts appearing later. For now, though, we will begin at the beginning, the building blocks of math. This chapter will teach you the foundational math skills necessary to answer many of the SAT Heart of Algebra questions by explaining the following four topics:

- Substitution

- Simplifying Expressions

- Percents

- Slope

Throughout the upcoming chapters, we will help you ingrain the growth mindset habits that will enable you to conquer any math problem. Here's a preview of how a growth mindset can help unleash your potential.

The equation $y = a(x - h)^2 + k$ represents a parabola with a vertex at (h, k). If the vertex of the parabola is $(2, 4)$ and passes through the point $(3, y)$, what is the value of y if a is equal to -1?

A) 2

B) 3

C) 4

D) 5

Although this question may appear challenging, especially to a beginner, in reality it is not difficult provided you approach it calmly and with an open mind. Answering this question correctly is more about using a combination of problem-solving skills and growth mindset than it is about understanding the intricacies of advanced math topics.

The key to finding the correct answer to this question, and many others, is completing the first step: begin by substituting 2 in for h and 4 in for k, resulting in:

$$y = a(x - 2)^2 + 4$$

Many students will give up before they even begin the first step on a problem like this, not trusting their own ability. Having a growth mindset, though, will enable you to overcome this initial reaction and attempt the problem with an open mind. When you do so, notice what happens. Once you complete the first step, the remaining steps will be revealed to you, and you'll realize that it's just another math problem that you possess the skills to answer. The next step is to substitute -1 in for a, leaving you with:

$$y = -1(x-2)^2 + 4$$

Look at how much easier this question became once numbers were substituted in for variables. The next step will require some creativity: since you know that the graph passes through the point $(3, y)$, you have to figure out what this means. Can you make any connections to something you already know? Think about how coordinate points are written—(x, y) should be familiar to you. This means that x is 3, which can be substituted into the equation, leaving you with $y = -1(3-2)^2 + 4$.

The only variable remaining is y, and with some simple yet careful calculations, you can simplify this to get 3, which is choice (B).

While most SAT math questions will require you to understand a variety of mathematical concepts that you will learn from this book, the purpose of this question is to demonstrate that you will also be rewarded for perseverance, creativity, and most importantly, the belief that you have the ability to correctly answer the question.

Substitution

The previous question was solved using substitution, which is very important because often it is the first step to solving problems. Many questions require substitution to be solved. Let's master the strategy by applying it to some basic math questions.

The word substitute means to replace one thing with another. On the SAT, this relates to substituting numbers, plugging in expressions, and inserting points. Take a look at the problem below:

$$y = 2x - 3$$

If x is equal to 5, what is the value of y?

By replacing the x with 5, the equation can be rewritten as:

$$y = 2(5) - 3$$

This can be simplified to:

$$y = 10 - 3 = 7$$

Order of Operations

When simplifying a mathematical expression, you must follow a certain sequence when performing different operations. In the example above, you multiplied 2 and 5 before subtracting the 3 because multiplication takes precedence over subtraction.

The order of operations will always be the following:

Parentheses → Exponents → Multiplication/Division → Addition/Subtraction

This is where the popular acronym PEMDAS comes from, and you want to be sure you are following it correctly on the SAT.

Here's another example in which understanding order of operations is crucial.

$$y = 12 - 3x^2$$

If x is equal to –2, what is the value of y?

Be careful with this question! You must square the –2 before multiplying by 3.

$$y = 12 - 3(-2)^2$$

$$y = 12 - 3(4)$$

$$y = 12 - 12$$

$$y = 0$$

Anytime a question gives you the value of a variable in an equation, immediately substitute the value in for the variable and rewrite the equation.

The techniques you just learned will be used to solve even the most difficult of questions. An example of this is what we call plugging in answer choices, which is substituting each answer choice into the equation given.

Plugging in Answer Choices

Plugging in answer choices is a great strategy that is entirely based on substitution and PEMDAS. It is very simple and can be used quite often. You start by substituting choice (A) into the equation to see if it makes the equation true. If it doesn't, move on to choice (B). Some students use this all over the test. You can even use this strategy to solve nonlinear equations.

Let's try an example:

$$2x^2 - 8 = 0$$

Which of the following is a solution to the equation above?

A) 0

B) 2

C) 4

D) 8

One by one, substitute each answer choice in for x and see which number would make the equation true.

By plugging in 0 for x, the equation would say $-8 = 0$, which is not true. When you plug in 2 for x, you end up with $0 = 0$, which is true, meaning that choice (B) could be the correct answer. Continue to plug in each answer choice to be sure that your answer is correct. Since choices (C) and (D) do not work, they are not the correct answer, meaning that (B) is the correct answer.

Evaluating Functions

You will also use substitution when evaluating functions, which are quite simple to work with once you understand what they are. On the SAT, the only difference between a function and an equation is the notation. An equation will usually start with y, whereas a function will start with either $f(x)$, $g(x)$, or $h(x)$. Take a look at this function:

$$f(x) = 2x + 6$$

This says "f of x," with f representing the name of the function, x being the input (what you plug in), and $2x + 6$ being the output.

When you evaluate a function, you will substitute a number or expression for the given variable. You will know to use substitution when you are given a number or expression inside the parentheses, such as $f(4)$. This is telling you to replace the variable on the right of the equals sign with the number 4.

Because you are using substitution, you must simplify the expression using PEMDAS. Here is an example of how you would find $f(4)$ using the function from above:

$$f(4) = 2(4) + 6$$

$$8 + 6$$

$$14$$

Here is another example with a different function. Pay attention to the order of operations after substituting for x:

$$\text{If } f(x) = 2x^2 + 6x, \text{ find } f(3).$$

$$f(3) = 2(3)^2 + 6(3)$$

$$2(9) + 18$$

$$36$$

Let's look at a few more examples, including some more advanced applications of substitution.

$$\text{If } g(x) = 3x - 2, \text{ what is the value of } g(2x)?$$

Make sure you replace x with the $2x$, meaning the original x should disappear.

$$g(2x) = 3(2x) - 2$$

$$6x - 2$$

Here is a more challenging question that requires you to evaluate two functions.

$$\text{If } f(x) = 5x - 4 \text{ and } g(x) = 2x + 1, \text{ find } f(g(3)).$$

Start by evaluating the inside function first, or $g(3)$.

$$g(3) = 2(3) + 1 = 6 + 1 = 7$$

Because $g(3)$ equals 7, now you are solving for $f(7)$. Plug in 7 for x to get:

$$f(7) = 5(7) - 4 = 35 - 4$$

$$35 - 4 = 31$$

Below are some practice problems that involve evaluating functions. These are a great opportunity to improve your substitution and order of operations skills.

PRACTICE A

1) If $g(x) = 4x^2 + 5$, find $g(5)$.

2) If $h(x) = 2 - x^2$, find $h(2)$.

3) If $g(x) = 3x - 4$, what is $g(g(2))$?

4) If $f(x) = x^2$ and $g(x) = x + 3$, what is the value of $f(g(4))$?

5) If $h(x) = 4 - 2x$, what is $h(3x)$?

6) Given the functions $f(x) = 3x - 2$ and $g(x) = 2x + 1$, what is value of $f(2) + g(-1)$?

Simplifying Expressions

The second building block to Heart of Algebra is simplifying algebraic expressions, which will later be required to solve or rewrite linear equations. Learning to rewrite complex equations as simpler ones is one of the keys to solving some of the most advanced questions on the SAT. Rather than being intimidated by equations with multiple parts, let's learn some ways to simplify them.

Combining Like Terms

You have most likely found the sum of (added) like terms before. Combining like terms is an integral part of any algebra class. Let's review the rules so we can point out some common traps the SAT sets.

- Like terms have the same variable and exponent. An example of two like terms would be x and $5x$, that when combined would be $6x$. $4x^2$ and $-3x^2$ are also like terms, and when combined, they would be x^2. Another example would be $2y$ and $4y$, which become $6y$. Similarly, the expressions xy and $2xy$ can be combined to $3xy$.

- Constants, or numbers by themselves, are like terms as well. The expression $2x + 4 + x + 1$ can be rewritten as $3x + 5$.

- Even imaginary numbers can be like terms. The same rules as stated above apply, so $4i + 3i$ will become $7i$.

- x^2 and x are *not* like terms since they have different exponents. Variables with different exponents *cannot* be combined.

It will help to circle, underline, or box like terms when combining them. Make sure to circle the sign (+ or −) in front of the term as well.

Take a look at this example, which includes a set of parentheses around two expressions. Do not let parentheses confuse you. In this case, you can simply remove the parentheses and then combine the like terms.

$$\text{Simplify } (x + 2) + (3x - 1).$$

$$x + 2 + 3x - 1$$

$$4x + 1$$

The Distributive Property

The distributive property allows you to multiply one term by each of the terms being added or subtracted inside of parentheses. Here is an example of the distributive property in action.

$$a(b+c) = ab + ac$$

On the SAT, you may need to distribute and combine like terms in the same question. This should be simple, as long as you break it down into two steps: distribute first, then combine the like terms. Always write your steps out and do not rush. Here is an example that contains the imaginary number, i.

$$\text{Simplify } 4(2 + i) + 3(1 - i).$$

$$8 + 4i + 3 - 3i$$

$$11 + i$$

Hint

Questions that contain imaginary numbers may tell you that $i = \sqrt{-1}$. Do not let this throw you off as it is most often not needed to solve these questions.

Distributing a Negative (−)

Distributing a negative is another type of simplifying and is a very important topic. It will most likely appear in some form on the test. In some cases, distributing a negative can turn a subtraction problem into addition. Your first step should always be to distribute any negative that precedes parentheses, which will change the sign of each term inside the parentheses. Try this question.

$$\text{Simplify the expression } (2x - 4) - (-3x + 2).$$

Be sure to distribute the negative to the −3x and the 2.

$$-(-3x + 2) =$$

$$3x - 2$$

You should always rewrite the expression with the negative distributed and without the parentheses. So, we can rewrite it as:

$$2x - 4 + 3x - 2$$

From here, you can just combine like terms and get:

$$5x - 6$$

This cannot be emphasized enough. You *must* remove the parentheses by distributing the negative to each term and then combine like terms.

PRACTICE B

Simplify each.

1) $4x + 3x$

2) $4x + 2 - 3x + 1$

3) $(2 + 3i) + (5 - i)$

4) $2x + xy + 5x - 3xy$

5) $x^2y - 3xy - x^2 + x^2y + xy + x^2$

6) $3(2x - 5) - 4x$

7) $-3(2a - 4) + 2$

8) $(x + 2) - (2x - 4)$

9) $(x^2y - 2xy + y^2) - (2x^2y + 6xy - y^2)$

10) $2(3 - 4i) - (2 - i)$

11) $3(x - 1) - 2(x + 5)$

Mindset Tip

A well-known math principle is that two negatives, when multiplied together, will equal a positive. In this way, math teaches us one of the most important pillars of growth mindset: the power to turn negatives (mistakes, obstacles, stress) into positives (learning, success, growth, and transformation).

Percents

Many questions on the SAT will test you on your understanding of percents. Although percents can have many applications, for right now, let's focus on finding percents of numbers.

While there are many methods for finding percents of numbers, converting the percent to a decimal is the most efficient on the SAT. When changing a percent to a decimal, move the decimal over two places to the left. So, 15% is equal to 0.15. Be careful when converting percents to decimals, especially with a percent like 1.5%, which would be converted to 0.015. Likewise, 115% would be 1.15.

The quickest way to find a percent of a number is to convert that percent to a decimal and multiply the two together.

What is 20% of 80?

Finding 20% of 80 with a calculator is simple, just multiply 0.20 and 80 to get 16. Since the SAT may require you to solve this without a calculator though, another way to solve the problem that allows you to do the math in your head is to first find 10% of 80, which is 8, and then multiply that by 2 to get 16.

Here is another example using percents that is phrased as a word problem.

Ethan bought a car for $22,600. If the sales tax was 7%, how much sales tax did he pay?

$$7\% \text{ of } 22{,}600 = 0.07(22{,}600) = \$1{,}582$$

Advanced Percents: Tax, Tips, and Discounts

Changing a percent to a decimal is also helpful with a tax, tip, or discount. A tax or tip represents an additional part to a bill. To find a total with a tax or tip, start by adding the percentage of the tip or tax to 1. One is equivalent to 100%, which represents the initial bill you are paying. For example, if you were paying a 7% sales tax, the total cost of the bill plus tax would be 107%, or 1.07. You would multiply this number by the original price to get your answer.

Since the sales tax is added to the bill, add 1 to the tax percent as a decimal, and then multiply that number by the original price. Here are some examples.

Lauren purchased a pair of headphones for $45 and paid 7% sales tax. What was the total she had to pay?

$$1.07(45) = \$48.15$$

Frankie wanted to buy a sweatshirt at a local store. It was originally priced at $24.99 but was discounted at 20% off. How much would Frankie pay for the sweatshirt? (Round your answer to the nearest cent.)

A discount means you are reducing the price, so subtract the percent from 1 and multiply by the original price.

$$(1 - 0.20)(24.99)$$

$$0.80(24.99) = \$19.99$$

PRACTICE C

Find each percent. Round each decimal to the nearest tenth.

1) 72% of 125

2) 118% of 74

3) 2.5% of 44

4) 10% of 80 (No Calculator)

5) 27% of 100 (No Calculator)

6) How much would you pay if your bill was $20 and the tax was 7%?

7) A shirt you wanted to buy was $40 with a 15% discount. How much would you pay to buy the shirt?

Slope

Slope is an essential topic on the SAT and a major part of any math class, including calculus. Understanding slope is a prerequisite skill to answering a variety of SAT questions.

The slope (m) is the measure of the rate of change. Think of it as the steepness of the line.

$$\text{SLOPE} = m = \text{RATE OF CHANGE} = \frac{y_2 - y_1}{x_2 - x_1} \text{ or } \frac{y_1 - y_2}{x_1 - x_2}$$

If you are given two points, use the slope formula.

What is the slope of the order pairs (3, –2) and (1, 8)?

It will help to label the points (3, –2) and (1, 8) to start.

$$x_1 \ y_1 \quad x_2 \ y_2$$

Simply substitute the numbers into the slope equation.

$$\frac{y_2 - y_1}{x_2 - x_1} = \frac{8 - (-2)}{1 - 3} = \frac{10}{-2} = -\frac{5}{1} = -5$$

Working with Fractions

Some questions involving slope may include fractions. Avoid the frustrations that fractions can bring by seeing them as opportunities to increase your intelligence. Adding and subtracting fractions can get a bit complicated, because you need to have a common denominator to do so. But if the denominators are the same, just add or subtract the numerators and keep the denominator the same. Let's try the example below.

The points $\left(\frac{1}{3}, -2\right)$ and $\left(\frac{4}{3}, 5\right)$ are on the same line, what is the slope of the line?

$$\frac{5 - (-2)}{\frac{4}{3} - \frac{1}{3}}$$

Since the numerator is 5 minus –2, it becomes 5 plus 2, which is 7. There are fractions in the denominator $\left(\frac{4}{3} - \frac{1}{3}\right)$, but since their denominators are the same, you can subtract the numerators of each fraction.

$$\frac{7}{\frac{3}{3}}$$

Simplify $\frac{3}{3}$ to 1, so the final answer will be $\frac{7}{1}$, or just 7.

Slope on a Graph

The slope of a line can be classified four ways: positive, negative, zero, or undefined.

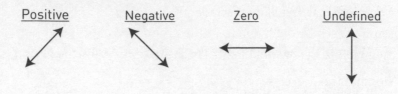

Slope can easily be found on the graph by calculating the rise over the run from one point to another. The rise is the number of units you count up or down (y), and the run is the number of units you count to the right (x). Always be aware of the units on each axis, as they do not necessarily increase by one each time.

When answering questions about slope, it will be helpful to know the basics about the coordinate plane that are shown below.

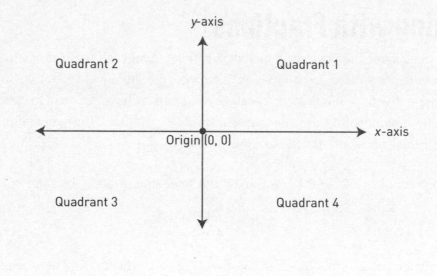

Hint

Drawing a graph is an awesome idea if the question does not provide one. However, make sure you do not waste time doing so. You want the graph to be neat and organized but be sure to do it quickly; you will not be scored on how perfect your graphs are.

PRACTICE D

1) What is the slope of the points (2, 4), (1, 7)?

2) What is the slope of the points (–1, 6), (2, 3)?

3) A line on a graph passes through quadrants 1, 2, and 3. What type of slope would that line have: positive, negative, zero, or undefined? (It may help to draw the graph.)

4) What is the slope of the line shown below?

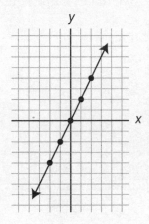

5) If a line passes through the points $\left(1, \frac{1}{2}\right)$ and $\left(3, \frac{5}{2}\right)$, what is the slope?

Mindset Tip

Now that you understand slope, let's see how it applies to your mindset. A student with a fixed mindset believes that their abilities are constant, or flat, while a student with a growth mindset believes their abilities can be developed or improved with time.

One of the main focuses of the growth mindset is incremental improvement. This means that you are always improving, always learning new things. Even small steps are important. Once a student adopts the growth mindset, their ability immediately starts to increase.

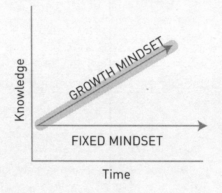

PRACTICE E

1) If $x = 4y + 6$, what is the value of $2x - 8y$?

2) Let r be equal to $3x$, s be equal to $5x$, and t be equal to $10x$. If $r + s + t$ is equal to ax, what is the value of a?

A) 8

C) 15

B) 13

D) 18

3) Let $r = 2x + 3$ and $v = x^2 - 4$. Which of the following is the sum of r and v?

A) $x^2 - 2x + 1$

C) $x^2 + 2x - 1$

B) $x^2 + 5x$

D) $x^2 + 2x + 1$

4) If $a = x^2 + 3$ and $b = 3x - 1$, which of the following is equivalent to $a + b$?

A) $x^2 + 5$

C) $x^2 - x - 2$

B) $x^2 + 5x$

D) $x^2 + 3x + 2$

5) Which of the following is a solution to $\sqrt{x-3} - 2 = 6$?

A) 7

C) 19

B) 11

D) 67

6) Based on the functions below, which of the following is equal to $2(f(x)) + g(x)$?

$$f(x) = 2x + 4$$

$$g(x) = 3x - 2$$

A) $7x + 6$

C) $5x + 6$

B) $7x + 2$

D) $5x + 2$

7) Mike's bill was $15, and he wanted to pay the server a 20% tip. Which of the following expressions could be used to find the total amount needed to be paid?

A) 0.20(15)

C) 0.15(20)

B) 1.20(15)

D) 1.15(20)

8) Steven purchased a pair of jeans for $32, which included a sales tax of 8%. Which of the following equations could be used to find the original price of the jeans?

A) $1.8x = 32$

C) $1.08x = 32$

B) $0.8x = 32$

D) $1.08 = 32x$

9) What is the sum of the expressions $(2x - 3)$ and $2(-x + 2)$?

10) Which of the following represents the slope of a line that passes through the origin and the point (4, 3)?

A) $\dfrac{4}{3}$

C) $-\dfrac{4}{3}$

B) $\dfrac{3}{4}$

D) $-\dfrac{3}{4}$

Answers

Practice A (page 31)

1) 105

2) −2

3) 2

4) 49

5) $4 - 6x$

6) 3

Practice B (page 34)

1) $7x$

2) $x + 3$

3) $7 + 2i$

4) $7x - 2xy$

5) $2x^2y - 2xy$

6) $2x - 15$

7) $-6a + 14$

8) $-x + 6$

9) $-x^2y - 8xy + 2y^2$

10) $4 - 7i$

11) $x - 13$

Practice C (page 36)

1) 90

2) 87.3

3) 1.1

4) 8

5) 27

6) $21.40

7) 34

Practice D (page 39)

1) −3

2) −1

3) Positive

4) $\dfrac{2}{1}$ or 2

5) $\dfrac{\frac{4}{2}}{2} = \dfrac{2}{2} = 1$

Practice E (page 40)

1) 12

2) D

3) C

4) D

5) D

6) A

7) B

8) C

9) 1

10) B

UNTIMED COLLEGE BOARD PRACTICE

Complete the following College Board practice problems from College Board's *The Official SAT Study Guide* or online at www.collegeboard.org. Review answers after completing.

Test 1, Math: No Calculator, #2, 5, 12

Test 2, Math: Calculator, #10, 26, 37

Test 3, Math: Calculator, #5, 6

Test 4, Math: No Calculator, #4, 9

Test 4. Math: Calculator, #4, 8

Chapter **2**

The Value of Growth Mindset

An important part of success is building the right habits in the beginning and applying them to every task, no matter how small or seemingly insignificant it may be. These habits and strategies will eventually give you the ability to tackle the bigger challenges. Taking the time to create the right habits is important. In fact, this is one of the things that separates self-made millionaires from others—they make an effort to create good habits, which leads them down a path of success.

Growth Mindset Millionaires

Interestingly, the majority of millionaires in America are self-made. How does one become a self-made millionaire? If you look at the experiences of the self-made super rich, such as Warren Buffett, Bill Gates, and Oprah Winfrey, certain unmistakable patterns emerge. These individuals value lifelong learning, perseverance, work ethic, and a dream-big attitude over innate ability.

Thomas C. Corley, author of *Rich Habits*, spent five years studying the habits of 177 self-made millionaires. These practices separate them from ordinary people:

- Read books to learn

- Wake up early

- Think positively

- Keep goals in sight

- Exercise

Corley understood that to become a millionaire, one must first adopt the correct habits. Each of the above actions can be done by any person; thinking positively, learning constantly, and keeping goals in sight are core growth-mindset principles. Following these practices, *anyone* can become a millionaire. In short, wealth creation is centered on adopting the correct mindset and building the right habits. By changing our mindset, we drastically improve our chances of success in any endeavor.

The Chicago Cubs: A Growth Mindset Success Story

The Chicago Cubs had gone without a championship for over 100 years. The team suffered from a toxic fixed-mindset culture: they shared a belief that there was some curse that the players could do nothing about, which continually sabotaged their chances of winning. This type of mindset breeds a sort of helplessness in the players. They felt powerless to change their reality, and that powerlessness eventually seeped into their actions on the field—their pitches, their hits, everything.

In 2015, they got a new manager, Joe Maddon, and in 2016, the Chicago Cubs won the World Series. What did Joe Maddon do that was special enough to stop a 100-year-long losing streak?

Well, here is what he didn't do. He didn't recruit countless superstars to his baseball team. He also didn't come up with some ingenious batting lineup, invent a new unhittable curveball, or feed them some super-duper energy drink.

Joe Maddon changed the culture of the Chicago Cubs from that of a fixed mindset to a growth mindset. He convinced the players to believe in their ability to win through hard work. Here are the core principles he preached:

- It takes zero talent to work hard every day.

- No one should be afraid of making mistakes.

- Don't worry about the result, focus on the preparation.

- Always be positive.

- Learn from one year and apply it to the next.

- Improve yourself and improve your team.

The Growth Mindset–Grade Connection

It's been proven that when students adopt a growth mindset, their grades are more likely to improve over time. In a 2007 study, researcher Carol Dweck examined seventh and eighth graders' beliefs about intelligence and how those beliefs correlated with their actual grades in mathematics. She found that the students who believed that "intelligence [was] malleable [experienced an] upward trajectory in grades over two years at junior high school, while students who believed that intelligence was fixed, experienced a flat trajectory in their grades." In essence, growth mindset caused grades to increase. Grade increase was not the only positive consequence of a growth mindset. Those students who had a growth mindset were much more likely to apply their effort toward "challenging tasks that [promoted] skill acquisition and [overcoming] difficulty."[1]

Hopefully, you are starting to see a pattern here. Every successful person believed they could achieve their goals through practice, effort, positivity, and learning from failure. This is growth mindset. It is what makes champions and what builds million-dollar fortunes. It is also what will make you conquer the SAT and attain the score you are seeking.

Reading Test: The Reading Method

Active reading is very different from reading on a beach or before bed. Active reading involves annotating, taking notes, and asking questions while you read. It is a habit of any successful person: reading with purpose to achieve your goals.

Think of active reading as a conversation between you and the text. You are not just passively absorbing the words on a page, but engaging with the text by underlining it, asking questions about it, and mining for information relevant to your specific tasks. On the SAT, this means filtering out unnecessary information, underlining as you read, not being distracted by technical jargon, and reading older, long-winded literature fluidly.

Below, we lay out an eight-step reading method, which has simple yet comprehensive steps to follow while reading a passage.

1) READ THE BLURB FIRST. The blurb is the introductory material that comes immediately before the passage. This material usually provides the author, title of the work from which the passage is excerpted, copyright, and often a general summary of what the passage will be about. As a result, reading this first can aid your understanding of the passage and clue you in to key ideas.

For example, you might read an introductory blurb that tells you the passage is a speech from 1792 by Elizabeth Cady Stanton at the Seneca Convention for women's suffrage. Even if you just remembered a few lessons from history, this information should allow you to predict that the passage might be about women and their rights and that the author will most likely be for women's rights.

2) READ FOR A GENERAL UNDERSTANDING OF THE PASSAGE. Try to determine PPTT—the **P**oint of view, **P**urpose, **T**one, and **T**heme—without getting bogged down in minor details. With paired passages, read passage 1 first then answer the questions that pertain to it. Then, when the questions prompt you to move on, read passage 2.

The most important aspects to understand about any passage are the reasons (purpose) the author wrote it, the tone of the author, and what point of view the author or character holds. These "author purpose" questions will always be asked, and knowing an author's point of view will help guide you to the correct answer for each question. With literature passages, instead of identifying purpose, you must determine theme.

3) ANNOTATE THE PASSAGE. Underline these items (which you read about in Chapter 1) as you come across them:

- contrast words and what immediately follows them

- repeated words, opinion words, or telling details

- colorful or extreme language

These words and phrases are the key to unlocking the passage's meaning and will also help you navigate the passage quickly when you are directed to find information to answer questions. Underlining as you read also keeps you engaged in the passage so you stay focused and do not drift off or space out while reading.

4) READ FLUIDLY. Reading fluidly means reading the passage without stopping and starting too often as you progress through the passage.

As stated in Chapter 1, your reading level is determined by two factors: level of vocabulary and short-term memory. This means that the more words you know and the more you can remember, the higher your reading level. The SAT is filled with passages written at a high level, with tough vocab and long winding sentences. When you segment your reading by stopping too often, you forget where the sentence began, thus impeding your comprehension and lowering your reading level.

5) LOOK WHO'S TALKING. Underline speaker changes in the passage.

You can be the smartest student in the world, but if you confuse Author X's point with Author Y's, or Author X's point with that of an expert being quoted, you will get the question wrong. Most passages have multiple opinions stated; that is the nature of academic writing.

6) ALWAYS, ALWAYS, ALWAYS GO BACK TO THE PASSAGE TO FIND THE ANSWER. This test is not about being creative. It is not about being imaginative. It is about thinking critically and methodically going back to find the evidence.

7) PREDICT THE ANSWER. Before your look at the answer choices, predict what you think the answer might be.

If this test were a short answer test without multiple choices to choose from, it would be much easier. The answer choices on the SAT are purposefully designed to be deceptive. The best defense against falling into a wrong-answer trap is to have a prediction in your head before you look at the answer choices.

8) ELIMINATE WRONG ANSWERS. More often than not, you will arrive at the correct answer by eliminating all the wrong answers. All savvy test takers eliminate answer choices as they go. This also reduces the possibility of making careless errors. Your test book should look like the writings of a madman, with cross-outs, arrows, and underlines.

Mindset Tip

Before you begin your first full practice passage, remember the first habit of self-made millionaires: they read books to learn. As you read this upcoming passage, read actively and genuinely learn from it. This level of focus will make the questions that follow a breeze.

PRACTICE

1 While many Americans associate the Park Service with the preservation of pristine natural places, few realize that almost two-thirds of the national
5 parks—Gettysburg, San Antonio Missions, Valley Forge, the Frederick Douglass House, and Little Bighorn, to name a few—were designated specifically to preserve an important
10 aspect or moment in our nation's history.

Moreover, the Service is directed by law to assist with historic preservation beyond park boundaries—on all federal 15 lands, on tribal reservations, and in the public and private sectors. Its responsibilities include administering the National Historic Landmarks program, which has designated more 20 than 2,300 nationally significant properties since 1935, and the National Register of Historic Places, which now includes more than seventy thousand sites. The Service provides matching 25 grants to restore public and privately owned historic places through the Historic Preservation Fund. The NPS-administered Historic Preservation Tax Incentives program, which encourages

30 the preservation of historic places in town and city centers, has accounted for more than $23 billion in private investment nationwide since 1976. In many ways, the National Park Service is
35 our nation's Department of Heritage.

Our historical heritage, however, faces important challenges in the twenty-first century. Many sites and structures have been degraded by neglect and
40 vandalism; others are at risk because of inadequate budgetary support or insensitive national, state, and local policies. Development encroaches upon our battlefields. Historic neighborhood
45 schools are abandoned. Prehistoric archaeological resources are looted or vandalized. Suburban sprawl consumes historic farmsteads and rural landscapes. Acid rain eats at cemetery
50 stones, memorials, and monuments.

America may be losing something else—its historic literacy. Of some 556 seniors surveyed at 55 of the nation's top colleges and universities, only 60%
55 placed the American Civil War in the correct half of the nineteenth century. Only 34% identified George Washington as the American general at the Revolutionary War battle
60 of Yorktown—37% thought the general was Ulysses S. Grant. At 78% of the institutions polled, no history whatsoever was required as part of the undergraduate program.

65 "It is not surprising," states the report by the American Council of Trustees and Alumni, "that college seniors know little American history. Few students leave high school with an adequate
70 knowledge of American history, and even the best colleges and universities do nothing to close the knowledge gap." As historian David McCullough observed in the same report, "We are
75 raising a generation of young Americans who are historically illiterate."

At the same time, another study found that many Americans not only feel a strong connection to their past but hold
80 historic sites and museums to be their most trustworthy sources of historical information, above movies, television, college professors, and even personal accounts from relatives.

85 The study of our nation's history, formal and informal, is an essential part of our civic education. In a democratic society such as ours, it is important to understand the journey of liberty and
90 justice, together with the economic, social, religious, and other forces that barred or opened the ways for our ancestors, and the distances yet to be covered. Visits to historic places,
95 whether managed by the Park Service or by others, allow us to take the measure of our history in immediate ways. Parks should be not just recreational destinations but

100 springboards for personal journeys of intellectual and cultural enrichment.

The Park Service must ensure that the American story is told faithfully, completely, and accurately. The story
105 is often noble, but sometimes shameful and sad. In an age of growing cultural diversity, the Service must continually ask whether the way in which it tells these stories has meaning for all our
110 citizens. The Service must look anew at the process and make improvements. For example, the relationship between environmental and human history should be seamlessly presented as
115 inseparable chapters of our life on this planet.

To the National Park Service, the challenge is critical. Our nation's history is our civic glue. Without it, our national
120 character is diminished.

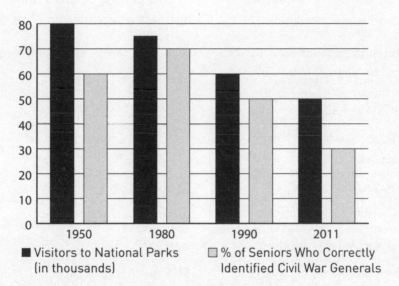

- ■ Visitors to National Parks (in thousands)
- ☐ % of Seniors Who Correctly Identified Civil War Generals

1) As used in line 3, the word "pristine," most nearly means

A) Perfect

B) Unspoiled

C) Primeval

D) Cleanly

Hint

Staying close to the author's point of view and tone will guide you to the correct answer.

2) The Park Service, as part of its duties, does all of the following EXCEPT

A) Provide matching grants for restoration

B) Administer the National Historic Landmarks program

C) Help preserve federal lands

D) Work with the Department of Heritage to encourage historic literacy

3) What is the primary purpose of paragraph 3?

A) To emphasize the diversity of change in the twenty-first century

B) To enumerate the many challenges facing America's historic heritage

C) To petition the reader to join the National Park Service

D) To condemn suburbia for consuming historic farmsteads and rural landscapes

4) In paragraph 4, the author uses all of the following rhetorical strategies EXCEPT

A) Relate a personal anecdote

B) Cite statistical evidence

C) Quote an expert

D) Make a prediction

5) According to the passage, what do Americans feel is the most trustworthy source of historical information?

A) Historic sites and museums

B) Personal accounts from relatives

C) College professors

D) Television and movies

6) What best describes the development of the passage?

A) The introduction of a commonly held view followed by a rebuttal by the author

B) The discussion of a dire need followed by a recommendation from the author

C) A careful analysis of a system and what makes it work

D) An extended comparison between two seemingly opposed principles

7) What is the rhetorical effect of repeating the word "our," in paragraph six?

A) It emphasizes the author's distance from his country

B) It conveys the author's belief that the American people are entitled to pristine parks

C) It emphasizes the author's belief that all Americans share a part in preserving and learning the country's history

D) It reinforces the idea that the author is an American and filled with national pride

8) As used in paragraph 6, line 100, what does the phrase "springboard for personal journeys" refer to?

A) A beginning for self-reflection and introspection

B) A tool used to enhance intellect and build knowledge

C) A recreational destination that incorporates activities

D) A catalyst to historical and cultural exploration

9) As used in paragraph 7, line 103, what does the phrase "American story" most likely refer to?

A) The victories and triumphs of America

B) The promise of the American Dream

C) The colorful history of America

D) The democratic ideals of America

10) Based on the passage, it can be reasonably inferred that the author…

A) Is a history professor at a college and wants others to value history

B) Is supportive of Americans knowing their historical heritage

C) Is retired from the National Park Service

D) Disdains the "historically illiterate"

11) What is the central purpose of the passage?

A) To persuade the public to visit more historic landmarks

B) To criticize those who do not have an understanding of their own history

C) To volunteer different ideas for renovating national parks and federal lands

D) To encourage people to see the importance of national parks to historic legacy

12) Which choice provides the best evidence for the answer to the previous question?

A) Lines 27–31: "The NPS-administered Historic Preservation Tax Incentives program, which encourages the preservation of historic places in town and city centers"

B) Lines 36–38: "Our historical heritage, however, faces important challenges in the twenty-first century"

C) Lines 74–76: "We are raising… historically illiterate."

D) Lines 102–104: "The Park Service must ensure that the American story is told faithfully, completely and accurately."

13) Based on the information in the graph, which year most supports the author's argument that visitation to National Parks will further historical literacy in America?

A) 1990

C) 1980

B) 2011

D) 1950

14) Based on the passage, one reasonable inference for the greater disparity in the year 2016 between the number of visitors to national parks and the percentage of college seniors correctly identifying the generals of the Civil War is…

A) The seniors were more lax with their studies toward the end of the year

C) History classes were not a requirement for many undergraduate colleges

B) Certain public universities lost funding in 2016 due to an economic recession

D) The American Council of Trustees banned history education

Answers

1) Answer B, Unspoiled, is the correct answer. Answers A and D, though common meanings of the word pristine, are too extreme or awkward in this context and do not consider the idea that nature is untouched by man. Answer C is off topic.

2) Answer D is the correct answer, because the Department of Heritage is a figurative term. Evidence for Answer A was stated in lines 24–25; B, in lines 16–17; and C, in lines 12–15.

3) Answer B is the correct answer. Answer A is too general; it does not discuss the National Parks Service specifically. Answer C is inaccurate, as the author does not try to petition the reader to join the NPS. Answer D is incorrect because it is too extreme; suburban sprawl is not the purpose of this paragraph.

4) Answer A is the correct answer; the author does not relate any personal anecdotes in the passage. The author does cite statistics, quote the expert David McCullough, and predict that "America may be losing something else—its historic literacy."

5) Answer A is correct; Answers B, C, and D are all opposite from what is stated in the passage.

6) The author does not provide a counter argument to his claims, investigate the inner workings of the National Parks Service, or compare the NPS to another body. Thus, Answer B is correct.

7) "Our" refers to the collective responsibility of Americans to preserve and learn from the country's history, so Answer C is correct. The author counts himself as an American, so A is incorrect. Answer B is incorrect because it is off topic, and Answer D is incorrect because it does not explain the author's purpose.

8) Answer D is correct because it directly relates to the theme of the passage. Answers A and C are incorrect because they rely on unrelated definitions of the words "personal" and "springboard," while Answer B is incorrect because it is too general in scope.

9) Answer C is correct because it relates directly to the theme of America's history. Answer A is an extreme example, so it is incorrect. Answer B is incorrect because it is an assumption based on an idiom, "The American Dream," and answer D is an assumption about the author's ideas.

10) Answer A incorrectly cites information from the passage—the author mentions a professor, but is not one. Answer C is an assumption, and Answer D is too extreme in tone. Thus, Answer B is correct.

11) Answer A is too narrow in scope: the passage addressed many other themes. Answer B is too extreme in tone. Answer C is also incorrect, because the author did not provide any ideas. Thus, Answer D is correct.

12) Answer D is correct. Answers B and C only partially cover the author's point, while Answer A is too narrow in focus.

13) Answer C is correct; on the graph, the two bars have the closest correlation in 1980.

14) Answers A and B are both assumptions that cannot be proven from either the passage or the graph. Answer D is too extreme and is off topic from the passage. Thus, Answer C is correct.

Mindset Tip

When reviewing answers, it does not matter how many questions you got right. Don't worry about the result right now; focus on the process. Did you apply the strategies? Did you read actively and fluidly, underline key points, note author purpose, and skip technical jargon? Did you see the wrong answers as opportunities to learn? If you did all or just some of these things, you are on your way to success.

Vocabulary Words 16–30

16) **empathy** (n). the identification with the feelings of another: *One of the things that made Joya an exceptional social worker was her empathy, which allowed her to deeply connect with her clients.*

17) **disparage** (v). to mock or make fun of: *Jack was a mean boy who often disparaged his fellow classmates.*

18) **yearn** (v). to have a strong desire; to long for: *Melanie yearned for a puppy.*

19) **resignation** (n). a) a formal notification of one's quitting of office or position; b) an accepting, unresisting attitude or state, etc.; submission; acquiescence: *After learning that his cancer was terminal, Pete went about life with resignation.*

20) **restraint** (n). a) a restriction or limit to freedom; b) holding back of feelings and/or behavior: *After Tim insulted him, Reggie showed great restraint, refusing to be goaded into a fight.*

21) **tremulous** (adj). timid and fearful: *Mary was tremulous in the face of the intimidating headmaster at her school.*

22) **portentous** (adj). ominous; warning; threatening: *Portentous, ominous black clouds seemed to amass on the horizon.*

23) **uncouth** (adj). ill-mannered, uncivilized, coarse, crude: *Eating with your mouth open and your elbows on the dinner table is uncouth.*

24) **avid** (adj). passionate, enthusiastic: *Andrew was an avid reader, which helped greatly on the SAT.*

25) **disdain** (v). to look upon or treat with contempt; despise; scorn: *Claire disdained doing housework, and thus put it off to the last minute.*

26) **sustenance** (n). means of sustaining life; nourishment, as in food and water: *After being stranded in the forest for several days, Patrick was in desperate need of sustenance.*

27) **cache** (n). a hiding place, especially one in the ground, for ammunition, food, treasures, etc.: *The thieves often visited their cache of stolen jewels to admire their handiwork.*

28) **ephemeral** (adj). short-lived, brief, fleeting: *The life of a fruit fly is ephemeral, often lasting only a couple of days.*

29) **egotism** (n). selfishness, self-centeredness, boastfulness: *The lawyer was often defeated by his own egotism; judges were turned off by his arrogance.*

30) **ccase** (v). to stop, halt, end: *After the company went bankrupt, all manufacturing ceased.*

Latin and Greek Roots 7–12

7) AMB: both, more than one (ambiguous, ambivalent, ambidextrous)

8) ANIM: life, mind, soul, spirit (animosity, animate, magnanimous)

9) ANTHRO: man, human (anthropology, android, misanthrope, philanthropy, anthropomorphic)

10) ANTI: against (antidote, antiseptic, antipathy)

11) APT/EPT: skill, ability (aptitude, adept, inept, apt)

12) ARCH/CRACY: governing body, leader, chief (monarchy, democracy, anarchy)

Math Test: Building Great Habits with Linear Equations

Linear equations are a great example of a starting point for building a good habit. If you want to be able to hit the game-winning home run, you first must learn to make solid contact off a tee. Similarly, in algebra, by learning to solve linear equations and building the right habits, you put yourself in a position to answer those intimidating questions the test will inevitably throw at you.

In this section, we are going to learn to solve linear equations, which are the bread and butter of algebra. The key to solving any equation is to get the variable you're solving for alone on one side of the equals sign by moving everything else away from that variable. To move something from one side of the equals sign to the other, you perform the inverse operation to cancel it out. For example, the inverse of addition is subtraction and the inverse of multiplication is division. To solve the equation $x + 2 = 5$, we would move the 2 by subtracting it from the left side.

No matter what type of equation you are solving, whatever you do to one side you must do to the other. In the equation above, since we subtracted two from the left we also had to subtract two from the right, which makes x equal to 3. Let's look at an example that demonstrates how to solve a two-step equation.

In the equation $2m - 4 = 6$, what is the value of m?

To solve this equation, you must first add 4 to both sides to eliminate the four, which leaves:

$$2m = 10$$

The second step to solving for m would be to simply divide both sides by two.

$$\frac{2m}{2} = \frac{10}{2}$$

$$m = 5$$

Since the variable m has been isolated on one side of the equals sign, the problem has been solved.

Variables on Both Sides

At some point, you will have to solve an equation with variables on both sides.

What is the value of x in the equation below?

$$3x - 1 = 6x - 3$$

Solving this equation will require multiple steps, and while there are different approaches, it's best to start by subtracting the $3x$ from both sides of the equation. If there are variables on both sides, start by moving the variable with smallest coefficient. The word coefficient refers to the number in front of the variable.

$$3x - 1 = 6x - 3$$
$$-3x \qquad -3x$$

$$-1 = 3x - 3$$

After completing the first step, you are left with a two-step equation that is just like the previous example, so you can solve it by first adding 3 to both sides and then dividing by 3. When adding –1 and 3, be sure to take the time to avoid a careless mistake.

$$-1 = 3x - 3$$
$$+3 \qquad +3$$

$$2 = 3x$$

$$\frac{2}{3} = \frac{3x}{3}$$

Make sure you divide by the correct number. Since the 3 is with the x, divide both sides by 3.

This becomes $\frac{2}{3} = x$, which can also be expressed as:

$$x = \frac{2}{3}$$

Building the Correct Habits

Whether you have found the previous examples to be easy or challenging doesn't matter. Either way, you can start to build the correct habits needed for long-term success. Here are some great habits to work on:

- Focus on the process; complete each step by writing it out.

- Check to see if your answer makes sense by plugging it back in to the original equation.

- Be on the lookout for more efficient ways of solving.

- Make connections to previously learned topics.

Let's try some practice problems. All the equations below are similar to what you will see on the SAT and may require skills learned in the previous chapter.

PRACTICE A

Solve each equation.

1) $2x + 8 = 10x$

2) $2x - 1 = x + 6$

3) $4(x - 2) = 18$

4) $x + 2 = 2x - 8$

5) $(3x - 4) - (2x - 5) = 5$

6) $2x + 4 = x$

7) $(2x + 4) + (3x - 1) = 13$

8) $2x + 4 + x - \frac{1}{2} = 5\frac{1}{2}$

9) $5a = 6a - 2$

10) $5b + 4 = 4b$

Solving Linear Equations with Fractions

At some point, you will encounter questions that require you to work with fractions. While they are not as simple as working with integers, they should not be something that you are afraid to do.

You know how to add and subtract fractions with common denominators, but what about when there is no common denominator and you have to make them the same? Here is an example:

Solve for x.

$$x - \frac{1}{3} = \frac{3}{4}$$

To solve this equation, you simply need to move the $\frac{1}{3}$ over to the right by adding $\frac{1}{3}$ to both sides.

$$x - \frac{1}{3} + \frac{1}{3} = \frac{3}{4} + \frac{1}{3}$$

Because they are inverse operations, the $-\frac{1}{3}$ and the $\frac{1}{3}$ cancel out on the left side of the equal sign. Now you just have to add $\frac{3}{4}$ and $\frac{1}{3}$, which will require you to find a common denominator. A common denominator means that the denominators of both fractions are the same, and can always be found by multiplying both denominators together, which is what we will do to add $\frac{3}{4}$ and $\frac{1}{3}$, making the common denominator 12.

To convert $\frac{3}{4}$ to have a denominator of 12, multiply both the numerator and denominator by 3 to get $\frac{9}{12}$.

To convert $\frac{1}{3}$ to have a denominator of 12, multiply both the numerator and denominator by 4 to get $\frac{4}{12}$.

$$\frac{9}{12} + \frac{4}{12} = \frac{9 + 4}{12}$$

$$x = \frac{13}{12}$$

You don't always need to multiply the denominators together to find a common denominator. For example, to add $\frac{1}{4}$ and $\frac{1}{8}$, you can multiply the first fraction by $\frac{2}{2}$ to get $\frac{2}{8}$, and their common denominator will be 8. This is called the least common denominator.

This next type of linear equation is one in which a variable is divided by a whole number (the variable is the numerator) or multiplied by a fraction. The key to solving these is to eliminate the fraction by multiplying both sides of the equation by the denominator. Here are some examples illustrating this strategy.

Solve for x.

$$\frac{x}{2} = 10$$

While there are multiple ways to solve this equation, one way is to multiply both sides by 2, which will eliminate the fraction on the left.

$$2 \cdot \frac{x}{2} = 10 \cdot 2$$

By multiplying both sides of the equation by 2, the 2 in the denominator will cancel out and leave you with $x = 20$.

Here is a similar example.

Solve for x.

$$\frac{3}{4}x - 2 = 6$$

Your first step should be to isolate the $\frac{3}{4}x$ by adding 2 to both sides. This results in $\frac{3}{4}x = 8$.

To finish solving this equation, multiply both sides of the equation by the reciprocal, or multiplicative inverse, of the fraction. In this case, the reciprocal of $\frac{3}{4}$ is $\frac{4}{3}$.

$$\frac{4}{3} \cdot \frac{3}{4}x = \frac{8}{1} \cdot \frac{4}{3}$$

When you multiply $\frac{4}{3}$ and $\frac{3}{4}$ on the left, you get $\frac{12}{12}$, which is equivalent to one, leaving x by itself. Once you multiply the fractions on the right you get $x = \frac{32}{3}$.

Remember, when you multiply fractions, you multiply straight across.

Solving Proportions

A proportion is another type of equation that uses fractions, and being able to solve proportions is crucial. A proportion is nothing more than two ratios, or fractions, that are equal.

$$\frac{a}{b} = \frac{c}{d}$$

The best strategy for solving a proportion is cross-multiplication, which is effective because it eliminates the fractions.

When cross-multiplying, you will multiply the top left number with the bottom right number, which looks like $a \times d$. Then, set that equal to the product of the bottom left and top right, $b \times c$. It will end up looking like this:

$$ad = bc$$

From there, you can just solve the equation. Here is an example:

$$\frac{3}{5} = \frac{x}{20}$$

Start by cross-multiplying the 5 with the x and the 3 with the 20.

$$3(20) = 5x$$

$$60 = 5x$$

$$x = 12$$

Let's take a look at a second, more challenging example involving proportions.

In the equation below, what is the value of x?

$$\frac{x-3}{4} = \frac{2}{3}$$

$$3(x - 3) = 2(4)$$

Make sure to use the distributive property.

$$3x - 9 = 8$$

$$3x = 17$$

$$x = \frac{17}{3}$$

Blind Spot

The strategies for solving proportions and multiplying fractions look similar, but they require different methods of multiplication. A proportion, which has an equal sign between the fractions, uses cross-multiplication to solve. When multiplying fractions, however, you must multiply straight across—multiply numerators by numerators, and denominators by denominators.

PRACTICE B

Solve each equation without using a calculator.

1) $\frac{1}{2}x = 6$

2) $\frac{x}{4} = 9$

3) $\frac{a}{2} = -8$

4) $-\frac{1}{4}y = 3$

5) $\frac{x}{4} - 1 = 13$

6) $\frac{2}{3}x = 12$

7) $\frac{4x}{5} = 20$

8) $4 + \frac{1}{2}x = 6$

9) $\frac{x}{6} = \frac{5}{4}$

10) $\frac{x+1}{2} = \frac{4}{5}$

11) $\frac{3}{4}x = \frac{2}{3}$

12) $\frac{1}{2}x = \frac{1}{8}$

13) $18 = \frac{1}{9}x$

14) $\frac{x+2}{3} = 4$

15) $\frac{1}{2}x + \frac{1}{4}x = 8$

Hint

Knowing the rules of simplifying fractions is important for the test. First, if you can use your calculator to simplify it, use it. If it is the non-calculator section, though, follow these rules:

- Just divide the numerator and denominator by the same number. In $\frac{22}{44}$, both numbers can be divided by 2, which becomes $\frac{11}{22}$.

- On the grid-ins, you can leave the fraction as it is (if the numbers are not too big). If it is a multiple-choice question, use the answers to guide you.

Solving Linear Inequalities

An inequality is set up like an equation but expresses a different relationship. It will include one of the following inequality symbols:

- Greater than (>)

- Greater than or equal to (≥)

- Less than (<)

- Less than or equal to (≤)

You solve an inequality the exact same way you would any other equation. However, the one thing you must remember when solving an inequality is this:

Anytime you multiply or divide by a negative, you reverse the inequality.

Take a look at the example below, which will require dividing by a negative number to solve.

Solve the inequality below.

$$4 - 2x < 16$$

To solve, start by subtracting 4 from both sides, which gives you:

$$-2x < 12$$

The final step would be to divide both sides by –2 and then reverse the inequality from less than to greater than. The answer would be:

$$x > -6$$

While solutions to linear equations are single values, an inequality will create what is called a solution set. This means that there are a multitude of possible values for x, as long as the value is greater than –6. This solution set could be graphed on a number line as shown below:

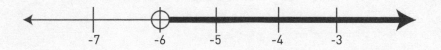

Hint

An integer is any positive or negative whole number, or zero. If the previous question had asked you to identify a possible integer value for $x > -6$, some answers include –5, –4, 0, 1, or 10.

PRACTICE C

Solve each inequality.

1) $2x - 4 < 18$

2) $4 - p \leq 5$

3) $-\frac{1}{2}x \geq 6$

4) $2m \leq -12$

5) $x - 4 > 3$

6) $-3y \geq 16 + y$

7) $4x < -12$

8) $-(x + 2) < 12 + 6x$

9) $12 \geq y - 2$

10) $\frac{1}{2}(2x - 4) > 6$

Mindset Tip

The Absolute Value–Growth Mindset Connection: imagine you complete a practice test. You answer 20 questions and you get all of them correct. You feel great. You complete a second practice test and get 20 questions wrong, and you feel great. How does this make any sense?

Answering 20 questions correctly shows that you mastered 20 topics. Answering 20 questions incorrectly gives you 20 opportunities to increase your score.

No matter what happens, the result is always positive. This is the absolute value of growth mindset.

Absolute Value

A simple way to think of absolute value is that the output, or result, will always be positive. An absolute value can never be equal to a negative. It is also referred to as the distance from zero on the number line.

The absolute value of −2, which is written as |−2|, is 2. The absolute value of 2, which is written as |2|, would also be 2.

Absolute value bars are a type of grouping symbol, so you will treat them as you would parentheses and complete the math inside them first using PEMDAS. Below is an example to help.

$$|2 - 6| = |-4| = 4$$

Solving Absolute Value Equations

Think about the equation $|x| = 3$. What number could you plug in to get 3?

You most likely answered 3, but −3 is also a solution.

Most absolute value equations will have two answers. To solve for them, get the absolute value by itself first. Then, write two equations, with one equal to the positive number and the other equal to the negative number. Finally, solve both equations.

Here is an example:

$$|x - 2| + 5 = 10$$

In the equation above, what is the value of x?

Begin by subtracting 5 from both sides and then rewriting two equations: one equal to 5 and the other equal to −5. Then solve for both answers.

$$|x - 2| = 5$$

$$x - 2 = 5 \text{ and } x - 2 = -5$$

$$x = 7 \text{ and } x = -3$$

You most likely have seen this in math class, as this is the algebraic way of solving. Another approach to solving, which can be more efficient at times, is one that you already learned: plugging in answer choices.

$$|x - 2| + 6 = 5$$

Which of the following could be the value of x?

A) 1

B) 3

C) 7

D) None

By substituting each answer choice in for x, you see that choices A, B, and C do not work, making choice D the correct answer. You could also have subtracted 6 from both sides, leaving:

$$|x - 2| = -1$$

Once you understand absolute value you will know that this is impossible, because *the absolute value can never be equal to a negative number!*

Consider the equation $|x| = -2$. What number can you plug in for x that would give you -2 in return?

If you plug in 2 or -2 in for x you get positive 2, so there is no number you can plug in and get -2. You can never have an absolute value equal to a negative number and expect to have a solution.

Be careful! The equation $-3|x| = -15$ will have solutions. When you divide both sides by -3 you get $|x| = 5$, which means the solutions would be 5 and -5.

PRACTICE D

Solve for x.

1) $|x + 3| - 2 = 3$

2) $-3|x - 2| = -15$

3) $|2 + x| - 6 = -4$

4) $|3 + 2x| + 5 = 3$

Translating Words into Math

The ability to translate words into mathematical expressions or equations is a very important skill for the SAT. While we will spend a lot of time on word problems later, let's start ingraining the habit of converting context into operations. Here is a table explaining the math vocabulary you need to know for the test.

+	Sum, plus, together, more than, total, combined, added to
−	Difference, minus, less than, fewer than
×	Product, times, twice, double, of
÷	Quotient, divided by, per, out of, ratio
=	Equals, is, same as

For example, the phrase "the sum of x and y" can be rewritten as $x + y$.

It will help to circle any of these words when you see them in a question, since they are mathematical cues that you will use to find the correct answer. The question may tell you what variable to use, as in the expression above, or it may not, in which case you should create your own variable. Anytime the question says "a number," you can simply replace it with x. Try this example:

> The sum of a number and five is the same as twice that number. What is the value of that number?

Start by converting the words to mathematical expressions:

$$\text{"sum of a number and five"} \rightarrow x + 5$$

$$\text{"is twice that number"} \rightarrow = 2x$$

Now you can put them together and solve.

$$x + 5 = 2x \rightarrow x = 5$$

Here is another example that uses percents.

> Thirty percent of what number is eighteen?

"What number" would indicate the need for a variable, such as x, and the word "of" says to multiply. To find a percent, multiply the percent as a decimal times the original, so you can write this as:

$$0.30x = 18$$

To solve for x, divide both sides by 0.30, and you get 60.

PRACTICE E

1) Two numbers, when combined, are 18. If one of those numbers is 12, what is the value of the other number?

2) The product of a number, x, and 4 is equal to the sum of five and that same number, x. What is the value of x?

3) 20% of a number is equal to 1.6. What is the value of that number? (Calculator)

Mindset Tip

Growth mindset is like putting the absolute value bars around your life. Everything you do, the obstacles you face, even the failures you encounter, can only amount to one thing: positivity. The Chicago Cubs, self-made millionaires, and the students in the study were all abiding by the rules of growth mindset. When you see everything, positive or negative, as stepping stones to success, you are living between the bars.

PRACTICE F

1) If $a = \frac{1}{2}$ and $b = \frac{1}{3}$, what is the value of $a + 2b$?

2) What is the value of x in the equation $(2x - 3) - (x - 1) = 8$?

3) In the equation $0.25m = 4$, what is the value of m? (Try this without a calculator)

4) One half of a number is the same as the sum of twice that number and 2. What is the value of that number?

A) -4 **C)** $-\frac{4}{3}$

B) 3 **D)** $\frac{4}{3}$

5) Which of the following is the solution to the inequality $5x - 1 > 2x + 11$?

A) $x > 4$ **C)** $x > 9$

B) $x < 4$ **D)** $x < 9$

6) Which of the following is one possible integer value of x for the inequality $2 < x - 4 < 10$?

A) 5 **C)** 13

B) 6 **D)** 14

7) If Weston bought a toy car for $34.99, which included an 8% sales tax, which of the following is closest to the original price of the toy car?

A) $2.80   **C)** $32.40

B) $32.20   **D)** $62.98

Answers

Practice A (page 60)

1) $x = 1$ **4)** $x = 10$

2) $x = 7$ **5)** $x = 4$

3) $x = \frac{26}{4} = \frac{13}{2}$ **6)** $x = -4$

7) $x = 2$

8) $x = \dfrac{2}{3}$

(Best first step is to add $\dfrac{1}{2}$ to both sides)

9) $a = 2$

10) $b = -4$

Practice B (page 64)

1) $x = 12$

2) $x = 36$

3) $a = -16$

4) $y = -12$

5) $x = 56$

6) $x = 18$

7) $x = 25$

8) $x = 4$

9) $x = \dfrac{30}{4} = \dfrac{15}{2}$

10) $x = \dfrac{3}{5}$

11) $x = \dfrac{8}{9}$

12) $x = \dfrac{2}{8} = \dfrac{1}{4}$

13) $x = 162$

14) $x = 10$

15) $x = \dfrac{32}{3}$

Practice C (page 66)

1) $x < 11$

2) $p \geq -1$

3) $x \leq -12$

4) $m \leq -6$

5) $x > 7$

6) $y \leq -4$

7) $x < -3$

8) $x > -2$

9) $y \leq 14$

10) $x > 8$

Practice D (page 68)

1) $x = 2$ and $x = -8$

2) $x = 7$ and $x = -3$

3) $x = 0$ and $x = -4$

4) No Solution

Practice E (page 70)

1) 6

2) $x = \dfrac{5}{3}$

3) 8

Practice F (page 71)

1) $\dfrac{7}{6}$

2) 10

3) 16

4) C

5) A

6) C

7) C (Use the equation $1.08x = 34.99$)

UNTIMED COLLEGE BOARD PRACTICE

Complete the following College Board practice problems from College Board's *The Official SAT Study Guide* or online at www.collegeboard.org. Review answers after completing.

Test 1, Math: No Calculator, #1

Test 1, Math: Calculator, #8, 11

Test 2, Math: No Calculator, #5

Test 2, Math: Calculator, #6

Test 3, Math: No Calculator, #17

Test 3, Math: Calculator, #7

Test 4, Math: No Calculator, #1

Chapter **3**

Brain Growth

In 2000, neuroscientist Eleanor Maguire wanted to see if all that driving around the winding, circuitous, impossible-to-navigate streets of London did anything to the cab drivers' brains. She analyzed the drivers' brains and compared them to the brains of average people.

What she found was extraordinary.

Cab drivers had enlarged memory centers in their brains. The "posterior hippocampi, or part of the brain used to facilitate spatial memory in the form of navigation, of taxi drivers were significantly larger relative to those of control subjects."[2] While this may not seem that significant in and of itself, its implications are life-changing.

Their brains literally grew! With this single study, Maguire confirmed beyond any shadow of a doubt that our brains will change and grow in response to the activities and exercises we do. This illustrates the concept of neuroplasticity, the ability of brains to grow and change over time. Applying the same concept proves that anyone can become a great test taker.

Imagine your brain as a mound of clay that can be molded and shaped by the things you do. This is one of the single most important ideas to appreciate when preparing for the SAT. Your intelligence or IQ is not fixed, permanent, or forever stuck at a certain level or number. Rather, your intelligence can grow over time in response to the learning you feed it, the activities that mold it. Think of your brain like a muscle—just as doing 10 reps of bench press increases your chest strength, 10 minutes of working in this book will increase your brain strength. So, what are some ways to boost that brain strength and capitalize on neuroplasticity?

- Repeated practice: the more you utilize the same area of your brain, the more that area of your brain grows.

- Embrace challenge: challenging problems and passages force your brain to stretch and expand.

- Shock your brain: vary your workout by trying new problems and passages you've never seen before. When you encounter that which is new and foreign, your brain is forced to grow.[3]

These strategies might sound familiar because they are the core of growth mindset. As you practice these exercises and understand more about neuroplasticity, you will actually change the way you approach learning.

Deliberate Practice

Chances are you have a friend who not only plays three sports, but is also the quarterback on the football team, starting point guard on the basketball team, and shortstop on the varsity baseball team. Or maybe you have a friend who plays four different instruments—drums, bass, guitar, piano—and perhaps she even sings. Maybe you know someone who is trilingual and picks up languages as if they were the easiest thing to understand in the world. Are these friends of yours superhuman? While there may be a very small number of people who are born with a particular talent, the truth is that many people develop these skills over time through practice. When you encounter such ability, you are just witnessing another unique aspect of the human brain: the neural pathway.

Our brains not only change in size, as shown in the cab driver example above, but also in structure based on the practice we do. There is a saying in the neuroscience world, "Neurons that fire together wire together." This means that if you deliberately practice the same thing over and over again, you will create stronger links among the neural pathways associated with that action. It's like wearing a groove in your mind or creating a superhighway. Your neurons will fire in sync when you do those things that require those same pathways and, as a result, those actions will become 10 times easier.[4] Why take the dirt road when you can ride on the superhighway? Here are some examples of the neural pathway in action during the SAT.

- Learn the strategy for identifying and correcting pronoun errors for the first time, and links start to form between neurons associated with this particular action.

- After factoring quadratics for the 20th time, the neural pathway strengthens and allows for speed and ease.

- After the twenty-fifth science passage graph analysis, muscle memory develops and you are guided to important information without having to actively think about checking the x- and y-axis.

- After taking five practice tests, you start to predict which types of questions are going to be asked.

This is another fundamental part of growth mindset. It's also why it is so much easier to learn a third language if you are already bilingual, and why musicians typically play multiple instruments with ease. When you learn a third language, you need only borrow the existing neural pathways associated with language learning that were formed when you learned the first. If you are a guitarist who wants to learn to the play the drums or piano, you can rely on the existing neural pathways associated with learning an instrument.

So, once you do the hard work in the beginning, doing similar work will be that much easier later. Your goal should be to form new SAT connections that can be strengthened over time through repeated practice.

Reading Test: Question Types

Most questions on the SAT reading section are wordy and have multiple parts. They may reference several aspects of the passage before actually asking you the question. The secret to never misreading a question is breaking the question down into the following four manageable parts.

WHERE. The place in the passage: to what part of the text is the question sending you?

> "The description in the fourth paragraph indicates that what Charles values most about Elaine is her…"

In this example, the place in the passage we are being sent to is the "fourth paragraph."

HOW. The contextual lens: the context required for your answer. In other words, what component of the text or part of the passage is your answer contingent upon? This determines how you should answer the question.

> "According to the events described in passage 2, whether the author's disciples continued to perform the same rituals was dictated by whether that particular ritual was…"

The contextual lens we must look though is "the events described in passage 2."

WHO. The person: to whom is the question referring? Whose opinion or point of view are you looking for in the passage?

> "One difference between the phenomena described in the two passages is that, unlike the experts quoted in passage 1, the author of passage 2…"

We are looking for the viewpoint of the "author of passage 2."

WHAT. The action: what is the question actually asking? Are you asked to compare, determine the author's response to a particular item, identify an attribute of an object, find the main purpose?

> "The passage most strongly suggests that Bernard used which of the following to infiltrate the precipitous mountain fortresses in the Himalayas?"

We want to know what the passage suggests Bernard used to infiltrate the fortress.

Takeaway

- If you break down the question and highlight, or at least take note of, these four components of any critical reading question, you will never misinterpret what is being asked of you or freeze on an intimidating question.

- Take note of the where (place in the text), how (context required), who (person of interest), and what (action you must take).

Mindset Tip

Remember that as you read and learn about question types, you are changing your brain. As you practice them and purposefully notice them within passages, you will begin to build a new neural pathway. Identifying types of questions and how to answer them will become muscle memory.

Question Types

Now that you know the fundamentals of reading questions, let's take a look at the six types of critical reading questions that will appear on the SAT.

Detail/Evidence

These "what" questions either require you to understand a detail that is directly stated, cite textual evidence, or summarize. These questions often require you go to the line number and examine the text carefully. Do not make leaps of deduction. It is also important to realize that the SAT will sometimes use synonyms for the words in the passage in the correct answer, so do not feel like the answer to the detail question needs to be the exact words of the passage.

When choosing evidence to support a previous question, you must be precise. The SAT tries to deceive you in this way by using overlapping line numbers. For example, one answer choice might list evidence in line 38, but another choice might list evidence in lines 38–42. If the idea or support is not included in just line 38, but continues over multiple lines, then you must choose 38–42.

Since the questions are typically laid out chronologically (meaning earlier questions will refer to earlier parts of the passage), when looking for evidence take note of what number question you are working on. If it is an earlier question, the correct evidence will usually be found in an earlier part of the passage.

"Which choice provides the best evidence for the answer to the previous question?"

"As stated in the passage, which of the following events occurred in response to the Great Fire?"

HOW TO ANSWER: Refer to the passage and check the line number cited. Do not make inferences; simply find the evidence or statement in the passage that you need to answer the question.

SKILLS TESTED:

- Connecting evidence to ideas

- Identifying support for an answer

Graph Analysis

These questions require students to read and interpret graphs or connect information within the graph to information within the passage.

Blind Spot

Sometimes evidence questions are not paired with the question that comes just before them and, if you are going too quickly, you might pick evidence based on the previous question. On occasion, the SAT will ask you to find evidence for a specific reason, unrelated to the previous question, as in, "which piece of evidence best supports the author's claim that elephants are hunted for their ivory?" Read carefully and answer these unique evidence questions correctly.

"According to the table, which of the following gives the correct percentage for Uber usage in NJ?"

"Does the data in figure 1 support the author's claim about the increase in Uber use over the last five years?"

HOW TO ANSWER: Read the title of the graph first, noting what information is being conveyed. Next, examine the x- and y-axes of the graph, noting how the information is measured. Finally, review any other additional points of information by checking two likely places: below the graph, where there may be a footnote, and the middle of the graph, where there may be an additional marker or piece of data.

Questions will sometimes try to fool you by including answer choices with information that is not measured in the graph.

SKILLS TESTED:

• Analyzing parts of a graph

• Comparing information in a graph to evidence in a passage

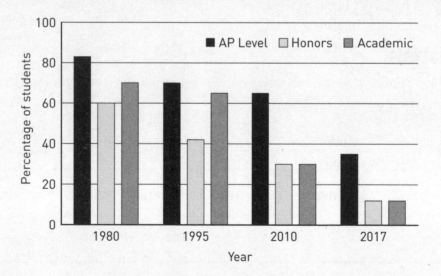

Percentage of Students who Believe in Value of High School Diploma

STEP 1: Note the title, which explains what the y-axis is measuring.

STEP 2: Check the x- and y-axes. Note that the y-axis shows a percentage up to 100, and the x-axis presents the different time periods in which the data was gathered.

STEP 3: Check the body of the graph and the information in the graph key. Based on this, you learn that each year measures three separate student groups: AP (black), Honors (light gray), and Academic (dark gray).

Now, look at this sample question:

1) Which statement is best supported by the information in the graph?

A) Between 1980 and 2017, the value of a high school diploma declined considerably

B) In 2010, the percentage of all students who believed a high school diploma had value was half that of 1980.

C) Between 1980 and 2017, the perceived value of the diploma dropped considerably among all three groups.

D) AP students were able to do more with a diploma than both honors students and academic students.

ANSWER:

1) Choice (A) is incorrect because it makes an assumption about the data. The graph measures student perception of a high school diploma's value, not the actual value. Choice (B) is too extreme and is a distortion of the values represented on the graph. Choice (D) is not represented on the graph. So, choice (C) is correct.

Vocab-in-Context

These questions require students to determine the definition of a word as used in the passage, based on context. For example:

> "As used in line five, 'currency,' most nearly means…"

Hint

Be careful with common meanings of the word. The SAT tests words with multiple meanings or older, uncommonly used words from eighteenth- to twentieth-century literature. As a result, your best strategy for identifying the meaning of a word is always predicting its meaning from its context. The word "currency" in this example probably does not mean money, but rather its less common definition: frequency of use, or popularity.

HOW TO ANSWER: Reread the line in which the word appears, then put your own word in its place before looking at the answer choices. Remember to think carefully about the context— what is the author trying to convey here? Then go to answer choices and match your word with an answer. Plug the answer choice into the sentence to see if it makes sense.

SKILLS TESTED:

- Prior vocabulary knowledge

- Determining a word's use in context

> "The majority of people in a waiting room, however, adhere to a typical decorum: wait and do not talk to the people next to you. Perhaps we can attribute this behavior to a common dread of what lies beyond the doors to the dentist/doctor/etc."

1) As used in the line 2, "attribute" most nearly means…

A) A characteristic

B) A defining quality

C) Assign

D) Offer up praise

ANSWER:

1) Though "characteristic" and "defining quality" are both popular meanings of the word attribute, they are incorrect in this context. "Offer up praise" is a distorted definition of the work based on part of the word, "tribute." "Assign" is the correct answer.

Central Idea

These questions ask students to understand the big picture and pull together points of the entire passage. These types of questions could ask about tone, purpose, point of view, summary, or main idea. Why did the author write the passage? What is the theme? What is the best summary of the first paragraph?

"The central idea of passage 1 is that conservation and recycling…"

"What best summarizes the main idea of the passage?"

"The primary purpose of the passage is to…"

HOW TO ANSWER: Reread the introduction and conclusion to see what the author emphasizes and repeats. Review repeated words and phrases as you read. Avoid secondary ideas and overly specific details.

SKILLS TESTED:

- Understanding the author's purpose in writing

- Understanding how repeated ideas and contrast create theme

- Differentiating between main idea and secondary information

Relationships and Structure

These questions require students to analyze text structure, shifts, development, and relationships between parts and ideas. Common structural relationships include problem/solution, cause/effect, and comparison/contrast. For example:

"Douglass develops his argument primarily through the use of…"

HOW TO ANSWER: Check your annotations (discussed in Chapter 2), especially the contrast words. These will help you determine shifts and evaluate how the author is developing his or her point. Reread the introduction and topic sentences of body paragraphs to note predominant structural patterns such as problem/solution, thesis/support, anecdote/explanation, and point/counterpoint.

SKILLS TESTED:

- Development of argument

- Shifts and digressions

- Organization of passage

Many people have been clamoring for change in their local governments, change in taxes, change in public safety, change in traffic ordinances, change in everything. And, they apparently believe that the best way to go about creating change is to sit at home or at dinner parties and complain about the current state of the town. This will not create change. To truly change the local government and workings of a town, one must engage in their civic duty of petition, letter writing, speeches at town hall, and of course, voting.

1) How would you describe the organization or structure of this short excerpt?

In the passage, the author first discusses a group of people, what they want, and the way they are going about getting it. He then disagrees with their plan of action and explains what he believes is the correct way to create change. This is an example of point/counterpoint.

Joshua looked around, finally taking notice of his surroundings. The carpets were covered in crumbs, the dishes lay the kitchen sink, and the mail had begun to pile up. Everything was in disarray; the house, without the care of his grandmother, succumbed to entropy. His little brother would never be able to pick up this slack. Charlie just was not of the sort of homebound, dutiful stock that was needed in times like these. Grandma was sick; she had been sick for a while and she was not getting better. Suddenly, with all the callous inhumanity of an abrupt shove on the subway, Joshua saw it all. He saw himself coming back home, putting his education on hold, and setting roots firmly in the house until Grandma passed. His book bag dropped with a loud thud.

2) How would you describe the development of this short excerpt?

Here, a character walks into a setting, surveys the scene, acknowledges a problem, and then comes to a realization. This could be described as a problem/solution or conflict/epiphany structure.

Function/Effect

This type of question asks students to understand the function or effect of a particular part of a passage or narrative technique of the author. They require students to answer the question: "What does it do?"

Think of the sentences in the passage not in terms of their content but in terms of their function, like support beams, or windows in a house. We don't care about the shape of the window, we care about what it does; it lets light into the house. For example:

"The author uses the phrase 'suit of armor' mainly to…"

"The author includes the quotes around the word 'art' in order to…"

"What is primary rhetorical strategy the author uses in the first paragraph?"

HOW TO ANSWER: Reread the entire context surrounding the line to which you are referred. Put yourself in the author's shoes and ask *why would I include this line? What does it do for my argument, what does my reader gain from it?*

SKILLS TESTED:

- Determining the effect of a particular part of the passage

- Identifying the function or purpose of a part of the passage

- Determining how a narrative technique advances the author's argument

- Determining how a component of the passage helps create theme

> "Last night Japanese forces attacked Hong Kong.
> Last night Japanese forces attacked Guam.
> Last night Japanese forces attacked the Philippine Islands.
> Last night the Japanese attacked Wake Island.
> And this morning the Japanese attacked Midway Island."
> *Excerpted from President Franklin Roosevelt's speech on Dec. 8, 1941*

1) What is the effect of this repetition? How does it make the listener feel? What point does it convey?

Perhaps you felt overwhelmed, surrounded, like the Japanese forces were everywhere and that the only way to escape the situation was to fight your way out. If you felt something along these lines, then FDR succeeded in using his rhetoric to create an effect. And so, in this case, the function of the repetition and parallel phrasing is to make us feel the urgency and the imminence of a Japanese takeover.

Inference

This type of question requires students to infer an answer based on information in the passage and the author's point of view.

For these it is often better not to predict, but rather get the correct answer by heading to the answer choices and eliminating the assumptions, distortions, and extreme wrong-answer traps (discussed in Chapter 4) one by one.

"Based on the passage, it can be reasonably inferred that in the city…"

"The passage most strongly suggests that rabies is…"

HOW TO ANSWER: Read the passage and note contrasting words and what follows them, as well as the point of view of the author. When directed to a certain line number, reread the entire section or at least two to three lines before and after the line number, keeping in mind the point of view of the author. Go to the answer choices and eliminate choices that are assumptions or distortions (partially true or partially false). Sometimes a single word or phrase will negate an answer. Remember, an answer must follow the material in the passage directly.

Skills Tested:

- Understanding point of view

- Avoiding distortions of the author's point

- Understanding the central idea of the passage

Vocabulary Words 31–45

31) **reverence** (n). a feeling or attitude of deep respect tinged with awe; veneration: *Joe felt a great reverence for the general.*

32) **trivial** (adj). unimportant, insignificant: *Most people don't remember such trivial information as the inches of rainfall in Seattle, WA, in 1986.*

33) **mutual** (adj). a) possessed, experienced, or performed by each of two or more people with respect to the other; reciprocal; b) having the same relation each toward the other; c) of or

relating to each of two or more; held in common; shared: *The love between Maria and Jake was mutual.*

34) **array** (n). a) order or arrangement; b) a large and impressive grouping of things: *The children walked into the candy store and stared in awe at the wide array of different treats.*

35) **cliché** (n). an overused, stereotyped expression: *A common cliché is "Don't take life for granted."*

36) **implicit** (adj). implied: *Although the teacher did not directly say that being absent would result in a penalty, it was implicit.*

37) **explicit** (adj). openly stated; fully and clearly expressed or demonstrated: *The vice principal explicitly told students that they would be suspended if they cut class.*

38) **compelling** (adj). captivating, fascinating; overpowering: *The news report was so compelling that viewers could not take their eyes off the screen.*

39) **ambivalent** (adj). having mixed feelings about someone or something; being unable to choose between two things: *Joshua was ambivalent about his girlfriend; he did not have any strong feelings one way or the other about her.*

40) **robust** (adj). strong, vigorous, hearty: *A robust economy is reflected in declining unemployment rates and stock market growth.*

41) **admonish** (v). to scold or reprimand: *Emma was admonished for eating several cookies before his dinner.*

42) **besiege** (v). to surround and attack: *The invaders besieged the castle for days.*

43) **engage** (v). a) to occupy oneself; become involved; b) to attract and hold fast: *The businessman was engaged in several different business ventures.*

44) **deter** (v). to dissuade, discourage, or put off: *Having a home security system will deter potential burglars.*

45) **emit** (v). to give off, produce, radiate, release: *The level of radiation that a microwave emits is dangerous to expectant mothers.*

Latin and Greek Roots 13–18

13) AUTO: self (autonomous, automatic)

14) BELL: war (rebellion, antebellum, bellicose, belligerent)

15) BEN: good (benefactor, benign, benevolent)

16) BI: two, twice (bipartisan, biannual, binoculars)

17) COGN: to know (incognito, cognizant, cognitive)

18) COSM: world (cosmos, cosmopolitan)

Mindset Tip

Try to practice the vocabulary and roots daily. Getting in your reps each day is very important to turning your regular brain into a vocab brain.

UNTIMED COLLEGE BOARD PRACTICE

Complete the following College Board practice problems from College Board's *The Official SAT Study Guide* or online at www.collegeboard.org. Review answers after completing.

Test 1, Reading Test, Passages 1 and 2, #1–21

Label the question types as you go and apply the strategies for answering them.

Math Test: Applications of Solving Linear Equations

In this section, you are going to learn the different ways questions will test your knowledge of solving linear equations. This is a great opportunity to grow your neural pathways by learning new skills while building on previously learned ones. Take the time to connect each part of the following chapter to something you have already learned.

Substituting for a Variable

At some point, you will be asked to solve an equation with multiple variables. To solve, check to see if the value of one of the missing variables is provided in the question. Then, use substitution and rewrite the equation.

Here is an example of a question with multiple variables, and also the information needed to solve.

$$\text{If } y = 3x - 4 \text{ and } y = 5, \text{ find } x.$$

This question becomes simple once you plug in 5 for y, but remember, it is important to rewrite the equation with the plugged-in variable.

$$5 = 3x - 4$$

Now just solve for x the same way you did in Chapter 2.

$$9 = 3x$$

$$x = 3$$

Some questions may not appear to be linear until you plug in a value, such as in the example below, which at first looks quadratic.

If $8 = a - 2x^2$, and x is equal to 3, what is the value of a?

By substituting 3 for x, the equation can be rewritten as $8 = a - 2(3)^2$, which can then be simplified to $8 = a - 18$. Don't forget about order of operations! You square 3 first and then multiply by -2.

Finally, to solve for x, just add 18 to both sides to get 26.

Sometimes, after substituting for a variable, it's easier to plug in answer choices than it is to solve the equation. This also reinforces an already established neural pathway. Substitution can allow you to answer questions that require skills that you may have not learned yet, as shown in the example below:

$$x = \sqrt{x+15} + b$$

In the equation above, what is the value of x if b is equal to 5?

A) 1

B) 5

C) 10

D) 21

Your first step should always be to rewrite the equation and plug in the number for the variable.

$$x = \sqrt{x+15} + 5$$

You may know how to solve for x, however, the most efficient and time-saving approach is to plug in the answer choices. Since plugging in answer choices requires substitution, be sure to follow the order of operations rules correctly.

A) $1 = \sqrt{1+15} + 5 \rightarrow 1 \neq \sqrt{16} + 5$

B) $5 = \sqrt{5+15} + 5 \rightarrow 5 \neq \sqrt{20} + 5$

C) $10 = \sqrt{10+15} + 5 \rightarrow 10 = \sqrt{25} + 5$

D) $21 = \sqrt{21+15} + 5 \rightarrow 11 \neq \sqrt{36} + 5$

The only correct answer is (C).

Take your time with these steps, as you would not want to make an unnecessary mistake.

Remember that anytime you are using substitution, order of operations is crucial, so be sure to follow PEMDAS.

Equations with Three Variables

Now this is getting complicated. Three variables? Come on, can you really solve that?

On the SAT, solving these questions is simple because the question must give you additional information. For these, you will most likely be plugging in two variables right away. Remember to rewrite the equation with the new information plugged in and see if you can solve for the remaining variable.

A question may also give you an equation with a coordinate point. Points on a graph are written in the form (x, y). For example, the point $(2, 4)$ can also be expressed as:

$$x = 2 \text{ and } y = 4$$

If you are given an equation, simply plug those values in. After that, you should be able to solve for the remaining variable.

Let's try this next example:

In the equation of the line $y = 3x + b$, b represents the y-intercept. If the graph of the given equation passes through the point $(2, 11)$, what is the value of b?

The key to this question is to find the third variable, in this case b.

Since you are given the point $(2, 11)$, you know that $x = 2$ and $y = 11$, so you can plug those values into the equation.

$$11 = 3(2) + b$$

$$11 = 6 + b$$

$$b = 5$$

You build the connections in the neural pathway by challenging yourself and stretching your mind. Each topic or answer you learn that you did not previously understand means your brain is growing.

Using Function Notation

SAT questions often write coordinate points in function notation. For example, the point (2, 4) could also be written as $f(2) = 4$. The number inside the parentheses is the x and the number on the opposite side of the equals sign represents the value of y. Here is an example:

In the function $g(x) = -4x^2 + k$, what is the value of k if $g(3) = 6$?

The statement $g(3) = 6$ tells you that $x = 3$ and $g(x) = 6$. Immediately substitute those values in and solve for k.

$$6 = -4(3)^2 + k$$

$$6 = -4(9) + k$$

$$6 = -36 + k$$

$$k = 42$$

Solving for an Expression

Some questions may give you an equation and, rather than asking you to solve for a single variable, they require you to find the value of an expression, such as $5x$ or $2x + y$. There are two ways to solve these problems. The first is just to solve for the variable and plug it into the expression. Here is an example:

If $2x + 4 = 10$, what is the value of $3x$?

To correctly answer this question, you first need to solve for x and then plug that value into the expression $3x$.

$$x = 3 \rightarrow 3(3) \rightarrow 9$$

Here is another example that will require adept problem-solving skills.

If $3x - 7 = 13$, what is the value of $15x$?

Begin this question by adding 7 to both sides.

$$3x = 20$$

If you solve for x you will be left with a fraction, which could make it difficult to find the final answer. However, since the question is asking you to find $15x$, you can multiply both sides of the equation by 5 to get:

$$15x = 100$$

This method, called pattern matching, is useful for solving an expression. In the example below, you cannot solve for either of the variables, so you must identify the pattern and then match one expression to the other.

If $x + y = 5$, what is the value of $2x + 2y$?

Especially with these question types, you must be aware of what the question is asking.

Notice if you multiply $x + y$ by 2, or $2(x + y)$, you get $2x + 2y$. Whatever you do to one side of an equation, must also be done to the other side, so you multiply 5 by 2 and you get 10. Since $x + y = 5$, then $2(x + y) = 5 \times 2$. Therefore, $2x + 2y = 10$.

PRACTICE A

Answer the following without using a calculator.

1) If $3a + 2b = 9$, what is the value of $9a + 6b$?

2) If $2x - 18 = 24$, what is the value of $3x - 6$?

3) If $(m + n) - 20 = 8$, what is the value of $(m + n)$?

4) What is the value of x^3 if $\frac{1}{2}x + 4 = 6$?

Rearranging Equations

Sometimes solving an equation doesn't mean finding a number value. It is common for an SAT question to require you to rewrite an equation in terms of a certain variable. This is what we call rearranging. In other words, how can you express the same equation or formula in a different way by rearranging the numbers and variables? You will use the same rules for solving equations, only with these questions, the equations will have more variables than numbers.

Here is an example of when to use rearranging:

$$2x + y = z$$

The formula above represents a line. Which of the following represents x, in terms of y and z?

A) $x = z - \dfrac{y}{2}$

B) $x = \dfrac{z}{2} - 2y$

C) $x = \dfrac{z - y}{2}$

D) $x = \dfrac{1}{2}z - y$

This question is simply asking you to move everything around, or rearrange the equation, so that x is isolated. Start by subtracting y from both sides, which would give you:

$$2x = z - y$$

Finally, to get x by itself, divide both sides by 2. Be sure to divide the entire right side by 2, so it should look like:

$$x = \dfrac{z - y}{2}$$

Looking at the answer choices, this would be choice (C).

Questions that require rearranging are easy to spot because the answer choices are all equations, and they even tell you the variable for which you need to solve.

Let's look at another example.

Which of the following is another way of writing $h = \frac{1}{4}m - t$?

A) $m = \frac{1}{4}(h+t)$

B) $m = 4h + t$

C) $m = h + 4t$

D) $m = 4h + 4t$

To rearrange this equation, start by adding t to both sides:

$$h + t = \frac{1}{4}m$$

To get m completely by itself, multiply by the reciprocal of $\frac{1}{4}$, which is $\frac{4}{1}$. Be sure to multiply the entire expression on the left side by 4:

$$4(h + t) = m$$

Since that answer is not a choice, you must distribute the 4 to get $4h + 4t$, so you get choice (D).

$$m = 4h + 4t$$

Here is another example involving rearranging:

The kinetic energy of an object is given by the formula $KE = \frac{mv^2}{2}$, with m being the mass of the object and v being the velocity (speed) of the object. Which of the following equations expresses v^2 in terms of m and KE?

A) $v^2 = \frac{mKE}{2}$

B) $v^2 = 2mKE$

C) $v^2 = 2KE - m$

D) $v^2 = \frac{2KE}{m}$

While this question looks intimidating, it is only asking you to rearrange the original equation so that v^2 is isolated. You can tell that this is what the question is asking because of the words "in terms of." Do not let the fancy language and formula fool you; just manipulate this the same way you would a simple equation. Begin by multiplying both sides by 2, which gives you:

$$2KE = mv^2$$

Finally, to get v^2 alone, divide both sides by m, and you get:

$$\frac{2KE}{m} = v^2$$

This is choice (D).

PRACTICE B

Solve for k by plugging in the given point.

1) $y = 3x - k$

$(2, 6)$

2) $y = \frac{1}{2}x + k$

$(4, 3)$

Solve for b using the given information.

3) $f(x) = \frac{1}{2}x - b$

$f(6) = -4$

4) $f(x) = x^2 + b$

$f(-2) = 8$

Solve each for t using the given information.

5) $h = \frac{1}{4}t$

7) $h = \frac{t-3}{4}$

6) $h = \frac{1}{2}t - 8$

8) $h = \frac{1}{rt}$

Solve for each expression:

9) If $2x + 4 = 8$, what is the value of $4x$?

10) If $5x - 3 = 16$, what is the value of $15x$?

Rewriting Rational Expressions

Questions that ask you to solve for expressions or rearrange equations may require you to rewrite rational expressions. The word rational refers to a fraction, and the first step in the process of rewriting these rational expressions is splitting up the fraction.

$$\frac{8x - 4}{4}$$

Say you need to simplify the expression above. Start by splitting the numerator into two separate fractions, both with the same denominator. Rewrite it as:

$$\frac{8x}{4} - \frac{4}{4}$$

Then, simplify each fraction to get:

$$2x - 1$$

This next example can be solved quickly by rewriting rational expressions.

$$3x - 6y = 12$$

What is another way to express the equation above?

A) $x - 2y = 12$

B) $x - 2y = 4$

C) $x - 6y = 12$

D) $x - 6y = 4$

The equation above can easily be simplified because 3, 6, and 12 are all divisible by 3. Just divide everything by 3 and you get:

$$\frac{3x - 6y = 12}{3}$$

$$\frac{3x}{3} - \frac{6y}{3} = \frac{12}{3}$$

The simplified answer would be $x - 2y = 4$, or (B).

Here is an example of a rearranging question that requires you to rewrite rational expressions.

Which of the following is equivalent to the equation $4x + 2y = 12$?

A) $y = 2x - 6$

B) $y = 2x + 6$

C) $y = -2x - 6$

D) $y = -2x + 6$

Start by subtracting $4x$ from both sides to isolate the y.

$$2y = 12 - 4x$$

Then, divide both sides by 2.

$$\frac{2y}{2} = \frac{12 - 4x}{2}$$

Since our answer is not a choice yet, we must rewrite the rational expression on the right.

$$y = \frac{12}{2} - \frac{4x}{2} \rightarrow y = 6 - 2x$$

Using the commutative property, you can switch the 6 and the $-2x$. The final answer could also be written as $y = -2x + 6$, or (D).

If these questions are intimidating at first, do not worry. This is a simple topic once you practice it a few times. Remember, these new skills and strategies are being wired into your brain right this very moment. You are taking steps to becoming the great test taker you are capable of becoming!

Mindset Tip

We all know that your muscles grow and your physique improves by working out. This is also true for the brain. Let's take you through a workout for your mind and demonstrate the ways by which you can improve your intelligence and capitalize on neuroplasticity.

These strategies might sound familiar because they are the core of growth mindset. As you practice these exercises and understand more and more of the truth of neuroplasticity, you are actually changing the way you approach learning.

PRACTICE C

1) The equation $y = 2x + b$ represents a line and b is a constant. If the point (2, 5) lies on the graph of the given equation, find y when x is equal to 8.

2) Solve for t.

$$h = \frac{3t + 6}{2}$$

A) $t = \frac{2}{3}h - 2$

C) $t = \frac{3}{2}h - 2$

B) $t = \frac{2}{3}h - 6$

D) $t = \frac{3}{2}h - 6$

3) Which of the following is equal to the equation $h = \frac{m - 4}{5}t$?

A) $t = \frac{m - 4}{5}h$

C) $t = h + \frac{m - 4}{5}$

B) $t = h - \frac{m - 4}{5}$

D) $t = \frac{5}{m - 4}h$

4) If $3y - 4 = 2y - 2$, what is the value of $\frac{1}{2}y$?

5) If $\frac{x}{3} = \frac{2x + 3}{7}$, what is the value of $\frac{3}{2x}$ given that x is not equal to 0?

6) If $\frac{1}{4}x - y = 10$, what is the value of $x - 4y$?

7) If $3a + 6b + 12c = 18$, what is the value of $a + 2b + 4c$?

Mindset Tip

Vary your workout by trying new problems and passages you've never seen before; when we encounter that which is new and foreign, our brain is forced to grow. Great problem solvers make a habit of searching out new puzzles, problems, and mysteries so their mind is always sharpening that skill and growing.

PRACTICE D

1) If $a + 9 = 2b$, what is the value of $4b - 2a$?

2) The expression $x^2 + 6x + 8$ is equal to 14. What is the value of $x^2 + 6x$?

3) In the equation $4x - 6y = 14$, if y is 2, what is the value of $8x$?

4) If $y = x^2 + 2x + k$ and passes through the point $(-3, 5)$, what is the value of $3k$?

5) A line has an x-intercept at the point $(a, 0)$. If the equation of the line is $y = 3x - 6$, what is the value of a?

6) If $a = \frac{1}{2}$ and $b = \frac{2}{3}$, what is the value of $\frac{a}{b}$?

7) Corbett's first test grade was 20% less than his second test grade. If his second test grade was a 90, what was his first test grade?

Math Mindset

Learning a new skill is hard in the beginning because you are building the connections for the first time. Your brain is literally stretching and growing. This is why riding a bike for the first time or learning a musical instrument is so hard. It is only after repeated practice that those skills become easier. The same can be said about the process of adopting a growth mindset.

Take a look at this simple chart that shows how you can change your outlook for nearly everything once you adopt a growth mindset approach to learning.

Fixed-Mindset Statement	Growth-Mindset Statement
I stink at fractions.	I haven't mastered fractions yet, but I am improving.
What's the point? I know what I can do and what I can't.	I can learn anything with the right mindset, practice, and strategies.
I am who I am.	There is no limit to who I can become.
I didn't recognize about 30 words in this passage. My vocabulary is horrible.	After I write down these 30 words and study them, I will be that much closer to building a solid vocabulary.
This test is five hours long, ugh.	This is a great opportunity to begin to build my SAT stamina.
I'm just not a creative person.	I used some creativity and imagination to correctly answer some of those "solving for expressions" questions. I wonder where else I can use some creativity where I wasn't using it before.
Everyone is finishing the sections faster than I am. I'm so slow!	Let me watch how others complete these sections so I can borrow and use some of their strategies and then begin practicing.
This problem looks difficult; I don't even want to attempt it because it might confirm my suspicions that I'm just faking it and not smart at all.	This difficult problem is an opportunity to learn strategies for facing other tough problems, so I'll be able to handle them on test day.
I've gotten the same type of question wrong again. Forget this, I'm done.	This helps me build resilience and grit. You can't become tough without facing repeated failure. Now I have a chance to rethink my approach to this type of question.

It doesn't matter what you thought before, this approach to learning will not only boost your SAT score but also unlock the doors to achieving whatever goal you have in life—doctor, Wall Street guru, millionaire entrepreneur. No matter your dream, growth mindset will help turn it into a reality.

Answers

Practice A (page 93)
1) 27

2) 57

3) 28

4) 64

Practice B (page 96)
1) 0

2) 1

3) 7

4) 4

5) $t = 4h$

6) $2(h + 8)$ or $2h + 16$

7) $4h + 3$

8) $\dfrac{1}{hr}$

9) 8

10) 57

Practice C (page 98)
1) 17

2) A

3) D

4) 1

5) $\dfrac{3}{18}$ or $\dfrac{1}{6}$

6) 40

7) 6

Practice D (page 99)
1) 18

2) 6

3) 52

4) $k = 2 \rightarrow 3k = 6$

5) $a = 2$

6) $\dfrac{3}{4}$

7) 72

UNTIMED COLLEGE BOARD PRACTICE

Complete the following College Board practice problems from College Board's *The Official SAT Study Guide* or online at www.collegeboard.org. Review answers after completing.

Test 1, Math: No Calculator, #7, 10

Test 1, Math: Calculator, #2, 4, 9, 10, 26

Test 2, Math: No Calculator #1

Test 2, Math: Calculator, #3, 33

Test 3, Math: No Calculator, #2

Test 3, Math: Calculator, #10, 11

Test 4, Math: No Calculator, #2, 6

Test 4, Math: Calculator, #5, 19

Chapter **4**

Growing Your Future: Mental GPS

Have you ever rehearsed something in your mind before you did it? Maybe it was a phone call, a free throw, or an audition for a part in the school play. If you have, then you have used a part of your brain called the premotor cortex. The premotor cortex is responsible for mapping out actions before they occur. Think of it like a mental GPS: plug in the route you want to take, and it maps it out before you actually start your trip. This is extremely important for practice and learning, especially in regard to the SAT. If you look at a brain scan while someone is using their premotor cortex to mentally rehearse an action, the parts of the brain required to do that action will actually light up.[5] This means that the neural pathways associated with that action will begin to link together just by thinking about it! So, when it comes time to actually perform the action, whether it is solving an algebraic equation or annotating a reading passage, your muscles and mind will already be primed and ready and that much more efficient.

Phil Jackson, who guided the Chicago Bulls to six championships and the Lakers to three championships, used the power of the premotor cortex by having his players visualize themselves executing the correct plays on the court and winning each game. Whether they knew it or not, these players were adopting a growth mindset. They were pre-paving the road ahead.

In essence, Phil Jackson was telling his players "think it, see it, do it."

Now it is your turn to *think it, see it, do it*, by committing to growth mindset and setting your first goals.

Goal Setting

Now that you have progressed through a few chapters, it is time to assess your goals and investigate the road you are on and where it is taking you. The goal-setting process is a fundamental part of any journey and crucial to unlocking your potential. So how do you correctly set a goal?

First, write down the goal you wish to achieve on a piece a paper. The act of writing it down makes it real and not just something that exists in your mind. It solidifies it so that it is harder for you to forget or change.

After you have set your goal, start thinking about what excites you about it. This emotional brainstorming will provide you with much-needed motivation to sustain your focus and drive throughout the entire journey. Once you have built up enough excitement around the goal you wish to achieve, you can create an action plan made up of manageable steps to take you there. Fortunately, for your SAT goals, this book lays out the steps for you; all you need to do is set a practice routine that states how often you will work with the book, on what days, and for how long.

The final two phases of the goal-setting process involve deeper self-reflection. Write down what obstacles you will face on your journey and how long it will take you. Be honest with yourself so that you can plan for these bumps in the road and accurately gauge when you believe you will attain the goal. Take a moment to fill out the chart below with this information so that you can prime your mind for successfully attaining your goal.

What score do you want?

What excites you about achieving this score?

What actions must you take to achieve this score?

What obstacles will you face in order to achieve this score?

How long will it take you to achieve this goal?

Remember, your ability to capitalize upon your growth mindset is only as good as the goals you set for yourself. These goals will be the fuel that sustains your practice, effort, and persistence through challenges.

Reading Test: Wrong Answer Types

The SAT test creators are diabolical in the ways that they design wrong answers. Fear not, though. There is a way to beat the SAT test makers at their own game: to take their greatest strength (deceptive, correct-sounding wrong answers) and turn it into their greatest weakness. Because wrong answers on the SAT are created to meet a standard, they follow the same patterns. Below are the five types of wrong-answer traps. Learn them and never be fooled again.

OFF TOPIC. These answer choices are either unrelated to the topic or discuss ideas beyond the scope of the passage.

GOLDILOCKS EFFECT. These are too extreme in tone or degree (either too general or too narrow). They will use language such as *always, never, loves, hates, totally,* and *all.* We call this the Goldilocks Effect because just like the porridge that was too hot or too cold, these wrong answers will be too far to one side or another.

ASSUMPTION. Look out for assumptions about the topic that make sense but are not supported in the passage. These could be extensions of the author's point or logical conclusions and extrapolations. As long as there are no direct facts in the passage to back them up, these assumptions will be incorrect.

MISINFORMATION. These answer types provide a detail or details stated in the passage that do not answer the question at hand. This wrong-answer trap uses the text to fool you by incorporating words, phrases, and/or ideas from the text that do not answer the question.

FUNHOUSE MIRROR. You will recognize something from the passage in these answer choices, but it will be twisted into something the author did not say. These wrong-answer traps will slightly alter, distort, or add to ideas you will remember the author stating; they could be partially true and partially false.

She seemed oblivious to his curious eye. As Thomas, mohawk carefully spiked, looked on from two desks behind her, Eva took notes, and notes, and notes. Her head never came up. The sound of the pencil pressing down hard as she wrote grated on Thomas' ears. But, what about all those tattoos? What about the lip ring, and the middle finger she casually rolled out for the cops who patrolled the school parking lot? Thomas felt his chest tighten. Had he been going about it all wrong? He ever so slightly adjusted his perfect slouch, sitting straighter, paused, and then took out his pencil.

1) Based on the passage, the reader can reasonably infer that Thomas's chest tightened because of:

A) His poor diet and lack of exercise *(assumption)*

B) Being ignored by Eva *(misinformation)*

C) His newfound love of Eva *(Goldilocks/assumption)*

D) His realization that he is mistaken in his views and actions **(correct answer)**

Mindset Tip

Remember as you practice that choosing a wrong answer is just as beneficial as finding the correct answer. With each wrong answer you choose, you will get that much closer to understanding wrong-answer patterns and developing wrong-answer radar.

PRACTICE

Joshua looked around, taking notice of his surroundings. The carpets were covered in crumbs, the dishes lay in the kitchen sink, and the mail had begun to pile up. Everything was in disarray; the house, without the care of his grandmother, succumbed to entropy. His little brother would never be able to pick up this slack. Charlie just was not of the sort of homebound, dutiful stock that was needed in times like these. Grandma was sick; she had been sick for a while and she was not getting better. Suddenly, with all the callous inhumanity of an abrupt shove on the subway, Joshua saw it all. He saw himself coming back home, putting his education on hold, and setting down firm roots in the house until Grandma passed. His book bag dropped with a loud thud.

1) The passage most strongly suggests that which of the following is true about Joshua?

A) He thinks his brother is a failure

B) He feels guilt for his grandmother's passing

D) He believes education is the only way to achieve his goals

C) He is willing to sacrifice his own dreams to help his family

2) What is the rhetorical effect of using the phrase, "an abrupt shove on the subway?"

A) It illustrates Joshua's dislike of subways

B) It shows that Joshua had a cluttered mind

C) It creates a smooth transition to the resolution of the passage

D) It conveys the suddenness and unwelcome nature of Joshua's epiphany

Answers

1) Answer (C) is correct because it is supported by the last two lines of the passage. Choice (A) is a funhouse answer, a distortion of the idea that Charlie won't help; choice (B) is an assumption; and choice (D) is a Goldilocks answer—it's too extreme.

2) Choices (A) and (B) are both assumptions that are not supported in the passage. Answer (C) is a funhouse answer: it does bring the reader to the resolution of the passage, but it doesn't offer a smooth transition, and it is not the main focus of the sentence. Thus, answer (D) is correct.

Vocabulary Words 46–60

46) **discomfiture** (n). shame, embarrassment, humiliation: *Robert felt great discomfiture after being sent to the vice principal's office for throwing an eraser at his friend Larry.*

47) **repudiate** (v). to reject, disavow, or deny as having no authority: *The celebrity repudiated the rumors that were circulated in the tabloids as being unfounded.*

48) **ignominious** (adj). shameful, disgraceful, embarrassing: *After missing the field goal kick, the player ignominiously walked off the field.*

49) **tactful** (adj). acting with a keen sense of what to say or do to avoid offending others; skill in dealing with difficult or delicate situations: *It would not be tactful to laugh during a funeral.*

50) **irksome** (adj). annoying, irritating, exasperating, tiresome: *Shyam found Billy's continuous sniffling quite irksome during the SAT.*

51) **tedious** (adj). long, tiresome, monotonous: *Filing all contracts dating back to 2008 for the entire office was a very tedious task for Cassandra.*

52) **promulgate** (v). to broadcast, announce, or promote: *The mayor called a town hall meeting to promulgate the new parking restrictions that would take effect in the new year.*

53) **tumult** (n). violent and noisy commotion or disturbance of a crowd or mob; uproar: *The children were awakened by a loud tumult coming from the basement.*

54) **persevere** (v). to persist in any undertaking despite obstacles: *Despite suffering many injuries throughout the season, Evan persevered and eventually was named MVP.*

55) **cherish** (v). to feel love for, to care dearly for: *When asked what they cherish most, many people answer "family."*

56) **antipathy** (n). dislike, hatred, aversion to: *Rebecca had great antipathy for her rival, Janine, who always seemed to find a way to put her down.*

57) **trifling** (adj). of little importance; trivial; insignificant: *Sarah tried to get her obsessive mother to stop worrying about trifling things like the length of the hedges in the front yard.*

58) **poignant** (adj). particularly affecting, regarding the emotions: *Mr. Riordan is an admirer of those who engage in poignant political discourse.*

59) **malign** (v). to slander, defame, speak untruths about: *Most of the characters in the movie* Mean Girls *malign each other secretly.*

60) **pittance** (n). a small amount or share: *Although his meager salary would never satisfy Isabella, Larry was quite content living on such a pittance.*

Latin and Greek Roots 19–24

19) CARD/CORD/COUR: heart (concordance, cordial, discord, cardiac, courage)

20) CAST/CHAST: cut (castigate, caste, chastise, chaste)

21) CENTR: center (concentrate, egocentric, heliocentric)

22) CERN/CERT/CRET/CRIT/CRIM: to judge, separate, distinguish, decide (discriminate, criteria, discreet, ascertain, certitude, discern)

23) CHRON/TEMPOR: time (anachronism, synchronize, temporal, extemporaneous)

24) CIRCU: around, on all sides (circumvent, circumlocution, circuitous, circumspect)

Mindset Tip

Before you begin the College Board Practice, take a moment, close your eyes, and visualize yourself spotting each of the wrong-answer traps as you go through the questions. You see a Goldilocks with a word like "all" or "totally," you see an assumption, a funhouse mirror, an answer choice that is way off topic, and a detail or piece of misinformation that does not answer the question asked. Spend a couple minutes working through a reading section in your mind and spotting these traps. Then do the practice.

UNTIMED COLLEGE BOARD PRACTICE

Complete the following College Board practice problems from College Board's *The Official SAT Study Guide* or online at www.collegeboard.org. Review answers after completing.

Test 1, Reading Test, Passages 3 and 4, #22–41

Try identifying one wrong-answer trap per question.

Math Test: Systems of Equations

We are sure you have heard about systems of linear equations in Algebra class, but you might not have realized how crucial they are to your success on the SAT. If there was one topic you would want to take the time to truly understand, it would be systems of equations, as many questions will test your knowledge of them. Although seemingly complex, systems of linear equations can be solved only one of two ways: substitution or elimination. Master these strategies, and watch your score greatly increase.

As you solve questions involving systems, ask yourself a few key questions:

- Which strategy can I use to solve the system?

- What is the question asking me to find?

In this section, we will outline the different methods for solving questions about systems of equations, but let's first start with the basics.

What Is a System of Equations?

Here is an example of a system:

$$3x + 2y = 21$$

$$x + 4y = 17$$

A system of equations is nothing more than two or more equations. In the example above, there are two equations, each with two variables.

Systems of equations have a solution at the point (x, y), which is where the (graphed) lines of the two equations intersect. The system of equations shown above, when graphed, would look like:

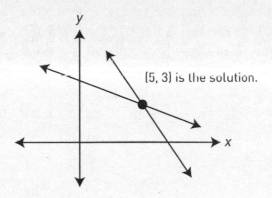

(5, 3) is the solution.

The solution to the system of equations shown above would be coordinate (5, 3), which means that $x = 5$ and $y = 3$.

Some questions may ask for the coordinate pair, and others may ask for just one of the variables where the lines intersect. Others may ask you to find the sum or the product of the two variables. Remember, sum means addition and product means multiplication.

Substitution Method

One of the most significant uses of substitution on the SAT is solving systems of equations questions. The same strategies used in the previous chapters can once again be applied to tackle some seemingly tough questions. To solve a system using substitution, you will be plugging in some type of expression to replace a variable.

You will know to use the substitution method when one of the equations contains a variable that is by itself. You can replace that isolated variable with its equivalent expression.

Here is an example below. Take note of the isolated y in the first equation, which tells you to use the substitution method.

Solve for x.

$$y = 2x$$
$$3x + y = 10$$

When solving a system using substitution, the goal is to eliminate a known variable so you can solve for the other, unknown variable or variables. By substituting the $2x$ for y in the second equation, x becomes the only remaining variable, allowing you to solve the equation.

$$3x + 2x = 10$$

$$5x = 10$$

$$x = 2$$

Finding the Second Variable

Sometimes, the first variable you solve for may not be what the question is asking you to find. After finding the value of one of the variables of a system of equations, you can plug that number into either equation to find the value of the other variable.

In the system above, x is equal to 2. To find y, plug 2 in for x in the equation with the isolated variable, and then solve for y. Even though you can plug 2 in for x in either equation, plugging into the equation with the isolated variable is the most efficient approach.

$$y = 2(2) = 4$$

The solution to the system could be expressed as $(2, 4)$, or $x = 2$ and $y = 4$.

Another type of systems of equations question may have two equations containing the same isolated variable. You can solve these with substitution by setting the two expressions equal to each other and solving for the remaining variable.

The next example below demonstrates this technique.

In the system below, the solution is a point (x, y). What is the product of x and y?

$$y = 2x - 4$$
$$y = 3x + 1$$

You can use substitution by setting the two equations equal to each other and solving for x.

$$2x - 4 = 3x + 1$$

$$-4 = x + 1$$

$$-5 = x$$

$$x = -5$$

Now plug −5 back into either of the original equations to find y.

$$y = 2(-5) - 4$$

$$y = -10 - 4$$

$$y = -14$$

This question is asking for the product of x and y, so multiply −5 and −14 to get 70.

$$xy = (-5)(-14) = 70$$

Blind Spot

Many times, the first variable you solve for is not the variable the question is asking you to find. It is easy to make a mistake, so slow down and know exactly what the question is asking for.

Substitution with Rearranging

Sometimes the best approach to solving a system of equations question may be substitution, yet neither of the equations have an isolated variable at first. With a little bit of rearranging, though, you can isolate one of the variables.

Let's try this next question, which builds on previously learned skills and, as a result, develops that neural pathway.

$$\frac{a}{2b} = 3$$

$$a + 2b = 24$$

In the system above, if $b \neq 0$, what is the value of a?

Since neither variable is isolated in either equation, you cannot use substitution yet, so you must rearrange the first equation to get a by itself. Do this by multiplying both sides by $2b$.

$$2b \cdot \frac{a}{2b} = 3 \cdot 2b \rightarrow a = 6b$$

Now that you have isolated a variable, you can substitute $6b$ in for a in the second equation.

$$6b + 2b = 24$$

$$8b = 24$$

$$b = 3$$

Since the question is asking for the value of a, you need to plug in 3 for b in either of the equations.

$$a = 6b \rightarrow a = 6(3) \rightarrow a = 18$$

PRACTICE A

Solve each for x and y.

1) $y = x + 4$

$2x + y = 10$

2) $y = 4x - 6$

$y = 3x + 10$

3) $4x + 3 = y$

$2x + 3y = 23$

4) $\frac{y}{2} = 1$

$2y + x = 12$

Elimination Method

Elimination is the second method you can use to solve a system of equations.

The great thing about elimination is that it is easy to know when to use it: when both equations have the same structure, with the variables and constants aligned vertically.

Use Elimination   Do Not Use Elimination

$$2y + 4x = 10 \qquad\qquad\qquad x = 12 + 2y$$

$$2y - 3x = 17 \qquad\qquad\qquad 2x - 4y = 6$$

Let's pay attention to two key points from the system that lets you know to use the elimination method.

- The xs, the ys, and the constants are aligned vertically.

- The coefficient, or the number in front of the variables, is the same, regardless of sign, for at least one of the variables (both ys).

Once you realize you can use elimination, find the variables that have the matching coefficient. In the example above, it would be the ys. If the signs (+/−) of the coefficients are the same, you will subtract the like terms of one equation from those of the other. If the signs are different, you will add the like terms of one equation to those of the other.

The purpose of adding or subtracting the equations is to eliminate one of the variables. This allows you to solve for the other variable. Here's an example.

What is the value of x in the system below?

$$-4x + 6y = 8$$

$$4x - 3y = 19$$

Since the coefficients of x are 4 and −4, *add* the terms, which results in −4x and 4x canceling each other out. Add the remaining variables and constants, and finally solve for y.

$$-4x + 6y = 8$$

$$\underline{4x - 3y = 19}$$

$$6y + (-3y) = (8 + 19)$$

$$3y = 27$$

$$y = 9$$

Once you have found the value of y, plug that back into one of the original equations to find x. Plug in 9 for y and solve for x.

$$-4x + 6(9) = 8$$

$$-4x + 54 = 8$$

$$-4x = -46$$

$$x = \frac{-46}{-4} = \frac{23}{2}$$

Here are two tips for using elimination:

- When subtracting, you want to subtract every term. Change the sign of each term of the equation and then add the corresponding terms of both equations together. Think of it as distributing a negative (−).

- The corresponding variables must be aligned with each other. If they are not, you must carefully rearrange them, making sure to keep the correct sign in front of each term.

Here is an example demonstrating both tips:

Solve for x.

$$2x + 8y = 10$$

$$8y - 4x = -14$$

Although the xs and ys in each equation do not align vertically, the first equation can be rewritten so they do. When moving the variables around, be sure to move the sign of the coefficient with them.

$$8y + 2x = 10$$

$$8y - 4x = -14$$

Now that the equations are correctly aligned, the $8y$ terms will cancel out if they are subtracted from each other. When subtracting, you must subtract each variable and constant, so it may help to write it like this:

$$8y + 2x = 10$$

$$-(8y - 4x = -14)$$

The next step is to distribute the negative, so the system is rewritten as:

$$8y + 2\text{x} = 10$$

$$-8y + 4\text{x} = 14$$

Now, using elimination is much easier, since the y terms will cancel. The equation $6x = 24$ is easily solved, resulting in $x = 4$.

Multiplying with Elimination

Sometimes, when answering systems questions, it will look like elimination can be used but none of the coefficients will cancel out. Before you can use elimination, at least one of the equations must be multiplied by a certain number so that the coefficients of the aligned variables are the same. You can multiply by any number, but make sure to multiply that number by each term. For example:

What is the value of y in the system below?

$$x + y = 4$$

$$-2x + 3y = 12$$

While this system can solved using substitution, it can also be solved using elimination, as you will see below. The quickest way to get the variables' coefficients to be equal is to multiply the first equation by 2. Make sure to multiply the entire equation by 2.

$$2x + 2y = 8$$

$$-2x + 3y = 12$$

Now that the coefficients of the x variable are the same in both equations, you can use elimination and add the two systems.

$$5y = 20$$

$$y = 4$$

A FEW KEY POINTS:

- You can multiply one equation by one number and the other equation by a different number.

- Try to multiply by a number that makes the equivalent coefficients opposite signs, so you can add the two equations.

Here is an example that can be solved by applying these key points:

$$4x + 3y = 10$$

$$3x + 2y = 8$$

What is the value of x in the system above?

Solving this question will require you to multiply both equations by different numbers in order to eliminate a variable. It will be easier to match the coefficients of the ys because the numbers will be smaller and eliminating the ys will solve for x, which is what the question wants you to find.

$$2(4x + 3y = 10) \rightarrow 8x + 6y = 20$$

$$-3(3x + 2y = 8) \rightarrow -9x - 6y = -24$$

The equations can now be added together and, after eliminating the ys, results in $-x = -4$. The final answer is $x = 4$.

There are many approaches to solving this question, but the one shown above is the most efficient.

Hint

Several SAT questions may have you find a point (x, y) as an answer.

Anytime you are asked to solve for a point and are provided with multiple-choice answers, you can always plug those choices into the system and see which answer choice is true. This is a great option for those tougher systems questions. Here a few hints when plugging in points:

• The point must work for both equations.

• You can pick the easier equation to plug into first.

• It will be safer to plug in all the answer choices, even if an early one works.

• Take your time when plugging in the numbers, as it is easy to make a simple mistake!

PRACTICE B

1) Solve for y.

$$2y + 4x = 10$$

$$2y - 3x = 17$$

2) What is the value of x in the system below?

$$2x + 4y = 6$$

$$y - 2x = 9$$

3) What is the value of x in the system below?

$$3x + y = 3$$

$$2y - 4x = -14$$

4) Which of the following points would be a solution to the system below?

$$\frac{y}{4} = 2x$$

$$x + y = 9$$

A) $(0, 8)$ **C)** $(1, 8)$

B) $(1, 0)$ **D)** $(8, 1)$

5) In the system of equations below, if (x, y) is the solution, what is the value of $x + y$?

$$\frac{1}{4}x = y$$

$$2x + y = 18$$

A) 2   **C)** 8

B) 4   **D)** 10

6) In the system below, what is the value of y?

$$5x - 2y = 10$$

$$2x + 7y = 7$$

A) $\frac{13}{5}$ **C)** $\frac{59}{39}$

B) $\frac{5}{13}$ **D)** $\frac{39}{59}$

7) If $f(x) = 3x - 4$ and $g(x) = \frac{5}{2}x + 6$, what value of x makes $f(x)$ and $g(x)$ the same?

Answers

Practice A (page 116)

1) $x = 2$ and $y = 6$

2) $x = 16$ and $y = 58$

3) $x = 1$ and $y = 7$

4) $x = 8$ and $y = 2$

Practice B (page 121)

1) $y = 7$

2) $x = -3$

3) $x = 2$

4) C

5) D

6) B

7) 20

UNTIMED COLLEGE BOARD PRACTICE

Complete the following College Board practice problems from College Board's The *Official SAT Study Guide* or online at www.collegeboard.org. Review answers after completing.

Test 1, Math: No Calculator, #8, 9, 11, 18

Test 2, Math: No Calculator, #2

Test 3, Math: No Calculator, #6

Test 3, Math: Calculator, #30

Test 4, Math: No Calculator, #3, 19

Chapter **5**

The Power of Your Thoughts

Positive thinking changes problems into puzzles, questions into opportunities, and worry into excitement.

What if we told you there was a way to instantly harness more of your brain power without doing more math problems or critical reading passages? Without any physical test prep? You would probably want to know what it was. It is actually quite simple, yet most students never even consider it as part of the test-prep process.

It's called positive thinking.

How you think, perceive problems, and frame the world around you is one of the most important components for success. When we are in a positive state of mind, the part of the brain in charge of higher-order thinking kicks into overdrive. We process more information, see different angles and perspectives, and critically think more efficiently. In other words, positive people are better problem-solvers. When we think positively, our brains work better. We see this every day in our classes—when a student is upset or holds any type of negativity toward the subject or themselves, their improvement comes to halt. This has also been proven in multiple research studies. In one study, Barbara Fredrickson and Christine Branigan found "that people experiencing positive emotions exhibit broader scopes of attention and [thought-action repertoires] than do people experiencing no particular emotion." Her experiments confirm "that positive emotion broadens the scopes of attention and cognition."[6] More recently, another study at Stanford showed that having a positive attitude was linked to greater math achievement.[7] The message is clear:

Positive Thinking → More Brain Power

Negative Thinking → Less Brain Power

Here are some of the many other benefits positive thinking can have on your SAT performance:

- More likely to take risks on tougher problems

- More willing to ask for help

- More likely to see a problem from a different perspective and find a shortcut

- More likely to persevere through a difficult passage

- More likely to use failure as a way to grow

- More willing to collaborate with others

Now, you might be thinking, "Well, what if I'm just not a naturally happy person? Does that mean I'm doomed for the SAT?"

The answer, of course, is no.

As with great test taking, positivity is an aspect of growth mindset and can be learned. Simply by adopting a growth mindset, you can become much more positive. If you believe you can change yourself and your future, it's possible to become much more optimistic about the process.

Here are some simple strategies for adopting a more positive outlook:

1) ADD SOME POSITIVE FUEL TO THE FIRE. You have the power to choose what you think about. Begin becoming more positive by remembering the things you did well in a given day or week. Too often, you only remember the negative—the math quiz you failed or the essay you forgot to hand in. Rather than harp on these, actively try to recall something you did, said, or accomplished that makes you feel proud of yourself: the right answer you got or the clever line you came up with.

2) SHIFT YOUR FOCUS FROM RESULTS TO EFFORT. When you base your success on your effort as opposed to the scores you receive, you have the power to win every time. Rather than dwell on a problem you got wrong, reflect on the amount of practice and effort you put in, and know that you are in control of your own effort.

3) BE GRATEFUL. One of the quickest and most overlooked ways to become more positive is through gratitude. Often, feelings of negativity and depression stem from lack. We believe we don't have something we need or that we lost something that is important to us. Being grateful for things we have has the power to automatically shift our thoughts from negative to positive. Anytime you are feeling down, think of things for which you grateful, including family, friends, or even your favorite flavor of ice cream.

4) GET MOVING. Sometimes the difference between a happy person and a depressed person just comes down to movement. Instead of sitting around and moping, get up and move. Take a walk, go for a bike ride, play a game of pickup basketball, or put on some music and dance around your living room. Don't believe us? Next time you're feeling down, get up and go for a walk.

These four strategies have the power to increase your positivity and should become part of your daily routine. In fact, to help solidify these habits, we'd recommend keeping a journal about daily achievements, determination and effort that you are proud of, and aspects of your life for which you are grateful.

Mindset Tip

Get your mindset right and higher scores will follow. Do you see your brain as half full or half empty?

Reading Test: Timing and Pacing

One of the most difficult aspects of the SAT is timing. On the reading section, students are asked to read five passages and answer 52 questions in 65 minutes. This is no small feat, especially for those of us who do not read often, and the idea of being timed sometimes finds its way into our negative thinking about the SAT. Students either decide to hate the test because of the timing, or begin to believe that something is wrong with their own ability if they cannot read quickly. If this sounds like you, we have the answer, and a sure-fire way to begin thinking more positively about the timing of the SAT.

Hint

It is important to remember that each question is worth the same number of points. You should not linger for too long on any one question, but instead move on to the next question to maximize your score.

By learning and applying one or both of the methods below, you can master the timing of the SAT and gradually eliminate that negativity that further hinders your growth.

PLAN A. If you do the math, you have roughly 12.5 minutes per passage, but you must remember that one of these five passages will be a paired passage, which merits a little more time. As a result, we recommend devoting 12 minutes to each regular 10-question passage set and approximately 14 minutes to the one paired passage of the test.

It is crucial to avoid lingering too long on any one question and to keep up your pace throughout the reading section. In addition, you should bring a watch with a second hand or a digital watch that measures seconds to help pace yourself. Try reading the passage in approximately 4–5 minutes (6–7 minutes for paired) and answering the questions accompanying the passage in the remaining 7–8 minutes.

If, however, you are an extremely slow reader (which can be helped over time), and you have never been able to finish a full Reading Test, no need to worry: we have a Plan B.

PLAN B. Instead of devoting equal time to each of the four regular (unpaired) passages, if you follow Plan B, you will devote less time to two of the passages, thus freeing up more time for the remaining passages.

Since graph questions typically do not require you to understand the entire passage and usually only come with 2–3 questions, you can save time by choosing two passages with graphs to not read fully—that's right, only *skim* these passages—and skipping right to the questions. For example, let's say you chose to avoid reading passages 3 and 4, maybe because passage 3 is hard science with a graph and passage 4 is on societal trends and has multiple questions on graphs. Each passage that you apply Plan B to will only take you approximately 9 minutes to complete, freeing up 6 minutes to be divided as you wish among the other passages that you do read. Here is what Plan B will look like if you decided not to read passages 3 and 4:

- Read passage 1, answer questions

- Read passage 2, answer questions

- Do *not* fully read passage 3, answer questions

- Do *not* fully read passage 4, answer questions

- Read paired passage 5, answer questions

So, how does this work? Can you really answer questions without fully reading the passage? It's actually quite simple due to the standardized nature of the SAT.

STEP 1: Take 2 minutes to read the blurb before the passage, then skim the introduction, the conclusion, and the first sentence of each body paragraph.

STEP 2: Go to the vocab-in-context questions. Answer them first.

STEP 3: Go to the graph questions. Answer them next.

STEP 4: Go chronologically to the questions that refer to line numbers and answer them by rereading 2–3 lines before and after the line in question. Read more if needed.

STEP 5: Answer the remaining questions using process of elimination, ending with central idea questions.

Hint

Always fully read the paired passages, as they have more questions that deal with understanding and comparing author's viewpoints.

PRACTICE: PLAN B

For this practice, you will answer vocab-in-context, graph, and detail questions, since these are the first questions to answer when using Plan B. We have also included a central idea question for you to attempt after completing the other questions.

Read the introductory blurb and then quickly skim the introduction, first sentence of each body paragraph, and conclusion. Then, start answering the questions, applying the reading method and your knowledge of reading question types.

The excerpt below is from "The Wright Brothers' Aeroplane" by Orville and Wilbur Wright. It details the brothers' early experiments in flight.

1   We began our active experiments at the close of this period, in October, 1900, at Kitty Hawk, North Carolina. Our machine was designed to be flown as a
5   kite, with a man on board, in winds from 15 to 20 miles an hour. But, upon trial, it was found that much stronger winds were required to lift it. Suitable winds not being plentiful, we found it
10   necessary, in order to test the new balancing system, to fly the machine as a kite without a man on board, operating the levers through cords from the ground. This did not give the
15   practice anticipated, but it inspired confidence in the new system of balance.

   In the summer of 1901 we became personally acquainted with Mr.
20   Chanute. When he learned that we were interested in flying as a sport, and not with any expectation of recovering the money we were expending on it, he gave us much encouragement. At
25   our invitation, he spent several weeks with us at our camp at Kill Devil Hill, four miles south of Kitty Hawk, during our experiments of that and the two succeeding years. He also witnessed
30   one flight of the power machine near Dayton, Ohio, in October, 1904.

   The machine of 1901 was built with the shape of surface used by Lilienthal, curved from front to rear like the

35 segment of a parabola, with a curvature 1/12 the depth of its cord; but to make doubly sure that it would have sufficient lifting capacity when flown as a kite in 15- or 20-mile winds, we
40 increased the area from 165 square feet, used in 1900, to 308 square feet—a size much larger than Lilienthal, Pilcher, or Chanute had deemed safe. Upon trial, however, the lifting

45 capacity again fell very far short of calculation, so that the idea of securing practice while flying as a kite had to be abandoned. Mr. Chanute, who witnessed the experiments, told us that
50 the trouble was not due to poor construction of the machine. We saw only one other explanation—that the tables of air-pressures in general use were incorrect.

Lifting Capacity When Flown as Kite
100% Lift is Required to Sustain Flight

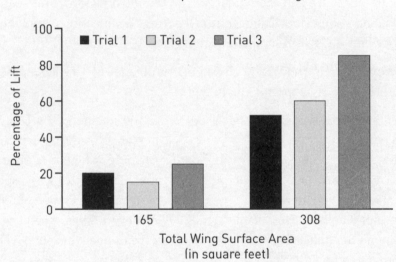

The graph above, which was adapted for SAT purposes only, shows the lift achieved during each of the three trials at the 165 and 308 wing areas.

1) As it is used in line 1, "active" most nearly means

A) On the go

B) Energetic

C) Hands-on

D) Full of life

2) In the context of the passage, "suitable" in line 8 most nearly means

A) Pleasant and warm

B) Appropriate in decorum

C) Sufficient for lift

D) Oriented in the correct direction

3) According to the table and the information in the passage, in which of the following trials did the Wright brothers achieve sufficient lift for flight?

A) 165: trial 2

B) 165: trial 3

C) 308. trial 3

D) Sufficient lift was never achieved

4) Based on the table, which of the following statements is true?

A) At 165 feet, the trials gradually produced greater lift than those at 308 feet

B) The area of the wings is directly proportional to the amount of lift achieved

C) Sufficient lift for sustained flight was achieved in trial 3 at 308 feet

D) At 308 feet, the lift achieved doubled from trial 2 to trial 3

5) As stated in paragraph 2 of the passage, what is one reason why Mr. Chanute approves of the Wright brothers' venture?

A) He enjoys watching people fail

B) He witnessed one flight of the power machine at Dayton, Ohio

C) The brothers were interested in flight regardless of expense

D) He spent several weeks at Kill Devil Hill

6) The main purpose of the passage is

A) To highlight the dangers of the Wright brothers' first flight experiments

B) To analyze the complex relationship between the Wright brothers

C) To detail the mechanics of lift in airplanes

D) To describe the Wright brothers' early experiments in flight

Answers

1) For this question, we need to reread the sentence with "active" in it and a couple sentences after in order to understand what an "active experiment" is. We would eliminate "energetic," "on the go," and "full of life" because they are common meanings of the word that do not make sense in context. This leaves us with choice (C).

2) This vocab-in-context question requires you to understand the surrounding context dealing with wind. When we reread that section, we realize that the wind is being referred to in connection with how sufficient it is to create lift, and so we will eliminate the common meanings "pleasant and warm" and "appropriate in decorum." "Oriented in the right direction" also does not have to do with lift, and so the answer is (C).

3) After you read the x and y-axis and look at the height of the bars in each trial, you should note that no trial achieved 100% lift, which is the lift necessary for sustained flight. Thus, choice (D) is the answer.

4) After measuring the bars on the graph, you will notice that each trial at 308 feet is greater than those at 165 feet. This means that as the wing area increased, so did the lift, which gives us (B).

5) Whenever you see "as stated in the passage," realize that this is a detail question and that the correct answer choice will either be directly stated in the passage or closely paraphrased. Choice (A) does not answer the question, and choices (B) and (D) use material from the passage to trick you. Although Mr. Chanute did indeed witness the flight of the power machine and spend several weeks in Kill Devil Hill, these are not the reasons he approves of the Wright brother's venture. Choice (C) is a close paraphrase of lines 20–24, which reveals the cause for Mr. Chanute's approval. This, question like the previous ones, does not require a full reading of the passage. In fact, reading the whole passage might actually mislead you by making other answer choices that misuse information from the passage seem much more appealing.

6) Having read the blurb and a good deal of the passage at this point, you should have a decent understanding of the central idea or purpose. You also know this passage is about the Wright brothers' aeroplane from the title. You can eliminate overly specific answer choices like (C) and eliminate choice (A) as only partially represented and too extreme. You can also eliminate choice (B) because it is off topic and not represented in the passage. This leaves you with choice (D).

Vocabulary Words 61–75

61) **composed** (adj). a) calm, tranquil, serene: *Despite the chaos around him, Fred remained composed*; (v). b) to make up or constitute a part of: *The new compound was composed of several different elements.*

62) **disparity** (n). lack of similarity; inequality; difference: *The metaphor of the Haves and the Have Nots was an easy way of explaining the wealth disparity in the Gilded Age.*

63) **distinct** (adj). a) characterized as being different; not identical; separate; b) clear and unmistakable; c) distinguishing or perceiving clearly: *Although alike superficially, fool's gold and real gold are distinctly different elements.*

64) **economy** (n). a) thrifty management; frugality with money or materials; b) the efficient or concise use of something: *Unlike Fitzgerald, Hemingway advocated a writing style grounded in economy of word usage, choosing to cut out all unnecessary words.*

65) **prevail** (v). a) to be widespread or current; exist everywhere or generally; b) to predominate; to be the most important feature: *Happiness and celebration prevailed in the Lin household after the acceptance letter from Princeton arrived.*

66) **denounce** (v). to condemn or censure openly and publicly: *After WWII, Hitler was denounced for the many atrocities he orchestrated.*

67) **adversity** (n). hardship, difficulty, misfortune: *Without facing adversity one will never develop the grit and determination necessary for success.*

68) **advocate** (n). a supporter or promoter; (v). to support publicly: *The new mayor advocated the use of bicycles as a form of public transportation to reduce obesity rates in his city.*

69) **absurd** (adj). ridiculous, strange, illogical: *A tiny elephant appearing on your shoulder during dinnertime would be quite absurd.*

70) **hypothesis** (n). a proposition assumed as the premise of the argument: *The scientists excitedly constructed the experiment to test their hypothesis.*

71) **relapse** (n). to slip back into a former state or practice: *It was discouraging to Amanda to have worked so hard to get healthy and then have a relapse.*

72) **succeeding** (adj). following, subsequent, coming after: *Macbeth grew paranoid when the three witches predicted that Banquo's son would be the succeeding king.*

73) **substantiate** (v). to establish by proof or evidence: *To write a solid essay, one must substantiate any claims he or she makes with quotes and evidence.*

74) **commodity** (n). an article of trade: *Coffee is a prized commodity among workers with early jobs.*

75) **precede** (v). to come before: *An engagement usually precedes a marriage.*

Latin and Greek Roots 25–30

25) CLA/CLO/CLU: closed off from (enclose, claustrophobia, recluse, cloister)

26) CO/COM/CON: together (coalesce, converge, collaborate, convivial, community)

27) CRED: belief or trust (credible, credulous, credentials, credence)

28) CULP: blame, guilt (culpable, exculpate, culprit)

29) DIA/TRANS: across, through (dialogue, dialect, diaphanous, translucent, transient, transitory)

30) DIS: not, away from (disparage, disease, disparity, disseminate, disperse, disingenuous, disinclined)

TIMED COLLEGE BOARD PRACTICE

Complete the following College Board practice problems from College Board's *The Official SAT Study Guide* or online at www.collegeboard.org. Review answers after completing.

Test 2, Reading Test, Passage 1, #1–10. Using the pacing strategy for Plan A, read the passage in 4–5 minutes and answer the questions in 7–8 minutes.

Next, try out Plan B by doing the second passage in the Reading Test for College Board Test 2, numbers 11–21. Apply the Plan B strategy of not fully reading the passage, making sure to time yourself and hit each of the steps in the appropriate order as listed above. Remember to also go through the usual process, using the reading method described in Chapter 2. Check your work. How did you do? How long did it take you?

Math Test: Mastering Linear Functions

This chapter will combine two essential components necessary to conquer the SAT: positive thinking and linear functions. We already know how powerful positive thinking is, so let's take a moment and see how it would look on a coordinate graph. Questions involving graphs come up frequently on the SAT, so it is important we take the time to learn them.

Below is an example of a possible linear function based on positive thinking. As pictured below, a linear function will always be a line.

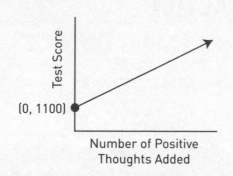

Number Positive Thoughts Added (x)	Test Score (y)
0	1100
1	1110
2	1120
3	1130
4	1140
5	1150

Here are the fundamentals of linear functions.

1) The slope of a linear function is the line's constant rate of increase or decrease. This means that the distance between each point will always be described by the same ratio. The slope is the change in y over the change in x. In the example above, notice how the x values increase by one each time and the y values increase by ten each time. Therefore, the slope would be $\frac{10}{1}$, or 10, which means that each positive thought will increase your score by 10 points.

2) The y-intercept is the point where the line crosses the y-axis. It is the starting point, or the initial amount, and is the first point you would graph. The y-intercept from above is (0, 1100) because the x value is equal to 0. If we are analyzing this, we would say that our test score remains the same if we do not add any positive thoughts.

3) The x-intercept is the point where the line crosses the x-axis. It is important to know that the y value is equal to 0 when the line crosses the x-axis, so to solve, you can plug in 0 for y. The x-intercept can also be referred to as a root or a zero.

Based on the graph on the previous page, you could say that as your number of positive thoughts increases, so does your test score. While the information was made up and generalized, the underlying principle is accurate. Our experiences have shown that there is a direct correlation between a student's improvement and his or her level of positivity. As a result, we can graph this relationship as a linear function with a constant slope.

Slope-Intercept Form

Most linear equations are written in slope-intercept form, which is shown below.

$$y = mx + b$$

The slope of the line is m, the y-intercept is b, and the x and y represent any point on that line.

Since $f(x)$ is essentially the same as y, slope-intercept form could also be written as $f(x) = mx + b$.

Writing Equations of Lines

To write an equation of a line, substitute the slope and y-intercept into $y = mx + b$. As you are writing an equation, it will help to remember these two keys:

• The m is the slope and is always multiplied by a variable.

• The b is the y-intercept, also called the constant, and has no variable.

Say we want to write an equation of a line in slope-intercept form with a slope of 5 and a y-intercept of $(0, 2)$.

By substituting in 5 for m and 2 for b, the equation can be written as $y = 5x + 2$.

Parallel and Perpendicular Lines

On the SAT, you will also need to write the equation of a line that is parallel or perpendicular to another line, so let's discuss what these two words mean.

- Lines that are parallel never intersect and thus, these lines have equal slopes.

- Perpendicular lines cross at a 90° angle and, as a result, they have opposite reciprocal slopes. This means you will change the sign and flip the fraction.

For example, a line with an equation of $y = -3x + 6$ is parallel to a line with an equation of $y = -3x - 2$, because they both have a slope of -3.

The line with the equation $y = -3x + 6$ will be perpendicular to any line with a slope of $\frac{1}{3}$ such as $y = \frac{1}{3}x + 4$.

Here is an example to demonstrate how your knowledge of these skills will be tested.

Which of the following lines is perpendicular to the line with the equation $y = \frac{2}{3}x + 5$?

A) $y = \frac{2}{3}x - 5$

B) $y = \frac{3}{2}x - 5$

C) $y = -\frac{3}{2}x + 5$

D) $y = -\frac{2}{3}x - 5$

The slope of the original equation is $\frac{2}{3}$, so to find the slope of a line perpendicular to it, take the opposite reciprocal, which is $-\frac{3}{2}$. The only answer choice with that slope is (C).

Rearranging to Find Slope-Intercept Form

The examples so far have been straightforward because the equations were written in slope-intercept form, making it easy to identify the slope. This next example presents an equation not written in slope-intercept form and will require you to use rearranging to identify the slope.

$$2x + 2y = 12$$

Which of the following is parallel to the equation above?

A) $y = x + 4$

B) $y = x + 6$

C) $y = 2x - 1$

D) $y = -x + 3$

Rearranging is a skill you have already learned and practiced. To find the slope of the original equation, you must first rearrange the equation so that it is written in the form $y = mx + b$. Remember, there are multiple ways of doing this.

$$2x + 2y = 12$$

Subtract $2x$ from both sides.

$$2y = 12 - 2x$$

Divide both sides by 2.

$$\frac{2y}{2} = \frac{12 - 2x}{2}$$

Rewrite the rational expression (fraction).

$$y = \frac{12}{2} - \frac{2}{2}x$$

Simplify both fractions.

$$y = 6 - 1x$$

It is important to remember that the slope is always the number with the variable. Here, the slope in the equation is -1. You can rewrite the equation as $y = -x + 6$ if you would like. Since the question wants you to find a parallel line, just identify the answer choice with the slope of -1, which is choice (D).

PRACTICE A

For questions 1–2, write an equation in slope-intercept form, using the given information.

1) $m = \frac{1}{3}$, $b = 2$

2) $m = -4$, $b = 3$

For questions 3–6, identify the slope and y-intercept for each line:

3) $y = 2x - 8$

$m = \underline{\hspace{2cm}}$, $b = \underline{\hspace{2cm}}$

4) $y = 10 - 3x$

$m = \underline{\hspace{2cm}}$, $b = \underline{\hspace{2cm}}$

5) $y = 2(x - 3)$

$m = \underline{\hspace{2cm}}$, $b = \underline{\hspace{2cm}}$

6) $y = \frac{1}{4}(x - 8)$

$m = \underline{\hspace{2cm}}$, $b = \underline{\hspace{2cm}}$

7) What is the slope of the line $4x + y = 2$?

8) What is the slope of a line parallel to $2x - y = 8$?

9) What is the slope of a line perpendicular to $y = -2x - 4$?

10) What is the slope of a line perpendicular to $x - 2y = 6$?

11) What is the equation of the line that passes through the point (2,6) and has a slope of –2?

12) What is the equation of a line that passes through the points (3,6) and (5,–2)?

Graphing Lines in Slope-Intercept Form

Graphing an equation that is written in $y = mx + b$ form is straightforward.

The y-intercept, which represents the starting point, will be the first point to plot. The graph of the equation $y = 2x + 1$, which has a slope of 2 and a y-intercept at $(0, 1)$, is shown below.

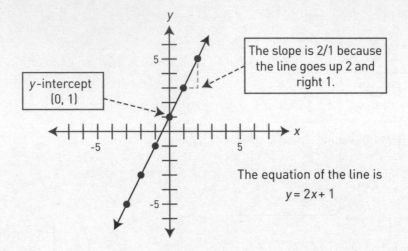

Let's try another example, this time with a negative slope.

$$\text{Graph the line } f(x) = -x - 3.$$

The y-intercept is at the point $(0, -3)$. Be careful with negative slopes! Since the slope is -1, it can be written as $\dfrac{-1}{1}$, telling you to go down 1 but still right 1.

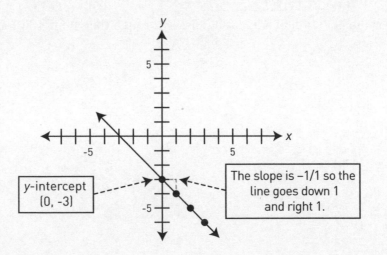

Graphing Linear Inequalities

Since an inequality is very similar to an equation, use the same process by plotting the y-intercept and using the slope to find the next point. There are, however, two additional steps required to graph a linear inequality.

1) With a greater than or equal to ($\geq$) inequality or a less than or equal to ($\leq$) inequality, the line will be solid, but both greater than ($>$) or less than ($<$) inequalities will be dashed lines.

2) One side of the graph will be shaded to represent all the possible solutions. If it is greater than ($>$) or greater than or equal to ($\geq$), the shading will be above the line. If it is less than ($<$) or less than or equal to ($\leq$), the shading will be below the line.

Here is an example that shows a graph of a linear inequality.

Graph the inequality $y < 2x - 1$.

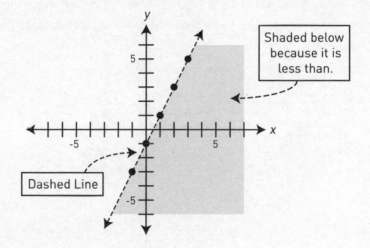

Shaded below because it is less than.

Dashed Line

System of Linear Inequalities

You may be asked to find a solution to a system of linear inequalities, as shown in the example below.

$$y \geq x - 1$$

$$y \leq 2$$

Which of the following points is a solution to the system of inequalities shown above?

A) $(5, 3)$

B) $(1, 1)$

C) $(0, -2)$

D) $(-2, -4)$

You could answer this question by plugging in answer choices, which would be an effective approach. However, let's explore the graph of these two inequalities prior to shading, as shown below:

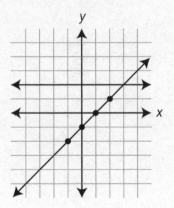

The key to solving a system of linear inequalities is to see where the shading of the two inequalities will overlap. Since you will shade above the line $y \geq x - 1$ and below the line $y \leq 2$, the overlap will be in between the two lines and to the left. The only answer choice that is in this section is (1, 1), or choice (B).

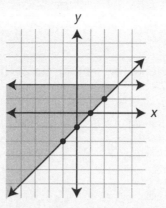

PRACTICE B

Graph each on the coordinate plane.

1) $y = \frac{1}{2}x + 3$

2) $y = -x + 1$

3) $y \geq 3x + 1$

PRACTICE C

1) Which of the following is parallel to $y = 2x - 3$?

A) $y = \frac{1}{2}x - 3$

C) $y = 2x + 4$

B) $y = -2x + 2$

D) $y = 2$

2) Which of the following is the x-intercept of the line $2x - 6y = 3$?

A) $\left(\frac{3}{2}, 0\right)$

C) $\left(-\frac{1}{2}, 0\right)$

B) $\left(\frac{2}{3}, 0\right)$

D) $(-2, 0)$

3) In which quadrant do the graphs of the functions $f(x) = x$ and $g(x) = x - 4$ intersect?

A) 1

C) 3

B) 2

D) None

4) Line l passes through the points $(4, 1)$ and $(-2, 5)$. Which of the following could be the equation of a line perpendicular line l?

A) $y = -\frac{2}{3}x + 1$

C) $y = -\frac{3}{2}x + 1$

B) $y = \frac{2}{3}x + 1$

D) $y = \frac{3}{2}x + 1$

5) Which of the following points is in the solution set of the system of inequalities listed below?

$$y \leq x + 2$$

$$y > -\frac{1}{2}x - 3$$

A) $(2, 8)$

C) $(-2, 1)$

B) $(2, -1)$

D) $(0, -4)$

Answers

Practice A (page 139)

1) $y = \frac{1}{3}x + 2$

7) -4

2) $y = -4x + 3$

8) 2

3) $m = 2; b = -8$

9) $\frac{1}{2}$

4) $m = -3; b = 10$

10) -2

5) $m = 2; b = -6$

11) $y = -2x + 10$

6) $m = \frac{1}{4}; b = -2$

12) $y = -4x + 18$

Practice B (page 143)

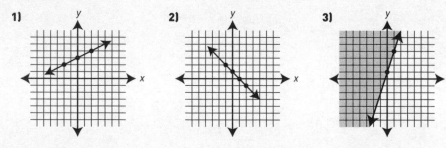

Practice C (page 143)

1) C

4) D

2) A

5) B

3) D

UNTIMED COLLEGE BOARD PRACTICE

Complete the following College Board practice problems from College Board's *The Official SAT Study Guide* or online at www.collegeboard.org. Review answers after completing.

Test 1, Math: Calculator, #18, 28

Test 2, Math: No Calculator, #6, 9

Test 2, Math: Calculator, #25, 28

Test 3, Math: No Calculator, #8

Test 3, Math: Calculator, #36

Test 4, Math: No Calculator, #8

Chapter **6**

Re-Visioning

> **"***The mind is its own place and in itself, can make a Heaven of Hell, a Hell of Heaven.***"** —Satan from John Milton's *Paradise Lost*

You know how important positive thinking is to conquering the SAT. So, how exactly do you become positive and look upon the SAT with happiness and hope rather than fear and dread?

You need to re-vision how you perceive the test. Re-visioning is purposefully changing the way you view something.

Your mind is always making judgments and assigning value to something as good or bad. Think about ice cream for a second. You probably got a little bit happier. You most likely like ice cream. Now think about the SAT. You probably do not get the same feeling you did when you thought of ice cream. Most students view the SAT with dread or, at the very least, mild anxiety.

We need to take a different approach and, as crazy as this may sound, learn to anticipate the test with excitement. Viewing the test as an opportunity to fulfill your dreams is a way to reverse the trend of negative thinking and invite new positive thoughts into your mind.

One way to re-vision the SAT is to look at it in terms of free tuition money. Many colleges offer tiered merit scholarships, which increase in monetary value with your score.

Take our student David, for example. After two attempts at the SAT without much of an increase in his math and English scores, you'd think David would have given up. His first score was under 1100, and that wasn't cutting it. The only way David was going to college was with a scholarship.

Enter growth mindset. David knocked on our door in the middle of his junior year and asked us for help with the SAT. David already had the drive; the only change we needed to make was in the way David viewed the test. Once David saw the test as a golden ticket to his future rather than an obstacle blocking him from his goal, he began to see his score steadily grow. The next time David took the test, his score had risen to 1200, which earned him that merit scholarship.

Ready to learn more? It's time to change your mind!

Reading Test: Timed Practice I

The next three chapters are each divided into two sections: strategy review and timed practice. In the strategy review section, we have included condensed, easy-to-read summaries of the strategies, along with some additional nuances and sample passages that model the strategy as a whole. In the timed practice section, you will be prompted to complete timed College Board practice with real SATs.

Strategy Review: The Reading Method

Before you begin your first full timed reading section, let's review the reading method for the reading comprehension section of the SAT, and then see how it is applied in a short excerpt.

1. Read the blurb first.

2. Read the passage fluidly and note the purpose, point of view, tone, and theme (PPTT).

3. Underline instances of contrast, repetition, extreme/colorful language, opinion words, and telling details.

4. Underline speaker changes.

5. *Always* go back to the passage when answering a question.

6. Predict the answer before looking at the answer choices.

7. Eliminate wrong answers.

With the reading method in mind, try your hand at this passage. We have modeled the steps for you. The following is an excerpt from the biographical account *Cardinal Wolsey* by Mandell Creighton, published in 1912, which explains the life and accomplishments of Cardinal Wolsey, a cardinal in the court of Henry VIII.

1   "All men are to be judged by what they do, and the way in which they do it. In the case of great statesmen there is a third consideration which challenges
5   our judgment—what they choose to do. This consideration only presents itself in the case of great statesmen, and even then is not always recognized. For the average statesman does from
10   day to day the business which has to be done, takes affairs as he finds them, and makes the best of them. Many who deliberately selected the issues with which they dealt have yet shrunk
15   from the responsibility of their choice, and have preferred to represent their actions as inevitable. Few can claim the credit of choosing the sphere of their activity, of framing a connected
20   policy with clear and definite ends, and of applying their ideas to every department of national organization. In short, statesmen are generally opportunists, or choose to represent
25   themselves as such; and this has been especially the case with English statesmen—amongst whom Wolsey stands out as a notable exception.

For Wolsey claims recognition on
30   grounds which apply to himself alone. His name is not associated with any great achievement, he worked out no great measure of reform, nor did he contribute any great political idea
35   which was fruitful in after days. He was, above all things, a practical man, though he pursued a line of policy which few understood, and which he did not stop to make intelligible.
40   No very definite results came of it immediately, and the results which came of it afterwards were not such as Wolsey had designed. Yet, if we consider his actual achievements,
45   we are bound to admit that he was probably the greatest political genius whom England has ever produced; for at a great crisis of European history he impressed England with a sense of her
50   own importance, and secured for her a leading position in European affairs, which since his days has seemed her natural right."

Let's apply each step of the reading method to this passage.

STEP 1: After reading the blurb, you learn valuable information: This is a passage about an important cardinal to King Henry VIII, and his accomplishments. It was published in 1912, which means the prose is wordier and has longer sentences, so you must read fluidly and more intently. You also should note that the excerpt is from a biography, which tells you that the passage will be focused on the cardinal himself and written from a single perspective.

STEP 2: From the final sentence of the passage, you get a good understanding of the author's point of view and tone. The author praises Cardinal Wolsey in the final sentence as "probably the greatest political genius," which reveals his admiration of the cardinal. Based on the type of work from which this is excerpted (a biography) and the formality of the sentences, you can identify this as informative and slightly laudatory (praising) in tone.

STEP 3: Take a look at the parts of the passage that have been underlined. Many of the phrases are extreme in degree, such as "all men," "only presents," "few can claim," "statesmen are generally opportunists," "Wolsey stands out as a notable exception," and "apply to himself alone." There is also the contrast word, "yet," that sets up an important point of the author: that Cardinal Wolsey was probably "the greatest political genius whom England has ever produced," which is also noteworthy because it is extreme in degree.

STEP 4: There are no speaker changes, so you can move to the questions.

STEPS 5 AND 6: To encourage you to predict, we have removed the answer choices for the three questions below. Write down answers in your own words, as if these were short answer questions. Remember to go back to the passage before you predict.

1) The author would likely attribute the greatness of Cardinal Wolsey to…

2) In the passage, the author characterizes the typical statesman as…

3) As used in line 35 of the passage, "fruitful" most nearly means…

Hint

Remember, your prediction does not have to be overly creative or insightful; it should simply answer the question by representing the material in the passage. You can even use a word from the passage as your prediction if that is easier.

STEP 7: Now, try these questions, which offer answer choices, and match your predictions to an answer choice. You might have to slightly adjust your predictions if they are not represented in the choices, but make sure to revisit the passage before you do so. Remember to eliminate answer choices as you go.

1) The author would likely attribute the greatness of Cardinal Wolsey to

A) The reform measures he succeeded in accomplishing

B) The practicality with which he approached all tasks

C) His success at elevating England's place and importance

D) The fact that he was the greatest political genius in the entire world

2) In the passage, the author characterizes the typical statesman as

A) Immoral

B) Self-serving

C) Untrustworthy

D) Compassionate

3) As it used in line 35 of the passage, "fruitful" most nearly means

A) Providing fruit

B) Abundant

C) Productive

D) Rewarding

Answers

1) Answer (C), which discusses Cardinal Wolsey's actions within England, is correct. Answer (A) is the opposite of what is stated in the passage, and answer (B) is misinformation: he was practical, but that was not the cause of his greatness. Answer (D) is a Goldilocks choice, because though Wolsey was thought of as great within England, it is hyperbolic to suggest he was the greatest in the world.

2) Answer (B) is correct because the author suggests that the typical statesman is self serving in lines 8–12 and lines 23–24. Answer (A) is extreme and slightly distorted and answer (C) is an assumption. One might logically assume that opportunistic people are untrustworthy, but this is not represented in the passage. Answer (D) is off topic.

3) Answer (A) is a purposeful confusion of the word "fruitful" with its literal components, whereas answers (B) and (D) are incorrect because, though they are common meanings of the word, they do not fit the meaning of the sentence. Thus, answer (C), "productive," is correct.

Anatomy of the Passage Extended

You have learned about the basic structure of the informational/argumentative passage and the narrative passage, but now let's look in more depth at some specific passage structures you will find on the SAT Reading Test.

Common Science Passage Structures

Science passages will appear either individually or as paired passages.

1) Hypothesis→ experiment→ findings

In these passages, the author will present a new hypothesis that he or she seeks to prove and then discuss an experiment or possible ideas for experiments. These passages typically conclude with findings of the experiment, although these findings need not provide any real answers. You may see passages on bees, DNA, ocean currents, climate, etc.

2) Phenomenon→ possible causes of that phenomenon

In these passages, the author will present a phenomenon, such as an animal's migration habits, technology's effect on job growth, or the movement of undersea waves, and then analyze the possible causes of that phenomenon. These passages often divide their paragraphs by explanation. In other words, paragraph 2 might be one explanation and paragraph 3 might be another.

3) Invention or new idea→ how new idea is received or invention changes society

In these passages, as with the passages concerning a hypothesis or phenomenon, the author will present a new idea, technology, or invention, and then use the rest of the passage to explain how this will change society. Certain passages might include the prospect of an off-world economy, the use of high-speed trains, or the invention of a new type of solar panel.

4) Theory A→ refutation (negation) of theory A→ theory B (author's theory)

This is perhaps one of the most common science passage structures and may appear within any of the above structures. For example, while reading about a new hypothesis or phenomenon, you might be presented with competing viewpoints or theories about its effect or origin. This structure might also appear as a paired passage with the first passage conveying the first theory or viewpoint and the second passage conveying a differing theory or viewpoint. With these passages, it is absolutely crucial to underline speaker changes and contrast words and understand each author's point of view.

Common History Passage Structures

1) Passage 1: Viewpoint one

2) Passage 2: Viewpoint two

As with the final science structure, this structure is based on contradictory viewpoints. The history passage will usually appear as a paired passage on the SAT because they typically involve different viewpoints on a topic in history. You may read passages related to women's rights or the role of women in society. These passages will typically be from a time period before women were granted equal rights. Passage 1 may be from the viewpoint of someone who believes women led an adequate life without the same rights as men, and passage 2 may present a viewpoint from someone who believes women must have rights. Other topics discussed in these passages include government and civil rights. For example, you might read one passage in which the author believes the only way to change laws is to follow the legal system and legislate, while the other author believes that rather than attempt to change unjust laws, one should simply break them.

1) Societal problem→ proposed solution

This passage structure will be found in unpaired history passages, which are less common on the SAT. Like the paired history passages, these examine societal problems and viewpoints. The author will present some issue that affects people and their rights or place in society, and will then discuss or petition for possible solutions. Like the authors in the paired passage, the author of the individual passage might be someone advocating for civil rights or women's rights, or someone examining an aspect of society and government that he or she deems unsatisfactory and wishes to change.

Common Literature Passage Structures

There are typically three types of literature passage structures on the SAT:

1) Character encounters a new situation and changes

2) Description of a unique character

3) Character in conflict with another character

Each of the three listed literature passage structures are contingent upon character and conflict. Anytime you read a literature passage, you must focus on telling details of character, and how that character changes throughout the passage.

Mindset Tip

Since this is the first time you are attempting a timed practice reading section, this is also the first time you will be faced with negative thoughts about timed reading. You might say to yourself, "Why do I need to do this? Timed reading is pointless," or, "I'll never be able to read fast enough." Rather than let these thoughts plague your mind, realize that this is a prime opportunity to begin re-visioning. Below are a few different ways to re-vision timed reading on the SAT. Repeat these re-visioned statements to yourself as you work through the timed section.

1) Since the reading section is timed, I am provided with a structure that allows me to better pace myself and stay on task.

2) By practicing with timing, I will become better at handling pressure so that in the future, I can excel at such tasks.

3) Timed practice allows the right habits and best neural pathways to be strengthened. Rather than reinforce a wandering mind, timed reading develops a focused, task-oriented mind.

4) If there is nothing at stake and no set parameters, I would not be pushed to grow.

Vocabulary Words 76–90

76) **engross** (v). to be completely absorbed or engaged in: *I was so engrossed in my book that I didn't hear the doorbell ring.*

77) **fundamental** (adj). a) essential: *One of the fundamental aspects of being an American citizen is paying taxes.* (n). b) part of the basic core structure: *Students must learn the fundamentals of arithmetic before moving on to advanced algebra.*

78) **anomaly** (n). a deviation from what is normal or common: *Ten consecutive days of 100 degrees in November is a scientific anomaly that needs to be studied.*

78) **phenomenon** (n). a) an occurrence worthy of observation; b) something interesting or impressive: *There are special UFO groups that study the phenomenon of alien visitors.*

80) **inversion** (n). a reversal, the opposite of: *It can be colder in the valley due to the temperature inversion in winter.*

81) **affluent** (adj). wealthy: *As we drove through the affluent neighborhood we were amazed at the size and beauty of the colossal mansions.*

82) **opulent** (adj). wealthy, lavish, luxurious: *The gala was held in the opulent grand ballroom of the palace.*

83) **feign** (v). to fake: *The little boy feigned illness to get out of going to school.*

84) **alleviate** (v). to make easier to tolerate; to lessen in severity: *I took an aspirin to alleviate the pain of my throbbing headache.*

85) **monetary** (adj). related to money: *The court awarded the worker monetary compensation for being injured on the job.*

86) **circumvent** (v). to go around or avoid: *John had the ability to circumvent any problems that arose with his charm and wit.*

87) **benevolent** (adj). kind and charitable: *The benevolent leader was loved and respected by his people.*

88) **recession** (n). a) the act of declining, a downturn; b) a state of economic depression: *Prices fall during an economic recession.*

89) **demographic** (n). a part of the population having similar characteristics: *Malibu Makeup is the newest in a line of makeup products aimed at the tween girl market demographic.*

90) **fiscal** (adj). relating to financial matters: *The company was accused of fiscal irresponsibility for misuse of funds.*

Latin and Greek Roots 31–36

31) DIC/DICT: speak, proclaim (contradict, dictate, dictator, diction, dictionary, indictment, prediction, verdict)

32) DEMOS/DEM: people (democracy, demographic)

33) DOC/DIDA: to teach (doctor, doctrine, didactic)

34) DOL: pain (dolorous, condolence)

35) DUPL: double (duplicate, duplicitous)

36) DUR: hard, stubborn (endure, obdurate, durable)

TIMED COLLEGE BOARD PRACTICE

Complete the following College Board practice problems from College Board's *The Official SAT Study Guide* or online at www.collegeboard.org. Review answers after completing.

Test 2, Reading Test

Do 3 of the 5 reading passages in this test, #22–52. Allot yourself 38 minutes to do one paired 14-minute reading passage and two regular 12-minute reading passages.

Math Test: Real-Life Linear Applications

Being able to convert real-life scenarios into expressions, equations, functions, and inequalities will help you answer many of the word problems you will encounter on the SAT.

Let's start by writing linear expressions, which, as we stated before, are made up of a combination of numbers and variables that can be written in the form $mx + b$.

There are two key components to a linear expression: the **slope** and the *y*-**intercept**.

Let's start with slope, represented by the variable m. As you recall, the slope is always multiplied by a variable and represents how much something is increasing (going up) or decreasing (going down). Another way to think about the slope is as the rate of change.

For example, if you made $10 an hour, you could write the expression as $10h$, with h being the number of hours, and 10 being the slope. This would mean you get $10 for every hour that you worked.

Here are some more examples:

You walk at a pace of 60 feet a minute (m) ➜ $60m$

Hot dogs (H) cost $3 each ➜ $3H$

Mike makes 20 muffins an hour (h) ➜ $20h$

Notice how all the examples combine a coefficient with a variable. This number is, in essence, the slope. So, anything that can increase or decrease will be attached to a variable.

The next step is to add in a constant, which is a number with a fixed value. The constant is the *y*-intercept (written as b) in $mx + b$. Here is an example:

You have $80 in your account and you add an additional $2 each day. Write an expression that represents the total money you have in your account after d days.

Since you start with $80, that is the constant, or y-intercept. The number that will be multiplied by the variable is the 2, because it represents the slope, or the amount of increase each day. Here is how the expression would be written:

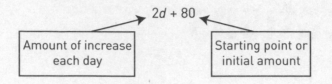

This expression could also be written as $80 + 2d$.

The key to writing an expression is to figure out which information will be represented with a variable and which will not. The table below contains some key words that will tell you what information is the slope and what is the y-intercept. It will help to underline, box, or circle them as you come across them in word problems on the SAT.

Slope (With a Variable)	Y-Intercept (No Variable)
Increase	Initial
Decrease	Tip
Per	Fee
Each	Starts at
Each time	Currently has
Grows	

Negative Slopes

All the previous examples had increasing rates, or positive slopes, but you will also need to write expressions that show a decreasing value, or a negative slope. The key here is that m will be negative.

The order of the slope and y-intercept can be changed and, oftentimes, the constant will come first, such as $100 - 2h$, but the expression could also be written as $-2h + 100$. Let's try some examples.

PRACTICE A

Write an expression for each of the following statements, in terms of the given variable.

1) Mia babysits and charges a $10 fee as well as $12 per hour, h.

2) It costs $40 a day, d, to rent music equipment and a security deposit of $120.

3) You start with 50 cookies and make an additional 48 per hour, h.

4) Kyle's grade is a 92 but will lose a point for each wrong answer, w.

Writing Linear Equations

The major difference between an expression and an equation is the equal sign, so writing equations will be very similar to writing expressions. An equation will have a variable that is isolated on one side of the equal sign. That variable will represent the total.

Here is an example of an equation you might see:

> A movie streaming company charges a five dollar fee to sign up plus an additional two dollars per downloaded movie. Write an equation to represent the total cost, in dollars, c, in terms of the total number of downloads, d.

$$c = 2d + 5$$

Writing Functions

It is common for some students to allow some negative thoughts to creep in whenever they see function notation, such as $f(x)$. Remember, the great test taker relishes the new terminology and realizes it is exactly the same as an equation. It is just a different way of writing the total amount.

You may see $c(x)$, $p(x)$, or $t(x)$. Treat these the same way you would a single variable. Here is the previous example written as a function instead of an equation.

$$c(d) = 2d + 5$$

There is no difference between the two strategies. Let's try the question on the next page.

Katie bought a membership to a fitness center. The startup fee was $50, and she will pay $20 for each month she is a member. If m is the number of months, which function C represents the total amount she will pay in dollars?

A) $C(m) = 20m + 50$

B) $C(m) = 70m$

C) $C(m) = 20 + 50m$

D) $C(m) = 50 - 20m$

The startup fee represents the y-intercept and the monthly fee would be the slope, so this function could be written as option (A):

$$C(m) = 20m + 50$$

Writing Inequalities

Everything you just learned can also be used to write an inequality, as long as you understand some key words involving inequalities. Below is a table of words translated as inequality symbols.

Greater Than >	More than, larger than, above
Greater Than or Equal To ≥	At least, minimum
Less Than <	Below
Less Than or Equal To ≤	Maximum, at most

Mindset Tip

When you are tasked with writing an inequality from words, take a few seconds to consider what the words mean. Phrases like *at most* or *at least* should help you determine the direction of the inequality.

It is more important to understand them than to memorize them. For example, if you see the expression *at most*, ask yourself what that would mean.

> John wants to make <u>at least</u> $800 working this summer. He will get paid $250 to house-sit and will get $32 an hour at a physical therapist's office. Write an inequality to express the number of hours, h, he would need to work to reach his goal.
>
> A) $32h + 250 \leq 800$
>
> B) $32h + 250 \geq 800$
>
> C) $32h + 800 \geq 250$
>
> D) $32h + 800 \leq 250$

Use the same approach you would for writing an expression. The 250 should be without a variable because it is a one-time fee. The 32 should be multiplied by the h because it is an hourly rate. So, the expression would be:

$$32h + 250$$

Since John needs to make <u>at least</u> $800, 800 represents the total, and can be isolated in this way:

$$32h + 250 \geq 800$$

We use greater than or equal to sign because we want the $250 plus his hourly rate to total at least $800.

Writing Equations in Standard Form

You may be asked to write an expression that represents a combination of two or more items. Not all expressions can be written in slope-intercept form, in which case you will want to use standard form, which looks like this:

$$ax + by = c$$

Notice that x and y will both have numbers in front, which means that you can treat them both as if they have a slope. This is how you know to write the equation in standard form: there are two slopes. Once again, c would represent the total.

Here is an example:

> Angel makes $4 per shirt and $8 per hat. Write an equation for the total, T, in dollars, he makes if he sells s shirts and h hats.

Since there are two different slopes for the two different variables, standard form must be used. It is important that you attach the correct rate to each variable. An effective strategy would be to circle both the "4" and the "s" and underline both the "8" and the "h".

The 4 is multiplied by s and the h is multiplied by the 8. When you combine, or add, the two together, you get the total, or T.

$$4s + 8h = T \longrightarrow T = 4s + 8h$$

Interpreting Linear Expressions

This next question type is simply the reverse of writing an expression, equation, or function. Rather than translating words into numbers and variables in an equation, you will be asked to explain the meaning of a certain part of an equation.

> Jenna's coaching charge is given by the expression $8h + 20$, with h being the number of hours. Which of the following could be the meaning of the 20?
>
> A) The amount she makes each day
>
> B) The initial amount she makes
>
> C) The amount of increase she earns per hour
>
> D) The increase in hours

In the question above, you are asked to *interpret* what the 20 could represent. When approaching this question, you should ask yourself:

Is the 20 with or without a variable?

Since the 20 is without the variable it is the constant, or the starting point. Therefore, the 20 could represent a tip, a fee, or any other initial value. It cannot represent an increase, decrease, or a rate. The correct answer to this question is (B).

Remember: The word *constant* is another way of saying the y-intercept, and it represents the total when x is equal to zero. It will be measured in the same units as the total. So, if the total is measured in dollars, the y-intercept will be as well.

If the question was asking for the interpretation of the 8, since it is being multiplied by the variable, you would first identify it as the slope. It would represent how much the charge increases each hour. Once again, the number with the variable represents how much the total increases or decreases.

Labeling to Interpret

Labeling is a strategy that works great with questions that ask you to interpret part of an equation. Rewrite the expression, equation, or function and label each part with the information that is given, such as the slope, y-intercept, and total.

It may help to label the information with the units as well. Remember, the y-intercept has the same units as the total. Apply the labeling strategy to the example below.

> In the function $T(m) = 80m + 10$, T represents the monthly cost, in dollars, Gloria paid for a beach membership. If m represents months, what could the 10 represent?
>
> A) The price per month, in dollars
>
> B) The initiation fee, in dollars
>
> C) The number of months it takes to pay $80
>
> D) You start paying after 10 months

This question is asking you to interpret the meaning of the constant, 10. Below is an example of how a great test taker would label the function.

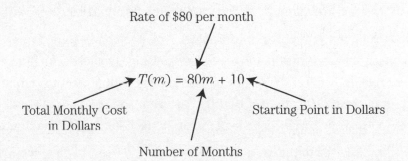

Since the units of the y-intercept will be in dollars, you can eliminate (C) and (D). Choice (A) refers to the increase, or slope, which should also be eliminated.

Since we are looking for the starting point in dollars, the answer that makes the most sense is choice (B).

Hint

The units of the constant and the total will always be the same.

Embracing Word Problems

Billionaire entrepreneur Richard Branson knows the power of growth mindset. His unique vision combined with his optimistic and adventurous approach to life are inspiring. Having started numerous companies using several of the concepts you have already learned in this book, he has become a self-made billionaire. One lesson we can learn from him is how he embraced obstacles as opportunities or, in other words, how he re-visioned problems.

You may have heard of Richard Branson's popular company, Virgin Airlines, but you might not know the story behind its origins. You see, Richard had a problem. His flight to Puerto Rico was canceled, leaving him and several other people stranded. So, what did Richard do? He didn't panic or give up; he began to search for a solution. As this was the last flight to Puerto Rico, he knew that there were other people in the same situation and he could take advantage of this unique predicament. Richard Branson decided to charter a plane. Now we know what you are thinking—it's crazy to charter a plane—but by convincing the other stranded passengers to join him, he found his solution. This ingenious re-visioning of a problem into an opportunity marked the beginning of Virgin Airlines.

What can we learn from this? How does starting your own airline apply to SAT math questions?

It is about viewing problems as opportunities instead of obstacles. We want to view word problems in the same way that Richard Branson and other extraordinarily successful business people view problems: as blessings in disguise. Word problems are a great opportunity to ingrain the correct mindset needed for success. The mindset that Richard Branson used to make billions is the same one needed to increase your SAT score. As the man himself said, "To launch a business means successfully solving problems."

So how can you apply the lessons from Richard Branson and the growth-mindset strategies he implemented in solving word problems?

The first thing is to use the skills you learned earlier in this chapter to conquer word problems. The second thing is to develop and apply a consistent method to solving word problems. Great test-takers have a systematic approach that they repeat for each question. This process is learned through practice over time.

When you approach a word problem, follow these steps:

1) Carefully read the question, collecting and organizing key information as you go.

2) Identify the type of problem and apply the appropriate strategy.

3) Solve the problem and make sure you correctly answered the question.

Let's try an example. Focus on the process and use the word problem–solving approach.

> A fast-food chain is running a special on some of its items for the month of November. They will be selling cheeseburgers for $1.50 each and French fries will cost $0.99 each. Which of the following expressions represents the total amount of money spent, in dollars, on c cheeseburgers and f French fries?
>
> A) $1.50c + 0.99f$
>
> B) $1.50c + 0.99$
>
> C) $0.99c + 1.50f$
>
> D) $1.50c - 0.99c$

STEP 1: While this question may look intimidating, it is a great example of how important Step 1 of the word problem–solving approach is. As you read the question, highlight the key information you think will help you find the correct answer.

> A fast food chain is thinking about running a special on some of its items for the month of November. They will be selling <u>cheeseburgers for $1.50 each and French fries will cost $0.99 each</u>. Which of the following expressions represents the <u>total amount of money spent</u>, in dollars, on <u>c cheeseburgers</u> and <u>f French fries</u>?

STEP 2: We can identify this word problem as a Writing Linear Expressions in Standard Form question and so we will apply the strategies we learned before.

$$\text{Cheeseburgers} = 1.50c$$

$$\text{French fries} = 0.99f$$

$$1.50c + 0.99f \text{ or (A)}.$$

The most common reason students struggle with word problems is because they expect to see the solution immediately and, as a result, they miss crucial steps in the process. The best thing you can do is take your focus off the answer and put that focus on your initial approach. By re-visioning the initial approach as the most important component of the word problem process, students will have much more patience, perseverance, and overall success on word problems.

> "*You don't have to see the whole staircase, just take the first step.*"
> —Martin Luther King Jr.

Here is another example for you to try. Focus on identifying the key information and finding a strategy to solve.

Jade has $200 saved and can earn $10 an hour interning for an architect. How many hours will Jade have to work to have $320?

A) 11

B) 12

C) 13

D) 14

The first information you collect can be organized into the expression $10h + 200$. The remaining information is $320, and since it represents the total or the final amount that Jade needs, this question can be written as an equation.

$$10h + 200 = 320$$

Since the question wants you to solve for the number of hours, you know to solve for h by subtracting 200 from both sides and then dividing by 10.

$$10h = 120$$

$$h = 12$$

This problem, like others, could be solved with different strategies such as writing an equation or plugging in answer choices. The key is to find the strategy that works for you.

Mindset Tip

Many SAT math questions contain a lot of words, but do not let them intimidate you. By staying positive, you give yourself the best chance at success. Remember, positive thinking = positive results.

Great problem solvers have a sense of curiosity, as they are always looking for information that will help them solve the question. They know how to connect the information they've been given to other skills they have learned. While some questions will tell you everything you need to answer the question correctly, others will require you to use information that is not given to you directly.

This next example is a great one to expand your word problem–solving abilities.

> The perimeter of a rectangle is 62 inches and the length is 12 inches. What is the area of the rectangle?
>
> A) 19
>
> B) 24
>
> C) 128
>
> D) 228

This will demonstrate how a great test taker will solve an SAT word problem.

What information am I given?

$$\text{I know } l = 12 \text{ and } P = 62.$$

Is there anything else that I know?

$$\text{I know that the perimeter formula of a rectangle is } P = 2l + 2w.$$

What strategies can I try?

$$\text{I can substitute these values into the equation and then simplify.}$$

$$62 = 2(12) + 2w \rightarrow 62 = 24 + 2w$$

I can solve for w and get 19.

What does the question want me to find?

The question is looking for the area of the rectangle, and since we know length and width, we can plug them into the area formula.

$$A = l \times w$$

$$A = 12 \times 19 \rightarrow A = 228$$

Blind Spot

Notice how 19, which is the width, is an answer choice. This is why it is so important to know what the question wants you to find. It wants you to find area, not width.

PRACTICE B

1) If ABC is equilateral and side AB is equal to $2x + 4$ and side BC is equal to $3x - 7$, what is the length of side AC?

A) 11

C) 33

B) 26

D) 44

2) The volume of a rectangular prism can be found by multiplying the length, l, width, w, and height, h. Which of the following equations represents the length, in terms of the width and height?

A) $l = whV$

C) $l = \dfrac{V}{wh}$

B) $l = \dfrac{wh}{V}$

D) $l = V - wh$

3) In 2010, Emily's math grade was an 84. Which of the following would represent her average rate of change, per year, if her math grade is a 98 in 2014?

A) 3 points per year

C) 4 points per year

B) 3.5 points per year

D) 4.5 points per year

4) Joey needs $15,000 for a new car and earns $30 per hour cleaning pools and $50 per hour playing piano at parties. If he already has $9,000 saved up and plans on working 100 hours cleaning pools, how many hours will he need to work playing piano to pay for the new car?

5) Tiffany is an airplane mechanic and the number of planes she has left to inspect can be modeled by the function $P(h) = -\frac{1}{2}h + 14$, with h being the number of hours she works. What is the meaning of the $-\frac{1}{2}$ in the given function?

A) The number of planes Tiffany can inspect per day

C) Tiffany can inspect one plane every two hours

B) The number of hours it will take Tiffany to inspect 14 planes

D) The number of planes she has remaining to inspect

6) So far while fishing, Matt has caught 34 fish. He catches fish at a rate of 6 per hour and needs to catch at least 80 fish before heading home. What is the fewest number of hours he would need to keep fishing before going home?

A) 6

C) 8

B) 7

D) 9

Answers

Practice A (page 159)

1) $10 + 12h$ or $12h + 10$

3) $50 + 48h$ or $48h + 50$

2) $4d + 120$ or $120 + 4d$

4) $92 - w$ or $-w + 92$

Practice B (page 168)

1) B (While x is equal to 11, side AC is 26.)

6) C

2) C

3) B

4) 60

5) C

UNTIMED COLLEGE BOARD PRACTICE

Complete the following College Board practice problems from College Board's *The Official SAT Study Guide* or online at www.collegeboard.org. Review answers after completing.

Test 1, Math: No Calculator, #3, 4, 6

Test 1, Math: Calculator, #32

Test 2, Math: No Calculator, #3, 8, 16

Test 2, Math: Calculator, #1, 8, 12, 17, 21, 35

Test 3, Math: No Calculator, #1, 4

Test 3, Math: Calculator, #8, 17, 18, 31

Test 4, Math: No Calculator, #7, 20

Test 4, Math: Calculator, #1, 2, 16, 17, 31, 32

Chapter **7**

Failure Phenomenon

> **"***Failure is not an option, it is a necessity!***"**
>
> —Anonymous

We hope you fail. Yes, you read that correctly; we hope you fail, and fail often.

Making mistakes is one of the most important components to success, and thus one of the most important aspects of re-visioning the SAT. Any successful individual, be they a sports icon, a politician, or a valedictorian, faced failure at some point. The difference between them and most students is that they learned how to use failure to benefit themselves and grow. All great endeavors involve risk, which at some point inevitably leads to a dead end, or "failure." Safe roads do not lead to success.

Take a moment and look at some of America's great "failures:"

- Michael Jordan was cut from his varsity high school basketball team as a sophomore.

- Abraham Lincoln ran for office seven times and was defeated seven times. His first significant win was being elected president of the United States.

- Steve Jobs dropped out of college, was fired from the company he founded, unsuccessfully founded a new company called NeXt, and eventually returned to Apple to save it from financial doom, making it one of the best companies ever.

We are programmed to think that mistakes and failures are bad. When you are failing in class, your teacher calls home. Failure means angry parents, lost privileges, and a slimmer chance at getting into the college of your dreams.

However, handled properly, failures are actually blessings in disguise. The student who never makes mistakes or never fails will never truly realize their potential. Take a second and reflect upon one family that understood the power of failure. When Sara Blakely, founder of Spanx, was growing up, her father would ask her the same question every night at dinner: "What did you fail at today?" This might seem like odd parenting, but in actuality, he was helping Sara re-vision failure by treating it as something positive, acceptable, and normal, rather than as a stigma or negative thing. As a result, Sara's father primed her for success at a young age. She would later recount how "[Her father's question] really allowed [her] to be much freer in trying things and spreading [her] wings in life."[8] Now one of the richest women in the world, Sara Blakely certainly took her father's lessons to heart and used failure to succeed.

A mistake or a failure says, "Look here at this question and learn from it." If you learn from a mistake, you will never make that mistake again, and that equals guaranteed points on the test.

In fact, the more mistakes you fix, the higher your score will be. This is the growth-mindset approach. When you re-vision failures and mistakes and see them as points on the test, you *take the power back from failure.* How can a failure depress you, demoralize you, or distract you from your goals when it is a vital part of why your score is skyrocketing?

The key to using mistakes to grow your score is to understand the different categories of mistakes and how each type serves a different purpose when approached correctly. The two most important categories of mistakes on the SAT are:

1) CARELESS MISTAKE. Careless mistakes occur when you are going too quickly or not applying the strategies correctly. Some careless mistakes include:

- Circling an answer that looks similar to the correct one

- Not answering the correct question

- Choosing a piece of evidence that seems correct before reading the other choices

Careless mistakes, when examined and reflected upon, teach us to fine-tune and adjust our test-taking process and approach. While they don't necessarily teach us new concepts, they force us to develop a discipline of mindfulness that is crucial for success on the test.

2) REVELATION MISTAKE. This is a mistake you make that has nothing to do with a lack of focus or something you did wrong. A revelation mistake is a mistake that *reveals* a need for growth of which you were not aware.

One type of revelation mistake can be when you are working within a familiar topic and make a mistake that reveals a gap in your knowledge, which you now realize must be filled. Had you not made the mistake in the first place, you would never have become aware of the gap in knowledge.

Another type of revelation mistake occurs when you are working on a very challenging problem and it reveals a new skill that you have not yet acquired.

To someone with a growth mindset, each of these mistakes triggers more thought, reflection, and eventual improvement. This is even backed by science: in the study *Mind Your Errors,* researchers investigated what occurs in the brain when we make an error. There findings were quite remarkable. When we make an error there is an accompanying electrical response in our brain called an ERP or Event Related Potential. Think of it like a spike in electrical current. When we mess up, our brain lights up. This occurs regardless of whether we know we made a mistake or not and is good news for us because the more electrical activity in the brain, the more brain growth.

There is, however, even better news for those with a growth mindset. The ERP that occurs at the onset of the initial error is not the only ERP (spike in electrical current). There is another electrical spike that follows the error, related to how you perceive the error. In the brains of people who believed they could grow from mistakes, the spike in electrical activity was much larger than the electrical spike in the brains of those who had a fixed mindset and did not believe they could learn from the error.[9] What does this mean?

When you combine a growth mindset and failure, it's like a laser light show in the brain. The more you fail, the more you grow.

Failure and mistakes are integral to your success on the SAT, so re-vision them and begin learning from them. Next time you face a challenge that you think you cannot overcome or a mistake you've just made, realize its hidden potential to light up your brain and make it grow.

What did you fail at today?

Reading Test: Timed Practice II

In this chapter, you will first reinforce your learning by reviewing the reading question anatomy and question types. Then, you will further develop your ability to identify question types and apply the correct strategy for answering by doing targeted practice. You will get to know your enemy so well that there will be no surprises, no tricks up the sleeve of which we are unaware. The reading questions will become so familiar that victory on the Reading Test will be inevitable.

Strategy Review: Question Types

As a reminder, these are the question components of an SAT reading question. These components will direct you toward the answer. Review these components again to ensure that you understand the anatomy of the reading question. Each of the following components is individually distinguished either by bolding, underlining, italicizing, or bolding and underlining the first word so that you can identify them in the example below.

- **Where**: To which location in the passage is the question referring you?

- *How*: Is there a part of the passage upon which this question is contingent or reliant?

- <u>Who</u>: To whom is this question referring? Is there a point of view to consider?

- **What**: What is the question actually asking?

In the passage example below, the **where** is bolded, the <u>who</u> is underlined, and the *how* is italicized. The **<u>what</u>** of the question has been bolded and underlined.

> *Based on the data presented in the graph*, <u>the author of passage 1</u> **<u>would most likely respond to the historian's statement</u>** about the Gilded Age in **lines 86–90** in which of the following ways…

It is important to remember the breakdown of the reading question and continually reinforce it by seeing it in every reading question because very few reading questions are one-dimensional. Many of them will require you to keep in mind several ideas and fulfill certain parameters; by breaking down the question, you are able to successfully answer.

Question Types

As we have learned in previous chapters, there are many different types of reading questions, and so it is important to continually practice identifying them; if you know all the faces and disguises of your enemy, you will ensure success in battle.

- Detail/Evidence: Refer to line numbers, and the answer is either stated directly or closely paraphrased. Don't overthink it: the answer choices give you line numbers to reference.

- Vocab in Context: These will ask about a word as it was used in the passage. Predict the meaning first and be careful with common meanings.

- Graph Analysis: Always read the graph's title, check the x- and y-axes, and look at the key or any other information. Be careful not to choose answers with information that is not measured or represented in the graph.

- Central Idea: These questions ask about main idea or the author's purpose. Check the introduction and conclusion and avoid overly specific answers.

- Relationships and Structure: This question type asks students to analyze text structure, shifts, development, and relationships between parts and ideas. Remember the common structures.

- Function and Effect: These are often "why" questions, asking about the purpose of part of the passage. They ask you to put yourself in the author's shoes. Reread two to three lines before and after the line numbers referenced to find the answer you need.

- Inference: These questions require you to make an inference about something not directly stated in passage. Be careful to avoid wrong-answer traps, especially funhouse mirrors and assumptions.

As you continue your reading timed practice, you might start focusing upon questions you have been answering incorrectly. You might start questioning your abilities. This is the perfect time to remember the failure phenomenon. In the words of Thomas J. Watson, chairman and CEO of IBM: "If you want to increase your success rate, double your failure rate." You must re-vision little mistakes and failures along the way in your reading timed practice and see them as opportunities for growth. Each incorrect answer in practice can be converted into a correct answer on the test.

Practicing Question Types

Let's dive deeper into the more difficult question types by examining the components of a few very important ones: function and effect, inference, relationships and structure, and vocab in context. The following is a condensed paired passage, from which we have eliminated much of the detail. What you have left is the basic skeleton of the passage. This stripped-down passage will help you better understand the subtle dynamics of each of these question types.

The first passage is written by Author X, a prominent researcher in the field of the psychology of human development, and the second passage is from Author Y, a prominent futurist in the field of technology and twenty-first–century society. (These passages were written solely for SAT practice and do not reflect any current research.)

Passage 1

1   Over the past ten years, the use of tablets and smart phones has increased dramatically among preteens. Now, at least 1 in 3 preteens owns and

5   operates a smart phone. The average use time has increased among preteens, and among teenagers, as well. Ten years ago, before the app boom (a period of time when the number of apps

10   available for smart devices tripled in one year), average use time was around 2 hours per day. In 2017, when study X was conducted, we found that the average use time had doubled

15   to 4 hours per day. Although many believe it teaches independence and accelerates intellectual growth, there are actually myriad negative effects of the increased reliance on and use of

20   smart phones in preteens and teens. Study X also found that increased use of smart phones severely stymied the development of preteens' interpersonal skills, while also contributing to a rise in

25 social phobias. Teenagers in high school
reported lower self-esteem, on average,
and trouble sleeping on a weekly basis.
Sure, smart phones can do a number of
great things, like provide directions,
30 call a ride, or look up a phrase in
Italian. But, while they might have some

benefits in the immediate present, their
cumulative effect on the social and
emotional development of our children
35 must be examined and reflected upon.
The future of our children is indeed in
jeopardy.

Passage 2

In the science fiction novel *Ender's
Game*, boys selected to enter battle
40 school train using simulators akin to
video games in order to prepare to
fight the alien threat, the Buggers. The
simulators create an immersive virtual
experience in which the battle school
45 cadets use a joystick and other controls
to navigate outer space and take out
Buggers. This simulation training is a
cornerstone of the novel and eventually
what saves humanity. What is important
50 to note about *Ender's Game*, though,
is not the foresight Orson Scott Card
showed with his rendering of a virtual
reality–type scenario, but the age he
chose to make the people tasked with
55 this simulator training and the job of
saving humanity. Adults are not chosen
to fly the simulators; children are. Why?
Why could it be that the very fate of the
planet is handed over to kids under the
60 age of 15? The answer is simple: they
are better at it. Children are adaptable,
malleable, and much more prepared to
engage with new, different technologies
than adults are. This is why it is illogical

65 to deny children—the ones most suited
for new technology—new technology.

Children must be raised in such a way
that allows them to engage with new
and different technologies because
70 these technologies represent new ways
of communicating and interacting with
information and society. The jobs that
the children of today will be applying
for will be grounded in these new
75 means of communication and
interaction. The inventions of tomorrow
will be born of the minds of the children
today, minds that need to be plugged
into the techno-socio framework of
80 society. Granted, there are reasonable
limits; infants should not be handed an
iPad instead of a rattle. But, not long
after these infants develop motor skills
and the ability to recognize the
85 world around them, they should be
introduced to these technologies. It
may not be from a hostile alien race,
but our tech-savvy children will most
certainly save humanity.

Function and Effect Questions

1) Author X uses the parenthetical in lines 8–11 in order to

A) Clarify a claim

B) Define a term

C) Analyze a response

D) Provide supporting evidence

This type of function question is quite common on the SAT. Essentially, it requires you to identify the purpose or rhetorical reason the author included an aside or supplemental piece of text. To answer this one, go back to the text and reread the phrase being referred to: "Ten years ago, before the app boom (a period of time when the amount of apps available for smart devices tripled in one year), average use time was around 2 hours per day."

Usually, you will need to reread more than just the two lines listed, but since this is referring to a chunk of text within the parentheses, it is okay to simply reread those lines.

Next, predict the answer by asking yourself, "If this statement were not here, what would I lose from the text?" Your answer should be a definition of "app boom," which leaves you with choice (B).

It is important to know the meaning of these author purpose verbs, like "define," which describe what the author does.

Analyze: to evaluate; to weigh the pros and cons; to break down and investigate

Clarify: to explain further or make clearer by adding more information

Highlight/underscore: to draw attention to, emphasize

Illustrate: to demonstrate or show

Provide support: giving additional evidence or data to back up a claim

Qualify: to modify, alter, or limit

Refute: to disprove, contest, or argue against

Reiterate: to repeat

Undermine: to undercut, weaken, or challenge

Let's try a similar function question:

2) The phrase "the ones most suited for the new technology" in lines 65–66 primarily serves to...

A) Reiterate the author's main point by highlighting a distinction

B) Undermine an argument proposed by Author X

C) Define a specialized term

D) Provide additional evidence for the main point of the author

For this question, follow the same method as above, rereading the sentence and predicting a purpose. The phrase "the ones most suited for new technology," repeats the author's point by singling out children as the ones who should be immersed in technology. Thus, our answer is (A). Nothing is defined in this statement, and no additional evidence is offered.

3) What function does author X's statement "Sure… Italian" in lines 28–31 serve?

A) It repeats the primary argument of the passage.

B) It provides an overview of potential drawbacks of the smart phone.

C) It acknowledges that there are some benefits to the smart phone.

D) It qualifies an earlier statement by giving additional data.

This function question illuminates a major rhetorical strategy found in informational/argumentative passages—acknowledging the counterpoint. After rereading the sentence, "Sure, smart phones can do a number of great things, like provide directions, call a ride, or look up a phrase in Italian," we can predict that this line is here to concede a point to the other side of the argument: that smart phones do have benefits. Thus, our answer is (C).

This same rhetorical strategy is present in the second passage, as well—"Granted, there are reasonable limits; infants should not be handed an iPad instead of a rattle"—in which Author Y makes a concession and acknowledges the other side of the argument. Knowing this function will help you greatly in understanding paired passage structure and answering these types of questions.

4) What function does the first paragraph in passage 2 serve for the passage as a whole?

A) To present the background of the app boom

B) To evaluate the research that led to the development of twenty-first–century society

C) Analyze the themes and main plot elements of the novel *Ender's Game*

D) Use a comparison to introduce the author's point about the importance of technology

Sometimes, function questions will ask about entire chunks of text, such as a whole paragraph. In these cases, it is important to remember to reread not only the paragraph being referred to but also the surrounding area (2–3 sentences before and after). In the question above, reread paragraph 1 and the first couple lines of paragraph 2. A common trap that students fall into is choosing an answer that merely summarizes the paragraph's content, rather than one that identifies its purpose in the passage. Choice (C) is the trap because it gives a possible summary of paragraph 1, by discussing the plot and content of *Ender's Game*. This, however, is not the paragraph's purpose. The paragraph's purpose is to set up the author's main argument about the importance of technology, and it does this by using an analogy to literature. Thus, the correct answer is choice (D).

Inference Questions

1) How would Author X most likely respond to Author Y's statement "But… technologies," in lines 82–86?

A) He would assert that the technologies being referred to are exorbitant in price and thus it is highly improbable to give each child a smart phone or tablet.

B) He would argue that the introduction of these technologies to children at such a young age has negative consequences in regard to mental and emotional health and well-being.

C) He would advocate accelerating the process by incorporating such technologies into every facet of the child's life.

D) He would claim that it is impossible to know when infants are able to recognize the world around them.

When answering this question, it is important to make sure you do not mix up the viewpoints of the two authors, and that you know which author's viewpoint the question is asking about. In this case, you want to know how Author X (the first author) would respond to a statement by Author Y (the second author), so you must keep in mind Author X's viewpoint: that technology has negative effects on children. By acknowledging this perspective, you can easily eliminate choice (C) because it is pro-technology. Choice (A) is not represented in Author X's essay, so you can eliminate it as well. This leaves you with (B) and (D). You can eliminate (D) because it also sidesteps Author X's main points: Author X never discusses infants and their ability to recognize the world around them. The answer is (B), which is in line with the author's point of view.

2) On which of the following points would the authors most likely agree?

A) Those who use technology at a young age will vastly improve their chances of getting a lucrative job.

B) The use of technology is becoming more prevalent in society.

C) Smart phones and tablets are becoming increasingly more expensive to buy and operate.

D) The use of smart phones and tablets among preteens generally has a negative effect on their self-esteem.

To answer this inference question, it is important to first remember the respective viewpoints of each author. Once you have noted that their viewpoints contrast with one another, you will realize they do not share much common ground, so you must choose something general. Think of this in terms of a Venn diagram: where would their opinions overlap?

Choice (A) represents only the viewpoint of Author Y, and choice (D) represents only the viewpoint of Author X. Choice (C) does not represent either, so (B) is the correct answer. Although each author differs in opinion as to whether the increased prevalence of technology is good or bad, they both in fact agree that technology is becoming more prevalent.

Relationships and Structure Questions

1) Which of the following best describes the overall relationship between the two passages?

A) Passage 2 elaborates on the problem presented in passage 1 by including further evidence.

B) Passage 2 strongly challenges the viewpoint presented in passage 1.

C) Passage 2 provides a solution to the problem presented in passage 1.

D) Passage 2 argues against the validity of the study presented in passage 1.

Whenever you have a paired passage, you will encounter a question like this one. This type of question requires you to identify the relationship between the two passages. To answer these, you must recall each author's viewpoint and determine how the two passages are related in content, point of view, and purpose. Paired passages will *never* be identical in their meaning and the viewpoint they offer, but they will not always be diametrically opposed. Think clearly about the purpose of each passage and then use the process of elimination. You can eliminate (A) and (C) because these options assume that passage 2 agrees to some extent with the claims of passage 1. You can also eliminate (D) because there is no mention of the study's validity in passage 2. This leaves you with (B).

Vocab in Context

1) As it is used in passage 2, what does "akin" most nearly mean?

A) Familial

B) Arranged next to

C) Affiliated

D) Similar to

Sometimes, vocab-in-context questions ask you about words, such as "akin," that you might not know immediately. For this type of question, as with all vocab-in-context questions, reread the line and predict a meaning. Be careful of traps such as "familial," which is purposefully confusing "akin" with "kin." After going back to the lines of the passage and predicting, you should understand that the author is comparing simulators to video games, and can thus choose (D).

Vocabulary Words 91–105

91) **lament** (v). to mourn, express sorrow for: *Johnny lamented the death of his pet hamster.*

92) **presume** (v). to assume: *Do not be so foolish as to presume you know everything just because you went to college.*

93) **subsequent** (adj). following, coming later: *The main character's motives will be discussed in subsequent chapters.*

94) **insolent** (adj). boldly disrespectful: *Insolent behavior will not be tolerated in Mr. Smith's classroom.*

95) **tyranny** (n). oppressive or unjust rule or leadership: *The slaves rebelled after living under the tyranny of the corrupt and vicious ruler.*

96) **provision** (n). a) something provided as in food or other necessities: *Before Peter and Jake went camping, they checked all their provisions to make sure they had enough food and water for a three-day hike;* b) an addendum or stipulation in a contract or clause: *The judge granted bail with the provision that the accused not leave town.*

97) **accommodate** (v). to provide suitably for; to oblige: *The banquet hall was so large, it easily accommodated a thousand guests.*

98) **renounce** (v). to reject, relinquish, disavow: *After arriving in the United States, many Cuban refugees immediately renounced the communist teachings of Fidel Castro.*

99) **precedent** (n). a) any decision or event that serves as a guide for future situations: *The college was setting an unfair precedent by expelling a student who protested the administration;* b) coming before; taking priority: *Murders and other violent crimes take precedence over traffic violations in a policeman's job.*

100) **assert** (v). to state strongly or positively: *The student strongly asserted his innocence when the teacher accused him of cheating on the exam.*

101) **plausible** (adj). believable: *It's plausible that there might be life on Mars because water has been found there.*

102) **contemporary** (adj). modern; belonging to the present time: *Some people think contemporary pop music is lacking in the vibrancy and passion of older classic rock.*

103) **skeptical** (adj). doubtful, unconvinced, disbelieving: *It's wise to be skeptical about information that you read on social media.*

104) **exemplify** (v). to illustrate or embody: *With her perfect diction and impeccable manners, Lady Astor truly exemplified class.*

105) **perturb** (v). to disturb or annoy: *Maria was greatly perturbed when she realized her boyfriend lied about where he had been the other night.*

Latin and Greek Roots 37–42

37) EQU: even, equal (equitable, equilibrium, equality)

38) ERR: to wander (erratic, erroneous, aberration)

39) EX: not, out, outside (extricate, exoskeleton, exonerate, exculpate)

40) EXTRA: beyond (extraordinary, extraneous)

41) EU: good, positive (euphemism, euphoria, eulogy, euphony)

42) FIN: end (finale, finite, infinity)

TIMED COLLEGE BOARD PRACTICE

Complete the following College Board practice problems from College Board's *The Official SAT Study Guide* or online at www.collegeboard.org. Review answers after completing.

Test 3, Reading Test, Passages 1–3, #1-30

Allot yourself 36 minutes, 12 minutes per passage.

Math Test: Embracing Challenging Topics in Linear Equations

> *"Strength and growth come only through continuous effort and struggle."*
> —Napoleon Hill

One of the pillars of growth mindset is embracing challenge and, in this chapter, we will unlock some of the keys to tackling challenging questions that involve linear equations.

Imagine a basketball player who wants to improve. Would he play against opponents who are not as good as him? Would a violinist striving for world-class talent play songs for beginners? Of course not. If you want to get better at something, you must try things that are hard for you. While it might be easier and more flattering to play it safe, you only get better if you start to take on some questions that cause you to struggle and make mistakes.

Remember, one key characteristic of great problem solvers is a vast skill set that is only increased by harder questions and topics.

To some students, a challenging question seems like a risk, because failing at it could potentially damage their self-esteem, making them feel like they are not smart enough to take on the SAT. In reality, the bigger risk is in not attempting these tough questions, because you could miss out on the immense amount of growth that comes from merely attempting them.

Below are some challenging topics that will help you to continue to expand your skill set. As you work through these difficult linear equation questions, remember that as you struggle and make mistakes, you are just growing that much more.

Writing and Solving a System of Equations

Some questions may require you to write two equations, or a system of equations. While writing the system may be all that's necessary to correctly answer the question, for most of these questions, you will need to solve for one of the variables. This may seem daunting, but once you write the system of equations correctly, solving the system is easy with the substitution or elimination method.

Here is an example to try.

> James and Sadie both work at a surf shop. James made $12 an hour plus a $10 tip and Sadie made $8 an hour plus a $30 tip. How many hours would James and Sadie have to work to make the same amount of money?

Begin by writing the two equations, using variables that are related to the given information, like J for James, S for Sadie, and h for the number of hours.

$$J = 12h + 10$$

$$S = 8h + 30$$

This system can easily be solved using substitution, and since the question is asking when James and Sadie's amounts are equal, set the two expressions equal to one another, and solve for h.

$$12h + 10 = 8h + 30$$

$$4h = 20$$

$$h = 5$$

Blind Spot

Remember to always check that your final answer is what the question is asking you to find.

Writing a System of Inequalities

You may also be asked to write a system of inequalities. Be careful with these questions! Many students will make a careless mistake while answering these because the answer choices look very similar to each other. Pay close attention to the direction of the inequality and eliminate incorrect answer choices. Here is an example.

> Sam makes \$10 an hour working at a restaurant and \$14 an hour fixing cars. She makes at least \$200 a week and works less than 18 hours. Given that r is the number of hours she works at the restaurant and c represents the number of hours she fixes cars, write a system of inequalities to model the situation.
>
> A) $10r + 14c \geq 200; r + c < 18$
>
> B) $10r + 14c \leq 200; r + c < 18$
>
> C) $10r + 14c \geq 200; r + c > 18$
>
> D) $14r + 10c \leq 200; r + c < 18$

This question requires you to identify and connect the key pieces of information. For example, the 10 gets multiplied by r and the 14 is multiplied by c to represent the money she makes working at the restaurant and fixing cars.

The 200 will represent the total amount of money earned in the inequality with the $10r$ and the $14c$. Since "at least" means greater than or equal to, an inequality can be written as:

$$10r + 14c \geq 200$$

Carefully cross off incorrect answer choices, making sure to be precise with the signs. You can eliminate answer choices (B) and (D).

Since the 18 represents total number of hours worked, simply add the two quantities r and c and set the inequality as less than 18.

$$r + c < 18$$

If you put the two inequalities together, you get choice (A).

$$10r + 14c \geq 200$$

$$r + c < 18$$

Writing Expressions with Percents

Some of the more challenging questions in Heart of Algebra will include writing an expression using either a tax, tip, or discount written as a percent.

A tax or tip will be added to 1 because they represent an additional amount, and a discount will be subtracted from 1 because the amount goes down.

After determining the correct rate to use, just multiply that initial number by the expression.

Here is an example for you to try.

> At a diner, Jake and Bryce will buy hamburgers, fries, and drinks. Hamburgers cost $4 each, fries cost $2 each, and drinks cost $1 each. Using h for hamburgers, f for fries, and d for drinks, which of the following would represent an expression for the total cost of their meal, including a 20% tip?
>
> A) $1.20(4h + 2f + d)$
>
> B) $0.20(4h + 2f + d)$
>
> C) $0.8(4h + 4f + d)$
>
> D) $4hfd + 2$

Start by matching the information to form an expression that represents the amount paid for only the hamburgers and fries.

$$4h + 2f + d$$

To find the total cost including the tip, multiply that expression by the percent as a decimal added to 1, which is 1.20.

Now you can multiply the percent and the expression.

$$(1.20)(4h + 2f + d)$$

Mindset Tip

Heart of Algebra questions are filled with opportunities to make careless mistakes, such as incorrectly solving for a variable, circling the wrong answer, or even making computational mistakes, such as simple addition. Making mistakes is normal and to be expected while working with linear equations. The key is to make these mistakes while practicing so that you can fine-tune your test taking-techniques, and not make them on the actual test.

Linear Functions as Tables

The SAT will have quite a few questions involving a table that is made from a linear function. These questions may require you to identify the slope, x-intercept, or y-intercept. The key to answering these questions is to view a table as a collection of points. Below is a table that represents a linear function and, with it, some examples further illustrating this concept.

x	$f(x)$
-2	-4
0	-3
2	-2
4	-1
6	0

1) Find the slope of the given function.

2) What are the x- and y-intercepts in the table above?

3) Write the function in slope-intercept form.

4) What is the value of $f(2)$?

5) What is the value of $f(0) + f(3)$?

6) What is the value of $f(f(2))$?

1) The best approach to finding the slope is to pick any two points and plug them into the slope formula. For example, if you use the points $(-2, -4)$ and $(0, -3)$, you get:

$$\frac{-3-(-4)}{0-(-2)} = \frac{1}{2}$$

You can also find the difference of each y-value and divide it by the difference of each x-value.

2) To find the y-intercept, identify the point where x is 0, or $(0, -3)$. The point $(6, 0)$ is the x-intercept because the zero is in the column on the right.

3) You can easily write the function in slope-intercept form by substituting the slope and y-intercept into $f(x) = mx + b$, which can be rewritten as: $f(x) = \frac{1}{2}x - 3$.

4) Since 2 is the x value, locate it on the table and find its corresponding $f(x)$ value, which is -2. Remember that $f(x)$ is the same as y.

5) To find $f(0)$, find the x value that is 0 and find the corresponding value of -3. Finding $f(3)$ is a bit more complicated since it does not have a value in the table. However, since it would be located between 2 and 4, then it would be halfway between -2 and -1, which is -1.5. Now you can just add -3 and -1.5 to get -4.5.

6) Start by finding $f(2)$, which is -2. Since $f(2)$ is -2, rewrite $f(f(2))$ as $f(-2)$, which is -4.

System of Equations: Special Cases

We learned that a solution to a system of equations is the coordinate point where the two graphs intersect. However, not all systems of equations will have a solution at a single point, as it is possible for a system to have no solution or even infinite solutions. These questions will not ask you to find the solution, but they do ask you to identify the number of solutions a system of equation will have.

Below is an example of a question in which you have to determine the number of solutions to a system of equations.

$$x + 2y = 4$$

$$2x + 4y = 8$$

How many solutions does the system above have?

A) None

B) One

C) Two

D) Infinite Number

You may have noticed that this question looks like a system that can be solved by using elimination. While it is not exactly the same, the approach is very similar. Let's begin by multiplying the top equation by 2 to get:

$$2(x + 2y = 4) \rightarrow 2x + 4y = 8$$

$$2x + 4y = 8$$

Once you transform the first equation by distributing the 2, you will notice that the two equations are exactly the same, making them the exact same line, which means that they intersect at an infinite number of points.

The correct answer would be (D).

Below is another example of a system of equations with an infinite number of solutions. However, this question will require you to solve for a missing coefficient. Try it out.

What value of a would make the system of equations below have infinite solutions?

$$ax + 6y = 8$$

$$x + 3y = 4$$

A) 1

B) 2

C) 3

D) 4

The secret to solving this question is to use the constants, or the numbers without variables, to determine what number to multiply by. Since a system will have an infinite number of solutions when the two lines are the same, the goal when answering these questions is to make the equations the same by multiplying one or both of them by a number that would accomplish this task. In order to make the two equations the same in this example, the second equation needs to be multiplied by 2. Do not forget to multiply the entire equation by 2.

$$ax + 6y = 8$$

$$2(x + 3y = 4) \rightarrow 2x + 6y = 8$$

Once the two equations are the same, just set the variable you are looking for, in this case a, equal to the coefficient in front of the x in the second equation.

In the problem above, a is equal to 2.

Hint

Although these question types may only show up once or twice on an SAT, because of their ability to grow your grit, perseverance, and self-confidence, they have the potential to earn you much more than just 10 points. Master these and watch your score grow by 10, 20, 30...

Systems with No Solutions

It is also possible for a system of equations to have no solution if the two lines are parallel, since they will never intersect. Two lines will never intersect on a graph if they have equal slopes but different y-intercepts, or constants.

Solving for a system with no solution is similar to solving a system with infinite solutions—the coefficients of the variables will be the same, but the constants will be different.

Here is a common question that involves a system with no solution.

$$4x - 2y = 20$$

$$2x - 3ay = 12$$

What value of a would make the system have no solutions?

To make the coefficients the same, you must multiply the second equation by 2.

$$4x - 2y = 20$$

$$4x - 6ay = 24$$

Now that two equations are the same except for the constant, the system of equations will have no solution, and you can now solve for a by setting -2 equal to $-6a$.

$$-2 = -6a$$

$$\frac{-2}{-6} = \frac{-6a}{-6}$$

$$a = \frac{1}{3}$$

Most systems of equations questions can be solved using substitution or elimination, as shown in Chapter 4. However, if the question is asking you to look for the solution because there are infinite or no solutions, then you want to use the procedures described above.

PRACTICE A

1) Alie and Kevin went out to lunch for hot dogs and cheeseburgers. They ate a combination of 6 hot dogs and cheeseburgers and the total bill came to $22. If hot dogs cost $3 each and cheeseburgers cost $4 each, how many hot dogs did they have?

2) The perimeter of a rectangle is 48 feet. If the length is equal to the width plus 4, what is the area of the rectangle?

3) Juan buys a new football for $34.99 and h number of hats that cost $14.99 each. If he paid a 6% sales tax, which of the following expressions would represent the amount of his final bill?

A) $1.06(34.99 + 14.99h)$

C) $34.99 + 1.06(14.99h)$

B) $1.06(34.99h + 14.99)$

D) $36.05 + 14.99h$

4) Solve for d so that the given system has no solutions.

$$2x + 3dy = 4$$

$$x + 4y = 1$$

5) Solve for c and d so that the given system has infinite solutions.

$$3x - 6y = 12$$

$$5cx - 2dy = 4$$

6) How many solutions does the system below have?

$$x + 2y = 6$$

$$2x + 4y = 8$$

A) None

B) One

C) Two

D) Infinite Number

7) How many solutions does the system below have?

$$x + 2y = 6$$

$$y = \frac{1}{2}x - 3$$

A) None

B) One

C) Two

D) Infinite Number

8) Using the given table, which of the following represents the given function?

x	$f(x)$
−2	2
−1	0
0	−2
2	−6

A) $f(x) = \frac{1}{2}x - 2$

B) $f(x) = -2x - 2$

C) $f(x) = -2x - 1$

D) $f(x) = 2x - 2$

9) Regis, Ray, and Paul visit a local restaurant while on family vacation. They like to order appetizers, which cost $8 each, and cheeseburgers, which cost $13 each. If they each order one cheeseburger and paid 8% sales tax, how many appetizers did they order if their final bill was $93.96, not including the tip?

A) 4

C) 6

B) 5

D) 7

10) A function is given by $f(x) = -2x + a$. If $f(-1) = 6$, which of the following is equal to $f(x - 4)$?

A) $-2x + 12$

C) $-2x^2 + 12$

B) $-2x - 4$

D) $-2x^2 + 8x + 4$

Answers

Practice A (page 193)

1) 2

6) A

2) 140

7) B

3) A

8) B

4) $\frac{8}{3}$

9) C

5) $c = \frac{1}{5}, d = 1$

10) A

UNTIMED COLLEGE BOARD PRACTICE

Complete the following College Board practice problems from College Board's *The Official SAT Study Guide* or online at www.collegeboard.org. Review answers after completing.

Test 1, Math: Calculator, #19, 20

Test 2, Math: No Calculator, #20

Test 2, Math: Calculator, #9, 34

Test 3, Math: No Calculator, #9, 15, 19

Test 3, Math: Calculator, #4, 22, 24, 27

Test 4, Math: No Calculator, #12

Test 4, Math: Calculator, #6, 26

TIMED COLLEGE BOARD PRACTICE

Complete Test 5, Section 4 (No Calculator). Time yourself, but do not look at the clock until you have finished the section. This will provide you with valuable information about your pacing so you can begin to adjust as needed for future timed practice.

Chapter **8**

Never Blame Yourself

Let's see if you can get the answer to this question in under a minute.

$$f(x) = \frac{2x^3 + 4x}{9x^2 - 24x + 16}$$

What value of x makes the function above undefined?

Were you able to figure out the answer in under a minute?

If you figured out the answer or were close, that is outstanding. If you did not get it, don't worry.

The purpose of this question is to see how much you've embraced the failure phenomenon and grown in your ability to re-vision mistakes and failures. How do you respond to problems that you do not understand or are pressured to complete in a short amount of time? Has anything changed in your mindset?

If, after doing this question, you blame yourself for not knowing how to answer it, or if you think less of your abilities, then there is one more mental barrier you need to break through. It all boils down to a simple change in thinking.

Blaming your abilities or intelligence and internalizing failure is a fixed-mindset approach and the wrong way to reflect upon an event such as not correctly answering an SAT question. When you continually blame yourself, you eventually develop a harmful "why bother even trying?" attitude.

Rather than blame yourself, you should be thinking that you just haven't learned this topic or practiced it enough yet. This is a growth-mindset approach—the idea that you are capable of improving by changing your actions. This way of reflecting upon or assessing the outcome of events is crucial to developing a positive self-image, resilience, and grit, which in turn allow us to persevere despite seemingly insurmountable obstacles.

To develop this no-fault approach, you need to change the way you view an event.

Here are the two major ways of viewing your role in making a mistake.

1) External: You attribute the cause of a mistake to external actions not internal qualities.

2) Internal: You attribute the cause of a mistake to internal qualities, not external actions, and thus hold the damaging belief that you are the reason you failed.

Here are two examples of these different perspectives:

Event	Positive: External	Negative: Internal
You trip in the hallway	I was walking too quickly in a crowded hallway and forgot to tie my shoelaces. I am not to blame, my actions are. I can change my actions.	I'm such a clumsy person; this is why I got cut from the basketball team and why girls find me unattractive. This internal quality can never be changed.
You get 7 of the 20 questions wrong on the No Calculator section of a practice test.	I moved through the test too quickly and forgot to make sure that I was answering the question that was actually being asked. I can change this behavior.	I'm a careless person and this carelessness always leads to mistakes in all aspects of my life. This internal quality is just my nature.

Now, think about the math problem from the beginning of this chapter. If you realize that it was a style of problem that you have not seen yet, or that you need more practice with timing, then you have a positive, growth-mindset approach when identifying the cause of an event. If you were unable to complete the problem, it was not because of your intrinsic ability; rather it was just something you have not mastered yet. *Do not* internalize the failure, believing the failure was due to your character, your intelligence, you. You are not to blame.

When combining this external no-fault approach with the view that failures and mistakes are opportunities for growth, you will be on your way to becoming a great test taker.

> *Your thoughts either solve problems or they create more problems. It's up to you to make the right choice.*

Reading Test: Timed Practice III

When you have truly ingrained the habits of the great test taker, you will have developed a sixth sense for understanding the tricks and traps of the test. Your enemy will become an old friend, one whose quirks and mannerisms are so familiar to you that you can see them before they appear. This type of ability is something that all people acquire when they immerse themselves in an activity without fear of failure. You will eventually develop this ability so that you will be able to predict the traps of the SAT. This is no different from the ability of a point guard who is in tune with his teammates on the court and passes the ball to where they *will* be, not where they *are*, or the golfer who is able to predict the dips and slight curves of the course and adjust seamlessly.

Strategy Review: Wrong Answer Types

Reinforce your knowledge of wrong-answer traps by reviewing and completing additional targeted practice.

1) Off Topic. The answer choice was not mentioned in the passage.

2) The Goldilocks Effect: The answer choice is too extreme in degree or tone.

3) Misinformation: The answer choice offers a detail or piece of evidence that is true for the passage but does not answer the question.

4) Assumption: The answer choice mentions something that you could logically assume based on the passage but is not actually stated or supported by the passage.

5) Funhouse Mirror: The answer choice warps or twists the author's words; it may be part true and part false.

The Goldilocks Effect

From the above list, there is one type of wrong answer that you can sometimes eliminate without reading the passage: the Goldilocks Effect.

Here, we have listed answers without a corresponding question or passage. Try identifying the Goldilocks Effect trap in each set of answer choices.

PRACTICE

1) Sample Question

A) It will allow scientists to study the effects of the ocean currents.

B) It will present researchers with a new tool for measuring data.

C) It will completely change the value of the field of oceanography.

D) It will give researchers new data to study in future experiments.

2) Sample Question

A) Provide evidence of her creativity

B) Illustrate the intense wickedness in her character

C) Give an example of the traditional values that she supports

D) Foreshadow her eventual resignation from her job

3) Sample Question

A) Receive an education that will prepare them for the workplace

B) Replace all men in the institutions in which they rule

C) Earn the right to happiness and financial independence

D) Grant them the right to vote

4) Sample Question

A) They are totally incapable of lawful behavior

B) They value a personal code of ethics

C) They underestimate the power of good will among fellow citizens

D) They misinterpret the legal system on occasion

Answers

1) Sample Question

A) It will allow scientists to study the effects of the ocean currents.

B) It will present researchers with a new tool for measuring data.

C) ~~It will completely change the value of the field of oceanography.~~

D) It will give researchers new data to study in future experiments.

Choice (C) is the Goldilocks Effect answer because it is too extreme in degree; be wary of language like "completely."

2) Sample Question

A) Provide evidence of her creativity

B) ~~Illustrate the intense wickedness in her character~~

C) Give an example of the traditional values that she supports

D) Foreshadow her eventual resignation from her job

Choice (B) is our Goldilocks Effect because it is too extreme in tone; we want to be wary of very harsh language such as "intense wickedness."

3) Sample Question

A) Receive an education that will prepare them for the workplace

B) ~~Replace all men in the institutions in which they rule~~

C) Earn the right to happiness and financial independence

D) Grant them the right to vote

Choice (B) is a Goldilocks Effect because it makes the generalization "replace all men." Be wary of answers with the word "all," because usually it is a wrong-answer trap that tests you on your ability to see sweeping generalizations and spot unsubstantiated assumptions.

4) Sample Question

A) ~~They are totally incapable of lawful behavior~~

B) They value a personal code of ethics

C) They underestimate the power of good will among fellow citizens

D) They misinterpret the legal system on occasion

Choice (A) is our Goldilocks Effect. As in question 3, the phrase "totally incapable" is extreme in degree.

Practicing Wrong Answer Types

Let's apply the wrong-answer trap strategy to the sample passage below. Read and answer the questions, and then write down the type of traps next to the wrong answer choices.

Below is an excerpt adapted from the first chapter of *The Extermination of the American Bison* by William T. Hornaday, which discusses the first encounters with the buffalo.

The discovery of the American bison, as first made by Europeans, occurred in the menagerie of a heathen king.

In the year 1521, when Cortez reached Anahuac, the American bison was seen for the first time by civilized Europeans, if we may be permitted to thus characterize the horde of blood thirsty plunder seekers who fought their way to the Aztec capital. With a degree of enterprise that marked him as an enlightened monarch, Montezuma maintained, for the instruction of his people, a well-appointed menagerie, of which the historian De Solis wrote as follows (1724):

"In the second Square of the same House were the Wild Beasts, which were either presents to Montezuma, or taken by his Hunters, in strong Cages of Timber, rang'd in good Order, and under Cover: Lions, Tygers, Bears, and all others of the savage Kind which New-Spain produced; among which the greatest Rarity was the Mexican Bull; a wonderful composition of divers Animals. It has crooked Shoulders, with a Bunch on its Back like a Camel; its Flanks dry, its Tail large, and its Neck cover'd with Hair like a Lion. It is cloven footed, its Head armed like that of a Bull, which it resembles in Fierceness, with no less strength and Agility."

Thus was the first seen buffalo described. The nearest locality from whence it could have come was the State of Coahuila, in northern Mexico, between 400 and 500 miles away, and at that time vehicles were unknown to the Aztecs. But for the destruction of the whole mass of the written literature of the Aztecs by the priests of the Spanish Conquest, we might now be reveling in historical accounts of the bison which would make the oldest of our present records seem of comparatively recent date.

Nine years after the event referred to above, or in 1530, another Spanish explorer, Alvar Nuñez Cabeza, afterwards called Cabeza de Vaca—or, in other words "Cattle Cabeza," the prototype of our own distinguished "Buffalo Bill"—was wrecked on the Gulf coast, west of the delta of the Mississippi, from whence he wandered westward through what is now the State of Texas. In southeastern Texas he discovered the American bison on his native heath. So far as can be ascertained, this was the earliest discovery of the bison in a wild state, and the description of the species as recorded by the explorer is of historical interest. It is brief and superficial. The unfortunate explorer took very little interest in animated nature, except as it contributed to the sum of his daily food, which was then the all-important subject of his thoughts. He almost starved. This is all he has to say…

PRACTICE

1) According to the passage, what is one reason the author describes Montezuma as an enlightened monarch?

A) He kept a written historical chronicle of his exploits.

B) He sought to educate his people.

C) He instructed his people daily on the lineage of nobility.

D) He was the most enterprising man in the Americas.

2) Based on the passage, it can be reasonably inferred that Alvar Nunez Cabeza…

A) Was the most significant pioneer in Spanish culture

B) Viewed the bison as a source of sustenance

C) Was a distant relative of Buffalo Bill

D) Kept a well-appointed menagerie

Answers

1) Choice (B) is the correct answer, because this is mentioned in the passage. Choice (A), though mentioned in the passage, is off topic. Choice (C) is a Funhouse Mirror trap: Montezuma did instruct his people, but he did not instruct them daily, nor on the topic of lineage and nobility. And choice (D) is far too extreme in degree, making it a Goldilocks Effect trap.

2) Choice (B) is correct, as this can be found in the passage. Choice (A) is a Goldilocks Effect trap; you can tell it is too extreme because of its use of the word "most." Choice (C) is a Funhouse Mirror trap, distorting what is said in the passage. Cabeza was a "prototype" of Buffalo Bill, but it is just an assumption that the two were related. Choice (C) is Misinformation; it was Montezuma who kept a well-appointed menagerie, not Cabeza.

Vocabulary Words 106–120

106) **subtle** (adj). hinted at, not obvious: *Even though Kate and Liz are identical twins, there are subtle differences in their looks.*

107) **superficial** (adj). a) lacking depth; b) insignificant: *Miguel's cousin has only a superficial knowledge of computers but acts like he knows everything.*

108) **imprudent** (adj). foolish, rash, without caution: *The young teenager was arrested due to his imprudent shoplifting.*

109) **inherent** (adj). intrinsic, inborn; a permanent quality: *My grandmother has an inherent ability to make anyone feel comfortable and at ease in her presence.*

110) **innate** (adj). inborn; native from birth: *Hitler spoke of the innate superiority of the Aryan race.*

111) **impair** (v). to weaken or harm in some way: *Being under the influence of alcohol will impair your driving ability.*

112) **mired** (v). hindered, stuck, slowed down: *Many Middle Eastern countries are mired in political, economic, and social unrest.*

113) **scrutinize** (v). to analyze, inspect, or study carefully: *The college professor meticulously scrutinized the term papers to ensure there was no plagiarism.*

114) **faculty** (n). a) a natural or acquired ability; mental powers or capability: *The family contested their father's will claiming he was not in possession of his full mental faculties when he wrote it;* b) members of the teaching profession: *The faculty went on strike after the board did not approve their contract.*

115) **articulate** (v). to communicate clearly: *The foreigner was unable to articulate thoughts clearly due to the language barrier;* (adj). b) eloquent and well-spoken: *The student was articulate and poised when delivering the speech in front of the board of education.*

116) **confound** (v). to confuse: *The detective was confounded by the lack of evidence at the crime scene.*

117) **incredulous** (adj). unwilling to believe; doubtful: *The boy's mother was incredulous when her typically disobedient son told her he had won an award for best behavior in class.*

118) **correlate** (v). to relate or connect: *Some have said that the size of one's brain directly correlates to how intelligent one is.*

119) **ingenious** (adj). clever, original, creative: *The ingenious invention of the hole puncher has made organizing papers easy.*

120) **apt** (adj). a) suited to the purpose: *The speech given by the best man at the wedding was heartfelt and apt for the occasion;* b) likely: *Due to John's fear of flying, he is more apt to take a train than a plane to go anywhere;* c) unusually intelligent: *Toni was an apt pupil when it came to mathematics.*

Latin and Greek Roots 43–48

43) FORT: strong, advantageous (fortress, fortitude, fortuitous, fortunate)

44) FRAG/FRACT: to break (fracture, fractious, fragmentary)

45) FRATER: brother (fraternize, fraternity, fraternal)

46) GRAPHY: to write (calligraphy, demography)

47) GREG: herd, group (gregarious, segregate, congregate, aggregate)

48) HER/HES: to stick (inherent, adhere, adhesive)

Mindset Tip

As you go through this final reading practice, take note of how you assign blame. Are you externalizing failures and mistakes, or are you internalizing failure and damaging your self-image? Keep these scenarios in mind:

- You get a few questions wrong in a science passage. Rather than say, "I just can't do science passages," acknowledge that you have not yet seen many of these, and therefore have not yet mastered the graphs.

- You run out of time on the paired passage. Rather than say, "I will never be able to finish a paired passage," say to yourself, "My reading speed will continue to improve with practice."

- You bomb an entire section. Rather than say, "Man, this means I'm actually much worse than I thought I was!," recognize it as a fluke and probably due to other factors.

TIMED COLLEGE BOARD PRACTICE

Complete the following College Board practice problems from College Board's *The Official SAT Study Guide* or online at www.collegeboard.org. Review answers after completing.

Test 3, Reading Test, Passages 4–5, #31–52. Allot yourself 26 minutes. 12 minutes per single passage and 14 minutes for the paired passage.

Math Test: Overview of Problem Solving and Data Analysis

Now that you have made it to this point in the journey toward better test scores and a better mindset, you are most certainly closer to becoming a great problem solver and master of linear equations. You are ready to begin the next area of the math SAT: problem solving and data analysis. While this section will require you to collect, organize, and interpret key information, the math skills that are necessary to answer these questions are ones you already know. These questions will most likely be written as word problems, which you are well prepared for at this point.

Data analysis and analytics are used everywhere, from sports teams like the Chicago Cubs to businesses like Google. They are used to predict stock market success and optimize medicine and healthcare. Being able to carefully read data is a skill that may help you land a great job one day, but for now you will use it to correctly answer many questions on the SAT.

To best understand data analysis on the SAT, you must learn to think like an analyst. Data analysts sort through sets of data, identifying, organizing, and interpreting the needed information. An exceptional data analyst must be observant and attentive to details, while not making conclusions or predictions until all the information has been collected and evaluated.

This is the essence of data analysis: letting the numbers speak to you without being swayed by emotional bias, and then correctly answering the questions based on the data.

Hint

17 of the 58 questions will come from this area, which is why data analysis is a great opportunity to boost your score.

This section of the SAT places a heavy emphasis on solving problems in a real-world context. To solve, apply the word problem approach you learned earlier:

1) Carefully read the question, collecting and organizing key information as you go.

2) Identify the type of problem and apply the appropriate strategy.

3) Solve the problem and make sure you correctly answered the question.

Data analysis questions will consist of the following topics:

1) Ratios, Percents, and Probability

2) Reading Data from Tables

3) Scatter Plots

4) Essential Topics in Statistics

5) Exponential Growth and Decay

Most, if not all, questions related to problem solving and data analysis will be in the calculator section. These questions are about collecting and analyzing data and then applying skills you already know.

> **"**Don't worry about looking good. Worry about achieving your goals.**"**
> —Ray Dalio

Ratios and Proportion

One of the simplest ways to analyze and organize data is with what we call a ratio, which is a comparison of two quantities. Ratios are used in all aspects of life, from sports to business. In fact, the batting average in baseball or softball is a ratio that compares the number of hits to the number of at-bats. If Derek Jeter had 35 hits in a total of 100 at bats, the ratio of hits to at-bats could be expressed as one the following:

$$35 \text{ to } 100$$

$$35 : 100$$

$$\frac{35}{100}$$

$$0.350$$

The most common way of writing a ratio is as a fraction. For example, the statement "moving at a rate of 10 feet per year" written as a ratio would be:

$$\frac{10 \text{ feet}}{1 \text{ year}}$$

Here is an example that requires you to write a ratio and pay close attention to detail.

In a class of 24 students, there are 13 girls. What is the ratio of girls to boys?

It is important to identify the information the question is asking you for. Since the question is asking for the ratio of girls to boys, first find the number of boys in the class by subtracting the number of girls from the total number of students, 24. While the ratio could be expressed in a variety of ways, it is best to write ratios as fractions for the SAT.

$$\frac{13 \text{ girls}}{11 \text{ boys}}$$

Questions like the example above will usually require you to identify the key data from a table or graph, but the same concept can also be used to answer word problems.

Here is an example that uses ratios to find a quantity.

Mike can fix three computers in five hours. He just received a large order to fix 27 computers. How many hours will it take him?

The best way to solve this question is to set up a proportion, which is nothing more than two ratios that are set equal to each other. These problems can be solved with cross-multiplication. When setting up the proportion, it is best to label the numbers so that you can keep the units consistent in each ratio. Notice how the numerators are computers in both ratios.

$$\frac{3 \text{ computers}}{5 \text{ hours}} = \frac{27 \text{ computers}}{x \text{ hours}}$$

$$3x = 27(5)$$

$$3x = 135$$

$$x = 45 \text{ hours}$$

The secret to solving questions like this is to correctly match up similar units on the top and similar units on the bottom. Here is an example that will show how important it is to label your ratios.

Keegan runs at a rate of 2.5 miles per hour. How many miles will he run in 5 minutes?

Begin this question by setting up a ratio of 2.5 miles over 1 hour and another ratio with x miles over 5 minutes.

$$\frac{2.5 \text{ miles}}{1 \text{ hour}} = \frac{x \text{ miles}}{5 \text{ minutes}}$$

Notice that the first ratio is in hours and the second ratio is in minutes. In this case, we want to change 1 hour to 60 minutes, as shown below:

$$\frac{2.5 \text{ miles}}{60 \text{ minutes}} = \frac{x \text{ miles}}{5 \text{ minutes}}$$

Then, to solve the proportion, just cross-multiply:

$$60x = 5(2.5)$$

$$\frac{60x}{60} = \frac{12.5}{60}$$

$$x = 0.21 \text{ miles}$$

Blind Spot

A common careless mistake students make is dividing by the wrong number. When solving an equation, be careful to avoid this careless mistake by always dividing by the number with the variable.

Unit Conversion

As in the previous example, many SAT questions will require you to convert units. Converting 1 hour to 60 minutes can be done very quickly using logic. However, not all questions are that straightforward, and it will be helpful to understand how to convert units using a more scientific approach. Let's go through the steps of this approach by converting 3 hours into 180 minutes. This approach is based on multiplying by a ratio and allows you to cancel out like units from the numerator and denominator, leaving only the desired unit.

$$3 \text{ hours} \times \frac{60 \text{ minutes}}{1 \text{ hour}}$$

Multiply 3 hours by $\frac{60 \text{ minutes}}{1 \text{ hour}}$ so that the hours would both cancel out, leaving only minutes.

$$\frac{3 \text{ hours} \times 60 \text{ minutes}}{1 \text{ hour}} = 3 \times 60 \text{ minutes} = 180 \text{ minutes}$$

Let's look at this question below, which also requires you to convert units.

There are 2 gallons of lemonade in a pitcher. How many glasses could you pour if each glass held approximately 16 ounces each? (1 gallon = 128 ounces)

The question is just asking how many small glasses would fit into a larger pitcher, which tells you to divide. However, since the quantities are in different units, you must convert one of them to match the other. Since the question is asking you to find the number of glasses, you will want to convert everything to ounces.

To convert them to similar units, multiply the quantity you are converting, or the 2 gallons, by the given ratio of 1 gallon = 128 ounces.

$$2 \text{ gallons} \times \frac{128 \text{ ounces}}{1 \text{ gallon}} = \frac{2 \text{ gallons} \times 128 \text{ ounces}}{1 \text{ gallon}} = 256 \text{ ounces}$$

This is the technical way of completing unit conversion, and it is important to understand this method. The key is to get all units except for those you want at the end (ounces, in this case) to cancel out. Since $\frac{\text{gallon}}{\text{gallon}}$ is equal to 1, they both will cancel out, and you are left with only ounces. Any unit that will not be a part of the answer will need to be canceled out.

Since you now know the pitcher contains 256 ounces and the units in the ratios match up, you can divide 256 by 16 to get a final answer of 16 glasses.

Hint

Most of the questions that require you to convert units will give you the conversion factor, such as 1 gallon = 128 ounces. However, some conversion factors may not be given to you and you should know the ones shown below:

1 foot = 12 inches

1 meter = 100 centimeters

1 kilometer = 1,000 meters

1 hour = 60 minutes

1 day = 24 hours

1 year = 365 days

Try this example.

Linda is knitting her own scarf using yarn. If 1 roll of yarn can stretch out to 80 feet, approximately how many yards can 4 rolls stretch out to? (3 feet = 1 yard)

A) 100

B) 105

C) 120

D) 960

The question wants you to find the number of yards of 4 rolls of yarn. You should begin by finding how many feet would be in 4 rolls, so multiply 4 and 80 to get 320 feet.

Next, you need to convert 320 feet to yards. To do this using ratios, multiply 320 feet by $\frac{1 \text{ yard}}{3 \text{ feet}}$ to that the units of feet will cancel out. Set up the unit conversion like this:

$$320 \text{ feet} \times \frac{1 \text{ yard}}{3 \text{ feet}} = \frac{320 \text{ feet} \times 1 \text{ yard}}{3 \text{ feet}} \approx 106.7$$

Since the question is looking for an approximation, find the closest answer choice, which is (B), or 105.

Some students may be able to complete the unit conversion by dividing 320 by 3, since to go from feet to yards, the number will get smaller. Both methods will work. However, you should be able to find the answer using the method previously described.

Blind Spot

Be careful! If you miss the word approximately in the question, your answer may not be a choice. The correct answer is not always the exact number you get.

PRACTICE A

1) A car travels at a constant rate and went 56 miles in 3 hours. At this rate, how many miles did the car drive in 5 hours? (Round to the nearest whole number)

2) Madison reads 120 pages per day. If each page has an average of 70 words, how many words does she read in one hour?

3) Alma's pancake recipe calls for 2 cups of flour and can make 9 pancakes. How many cups of flour are needed to make 27 pancakes?

4) Alexis and Griffin are driving to the beach, which is 70 miles away. If they drive at an average speed of 40 miles per hour, how many minutes will it take them to arrive at the beach?

5) Jones made a putt of 25 feet. How many centimeters was the putt? (1 inch = 2.54 cm)

Percents as Ratios

In previous chapters, you learned the basics of percents. Now, we'll expand on percents and teach you how to solve for a percent from a set of data.

A percent can be written as a ratio with a denominator of 100. For example, 10% means 10 out of 100, and 35% means 35 out of 100. To find the percent, just write out the ratio and multiply the ratio by 100.

Think about a math test that has 20 questions. If you answered 18 questions correctly, your percentage would be:

$$\frac{18}{20} \times 100 = 90\%$$

Here is an example that asks you to find a percentage.

> If there are 41 girls and 48 boys in a school, what percentage of students
> are girls? Round your answer to the nearest percent.

This question can be answered by setting up the ratio of girls to total students in the school, and then multiplying that number by 100. Just like with ratios, be sure to use the correct data. You are not given the total number of students, so you have to add the 41 girls with 48 boys to get the total.

$$\frac{41}{89} \times 100 = 46\%$$

Hint

It may help to think of a percent as a ratio of the part to the total.

Percent Increase and Decrease

Some questions may ask you to determine the percent of increase or decrease, in which case you should use the formula given below:

$$\% \text{ Increase/Decrease} = \frac{\text{Amount of Increase/Decrease}}{\text{Original Amount}} \times 100$$

To find the amount of increase or decrease, start by subtracting the starting amount and the new amount. Here is an example for you to try.

> Ivy purchased a stock valued at $14 in 2017. In 2018, the stock price jumped to $31.
> Approximately what was the percent increase from 2017 to 2018?
>
> A) 17%
>
> B) 45%
>
> C) 120%
>
> D) 250%

To find the amount of increase, start by subtracting $31 and $14 to get $17, which represents the amount the stock price increased. Use that number and the original to create a ratio and multiply by 100.

$$\frac{17}{14} \times 100 = 121.4\%$$

The question wants the *approximate* answer, which is the answer choice that is closest. In this case, the correct answer would be (C).

Probability

Probability is another type of ratio that can be written as a fraction and refers to the likelihood of something happening. It can be written in this way:

$$\text{Probability} = \frac{\text{Number of items you want}}{\text{Total number selecting from}}$$

If there are 60 boys and 40 girls and one is randomly selected, the probability of selecting a boy is $\frac{60}{100}$, which can be simplified to $\frac{3}{5}$.

Probability can be written as a fraction, a decimal, or a percent. Here are a few key things to know about probability:

- When written as a fraction, the answer can be simplified by dividing both the numerator and denominator by the same number.

- To write the probability as a decimal, just use the calculator to divide the numerator and denominator, so $\frac{60}{100}$ would equal 0.6.

- To find the probability as a percent, divide the numbers on the calculator and multiply by 100. For example, $\frac{60}{100} \times 100 = 60\%$.

Two-Way Tables

The SAT will ask questions that test you on your ability to read two-way tables, which are nothing more than graphic representations of data that have multiple categories. Two-way table questions, which you will see in the example that follows, will usually involve the skills covered in this chapter: ratios, percents, and probability.

The first step to correctly answering a two-way table question is to determine the total, or the denominator of the ratio. One way the SAT will test your knowledge is with what is called unconditional probability, which uses the total population rather than the total of a single category.

In a poll of 100 people at a local restaurant, people were asked if they watched the Olympics. The results are shown in the table below:

	Watched the Olympics	Did Not Watch the Olympics	Total
Children	8	12	20
Adults	60	20	80
Total	68	32	100

What is the probability that a person at the restaurant, chosen at random, watched the Olympics?

A) $\dfrac{68}{100}$

B) $\dfrac{60}{100}$

C) $\dfrac{8}{60}$

D) $\dfrac{68}{32}$

In this question, since any person could have been asked, the total is the entire population, or in this case, 100. This number will be the denominator. Now, just determine the number of people in that population who watched the Olympics, which is 68. This number will be the numerator, making choice (A) the correct answer. Since the question is asking for the probability as a fraction, the answer choices would most likely have been simplified. The correct answer could also be written as $\dfrac{17}{25}$.

Here is another example that uses the same table.

What is the probability that a person at the restaurant, chosen at random, was an adult who watched the Olympics? Round your answer to the nearest tenth.

Once again, this question is using the entire population, so the denominator will be 100. Since you need to find the number of adults who watched the Olympics, you will use 60 as the numerator, which represents just the adults who watched the Olympics. The correct answer would be 0.6, which could also be entered as $\frac{6}{10}$ or $\frac{3}{5}$.

The SAT will also use two-way tables to test you on another type of probability, conditional probability, that involves two events or two steps. You will first have to identify which subset of the population the question is asking about, and then determine the probability of the second event occurring within that subset. Here is an example to try.

	Drives to School	Walks to School
Juniors	43	47
Seniors	80	30

Based on the two-way table above, what percent of seniors drive to school? Round your answer to the nearest tenth. Write the answer as a percent.

This question is an example of a conditional probability because, unlike the previous question, it is not referring to the total of the entire table, but only the seniors. However, at first glance, you don't know the total number of seniors; you only see information about certain subsets of the senior population. To find your denominator for this problem, you have to add the number of seniors who drive to school and the seniors who walk to school to find the total. The denominator will be a combination of 80 and 30, which is 110. Continue by finding the desired numerator, which in this case is the number of seniors who drive to school, or 80. To find the percent, just multiply this ratio by 100.

$$\frac{80}{110} \times 100 = 72.7\%$$

PRACTICE B

The table below gives the breakdown of athletes who play sports at Millstown School.

	Plays Basketball	Plays Soccer	Total
6th Graders	43	35	78
7th Graders	32	38	70
8th Graders	39	33	72
9th Graders	45	21	66
Total	159	127	286

Use the table to answer the following questions:

1) What proportion of Millstown students are 7th-grade soccer players?

2) What percent of students at Millstown School play basketball? (Round your answer to the nearest tenth percent.)

3) If a student at Millstown School is selected at random, what is the probability he or she plays soccer? (Write the answer as a fraction.)

4) If an 8th-grader is randomly selected, what is the probability he or she plays soccer? (Write the answer as a decimal rounded to the nearest hundredth.)

5) If a student at Millstown School is selected who is an 8th-grader or older, what is the probability he or she plays soccer? (Round the answer to the nearest percent.)

6) If a soccer player is selected at random, what is the probability of that student being a 7th- or 9th-grader? (Write the answer as a fraction.)

Advanced Questions Using Tables

Some challenging questions that involve tables may require you to use skills you have already learned, like percent increase and percents. Here are some more examples that may show up on test day. Remember, challenging questions are great opportunities for growth!

The table below shows a company's vehicle sales for the past 3 years.

	2014	2015	2016
Cars	$418,000	$445,800	$515,725
Trucks	$321,600	$318,200	$421,600
Vans	$675,250	$689,100	$700,100

What is the ratio of sales of cars to trucks for the year 2016?

Solve by setting up a ratio.

$$\frac{\text{Sales of cars in 2016}}{\text{Sales of trucks in 2016}} = \frac{\$515,725}{\$421,600}$$

What is the percent increase of the sales of vans from the year 2014 to 2015? (Round to the nearest percent.)

To find the percent increase, find the difference between the years 2014 and 2015, divide by the original and multiply by 100.

$$\frac{689,100 - 675,250}{675,250} \times 100 = \frac{13,850}{675,250} \times 100 = 0.02 \times 100 = 2\%$$

What is the difference between van sales and car sales in the year 2014?

The word "difference" means to subtract.

$$\$675,250 - \$418,000 = \$257,250$$

What is the average yearly rate of change for truck sales from 2014 to 2016?

Since average rate of change is just a fancy way of saying "slope," use the slope formula and the two data points, (2014, 321,600) and (2016, 421,600).

$$\frac{421,600 - 321,600}{2016 - 2014} = \frac{100,000}{2} = \$50,000 \text{ per year}$$

PRACTICE C

1) While playing golf, Eric hit his tee shot 285 yards. If one meter is equal to about 3.28 feet, approximately how far was his tee shot in meters? (Hint: 1 yard = 3 feet)

A) 260

C) 865

B) 270

D) 2850

2) A restaurant asked its patrons which of the three pizza types they preferred. If a person at the restaurant is chosen at random, what is the probability that a person was an adult who preferred mushroom pizza?

	Pepperoni	Mushroom	BBQ Chicken
Children	10	8	7
Adults	6	10	9

A) 0.1

C) 0.4

B) 0.2

D) 0.6

3) An American football field has a width of $53\frac{1}{3}$ yards while a Canadian football field has a width of 65 yards. What is the difference in feet between the width of the Canadian football field and the American football field? (Round your answer to the nearest whole number.)

A) 12

C) 30

B) 20

D) 35

4) Jess and Nicholas are making waffles for a school fundraiser. The recipe calls for one cup of water for every 10 waffles; however, they do not have a measuring cup. If one cup of water is equivalent to 16 tablespoons, how many tablespoons would be needed to make 50 waffles?

	Skiing	Snowboard	Curling	Ice Skating	Hockey	Total
Students	5	8	9	4	6	32
Teachers	4	3	8	2	9	26
Parents	3	5	6	3	5	22
Total	12	16	23	9	20	80

5) The two-way table on the previous page shows the results of a survey that asked students, parents, and teachers what their favorite Winter Olympic event was. Based on the table, what is the approximate probability that a randomly selected teacher prefers curling?

A) 0.10   C) 0.34

B) 0.31   D) 0.35

For questions 6–8 use the following table.

The table below shows the average scholarship money in dollars awarded to students at a local university, as categorized by major.

	2015	2016	2017	2018
Engineering	$20,500	$21,800	$29,000	$32,500
Computer Science	$19,000	$24,500	$28,600	$35,900
Finance	$23,600	$25,800	$26,400	$31,600

6) Which of the following best approximates the average rate of change, per year, of the scholarship money of students majoring in finance from the years 2015 to 2018?

A) $2,000 per year   C) $2,900 per year

B) $2,700 per year   D) $3,500 per year

7) Which of the following is closest to the percent increase in scholarship money for computer science majors from 2016 to 2017?

A) 15%   C) 19%

B) 17%   D) 20%

8) If scholarship money of for each major increased by 10% each year from 2018 to 2020, what would be the average amount of scholarship money awarded to engineering majors in 2020, rounded to the nearest dollar?

A) $65,000   C) $39,325

B) $39,000   D) $40,620

Answers

Practice A (page 214)

1) 93

2) 350

3) 6

4) 105

5) 762

Practice B (page 219)

1) $\frac{38}{286} = \frac{19}{143}$

2) 55.6%

3) $\frac{127}{286}$

4) 0.46

5) 39%

6) $\frac{59}{127}$

Practice C (page 221)

1) A

2) B

3) D

4) 80

5) B

6) B

7) B

8) C

UNTIMED COLLEGE BOARD PRACTICE

Complete the following College Board practice problems from College Board's *The Official SAT Study Guide* or online at www.collegeboard.org. Review answers after completing.

Test 1, Math: Calculator, #6, 13, 21, 22, 23, 27, 31, 34

Test 2, Math: Calculator, #2, 4, 5, 11, 15, 16, 31, 32

Test 3, Math: Calculator, #2, 9, 14, 19, 29, 37, 38

Test 4, Math: Calculator, #3, 7, 9, 33, 34

Chapter **9**

The Stress Response

Imagine you are on the plains of the African Serengeti, the sun is beating down fiercely, and you are just about to take a sip from your canteen when you hear a rustling in the brush behind you. You turn around to see a hungry-looking lion staring back at you. In the next moment, you are running for your life.

What goes through your head? Critical reading question types? Misplaced modifiers? Subject-verb–agreement errors? The quadratic formula? Not likely. The only thing that will be going through your head is "run fast, run very fast, and don't get eaten."

Unless you are a superhero, you are not going to be solving algebraic equations in your head as you run from a lion. Why? The answer to this question takes us into the inner workings of the human brain and our ancient, unchanged nervous system.

When we are faced with highly stressful situations, we go into fight-or-flight mode and our sympathetic nervous system is activated. When this occurs, our body is flooded with stress hormones, which optimize the glucose in our body, sending it to our heart and extremities so we can run, climb, punch, etc. Our body is directing all its resources to physical survival.

When our brain floods with these chemicals, we essentially get cognitive tunnel vision. Since being able to find the circumference of a circle is not going to help us outrun a lion, our brain shuts down that function. Higher order thinking is severely impeded.

"So what?" you say. I'm not outrunning a lion anytime soon, so why does this matter? It matters because our brain and central nervous system cannot tell the difference between a hungry lion and an extraordinarily intimidating algebra II word problem. They react the same way. To your stressed mind, the lion is the same as the SAT. In that case, instead of helping you survive, the stress hormones that flood your body and brain only impair your ability to reason and think critically. They also affect your attention, disrupt your working and long-term memory, and hinder your ability to reason and integrate new knowledge.[10] So, on the test, you end up tensing up, sweating lightly, and blanking out on the problem as your cognitive tunnel vision sets in.

Although it may very well save your life one day, the ancient nervous system and its fight-or-flight stress response is the enemy on the SAT. You need to learn to manage your stress response.

Your growth mindset and all the practice you've completed in the previous chapters have begun to change the way you view the SAT. You no longer instinctively run away from the difficult problems, and your brain no longer shuts down in the face of obstacles. You have come a long way to conquering stress, but to finish it off, you need one more secret weapon: your breath.

When your body floods with stress hormones and you go into fight-or-flight mode, not only do you get cognitive tunnel vision, but your heartbeat also speeds up and your breathing becomes shallow. Have you ever felt your heart racing before a big presentation or gotten light-headed on the free-throw line when the score was tied and there were three seconds left in the game? It's all connected to your breath.

This is why proper breathing is effective in managing stress. The key is slowing your breathing down by doing several Deep Breath Resets: inhaling through your nose for 3–5 seconds and exhaling through your nose for 3–5 seconds. Deep Breath Resets are designed to lower your stress response. You will develop an immense calm through this exercise, allowing for higher order thinking and creative problem solving. Your learning curve will broaden rather than narrow.[11]

You're back in another stressful situation, only this time it's not on the plains of the African Serengeti with a hungry lion behind you, but seated at a desk taking your first SAT. Rather than freak out and panic, you are calm, collected, and ready.

Writing and Language Test: Overview

The Writing and Language Test is divided into two major categories: conventions of English and expression of ideas. Some of the questions are designed to test your knowledge of grammar, and others are designed to test your understanding of how to accurately express ideas. As with the SAT Reading Test, you will be reading passages, only this time questions will be based directly on underlined parts of a passage, which you may be asked to correct.

It is important to remember that since all questions are grounded in the context of a passage, understanding the content and the author's ideas is just as important to the correcting process as your knowledge of grammar and conventions of English. It would be a mistake to correct each sentence as if it existed in a vacuum and was unrelated to the passage. The SAT test makers are trying to create a real-life, editing experience.

To help you conquer this section, the following chapters provide you with:

- The anatomy of the grammar passage

- The method for answering questions on the writing section

- Identification of the most common grammar error types and how to correct them

- The SAT's top characteristics of good writing, which can be summed up in one phrase: get to the point!

BASICS OF WRITING:

Good Writing	Bad Writing
Concise	Repetitive
Clear	Awkward
Consistent	Inconsistent
Cohesive	Off-topic
Logical	Irrelevant

The Anatomy of the Grammar Passage

Below is a typical grammar passage with questions. The following bullets explain how each part of the passage functions and what the test asks of you.

- The shaded numbers, which look like **1**, correspond to each question number. You must replace or fix whatever underlined portion comes immediately after the shaded number by choosing one of the corresponding answer choices.

- Most questions will include NO CHANGE as answer choice (A). You would choose this if you thought the sentence was correct as written.

- Most questions will not actually ask you a question, as in number 1 below, but will simply present answer choices. Your job is to choose the answer choice that best corrects the sentence.

- Some questions, like numbers 2 and 3 below, will require you to change the way the writer expresses himself, essentially making decisions about the content of the passage as if you were the editor.

- Some questions, like number 4 below, will require you to combine two sentences at an underlined portion.

- Some paragraphs in the passage will have bracketed numbers, which look like [1]. These bracketed numbers label sentences that may need to be relocated within the passage. As in number 5 below, your job is to decide if the sentence belongs where it is or should be placed in a different part of the passage.

[1] The carpets were covered in crumbs, the dishes lay in the kitchen sink, and the mail had begun to pile up. [2] Everything was in **1** disarray, the house, without the care of his grandmother, succumbed to entropy. [3] His little brother **2** would never be able to pick up this slack. [4] Charlie just was not the sort of homebound, dutiful stock that was needed in times like these. [5] **3** Grandma was sick— she had been sick for a while, and she was not getting better. Suddenly, with all the callous inhumanity of an abrupt shove on the subway, Joshua saw it all. He saw himself coming back **4** home. He would put his education on hold, setting roots firmly in the house until Grandma passed. His book bag dropped with a loud thud. [6] Joshua looked around, finally taking notice of his surroundings. **5**

PRACTICE

1

A) NO CHANGE

C) disarray?

B) disarray;

D) disarray, but

The writer wants the underlined portion of the sentence to convey the same idea, but in a more formal way. Which of the following choices accomplishes this goal?

A) would never be able to do it

C) would never be able to assume these responsibilities

B) would not be any good at it

D) would never be able to make the grade

3 The writer is considering deleting the underlined sentence. Should the sentence be kept or deleted?

A) Kept, because it provides a counterpoint to the previous statement about Charlie

C) Deleted, because it undermines the main point of the passage

B) Kept, because it provides an important detail relevant to the passage

D) Deleted, because it is irrelevant to the passage

Which choice most effectively combines the sentences at the underlined portion?

A) home, but he

C) home, putting

B) home; putting

D) home, and put

5 To make this paragraph most logical, sentence 6 should be placed…

A) where it is now

C) before sentence 3

B) before sentence 1

D) before sentence 5

Mindset Tip

Understanding the principles of good writing, familiarizing yourself with the Writing and Language Test, and learning the eight steps for approaching the grammar section are the best ways to reduce stress on the Writing and Language Test. In the following chapters, we will examine each error type on the Writing and Language Test and how to answer them. By doing so, we will build a strong buffer against any stress that might surface during this section. Remember, the easiest way to conquer stress and tame the lion is through thorough preparation.

Answering Questions: The Writing and Language Test

The following eight strategies can be used for the Writing and Language section of the SAT.

1) READ THE TITLE OF THE PASSAGE. While jumping right into the passage sounds like a time-saver, it actually might hurt you on content-related questions. The Writing and Language Test assesses both grammar and content development, so knowing the main idea (which is often presented in the title) always helps.

2) READ THE PASSAGE AS YOU WORK THROUGH THE QUESTIONS. It is very important to understand main idea and context as you correct each error, because most of the errors are connected to previous sentences or larger points. Thus, read the passage as you work through the questions.

3) READ THE SENTENCE IN THE QUESTION ALOUD. When we read silently, our minds—often without our knowing—correct grammatical errors. Basically, our minds act like our phones, spell-checking and self-correcting. This is great for comprehension, but it undermines us when we are looking for grammatical errors. So, on this section of the test, it is best to practice by reading the sentences in the question aloud. When you hear them, you will catch the errors. It's just like when your English teacher tells you to reread your papers out loud. Eventually, you will internalize this ability.

4) CHECK THE ANSWER CHOICES! Note what is different in each answer choice to learn what you need to correct. Most of the questions actually have no questions, and so to figure out what they are asking you to correct, you have to look at the answer choices.

5) ELIMINATE, ELIMINATE, ELIMINATE. As with the Reading Test, it is important to eliminate wrong answers. More often than not on these sections, you will arrive at the correct answer by eliminating all the incorrect answers.

6) PLUG IT IN. Before you can be sure your choice is correct, you must plug it into the passage and read it back. This is very important. Sometimes, you will find that when you plug in an answer choice, you created a new error, such as a sentence fragment or run-on. Always plug it in.

7) SHORTER IS BETTER. As with all writing, if you can phrase something more concisely, you should do so. This is especially true on the SAT, so be wary of those longer, wordier answer choices. This does not mean the shortest choice is always correct, but when all things are equal between two choices, and both choices correct the error in the sentence, choose the shorter, simpler one.

8) CONSISTENCY IS KING. Whenever possible, keep items in the sentence consistent, such as tone, diction, verb tense, pronoun case, subject-verb agreement, pronoun/antecedent agreement, and parallel sentence parts, like items being compared in a list. We'll talk more about each of these elements in the following chapters.

Answers

1) B

2) C

3) B

4) C

5) B

Vocabulary Words 121–135

121) **strenuous** (adj). demanding or laborious: *The coach put his players through a strenuous workout to get them in shape for the big game.*

122) **onerous** (adj). burdensome and tiring: *The janitor had the onerous task of cleaning the stadium after the game.*

123) **conserve** (v). to preserve, save, or prevent the waste of: *We need to conserve our water if we are going to make it through the long hike.*

124) **contend** (v). to resist or strive against; to compete with or oppose: *The Olympian had to contend with harsh training conditions and inferior equipment.*

125) **efficacious** (adj). effective: *The new drug on the market is efficacious in lowering blood pressure in heart disease patients.*

126) **virtuous** (adj). moral, honest, conforming to ethical principles: *The preacher's virtuous behavior made him an excellent role model for his congregation.*

127) **dispassionate** (adj). impartial; lacking emotion: *The judge delivered the death sentence to the criminal in a cool, dispassionate tone.*

128) **oppression** (n). tyranny, or the use of power in a cruel or unjust manner: *It is a citizen's right to have freedom from government oppression and control.*

129) **subjugate** (v). to control, conquer, or master: *The alien invaders felt they were a superior race and had the right to subjugate the lowly humans.*

130) **usurp** (v). to seize without legal right: *The college students were plotting to usurp the authority of the administration by staging protests on campus.*

131) **prescribe** (v). to direct or dictate: *The punishment the army prescribed for deserters was extremely harsh and cruel.*

132) **privileged** (adj). favored; advantaged: *Only the privileged few who were deemed worthy were granted an audience with the king.*

133) **ensure** (v). to guarantee; to make safe from harm: *It is a school's responsibility to ensure the safety of their students.*

134) **qualify** (v). a) to meet the requirements of eligibility: *To qualify for entering the contest one must be an American citizen*; b) to limit or modify in some way: *The researcher qualified his statement by including data and previous case studies.*

135) **susceptible** (adj). a) prone to, liable, or predisposed to be subject to some influence: *If you get plenty of sleep and eat a healthy diet, you will be far less susceptible to illness*; b) capable of being affected emotionally; impressionable: *The naïve young girl was very susceptible to the sweet talk of the handsome young man.*

Latin and Greek Roots 49–54

49) GRAND: big (grandiose, grandiloquent, grandeur)

50) ID: one's own (identity, idiosyncrasy, idiot)

51) IN/IM: inside/not (innate, introvert, immutable, immortal, inept)

52) JUS/JUD: law (judicial, justice, judge, adjudicate)

53) LEV: light, rise (elevate, levity, alleviate)

54) LIBER/LIVER: free (libertine, liberate, deliverance, libertarian)

Math Test: Scatter Plots

Scatter plots and line graphs are two more ways the SAT will use visual representations of data to test your problem-solving skills. Fortunately, though, questions about both types of diagrams will use many topics you learned in previous chapters. Let's begin with line graphs, which have a lot in common with graphs of linear equations.

Reading Line Graphs

Most questions involving line graphs will be simple and straightforward. Here are a few key definitions that will help you answer questions involving line graphs.

INCREASING: From left to right, the line is going up and the value is getting larger.

DECREASING: From left to right, the line is going down and the value is getting smaller.

MAXIMUM: The greatest (highest) point on the graph.

MINIMUM: The smallest (lowest) point on the graph.

GREATEST CHANGE: The biggest amount of increase or decrease from point to point. Remember, rate of change is another way of saying slope. To find the greatest change, you are essentially looking for the largest absolute value of the slope. The steeper the segment, the greater the change. The segment as pictured like this: / will have a greater change than the segment pictured like this: ⁄ .

PRACTICE A

Average Yearly Salary

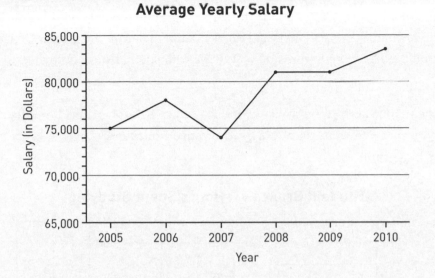

1) Did the average salary increase or decrease from 2007 to 2008?

2) What is the ratio of the average salary in 2007 to the average salary in 2008?

3) What is the minimum average yearly salary from 2005 to 2010?

4) In what year did the average salary stay the same?

5) What year did the average yearly salary decrease?

6) In what year did the maximum average yearly salary occur?

7) Which year had the greatest change in average yearly salary?

Hint

You can use these slope concepts when working with a line graph. Make sure to always read the graph from left to right.

- A positive slope, or increasing values, goes up.

- A negative slope, or decreasing values, goes down.

- A zero slope, or no change, is a flat line.

Working with Scatter Plots

A scatter plot is a type of graph in which two sets of data are graphed as points on a coordinate plane. Graphing points on a scatter plot is the same as graphing points on the coordinate plane—just find the first number on the x-axis and the second number on the y-axis. On the scatter plot below, the point (1, 62) would represent a student who spent 1 hour studying and scored a 62 on the test.

Scatter plots can also show how two sets of data relate to each other. Looking at the scatter plot below, you can see that, on average, the more hours a student spends studying, the higher his or her grade will be.

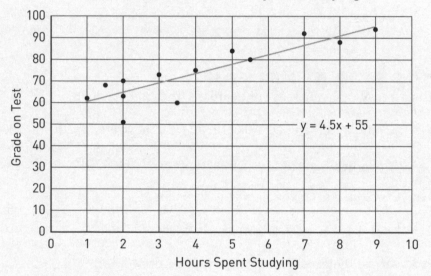

Answer the following questions using the scatter plot above.

1) How many hours did the student with the lowest grade study?

2) As the number of hours spent studying increases, the grades on the test

A) Increase

B) Decrease

C) Stay the same

D) Increase, then decrease

In the first question of the previous example, the lowest grade any student got was a 50. Simply find the value of 50 on y-coordinate, then locate the corresponding x-coordinate to see that the student studied for 2 hours.

The second question is asking you to spot the trend in the data. As the number of hours spent studying increases, the grades on the test increase as well, which is choice (A).

Hint

When answering questions involving scatter plots, it is important to be observant of each part of the scatter plot, such as the axis and units. Always pay close attention to each axis on a graph. Lines may increase by 1, but they can also increase by 2, 5, 10, or more. You will always be rewarded when paying close attention to the small details.

Using the Line of Best Fit

A line of best fit is nothing more than a line drawn through the "middle" of the points.

The line of best fit, shown on the scatter plot on the next page, can also be called a predictor line because it can **predict** what a value would most likely be for a point on the graph that is not plotted as an actual data point. Once again, it is important to determine what the question is asking you to find. If the question asks you to predict, use the line of best fit.

The line of best fit will quite often show the relationship between the x and y data sets. In the scatter plot from the previous example, since the line of best fit has a positive slope, the data increases as the hours increase. You could even predict the grades of students based on how many hours they studied.

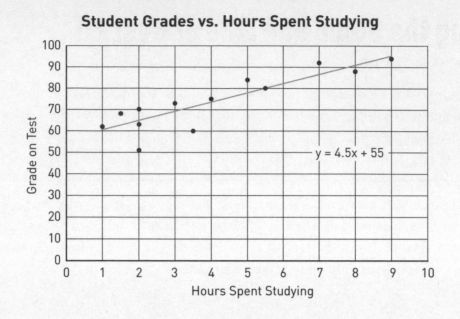

Student Grades vs. Hours Spent Studying

$y = 4.5x + 55$

Using the line of best fit, if a student studied for 5.5 hours,
what would their predicted test grade be?

To answer, go to 5.5 on the hours axis and go straight up to the line of best fit. You should hit 80 on the y-axis, which is the predicted grade on the test.

Using the Given Equation

You may be given the equation of the line of best fit written in $y = mx + b$ form. In the scatter plot above, the line has the equation $y = 4.5x + 55$. If given the equation, you can plug in a value for x and figure out the exact number for y, or the grade on the test. For example, if we plug in 2.5 hours for x, you get 66.25. Since this equation represents the line of best fit, this number would be the predicted amount, not the actual amount.

Using the scatter plot Student Grades vs. Hours Spent Studying, what is the difference
between the predicated grade and the actual grade of a student who studied for 3.5 hours?

Start by finding the predicted grade using the line of best fit equation by plugging 3.5 in for x to get the exact number 70.75. Next, find the actual point at 3.5 hours, which is 60. Remember, difference means subtract, so subtract 70.75 and 60 to get 10.75.

Finding the Slope of a Line of Best Fit

You may be asked to find the slope of a line of best fit. In the previous example, the equation is given to you, so it would be easy to find the slope, since the number with the variable is 4.5.

However, if you were not given the equation, you would need to find the slope using two points. Simply choose two points that are close to the line and are easy to read from the graph. To make it even easier, pick points that you can clearly locate on the scatter plot. From the scatter plot above, you can use the points (2, 65) and (8, 90) and then plug them into the slope formula.

$$\frac{90-65}{8-2} = \frac{25}{6} = 4.17$$

4.17 is not exactly 4.5, but it is close. The answer choices will be different enough that you will be able to identify the correct answer.

Mindset Tip

It is not about being 100% positive that your answer is correct. It's about having the ability to approximate, estimate, and, most importantly, eliminate the incorrect answer choices. Believe it or not, knowing that you don't have to arrive at the exact answer increases your likelihood of arriving at the correct answer. It frees your mind to think with less stress.

Writing the Equation

Some multiple-choice questions may ask you to write the line of best fit in $y = mx + b$ form. To do this, just substitute the slope and y-intercept in for m and b, respectively. Look at this scatter plot and the example that follows.

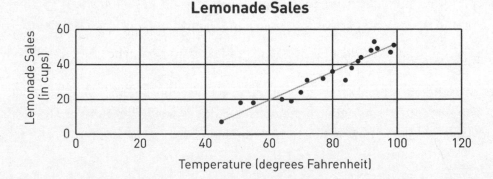

In the scatter plot above, the relationship between the temperature, t, and the lemonade sales, s, is represented by a linear function. Which of the following functions could it be?

A) $s = 0.8t + 29$

B) $s = 0.8t - 29$

C) $s = 2.8t + 29$

D) $s = 2.8t - 29$

The first step to answering this question is to see if you can eliminate any answer choices. If you were to estimate the y-intercept by extending the line of best fit, the intercept would be negative, which means choices (A) and (C) can be eliminated. Since the slope of the line is positive, you could eliminate any answer choices with negative slopes. In this question, however, there are none.

To determine the correct answer between the two remaining choices, you need to find the slope from two points. Pick two points on the line of best fit, such as (60, 20) and (80, 35). Just plug those points into the slope formula.

$$\frac{35 - 20}{80 - 60} = \frac{15}{20} = \frac{3}{4}$$

Since $\frac{3}{4}$ is 0.75, the best answer choice here is (B). Notice how you do not have to be exact with the number. You just want the closest answer.

Interpreting the Line of Best Fit

Some questions may ask you to interpret parts of the equation for the line of best fit. This is the same as interpreting liner expressions, which you learned in Chapter 6. If you are asked to interpret a part of the equation, treat it the same way you would any other problem.

Think about the equation from the scatter plot showing students' grades, $y = 4.5x + 55$.

Let's start with the 55, which is the constant, and represents the line's starting point. Since it is also the y-intercept, it also signifies the score a student would get if he or she studied for 0 hours. The 4.5 is the slope, or how much the score increased (since it is positive) for each hour of studying.

You can apply the rules you learned before. If a number is multiplied by a variable, it represents the amount of increase or decrease. If a number is a constant, it represents the y-intercept.

Nonlinear Models

So far, each line of best fit we have worked with has been a linear model. However, not all "lines" of best fit have to be linear. Take a look at this next example.

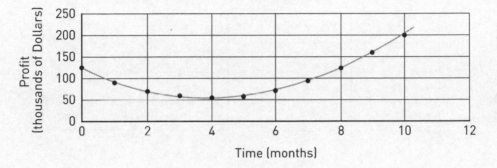

Profit of Crush Company

The scatter plot shown above displays Crush Company's profit during its first 10 months. Which of the following statements is true?

A) The profit increased at a linear rate.

B) The profit decreased at a linear rate.

C) The profit decreased and then increased.

D) The profit increased and then decreased.

Let's examine the movement of the points. From the first month all the way to the fourth month, Crush Company's profit decreased. However, from the fourth month on, the profit increased, making choice (C) the correct answer.

Association

Some SAT questions may ask you to describe the association between points on a scatter plot. Association means how well the data points relate to each other. They can be categorized as having a strong or weak association. For a scatter plot with a strong association, you can tell if the trend is increasing or decreasing, whereas a scatter plot with a weak association makes it more difficult to identify the trend. While both scatter plots below have an increasing pattern to them, the scatter plot on the left has a stronger association of the points than the one on the right.

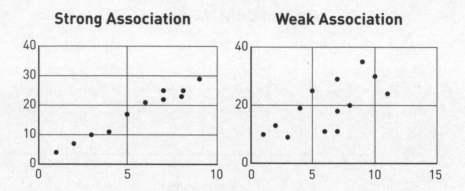

Data that has a strong association can be described as positive or negative. Below, the scatter plot on the left has a strong positive association because the points trend upward, whereas the scatter plot on the right has a strong negative association because the points trend downward.

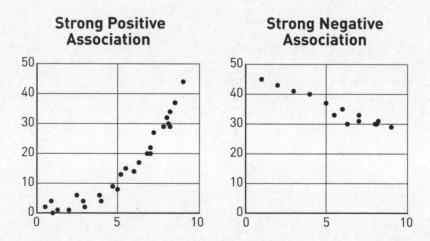

Now answer this question: is the strong positive association above a linear or nonlinear model?

Notice the slight curve to the points on the left. This curve means that the graph is a nonlinear model. We would call this an exponential model, which you may have heard of in algebra class. We will be discussing them soon.

Outliers

An outlier is a data point that doesn't fit the rest of the data. The scatter plot below, which represents a student's test scores on eight practice tests, contains an outlier.

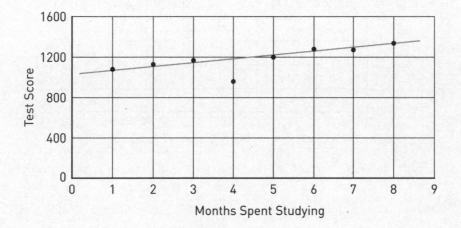

Most of the test scores fit the trend of improving at a constant rate, meaning that the data would have a strong positive association and be linear. The fourth practice test, which earned around a 900, does not fit the rest of the data, making it the outlier.

Mindset Tip

You might encounter outliers as you work through this book and prep for the SAT, such as a bad practice test or section. Do not be fazed by these outliers. Your practice using growth mindset is similar to the line of best fit: even though you might have some bad days, the general trend is upward.

PRACTICE B

1) The junior year grades for seven students in the technology club are shown in the scatter plot below.

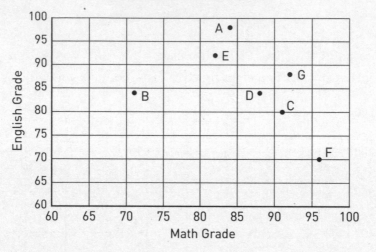

Junior Year Final Grades

Using the scatter plot, determine which student had a ratio of math to English grades closest to 1.

A) Student A

B) Student B

C) Student C

D) Student D

2) Using the line graph below, which months had the greatest rate of change?

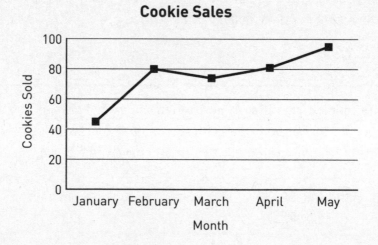

Cookie Sales

A) January to February   **C)** March to April

B) February to March   **D)** April to May

3) In which years did Jason's daily fee change more than Adam's daily fee did?

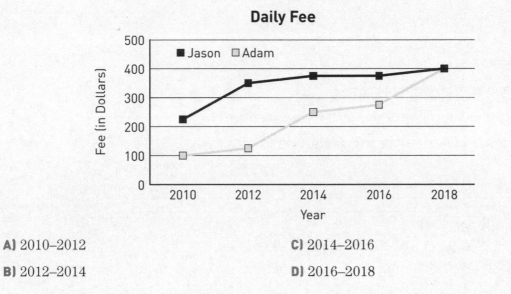

Daily Fee

A) 2010–2012   **C)** 2014–2016

B) 2012–2014   **D)** 2016–2018

The scatter plot below shows the temperature in degrees Fahrenheit and how many people visited Winter Adventure Park. Use the scatter plot to answer questions 4 through 6.

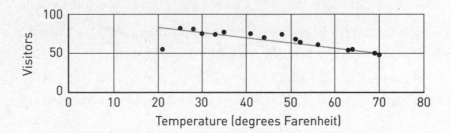

Visitors to Winter Adventure Park

4) Using the line of best fit, which of the following could the predicted number of visitors be if the temperature was 60° Fahrenheit?

A) 45   **C)** 60

B) 50   **D)** 70

5) Which of the following best describes the association of the data?

A) Strong Positive   **C)** Weak Positive

B) Strong Negative   **D)** Weak Negative

6) If the line of best fit was defined by the equation $y = -0.52x + 90$, with x being the temperature in degrees, and y being the number of visitors each day, what would be the best interpretation of the -0.52?

A) The amount of visitors each day

B) The number of visitors when $y = 0$

C) The expected decrease of visitors for every increase of 1°F

D) The number of degrees the temperature drops each day

Answers

Practice A (page 233)

1) Since the line goes up from 2007 to 2008, it increased.

2) $\dfrac{\$74,000}{\$81,000} = \dfrac{74}{81}$

3) $74,000. The year 2007 is the year that the salary was the lowest. Anytime you are answering questions that involve a maximum or minimum, make sure you know what the question is asking for. In this case they are asking for the salary, which is the number on the y-axis.

4) 2009. Since the line is flat, the salary neither increased nor decreased.

5) 2006 to 2007. That is the only time the graph is going down from left to right.

6) 2010. The maximum (highest point) of the graph is around $83,000. Since the question is asking you to find the year, you take the number from the x-axis.

7) 2007 to 2008. You can find the part of the line where the slope of that part is the steepest, and you can also determine the amount of increase or decrease for each year by subtracting.

        2005–2006: $78,000 – $75,000 = $3,000

        2006–2007: $78,000 – $74,000 = $4,000

        2007–2008: $81,000 – $74,000 = $7,000

        2008–2009: $81,000 – $81,000 = $0

        2009–2010: $83,000 – $81,000 = $2,000

Now, determine which difference was the greatest. In this case, it was 2007 to 2008. It does not matter if a section is increasing or decreasing, you are just looking for the largest difference.

Practice B (page 242)

1) D

2) A

3) A

4) C

5) B

6) C

UNTIMED COLLEGE BOARD PRACTICE

Complete the following College Board practice problems from College Board's *The Official SAT Study Guide* or online at www.collegeboard.org. Review answers after completing.

Test 1, Math: Calculator, #1, 5, 15, 16, 17, 33

Test 2, Math: Calculator, #14

Test 3, Math: Calculator, #1, 3, 20

Test 4, Math: Calculator, #10, 11, 27

Chapter **10**

Future Power Statements

> **"***Whether you think you can or you think you can't, you're right.***"**
> —Henry Ford

It's time to give your SAT score an energy boost. We talked about coming up with a number, a dream score to shoot for. And we asked you to figure out why it was important and how you're going to get there. Now it's time to take goal setting to a whole new level. This next tip has the potential not only to help you achieve your SAT score, but also to transform all aspects of your life—school, music, relationships, athletics, you name it. It is time to change the way you think about your goals.

Rather than focus on the SAT score you want and how many more questions you need to get right to achieve it, we now want you to think about the personal characteristics and habits you need to adopt to become the person who gets that score. Who do you want to be? How do you want to carry yourself? What is holding you back from becoming this person? To answer these questions and move into the next phase of goal setting, you must create Future Power Statements.

Future Power Statements are concise statements of targeted actions. They're framed in the present tense, as if they exist already. They are designed to develop the ability to manifest the future goal you desire. Here are some examples:

> *Example One:* Aaron needed more disciplined study habits. He always wanted to study but found himself getting easily distracted with text messages and social media.

> A typical goal Aaron might set would be: "My goal is to get an A on the next history test by studying more."

Aaron is on the right track—he has a goal and an action plan to attain it. This is a great start, but to take Aaron's goal setting to the next level, he needs to take some of his focus off the goal and place it on the actions and habits needed to attain it. By writing Future Power Statements in the present tense as if they already exist, Aaron makes the decision to adopt the correct habits today that will allow him to attain his goal tomorrow.

Aaron's Future Power Statements:

- I'm the person who has a schedule with 30 minutes each day dedicated to studying history.

- I'm the person who goes to bed and wakes up when he's supposed to.

- It's just like me to eat my lunch in the library to get extra studying in.

> *Example Two:* Julia needed help handling stress. She found that whenever a test day rolled around, she became very anxious and could not focus on the process.

Julia's Future Power Statements:

- I'm the person who prepares well in advance for every possible curveball and type of problem on the test.

- I'm the person who visualizes myself taking the correct approach on test day.

- It's just like me to do a Deep Breath Reset when I feel a touch of anxiety coming on.

Now, it's your turn. Create three Future Power Statements tailored to your specific personal improvement goals.

_____

_____

_____

Writing and Language Test: Sentence Structure

The next four chapters will review the most common errors tested on the Writing and Language Test and how to correct them. Each chapter will provide examples of how these errors might appear on the SAT. Try to correct them on your own before checking the answer choices that follow.

The Sentence

In order to master the rules of punctuation, you must first learn the basic structure of a sentence and some important terminology.

What makes a sentence a sentence all comes down to the type of clauses that exist within it. A **clause** is a grammatical unit consisting of a subject and verbal phrase. There are two types of clauses: independent and dependent.

An **independent clause** can stand alone as a simple sentence because it expresses a complete thought, whereas a **dependent clause** cannot. Dependent clauses can provide additional information but *depend* on other parts of the sentence. They cannot stand alone. A sentence must have at least one independent clause (subject, verb, complete thought) to be considered a full sentence.

Take a look at these examples:

- "Joe bought a pair of shoes" is an example of a sentence and an independent clause.

- "Joe bought a pair of shoes and then he decided to go running in the park" is an example of a sentence containing two independent clauses.

- "Joe, who likes buying shoes," is a sentence fragment because it is a dependent clause that does not express a complete thought.

The other major type of a sentence fragment is a **phrase**. Unlike a clause, a phrase is missing either a subject or a verb and thus cannot stand alone as a sentence.

"Buying a pair of shoes," is a phrase because it is missing a subject.

Hint

Differentiating between sentences and non-sentences is the single most important skill for answering all the punctuation error questions correctly.

Punctuation

The role of punctuation is to provide meaning and structure to written language. Punctuation helps us understand what the writer is trying to communicate. Take, for example, this often-cited (and humorous) illustration of the importance of punctuation:

Version 1: Let's eat, Grandma.

Version 2: Let's eat Grandma.

The comma in version 1 is quite crucial to the meaning of the sentence, and to Grandma's survival.

Punctuation also provides order by connecting independent and dependent clauses, something that will be tested often on the SAT. If we use the wrong punctuation mark to connect one clause with another, we can change the meaning of the writing.

Commas

Commas must serve one of the following purposes:

1) TO CONNECT A DEPENDENT CLAUSE OR PHRASE TO THE REST OF THE SENTENCE WITH A CONJUNCTION

A conjunction is a word used to connect clauses or phrases while also establishing the relationship between them. A good way to remember your conjunctions is with the acronym FANBOYS, which stands for For, And, Nor, But, Or, Yet, So.

I bought several items at the <u>store; but still</u> ended up with
money in my pocket when I got home.

A semicolon does not work here because the conjunction "but" makes the second part of the sentence a dependent clause, which needs a comma.

CORRECT: I bought several items at the store, **but** still ended
up with money in my pocket when I got home.

2) TO LIST THREE OR MORE THINGS

Bobby enjoys biking, <u>eating- and swimming</u>.

This is incorrect because commas need to be consistently used for items in a list.

CORRECT: Bobby enjoys biking, eating, **and** swimming.

3) TO SECTION OFF A PART OF THE SENTENCE THAT CONTAINS NONESSENTIAL INFORMATION

This means sectioning off a nonessential sentence part that can be deleted without affecting the sentence's meaning. The two main types of nonessential sentence parts that interrupt the sentence to add nonessential information are appositive phrases and nonrestrictive clauses.

An appositive phrase renames or further describes the subject, and a nonrestrictive clause adds extra, nonessential information into the sentence. The key with both of these sentence parts is that when you eliminate them the sentence's meaning does not change. They do not need to be there. Try eliminating the sentence part that you think is nonessential. If the meaning of the sentence is unchanged, then you need to surround the nonessential sentence part with commas, dashes, or parentheses.

There is, however, one exception that sometimes fools students: the restrictive clause. This clause also interrupts the sentence by separating the subject and verb, only it is essential to the sentence's meaning. Like the name implies, the restrictive clause is not free, but instead restricted to the sentence.

For example, in the sentence, "Children who play outside are much happier," the clause "who play outside" is essential to the meaning of the sentence. If we took it out, the sentence would read

"Children are much happier," which loses the idea that being outside is what made the children happy. Therefore, this clause is essential to the meaning and should not have commas around it.

Let's take a look at some nonessential sentence parts:

Jonathan, a <u>compulsive liar often cuts</u> class to go drive around with friends.

A second comma is needed to section off the nonessential appositive phrase "a compulsive liar," and keep the consistency of punctuation .

CORRECT: Jonathan, a compulsive liar**, often** cuts class to go drive around with friends.

* * *

The <u>boy who loves ice cream fell</u> out of the treehouse and broke his arm.

The nonrestrictive clause "who loves ice cream" can be eliminated from the sentence without changing its meaning, and so it must be surrounded by commas.

CORRECT: The boy**, who** loves ice cream**, fell** out of the treehouse and broke his arm.

4) TO CONNECT INTRODUCTORY DEPENDENT CLAUSES OR PHRASES TO THE REST OF THE SENTENCE

Whenever a dependent clause begins a sentence, it must be followed by a comma.

Always friendly and never <u>angry: Claire</u> was loved by all.

The colon is misused in this example because the part of the sentence before the punctuation cannot stand alone as a sentence. Thus, a comma is needed to connect the introductory phrase to the rest of the sentence.

CORRECT: Always friendly and never **angry,** Claire was loved by all.

* * *

Hint

Remember that when you section off a nonessential interrupting phrase you must use consistent punctuation both before and after the interrupting phrase. An interrupting phrase introduced by a comma must be followed by a comma, and an interrupting phrase introduced by a dash must be followed by another dash.

Barreling down the highway at breakneck <u>speed; the</u> truck veered off into a ravine.

There needs to be a comma after "speed" because the sentence begins with a dependent clause that modifies or describes "the truck." A semicolon is not correct because both sentence parts cannot stand alone as sentences themselves.

CORRECT: Barreling down the highway at breakneck speed**, the** truck veered off into a ravine.

Takeaway

- Commas serve one of the above purposes and should never just be placed in a sentence haphazardly.

- Do not be a comma fairy, sprinkling commas willy-nilly into a sentence. If you are unsure if it needs to be there, take it out.

Hint

Try reading the sentence without the comma. If it sounds fine without the pause and perhaps even smoother, then the comma is most likely misused.

Periods and Semicolons

Although a period is used to end a thought and a semicolon is used to connect two thoughts, grammatically, periods and semicolons function in relatively the same way. On the SAT, the only rule you need to remember is that a period and a semicolon can both be used to separate two independent clauses. This means that each sentence part before and after these punctuation points must be able to stand alone as a complete sentence. Determining if this is true is so important for punctuation errors on the SAT that we have highlighted it as its own strategy: the sentence test. This is a test that determines if the parts before and after the punctuation are both independent clauses and can stand alone as sentences. Whenever you are dealing with punctuation errors, perform the sentence test.

Bob is a firefighter; who works late hours on weekends.

By replacing "who" with "he" we make the clause after the semicolon independent and thus fulfill the grammatical rules of the semicolon.

CORRECT: Bob is a firefighter; **he** works late hours on weekends.

* * *

Josephine has a special bond with her planner; which never leaves her side.

Again, our job is to make sure the clauses before and after the semicolon can stand alone as sentences. "Which never leaves her side" cannot stand alone as a sentence and thus must be changed. By replacing "which" with "it," we are able to turn the phrase "Which never leaves her side" into an independent clause.

CORRECT: Josephine has a special bond with her planner; **it** never leaves her side.

Hint

Knowing when to use a comma and when to use a semicolon is an easy 30 points on the SAT. Commas do not separate independent clauses, but semicolons do.

Using a Semicolon	Using a Comma
Fredrick did not believe in marriage; he thought it was a useless social construct.	Frederick did not believe in marriage, thinking it a useless social construct.
The judo tournament was tomorrow; Ramone was ready.	The judo tournament was tomorrow, and Ramone was ready.

Takeaway

Perform the sentence test when dealing with punctuation errors. If you can substitute a period in for a semicolon, then the semicolon is being used correctly.

Colons

Colons are used to set up a list or example and often follow an independent clause. The clause after the colon can be dependent or independent.

Emily liked all sorts of vintage clothing: platform shoes, overalls, jean jackets.

You might ask, "If a colon and a semicolon can both separate two independent clauses, then how can I know which one to use?" A semicolon separates two related thoughts, but a colon sets up an explanation, example, or list that the sentence part before the colon is introducing. Usually, colons are followed by dependent clauses or phrases (non-sentences), but in rare cases, they are followed by independent clauses. Just remember their function: giving an explanation, example, or list.

Carlos wowed the crowd in the last few minutes with just
what they were hoping <u>for; an</u> amazing goal.

A semicolon would not work in this example because "an amazing goal" cannot stand alone as a sentence.

CORRECT: Carlos wowed the crowd in the last few minutes with
just what they were hoping **for:** an amazing goal.

＊ ＊ ＊

The park was closed due to one major <u>issue; its</u> water main burst, flooding the field.

Even though both clauses can stand alone as sentences, this sentence needs a colon because the clause after the colon ("its water main burst") explains the clause before the colon ("the park was closed").

CORRECT: The park was closed due to one major **issue: its** water main burst, flooding the field.

Dashes

Dashes are used to set up a list or example, but they can also be used as a comma to section off a nonessential interrupting phrase from the rest of the sentence.

Chloe is very talented—she's an actress, a writer, and a soccer player.

Chloe—an amazing actress—got the lead role in the play.

Here are some examples of how these errors might appear on the SAT:

Sarah believed another factor got her cut from <u>NHS. Her</u> frequent absences.

A period would not work because "her frequent absences" cannot stand alone as a sentence. "Her frequent absences" is the factor being referred to earlier in the sentence, which means we need a colon or dash to set up this example.

CORRECT: Sarah believed another factor got her cut from **NHS—her** frequent absences.

* * *

Geoffrey—the best player on the <u>team, scored</u> seven goals.

A comma is incorrect because the punctuation must be consistent: either two dashes or two commas.

CORRECT: Geoffrey—the best player on the **team—scored** seven goals.

Takeaway

Colons and dashes set up lists, examples, or explanations.

Blind Spot

If the phrase "such as" appears in the middle of the sentence, it should go between commas. For example, Migratory birds, such as geese, fly south for the winter.

Apostrophes

Apostrophes are used for making a noun possessive or forming a contraction of two words. On the SAT, you will be tested on using apostrophes with singular and plural nouns, as well as the word *its*.

<u>Natalias' shoelaces</u> came untied as she ran to catch the bus.

The apostrophe must come before the "s" because "Natalia" is singular.

CORRECT: Natalia's shoelaces came untied as she ran to catch the bus.

* * *

The vice principal searched three <u>student's lockers</u> at the end of the school day.

The apostrophe must come after the "s" because "students" is plural.

CORRECT: The vice principal searched three **students'** lockers at the end of the school day.

* * *

The groggy bear emerged from <u>it's cave</u> after a long winter hibernation.

"It's" with the apostrophe is the contraction for "it is," which does not make sense here. Instead, use "its," which is the possessive form.

CORRECT: The groggy bear emerged from **its cave** after a long winter hibernation.

Takeaway

With singular nouns, the apostrophe comes before the "s" to show possession, and with plural nouns, the apostrophe goes at the end of the word after the "s."

Hint

Earn 20 points by making sure you know that "its" is already possessive. For example: Just after he got the car, Joe broke its windshield. "It's" would be incorrect since it is the contraction for "it is."

PRACTICE PUNCTUATION ERRORS

1) Bobby had what it took to compete in the <u>chess tournament; mental</u> acuity, a steel resolve, and foresight.

A) NO CHANGE

B) chess tournament. Mental

C) chess tournament: mental

D) chess tournament mental

2) Wealthy benefactors donated some of the museum's most <u>famous pieces—three</u> Picassos and two Monets.

A) NO CHANGE

B) famous pieces; three

C) famous pieces three

D) famous pieces. Three

3) A recent documentary revealed an interesting change in primate behavior between 1425 and <u>1830,</u> apes had begun to use more elaborate tools.

A) NO CHANGE

B) 1830;

C) 1830

D) 1830, when the

4) The attempted assassination of a US senator is changing the way lawmakers view the following amendments of the <u>Constitution;</u> the right to bear arms, the right to free speech, and the right to organize.

A) NO CHANGE

B) Constitution, and

C) Constitution:

D) Constitution

5) Napalm is a highly flammable <u>bomb,</u> that was used extensively in the Vietnam War.

A) NO CHANGE

B) bomb; that

C) bomb that

D) bomb: that

6) The small puppy wagged <u>it's</u> tail once the family entered the kennel.

A) NO CHANGE

B) their

C) its

D) one's

7) The lead graphic designer—<u>an irritable perfectionist—</u>berated his assistant for returning with regular coffee instead of hazelnut.

A) NO CHANGE

B) —an irritable perfectionist,

C) an irritable perfectionist

D) ; an irritable perfectionist

8) Osprey and turkey vultures are both large, gliding <u>birds, they can be distinguished by</u> the difference in their eating habits. Osprey hunt and kill smaller birds, whereas turkey vultures scavenge already-dead animals.

A) NO CHANGE

B) birds? They can be distinguished

C) birds. They can be distinguished

D) birds. Distinguished

9) In order to avoid losing the <u>case. The</u> lawyer stayed up all night, meticulously studying each relevant document, making sure to read all case-law precedents.

A) NO CHANGE

B) case; the

C) case, the

D) case the

10) Dan obsessively washed his car during the <u>week. And</u> also on the weekends.

A) NO CHANGE

C) week; and

B) week, and

D) week: and

Mindset Tip

Sometimes questions will involve sentences with several confusing grammatical errors, which makes it difficult to figure out what is actually going on. With these, it is important to not get overwhelmed, but instead find a starting point and then work methodically. Do a Deep Breath Reset and find your starting point.

For example, read the following sentence:

It did not look like the Board of Trustees would be willing to make any changes, <u>but the professors worked tirelessly to get the new book approved, however, it soon became a</u> hit among the students.

A) NO CHANGE

B) but the professors worked tirelessly to get the new book approved, it soon became a

C) but the professors worked tirelessly to get the new book approved, however; it soon became a

D) but the professors worked tirelessly to get the new book approved. It soon became a

You might see right away that this is a run-on, but you might not know how to fix it. A great starting point for questions involving punctuation is the sentence test. Ask yourself whether the part before or after the second comma can stand alone as a sentence. Both parts can, so it does pass the sentence test, which means the comma is incorrect. Once you know this, narrowing down the answer choices becomes easy. Choices A and B both use a comma and so can be eliminated.

Next, to choose between C and D, you should realize that (C) is redundant because of the use of "however," which leaves you with the correct answer, (D).

Answers

1) Choice (C) is correct because it uses a colon to set off the list. Choice (B) incorrectly inserts a period, which can only be used to separate two complete thoughts, and choice (D) eliminates the punctuation between "chess tournament" and "mental acuity, a steel resolve, and foresight," which does not adequately set up a list.

2) Choice (A) is correct because it appropriately uses a dash to punctuate the break between the independent and dependent clauses. Choices (B) and (D) are incorrect because the second clause is dependent and cannot stand alone. Choice (C) eliminates punctuation to create a run-on sentence.

3) Choice (B) is correct because it properly uses a semicolon to punctuate the break between two independent clauses. A comma cannot separate two independent clauses, which is why choice (A) is incorrect. Choice (C) makes the sentence a run-on, and choice (D) adds unnecessary language.

4) Choice (C) is correct because a colon effectively sets off the subsequent list, unlike "and" in choice (B). Choice (A) is incorrect because a semicolon should not be used to introduce a list, and choice (D) is incorrect because the dependent clause needs additional punctuation to connect it to the rest of the sentence.

5) Choice (C) is the best answer because it eliminates the comma, which unnecessarily separates the restrictive clause "that was used extensively" from the statement.

6) Choice (C) is the correct answer because "its" is a possessive pronoun, whereas "it's" is a contraction. Choice (B) is incorrect because "their" is a plural pronoun and "small puppy" is singular; likewise, "one's," in choice (D), changes the pronoun case and no longer refers to "the small puppy."

7) Choice (A), NO CHANGE, is the correct answer. The dashes used are parallel and function as commas to separate nonessential information from the sentence.

8) Choice (C) properly uses a period to separate two independent clauses. Choice (D) is incorrect because by removing "They" from the second clause a new sentence error is introduced: the second clause becomes dependent and can no longer stand alone.

9) The comma in choice (C) is correct, because the comma connects the dependent clause, "in order to avoid losing the case," to the rest of the sentence. The original period is incorrect, because "in order to avoid losing the case" is a dependent clause and cannot stand alone. For this reason, choice (B) is also incorrect.

10) Choice (B) correctly uses a comma to connect the dependent clause "and also on the weekends" to the rest of the sentence. A period or semicolon is inappropriate because "and also on the weekends" is not a sentence; it is not a list or an example, either, so a colon is incorrect too.

Mindset Tip

Now that you have begun to hone in on the most common errors on the SAT and the exact ways they will be tested, it is time for some College Board practice to reinforce those new neural pathways. This is also a great time to write a new Future Power Statement about grammar and writing. No matter what you originally believed about yourself and your grammatical ability, this statement will have power if you continue building the pathways through targeted practice. Say or write: "I am the type of student who spots grammatical errors: I hear them and see them and I know what is good writing and what is bad writing."

Vocabulary Words 136–150

136) **ecosystem** (n). a community of interrelated elements such as organisms like animals and plants: *Ecosystems are fragile and complex and need to be protected for a better world.*

137) **profound** (adj). deeply insightful: *Buddha is known for the profound statements he made on the human condition.*

138) **rampant** (adj). raging; spreading wildly; unchecked: *Drinking is rampant on many college campuses.*

139) **conceivable** (adj). believable, plausible, possible: *In light of current research, it is conceivable that there is life on other planets.*

140) **conjure** (v). to call forth, to summon: *The purpose of a séance is to conjure the dead relatives of the living.*

141) **prosperous** (adj). successful, wealthy: *The prosperous merchant gave a great deal of his money to charity.*

142) **metropolitan** (adj). relating to a large city; urban: *Having grown up in the New York metropolitan area, I found it hard to adjust to country life.*

143) **degrade** (v). a) to lower in dignity or status; worsen: *When you associate with criminals and drug addicts, you degrade yourself*; b) to lower in character or quality: *Salt water will degrade and rot wood.*

144) **conduct** (v). a) to behave or act: *People will judge you by the way you conduct yourself in a professional environment*; b) direct or manage: *The fire marshal will conduct the students out of the building during the fire drill.*

145) **novel** (adj). new and different: *The artist had a novel way of using objects found in the trash for his collages.*

146) **therapeutic** (adj). curative; helpful in the soothing or curing of disease: *Meditation is very therapeutic for relieving stress.*

147) **apprehension** (n). anxiety or fear over the anticipation of future misfortune: *There is a growing apprehension that there will be a stock market crash in the near future.*

148) **abstract** (adj). theoretical, intangible; difficult to understand: *The philosopher's ideas were so abstract, no one could understand them.*

149) **subservient** (adj). obedient and submissive; acting like a servant to another: *Throughout history, women were expected to act in a subservient way.*

150) **ambiguous** (adj). unclear, vague: *The directions were so ambiguous that no one could understand them.*

Latin and Greek Roots 55–60

55) LITERA: letter (literature, literary, illiterate, alliteration)

56) LONG: (longevity, elongate, longitudinal)

57) LU/PHOS/PHOT: light (translucent, lucid, luminous, lackluster, elucidate, illustrious, Lucifer, photon, photography, phosphorescent, phosphorous)

58) LOC/LOG/LOQU: word, speech (eulogy, soliloquy, epilogue, dialogue, loquacious, eloquent, colloquial, obloquy)

59) MAG/MAJ/MAX: big (magnanimous, magnitude, majestic, maximum)

60) MAL: bad, ill, evil (malignant, malicious, malevolent, malaise)

UNTIMED COLLEGE BOARD PRACTICE

Complete the following College Board practice problems from College Board's *The Official SAT Study Guide* or online at www.collegeboard.org. Review answers after completing.

Test 1, Writing and Language, #3, 4, 11, 15, 16, 26, 32

Test 2, Writing and Language, #13, 14, 20, 27, 33, 40

Test 3, Writing and Language, #4, 14, 21, 29, 34, 35, 41

Test 4, Writing and Language, #3, 22, 29, 35, 36

Math Test: Statistics 101

This section will explain the use of statistics on the SAT. It will also explain the advanced statistical concepts, which will separate you from the group of average test takers.

The bedrock of statistics is the mean, a number that identifies the average point in a set a data and can be used in a variety of ways, from grades to salaries to stocks. The mean describes the typical result for a group. In other words, it describes what is normal.

You can find the mean of a set by taking the sum of all the values and dividing by the number of items in the set. The formula is as follows:

$$\text{mean} = \frac{\text{sum of items}}{\text{number of items}}$$

Here is an example that requires you to use the definition of the mean.

Using the data listed below, find the difference between the mean with the outlier and the mean without the outlier. Round your answer to the nearest whole number.

$$\{12, 32, 38, 16, 28, 40, 18, 28, 84, 17\}$$

Start by finding the mean of the entire set by adding all the numbers to get the sum, and then dividing by the number of items in the set.

$$\frac{12+32+38+16+28+40+18+28+84+17}{10} = \frac{313}{10} = 31.3$$

Now, find the mean of the numbers without the outlier, or value that differs greatly from the rest of the data. In this question, the outlier would be 84, since it is farthest away from the rest of the values. You can find the total by adding the nine numbers together or by subtracting 84 from 313. Since you are removing an item from the set, make sure you reduce the denominator by one.

$$\frac{12+32+38+16+28+40+18+28+17}{9} = \frac{229}{9} = 25.4$$

The question is asking you to find the difference between the two means, so you can subtract the two from each other and get:

$$31.3 - 25.4 = 5.9$$

Since the question tells you to round to the nearest whole number, the correct answer is 6.

Here's another example:

Coach Allan's team scored a combined 42 goals in their first four games. If the team scores an additional eight goals in the next game, what will be their average number of goals per game?

To find the average, you first need to find the sum of all the numbers in the set. Since the team has played five games, the sum would result from adding 42 and 8, which is 50. Finally, divide 50 by five, which is the number of items in the set, to get an average of 10.

Now, let's try this example.

Tommy went on a golf trip and after three rounds, his scores were 81, 84, and 80. What would Tommy need to score on his fourth round to average 79 for all four rounds?

The best way to solve this question is by writing an equation that uses the average formula. It would look like this:

$$\frac{81+84+80+x}{4}=79$$

Notice that x is placeholder for the fourth score because we do not know that value. Once the equation is correctly written, you can solve for x by using the same methods you mastered while solving linear equations. Begin by combining like terms.

$$\frac{245+x}{4}=79$$

Since this equation involves a fraction, eliminate it by multiplying both sides by 4.

$$4 \cdot \frac{245+x}{4}=79 \cdot 4$$

$$245+x=316$$

Finally, to solve for x, subtract 245 from both sides to get 71.

Here is similar example that will really challenge you.

Vito is a skilled bowler and is competing in the state championship. The winning score is determined by the highest average of three games. So far, through two games, Vito has an average of 255, but he needs a 265 average score to win. What would Vito need to score in his final game to average a 265?

A) 283

B) 284

C) 285

D) 286

This is a challenging question that can be answered using the same word problem approach we learned in Chapter 6. Start by collecting and organizing the important information as shown below:

$$\frac{\text{sum of the first 2 games}}{2} = 255$$

$$\frac{\text{sum of all 3 games}}{3} = 265$$

These two equations come from plugging the given information into the average formula. The next step you can take is to eliminate the fraction in both equations by multiplying both sides by their respective denominators.

$$\text{sum of first 2 games} = 510$$

$$\text{sum of all 3 games} = 795$$

This problem can now be solved using substitution, since the sum of the all three games (game 1 + game 2 + game 3) contains the sum of the first two games. Your equation can be rewritten as:

$$510 + x = 795$$

The variable x would represent the score from the third game, which is what the question is asking you to find, and can be solved by subtracting 510 from both sides. The correct answer is 285, or (C).

This question could have been solved in a variety of ways, and the method above is only one of them. Another method that some students prefer is to plug in the answer choices. The key is to follow the problem-solving method and choose the strategy that works for you.

You know the power of struggle and embracing challenge. Although one or more of these questions may be tough for you, it's time to recognize your future power. You are the student who not only works through these, but enjoys them, because you know that every example that you attempt, regardless of failure or success, is equivalent to tangible future power in the form of new learning, boosted confidence, and a greater separation from the mean.

Other Measures of Center

The mean is only one of the three types of measures of central tendency, which are methods of identifying the center of the data set. There are two other ways of identifying this point: the median and mode.

The median is the value located in the middle of a number set. For example, the median of 1, 2, and 3 would be 2. Sometimes, though, when there is an even number of items in a set, there is no middle number. In these cases, the median is the average of the two middle numbers. For example, the median of 1, 2, 3, and 4 would be $\frac{2+3}{2}$, or 2.5.

The mode is the number that appears most often. There can be more than one mode.

If you have to find the median or mode, you should rewrite the numbers in order from least to greatest.

$$\{13, 24, 22, 8, 12, 24, 20, 43, 23, 9\}$$

Using the data set above, find the median and mode.

To find the median and mode, rewrite the data set in order from least to greatest.

$$\{8, 9, 12, 13, 20, 22, 23, 24, 24, 43\}$$

Hint

Anytime you are writing the numbers in ascending order, make sure to be careful and precise, as it is easy to miss a number.

To find the median, or middle value, cross off a number from the left and then the right until you are at the middle.

$$\{8, 9, 12, 13, 20, 22, 23, 24, 24, 43\}$$

Since 20 and 22 are the middle two numbers, find the average of the two by adding them together and dividing by 2.

$$\frac{20 + 22}{2} = \frac{42}{2} = 21$$

The mode is 24 since it is the number that appears most often.

Using Data from Tables

You may be required to find the mean, median, or mode from data displayed as a table. Let's start with an example that uses a table that is actually just a list of numbers.

3	8	2	9	7
7	3	9	1	8
4	4	6	3	7
2	1	8	8	5

Based on the table above, how much greater is the median than the mean?

If you are given a table like the one shown above, it will be helpful to write out the numbers as a number set and reorder them for the purpose of finding the median. It will look something like this:

$$\{1, 1, 2, 2, 3, 3, 3, 4, 4, 5, 6, 7, 7, 7, 8, 8, 8, 8, 9, 9\}$$

The next step would be to find the mean and the median.

$$\text{Mean: } \frac{105}{20} = 5.25$$

$$\text{Median: } 5.5$$

Since the question is asking you how much greater the median is than the mean, you must subtract the two numbers to get 0.25.

Frequency Table

The word *frequency* appears a lot in statistics and refers to the number of times a value appears in a set. In the set {4, 5, 5, 6, 6, 6}, the 4 has a frequency of 1, the 5 has a frequency of 2, and the 6 has a frequency of 3.

Data sets will appear on the SAT in the form of a frequency table as shown below:

Students in Choir

Grade	Number of Students
8	2
9	4
10	5
11	7
12	4

The frequency table above is telling you that there are two eighth graders, four ninth graders, five tenth graders, seven eleventh graders, and four twelfth graders. This information can be written as the following data set:

{8, 8, 9, 9, 9, 9, 10, 10, 10, 10, 10, 11, 11, 11, 11, 11, 11, 11, 12, 12, 12, 12}

Once you rewrite the data this way, determining the mean, median, and mode is much easier. Try the example below.

Using the frequency table above, which is greatest: the mean, median, or mode?

Your first step should be to rewrite the data as a set, as shown above. From there, it is simple to identify the mode, which is 11. You can also easily find the median, which would be 10.5.

Finding the mean is the most time consuming, but we have a method for this that may save you some time:

$$8 \times 2 = 16$$

$$9 \times 4 = 36$$

$$10 \times 5 = 50$$

$$11 \times 7 = 77$$

$$12 \times 4 = 48$$

$$\frac{16 + 36 + 50 + 77 + 48}{22} = \frac{227}{22} = 10.32$$

Once you have found the mean, median, and mode, just compare all three numbers to see that the mode is the largest.

Frequency Graphs

Below is what we call a frequency graph, which displays the frequency as a bar graph.

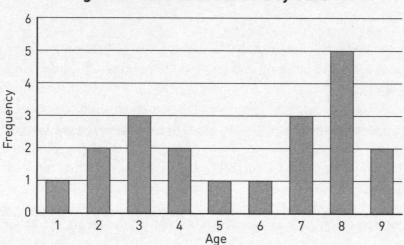

Ages of Children at Sara's Day Care

The height of each bar represents how many times that number appears in the set. For example, there are three 7-year olds.

Here is a list of the numbers if you write them out:

$$\{1, 2, 2, 3, 3, 3, 4, 4, 5, 6, 7, 7, 7, 8, 8, 8, 8, 8, 9, 9\}$$

Now it is simple to find the mean, median, and mode.

$$\text{Mean: } \frac{112}{20} = 5.6$$

$$\text{Median: } \frac{6+7}{2} = 6.5$$

$$\text{Mode: } 8$$

Finding the Median of Large Sets of Numbers

Sometimes a question will require you to find the median of a data set that has so many items that listing out all the values would take too much time. This next example will require you to use another method of finding the median.

If there are 100 students at an elementary school with 14 six-year-olds, 24 seven-year-olds, 21 eight-year-olds, and 41 nine-year-olds, what is the median age of the students?

In this question, we have a data set consisting of 100 students and we are tasked with finding the median student age. It would take way too long to convert the ages of the students and write those numbers out from least to greatest. So instead, let's visualize the problem and predict what the median would be. The median is the middle number, but since it is an even number set, it will be the average of the two middle numbers.

To solve, imagine the ages listed out from least to greatest. The first 14 numbers in the set would be 6 and the next 24 would be 7, meaning so far, we have listed 38 ages. The age of 8 will take up spots 39 through 59, which means that we have passed the "middle" of the data set. The median age would have to be 8.

Measures of Spread

In statistics, the word *spread* refers to how far apart data points are from one another and from the center. The most common way of measuring the spread of a set of data is by the range, which is the difference between the largest value and the smallest value.

The next example combines mean, median, mode, and range, and requires you to read a histogram, which is very similar to a frequency graph. This question also contains roman numeral statements and requires you to verify each one individually. Try it out.

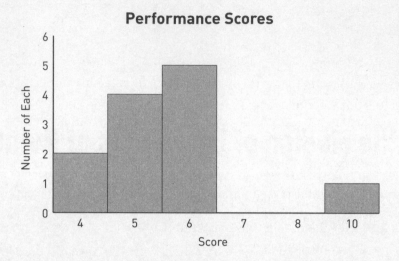

Performance Scores

Using the histogram above, which of the choices correctly describes the given data if the outlier is removed?

I. The mean will change

II. The mode will not change

III. The median will change more than the range

A) I only

B) I and II only

C) I and III only

D) None

Let's start by simply reading the data from the histogram. Here is a breakdown of the set:

$$\{4, 4, 5, 5, 5, 5, 6, 6, 6, 6, 6, 10\}$$

The outlier is 10 because it does not fit in with the rest of the data points. How would eliminating the outlier, 10, affect the mean, median, mode, and range? Let's go through each:

MEAN: The mean will definitely change. Eliminating 10 would be like dropping your highest test score in math class. Wouldn't your grade decrease? Of course it would. This means that (I) is true. (If you feel more confident finding the mean, that is fine as well. You should get approximately 5.7 with the outlier and 5.3 without it.)

MODE: The mode is 6 with or without the outlier, which means choice (II) is also correct.

MEDIAN: The median is 5.5 with the outlier and becomes 5 with the outlier removed.

RANGE: The range is 6 with the outlier and 2 without it.

Choice (III) says the median will change more than the range, which is incorrect. This leaves (I) and (II) correct, or choice (B).

Histograms can vary a bit. Some histograms will only give you a range rather than individual numbers. If you look at the histogram on the next page, we do not have the exact score for each student. We only know the frequency of the certain grade ranges.

Hint

While removing an outlier will change the mean and the range significantly, it will have very little effect, if any, on the median or mode.

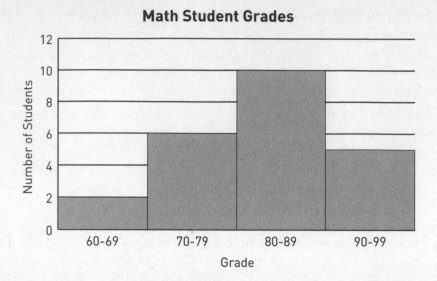

Math Student Grades

While we would not be able to determine the exact mean, range, or mode, we can still determine the median using a similar process to finding the median of a large set of numbers. Let's start by visualizing a list of possible scores.

$$\{60, 60, 70, 70, 70, 70, 70, 70, 80, 80, 80, 80, 80, 80, 80, 80, 80, 80, 90, 90, 90, 90, 90\}$$

Although these are not the exact scores, this estimation is sufficient to find the median. Think back to finding the median of large number sets.

There are 23 students, so the median would be the grade of the twelfth student. To find the twelfth student, start listing the grades in order from least to greatest. You will notice that there are two grades in the 60s and six in the 70s, which brings us to eight grades. There are ten grades in the 80s. This means that the twelfth grade must be in the 80s, and the median is somewhere in the 80s.

Standard Deviation

Standard deviation is another way of measuring the spread of data. It can be defined as the measure of how spread apart the data is from the mean; in other words, the average distance from the mean. It is considered an advanced topic on the SAT. Since you understand growth mindset and the power of challenge, you realize that by understanding what standard deviation is, you separate yourself from the norm (other students) and increase your own standard deviation—a prerequisite for SAT success. You see, standard deviation measures how far apart the values are from the mean, or how spread out the data is. So, when it comes to your SAT prep, aim to create a higher standard deviation by scoring above the rest of the pack. If most students score around 1000 and 1100 and you score 1400, you have increased the standard deviation.

Here is an example of standard deviation. Picture your math class having a pop quiz. Some students do horribly and get a 40%. Other students ace it with a 100%. This tells us that the range is very large, but standard deviation is a little bit different than range. Let's say the class scores were 40, 50, 60, 70, 80, 90, and 100. The class average would be 70.

These scores are spread out from each other, not clustered together. Since there is a large variety to the grades and not many scores are close to the center, the standard deviation would be large.

How about the scores 40, 68, 69, 70, 71, 72, and 100? The class average is again a 70. They have the same range as the first set of scores, but what do you notice about the majority of the scores? They are much closer to the class average.

These scores would represent a smaller standard deviation.

Let's recap the fundamentals of standard deviation:

- If the numbers are grouped more toward the average, the standard deviation is small.

- If the numbers are spread out with a lot of numbers farther away from the mean, the standard deviation is larger.

You will most likely be asked to compare the standard deviations of two sets of data. Here is an example:

Determine which set of numbers has a larger standard deviation:

A. {21, 34, 53, 61, 68, 71, 74}

B. {20, 44, 47, 49, 51, 53, 75}

A) The standard deviation of set A is larger than the standard deviation of set B.

B) The standard deviation of set B is larger than the standard deviation of set A.

C) The standard deviation of set A is the equal to the standard deviation of set B.

D) No conclusion can be made regarding the standard deviation of the sets.

The mean of data set A is approximately 55 and the mean of data set B is approximately 48. The standard deviation of the first is greater than the second, making the correct answer choice (A). Notice how the numbers are very spread out in the first set. However, in the second set, even though the first and last numbers are far apart, the rest of the numbers are more toward the middle.

Hint

It may help you to identify the mean of each data set to correctly answer questions pertaining to standard deviation.

Working with Populations

You may be shown the results of a survey conducted among a randomly selected subset of a population and then asked to use those results to make predictions for the entire population. You can use the information from the survey to estimate the results for the entire population.

Here is an example.

Blue Ridge High School has 2,200 students. The following table represents the results of a survey that asked a randomly selected group of students to name their favorite type of music.

Type of Music	Number of Students
Pop	26
Rock	32
Country	24
Rap	18

If the results of the survey are consistent with the whole school, how many students in the school consider country as their favorite type of music?

The first step is to use the data from the table to determine the percent of students surveyed who like country music. Since 24 students like country out of the 100 total students in the survey, find the percent by multiplying the ratio $\frac{24}{100}$ by 100 to get 24%.

Now we need to find 24% of the total number of students in the school, which is 2,200. Multiply 2,200 by 0.24 to get 528 students.

Random Sampling

The previous example used the expression "randomly selected," meaning that each of the students chosen for the survey had an equal likelihood of being selected. Random selection questions focus on the outcome. Other questions may focus on the sampling techniques and how random they are, rather than the results of the survey.

Answering these questions correctly is just a matter of eliminating answers that do not make sense.

Picture this scenario: You and a friend have a bet. You say that most people prefer sushi to pizza, but your friend thinks it's the other way around. To settle the bet, you decide to conduct a survey. Your friend wants to conduct the survey at a local pizzeria. Would you be okay with this as a way to settle the argument?

Of course not. That would be totally unfair. Most people at the pizzeria are going to favor pizza. This survey would be biased and not random, meaning you cannot draw any conclusions from it. Proper randomization can eliminate bias so conclusions are accurate. The more unbiased and random the sampling methods of a study, the more conclusions can be drawn. Likewise, if the sampling methods of a study are not random, fewer conclusions can be drawn.

Here is another scenario. Imagine you polled 100 people at the pizzeria, asking if they preferred cheese or pepperoni pizza, and 80% said pepperoni pizza. What conclusions could we make based on this survey?

- 80% of people in the world must like pepperoni pizza better than cheese pizza.

- 80% of people in California prefer pepperoni pizza to cheese pizza.

- If 100 more people were surveyed, exactly 80 of them would prefer pepperoni pizza to cheese.

None of the answers above are necessarily true, because they draw incorrect conclusions. Since the survey was being conducted at the pizzeria, you can only make conclusions about people from the pizzeria.

Here is a statement that is true:

> Most people at the pizzeria prefer pepperoni pizza to cheese pizza.

When dealing with questions that involve studies that did not use random sampling methods, eliminate answers that apply to a population of people outside of the sampling population. Those answers are most likely incorrect. For instance, if you randomly polled people in New Jersey, you can only make conclusions about people in New Jersey.

PRACTICE

1) The bench press weights for the Cardinals are listed in the table below:

| 235 | 315 | 185 | 145 | 215 | 225 | 195 | 155 |

Approximately what is the difference between the mean with the outlier and the mean without the outlier?

A) 11

B) 13

C) 15

D) 17

2) Christine teaches at a school. After grading 14 exams, the class average is an 84. Kayla, her fifteenth student, received a 100. What is the new class average rounded to the nearest whole number?

3) Katie is studying the eating habits of people in her town. She conducts a survey of 250 adults at the local fitness center and finds that 75% of the participants eat healthy. Which of the following is true about Katie's study?

A) 75% of children in her town eat healthy.

B) 75% of adults in her town eat healthy.

C) 75% of adults that visit the local fitness center eat healthy.

D) 75% of adults at the fitness center are in good shape.

Use the histogram below, which shows the final exam grades of Mrs. Matak's math class, to answer questions 4 and 5.

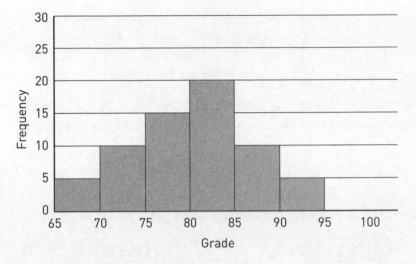

Final Exam Grades

4) Of the 65 final exam grades, which of the following could be the median?

A) 78

C) 86

B) 82

D) 87

5) Mrs. Matak had a few more grades to add to the list, which included a 95, 82, 63, 98, and a 54. Which of the following is true about the new data?

A) The standard deviation increased

C) The standard deviation stayed the same

B) The standard deviation decreased

D) There is not enough information to determine

6) In the system of equations below, the solution is (x, y). What is the average of x and y?

$$y = 4x + 3$$

$$2y + 3x = 17$$

A) 1

C) 7

B) 4

D) 8

7) The frequency table below displays a randomly selected sample of 80 students at Jefferson High School and their method of transportation.

Mode of Transportation	Frequency
Bus	30
Car	28
Walk	4
Bike	18

If there are 680 students in total at Jefferson High, which of the following is the best approximation of the total number of students that take the bus to school?

A) 190

B) 210

C) 225

D) 255

8) The frequency table below shows the ages of the 60 teachers at Pompton High School.

Age Range	Frequency
22–29	19
30–39	8
40–49	22
50–59	11

Which of the following could be the median of the ages of the teachers?

A) 34

B) 39

C) 45

D) 50

Answers

1) C

2) 85

3) C

4) B

5) A

6) B

7) D

8) C

UNTIMED COLLEGE BOARD PRACTICE

Complete the following College Board practice problems from College Board's *The Official SAT Study Guide* or online at www.collegeboard.org. Review answers after completing.

Test 1, Math: Calculator, #7, 12, 14

Test 2, Math: Calculator, #13, 18, 19, 20

Test 3, Math: Calculator, #15, 32, 35

Test 4, Math: Calculator, #21, 22, 23, 29

Chapter **11**

The Abyss

You're halfway through the book, and you are getting sick of the SAT. You are tired, frustrated, and a bit bored with the monotony of practice. Or maybe you have started thinking that you don't believe in hard work anymore, that if this process is so genius, you should be able to master it quicker. Maybe you haven't seen enough improvement to believe that this is actually working. Maybe old doubts start to resurface.

Welcome to the Abyss.

At some point in any journey, you will feel a low. If you envision your journey as a circle, with the top of the circle as the beginning, this is directly opposite the beginning. This is where most students fail to change; this is where they cease to build a new positive vision of themselves. They simply stop the journey, habit, or practice because it has become too tedious or difficult, or they no longer believe it has the power the help them. But this, the Abyss, is the most important part of the journey because it is here that true transformation takes place.

True transformation is not easy, and there will be growing pains. The old you is not going to die without a fight. It will cling, wrestle, connive, beg, barter, and steal to continue to exist. This is why the Abyss must exist—to vanquish the old self.

At this part of the journey, the pressure will be too strong—you must succumb to it and let it break you down so you can be rebuilt, reborn. All your weaknesses and poor habits will be burned right out of you.

Think about it. In every journey, at some point, the hero must enter the dragon's lair and slay the dragon. This dragon that you slay, though, is not some fictitious, folkloric creature, but rather that part of you that no longer serves your best interests. The dragon is whatever is holding you back.

So how do you prepare for the Abyss?

1) Recognize that at some point in your journey of change, the desire to give up will be overwhelming. Knowing that it will happen will help you get ready to face it.

2) Keep your goals in mind. This is why goal setting is so important. Goals are the light at the end of the tunnel. They will keep you going when the going gets not just tough, but darn near impossible. The better the goal and the more you have visualized attaining it, the more likely it will serve as your shield against the fire-breath of the dragon.

3) Realize that small improvements are continually occurring that you cannot even see. Change is occurring; it just may not be visible yet.

Writing and Language Test: Sentence Part Agreement

The focus of this chapter is consistency among related grammatical elements. You will learn about subjects and verbs, pronouns and antecedents, items being compared, and items in lists, all of which follow similar rules of consistency.

Subject/Verb Agreement and Tense

Subjects and verbs form the backbone of sentences and are integral parts of the conventions of English. To communicate the intended meaning of a sentence or paragraph, you must be able to determine if subjects and verbs agree and if verbs are in the appropriate tense.

A **verb** is a part of speech that is used to describe an action, occurrence, or state of being. Verbs fall into three major categories:

- Action verbs, which describe an action. Example: *Rejhan **sang** in the school play*.

- Linking verbs, which link the subject of the sentence to an adjective or noun that describes the subject. Example: *Maria **is** rambunctious during recess*.

- Helping verbs, which are used to "help" the action or linking verb by adding another layer of information, usually concerning possibility or time. Example: *Charles **can** dance quite well*.

The **subject** of a sentence is the person, place, thing, or idea that connects to the verb. With an action verb, the subject is the noun that is *doing* something, and with a linking verb, the subject is the noun that is *being* something. To find the subject, ask yourself, "Who or what is doing or being?"

Every verb is connected to a subject, and your job on the SAT is to determine if the subjects and verbs agree with one another in number. This means you must match singular subjects with singular verbs and plural subjects with plural verbs. Typically on the SAT subject/verb agreement is tested with third person verbs and subjects. Third person subjects include pronouns like *he*, *she*, *it*, or *they* and nouns like *the researchers* or *Jane*.

In the following two examples, we have bolded the subject and underlined the verb to which it corresponds. Try to correct the subject/verb agreement errors.

> **John** <u>swim</u> for at least one hour each morning.

> **They** <u>is</u> happy all the time.

You might hear that the subjects and verbs do not agree. This is because the ear is the best tool for identifying grammar errors. This is especially true in subject/verb agreement. The singular subject "John" does not match the plural action verb "swim," and the plural subject "They" does not match the singular verb "is."

Another way to verify if an action verb is singular or plural in the present tense is to check to see if it ends in an "s" or not. Contrary to what you might assume, plural action verbs, such as "bark" in "The dogs *bark*," do not end in "s," and singular action verbs, such as "runs" in "Charlotte *runs*," do. So, the sentences above should be corrected to:

> **John** <u>swims</u> for at least one hour each morning.

> **They** <u>are</u> happy all the time.

Now, if you think these seem too easy for the SAT, you are right. The SAT will rarely present simple sentences such as these with only one subject and verb. Instead, the SAT makes these subject/verb agreement questions more difficult by creating longer, more complex sentences with multiple subjects and verbs and interrupting phrases and clauses. Below are the main ways the SAT tries to fool you into misreading a subject/verb agreement question:

Subject/Verb Amnesia

This is when you forget what subject the verb corresponds to because the subject and verb are separated by so many interrupting phrases or clauses that you lose track of the beginning of the sentence.

In order to see if the subject and verb agree, cross out the interrupting phrases or clauses that come between the subject and verb. These could be appositive phrases, nonrestrictive or restrictive clauses, and prepositional phrases. Regardless of what they are, if they come between the subject and the verb, cross them out.

Bob, a reliable friend and trusted colleague, never <u>cancel</u> his social commitments.

By crossing out the appositive phrase "a reliable friend and trusted colleague," you can easily identify the subject/verb agreement error: Bob, the subject of the sentence, is singular, but the verb "cancel" is plural.

CORRECT: Bob, a reliable friend and trusted colleague, never **cancels** his social commitments.

* * *

Jason, who just got his driver's license, <u>are</u> a talented cellist.

Again, by crossing out the interrupting sentence part, in this case the clause "who just got his driver's license," you can clearly see that "Jason" is singular and "are" is plural.

CORRECT: Jason, who just got his driver's license, **is** a talented cellist.

Prepositional phrases can also cause subject/verb agreement problems on the SAT. A prepositional phrase is a group of words that begins with a preposition and modifies a noun or verb in the sentence by adding additional information about location or time. In the sentence "The cat jumped over the fence," "cat" is the subject, "jumped" is the action verb, and "over the fence" is the prepositional phrase. "Over the fence" modifies the verb by explaining where the cat jumped.

PRACTICE

Identify the prepositional phrase and preposition in each of the following sentences.

1) Billy ran through the plate-glass door.

2) Skyler was worried about the elephants.

3) Jess ate three burritos in one sitting.

4) His name is Peter but most call him Pete for short.

5) Sandra fell in love.

6) Megan accused Charles of stealing her popcorn.

7) Smoking is harmful to your health.

Answers

1) Billy ran **through** the plate-glass door.

2) Skylcr was worried **about** the elephants.

3) Jess ate three burritos **in** one sitting.

4) His name is Peter but most call him Pete **for** short.

5) Sandra fell **in** love.

6) Megan accused Charles **of** stealing her popcorn.

7) Smoking is harmful **to** your health.

On the SAT, you will see subject/verb agreement errors that try to trick you into believing a part of the prepositional phrase is the subject that corresponds to the verb. Take a look at this example:

> One of the three actors were caught stealing props from the set.

This can be a little tricky because, if you are going too quickly, you might think the subject is "actors," which is plural. The subject is, in fact, "onc" of those actors, which is singular. "Actors" cannot be the subject because it is a part of the prepositional phrase modifying the subject "One." The prepositional phrase "of the three actors" gives further description as to what the "one" is referring to, but it is not the thing itself that is doing the action.

> **CORRECT:** One of the three actors **was** caught stealing props from the set.

Here is another example:

> Not all research into space colonization possibilities
> require such technology and manpower.

This example is also tricky because you might confuse the subject "research" with a part of the prepositional phrase "possibilities." It is tempting to think "possibilities" is the subject that corresponds to "require" because the words are next to each other, but this is *exactly* what the SAT will do to give you subject/verb amnesia and make you believe the subject is a different noun than it is. "Into space colonization possibilities" is a prepositional phrase that gives additional information about the research, which is the real subject of the sentence.

A good question to ask yourself to determine if you have correctly identified the subject and not the prepositional phrase is: "Is this the thing? Or, does this describe the thing?" Once you determine the subject to be "research," cross out the interrupting phrase "into all space colonization possibilities" to isolate the subject and verb and then read aloud. You should hear that "research...require" does not sound right because "research" is singular and "require" is plural.

> **CORRECT:** Not all research into space colonization possibilities
> **requires** such technology and manpower.

Compound Subject Confusion

Another way subject/verb agreement is made more complicated on the SAT is through the use of compound subjects. A compound subject is when two or more subjects correspond to the same verb. Compound subjects can be singular or plural, depending on how the individual subjects are connected. There is only one rule you must remember to determine whether or not a compound subject is plural:

And is the only word in the English language that can combine two singular subjects to make a plural subject.

And is special, like a unicorn, because no other word can perform this function. *Either*, *or*, *neither*, *nor*, *along with*, *in addition to*, *as well as*, and *but* all create singular compound subjects.

Take, for example, the sentence "Lara and Jess enjoy shopping." Because it joins the individual subjects "Lara" and "Jess" with the word "and," the compound subject is plural and so the plural verb "enjoy" is correct.

If, however, we said "Neither Lara nor Jess enjoy shopping," we would have made a subject/verb agreement error. "Neither...nor" creates a singular compound subject by essentially dealing with each person separately, Lara and then Jess. Although you might not hear the error initially, it is still incorrect; the sentence should be corrected to "Neither Lara nor Jess **enjoys** shopping."

Hint

The SAT will always make the actual subject of the sentence and the noun in the prepositional phrase different in number. That's how it fools you into picking a plural verb when it should be singular or a singular verb when it should be a plural.

Try this example:

Either the cold temperature outside or the annoying
whining of his little brother <u>are</u> making Thomas irritable.

The first thing you should do is identify the compound subject, in this case "the cold temperature outside or the annoying whining." Then you should notice that this compound subject is connected by "either/or," making it singular. Finally, see if it matches with its corresponding verb, "are." It does not, so we must change "are" to the singular "is."

CORRECT: Either the cold temperature outside or the annoying
whining of his little brother **is** making Thomas irritable.

Blind Spot

When connecting two subjects of differing number by either/or and neither/nor to create a compound subject, the verb must agree with the subject that is closest to the verb.

Subjects That Come After Verbs

Sometimes on the SAT, the subject will come after the verb, which might make it more difficult to identify which noun is the subject and to which verb it corresponds. Although this might seem backwards, we actually speak like this quite often, saying things like "There are many different styles of music in the world today" or "There is a huge problem here." In both these sentences, the verbs come first and the subjects "styles" and "problem," respectively, come second. Two effective strategies for mastering these questions are to draw a line from the subject to the verb to be sure that you match them correctly, and to flip the sentence around so subject comes first.

Atop the peak of the tallest mountain in Romania rest the Castle of Vlad Dracul.

When the verb precedes the subject in a sentence, flip the sentence around. It will make it easier to see if the subject and verb agree. When you flip this sentence around so it starts with "The Castle of Vlad Dracul," you'll see that the verb doesn't match the subject.

CORRECT: Atop the peak of the tallest mountain in Romania **rests** the Castle of Vlad Dracul.

Singular Subjects that Appear Plural

The SAT is fond of testing you on certain subjects that appear to be plural but are not. Sometimes these subjects even sound like they should be plural when they are in fact singular, so your ear might not help you here. Do not worry, though; by memorizing a simple list of deceptive singular subjects and learning the rules for these tricksters, you will be able to spot them easily on the SAT.

THE COLLECTIVE NOUN. The collective noun is a collection or group of singular nouns that is acting as one and thus treated as a singular. Common collective nouns include:

- Class

- Team

- Group

- Mob

- Band

- Number

> The band hope to sign with a major record label one day.

Although a band is made up of multiple members, in this sentence it is treated as a collective singular unit. So, "hope" should be made singular.

> **CORRECT:** The band **hopes** to sign with a major record label one day.

* * *

> The collection of craft materials used by the art department are extensive.

In this sentence, "The collection" is a collective noun made up of different materials. It corresponds to the verb "are." Since "collection" is singular and "are" is plural, we have a subject/verb agreement error. If you are going quickly, you might think the subject is "materials," which is why this sentence is tricky.

> **CORRECT:** The collection of craft materials used by the art department **is** extensive.

* * *

> The number of people shopping at farmer's markets have doubled in the last year.

In this example, you might think the subject of the sentence is plural because the sentence is referring to multiple people, but this is incorrect. The "number" of people is the subject, which is a singular, collective unit, and so to fix the sentence you must change "have" to "has" in order to match the subject and verb.

CORRECT: The number of people shopping at farmer's markets **has** doubled in the last year.

Blind Spot

Some subjects might appear to be plural because they have an "s" at the end, but they're actually singular. Common tricksters here include book titles, like *A Tale of Two Cities*; measurements, like three-fourths; or areas of study, like politics or economics.

Gerunds

Gerunds are verbs acting like nouns or adjectives in a sentence. These impostors are tricky because they are verbs, but they are being *used* as something else. Take a look at this example:

Remodeling keep the builders busy.

In this example, it might be hard to spot the subject initially. This is because the subject is actually a gerund, or a verb masquerading as a noun. Verbs that end in "ing" can be used as nouns, as in the sentence above. "Remodeling" is the thing doing the action (keeping the builders busy), so it is the subject of the sentence. To address the error in the sentence you must change the plural verb "keep" to singular "keeps" to match the singular action of "remodeling."

CORRECT: Remodeling **keeps** the builders busy.

Takeaway

Subject/verb agreement errors are purposefully designed to be tricky. Avoid the traps by remembering the rules of subject/verb agreement listed above and by isolating the subject and verb to see if they agree.

Bad Habits: Singular Subjects

When we speak, we take shortcuts. We use slang, abbreviations, and convenient ungrammatical phrasing. It's just easier. But all these shortcuts build bad grammar habits in us. We end up believing that certain types of nouns are plural even though they are singular because we heard them and used them that way in speaking.

All of the following words are actually singular:

- Each

- Everybody

- Everyone

- Everything

- Not one

- Someone

- Anybody

- Anyone

- Anything

- No one

- Nobody

- Nothing

- Somebody

- Something

All these refer to one person, one place, or one idea that is not specifically named.

Everyone <u>are</u> going to the party.

In this example, the subject "everyone" refers to every *single* person, one at a time, and thus "are" needs to be changed to the singular.

Hint

When you see the word "one," "body," or "thing" in the subject, then you are most likely dealing with a singular noun.

CORRECT: Everyone **is** going to the party.

* * *

Each of the students need to get a parking pass by the end of the day.

In this slightly more difficult example, the subject is "each," which is singular. If you cross out the prepositional phrase "of the students," you can avoid the trap of believing that "students" is the subject. To fix, simply change the plural "need" to singular.

CORRECT: Each of the students **needs** to get a parking pass by the end of the day.

* * *

Not one of the athletes are running the mile relay.

In this example, the subject is "one," which is singular, so the plural verb "are" is incorrect.

CORRECT: Not one of the athletes **is** running the mile relay.

Verb Tense

A verb exists either in its base form as an infinitive (to be, to eat, to run) or in its conjugated form as a particular tense. Verb tenses show whether the action of the verb takes place in the past, present, or future. There are three main tenses and two secondary tenses:

Past tense refers to an event that occurred once in the past and is now over.

Examples: *I was, she loved, we worked, he slept*

Present tense refers to something that is currently happening, that is always true, or that happens regularly.

Examples: *I am happy, she loves me, she has long hair, we meet for tea every Friday*

Future tense refers to things that have not happened yet, but will likely occur in the future.

Examples: *I will be, she will love, we will work, he will sleep*

Continuous tense refers to something that is happening continuously over a period of time.

Examples: *I am breathing, she is walking, we are swimming.*

Perfect tense refers to an action or state that has been completed, or "perfected," by the present time, at some point in the past, or will be completed in the future.

Examples of present perfect: *I have grown, Charles has run, we have laughed*

Examples of past perfect: *I had grown, Charles had run, we had laughed*

Examples of future perfect: *We will have grown, Charles will have run, we will have laughed*

Now, you might be thinking, "that's a whole lot of terminology." But do not worry, there are only a few rules to remember when evaluating if a tense in a sentence is correct. Follow these simple steps:

1) Determine the time in which the action takes place by the context of the sentence. Match it with the appropriate verb tense.

2) If there is more than one verb in a sentence, check to see if the verb tense switches unnecessarily. This means that if nothing in the context of the sentence is telling you that the actions are occurring at different times, the verb tense should remain the same. Verb tense should only change if there is a shift in time.

I walked to the playground and I play with my friends.

In the example above, "walked" is past tense and "play" is present tense, but the context of the sentence does not tell us that there is a shift in time. So, there is verb tense error here. To fix this, you must change "play" to "played" to make it consistent with "walked."

CORRECT: I walked to the playground and I **played** with my friends.

Hint

Check time words that indicate a sequence of events such as *today, yesterday, tomorrow, last, first, next, then, later, now.*

* * *

I see my cousin at the party and I tried to get his attention.

Again, this sentence has a shift in verb tense but does not indicate a shift in time. "See" is present tense, but "tried" is past tense. Change "tried" to "try" to make the verb tense consistent.

CORRECT: I see my cousin at the party and I **try** to get his attention.

Let's try an example when a tense change is necessary due to a shift in time.

Yesterday, Jonathan visited his brother in Wisconsin,
and next week he flew home.

IN THIS EXAMPLE, THERE IS A SHIFT IN TIME: Jonathan visited his brother yesterday, but he is not flying home until next week. Therefore, the second verb, "flew," should be written in the future tense as "will fly."

CORRECT: Yesterday, Jonathan visited his brother in Wisconsin,
and next week he **will fly** home.

If the context of the sentence does not require a perfect verb tense, use simple present or simple past.

I have walked for a mile yesterday.

In this example, the present perfect "have walked" is unnecessary because the period of time in which the walking occurred is over and does not extend to the present moment. Therefore, you would use the simple past tense "I walked."

CORRECT: I **walked** for a mile yesterday.

I walked two miles already but still have not reached my destination.

In this example, the simple past tense "walked" is incorrect and the present perfect tense is needed because the walking still occurring and extends to the present moment.

CORRECT: I **have walked** two miles already but still have not reached my destination.

Hint

Use specific adverbs as clues to indicate the need for present perfect such as *already, before, now, lately, a while*, etc. Each of these adverbs alludes to something that occurs over a span of time.

Emily traveled to five countries by the time she was 15.

The example above indicates an action, traveling, that was completed before another action in the past. If the action in the past is described as having happened before another action that also occurred in the past, then you need to use past perfect. Emily traveled to five countries *before* she *was* 15. This means that the action occurred before or up to the time she reached that age. Thus, we need to change the simple past "traveled' to past perfect, "had traveled."

CORRECT: Emily **had traveled** to five countries by the time she was 15.

Hint

When choosing the correct verb tense, choose the simplest tense possible that fits. Sometimes we use "had been" to sound more formal, but this is usually incorrect.

PRACTICE: SUBJECT/VERB AGREEMENT ERRORS

1) Each of the three actors <u>were memorizing</u> lines for the play when the director walked backstage.

A) NO CHANGE

B) was memorizing

C) have been memorizing

D) memorizing

2) Neither Jake nor Larry <u>were ready</u> for the cumulative biology exam.

A) NO CHANGE

B) ready

C) had been ready

D) was ready

3) High above the Rocky Mountains <u>soars golden eagles</u>.

A) NO CHANGE

B) soaring golden eagles

C) soar golden eagles

D) sore golden eagles

4) Every one of the students <u>need to pick up</u> a permission slip by the end of the day.

A) NO CHANGE

B) needs to pick up

C) needs to picks up

D) needing to pick up

5) Lara and Nancy, who have been best friends for <u>years, is going to rent</u> a house down the shore together.

A) NO CHANGE

C) years; are going to rent

B) years, is go to rent

D) years, are going to rent

Pronouns

A **pronoun** is a word that takes the place of a noun or a group of words acting as a noun. An **antecedent** is a term used to describe the noun that the pronoun is replacing.

We use pronouns to add variety and avoid repetition in a sentence. Take a look at the following example that includes one sentence without pronouns and one with pronouns.

Version 1: Aunt Irene was late because Aunt Irene had to wait for Aunt Irene's niece to arrive.

Version 2: Aunt Irene was late because she had to wait for her niece to arrive.

Clearly, pronouns are quite necessary to make the sentence less repetitive and more interesting. In this example, *she* and *her* are both pronouns and *Aunt Irene* is the antecedent.

Major Categories of Personal Pronouns

Person	Pronouns	Description
First person singular	I, me, my	Refers to the person speaking
First person plural	we, us, our	Refers to the person speaking and other people
Second person	you, your	Refers to the person or people being spoken to
Third person singular masculine	he, him	Refers to the male person
Third person singular feminine	she, her	Refers to the female person
Third person plural	they, them	Refers to many people or things
Third person neuter	it, its, one	Refers to an inanimate object, nonperson, or unknown person

Pronoun/Antecedent Agreement

A pronoun must agree with its antecedent in person, gender, and number.

PERSON ERROR. This is when a pronoun is written in a different person or point of view than the antecedent to which it refers.

Urbe surprised the teacher when you pulled out a harmonica in the middle of class.

In this example, Urbe (third person singular) is the one who surprised the teacher, but the pronoun that refers to him is "you" (second person). It makes no sense for "you" to be pulling out the harmonica because, based on the context, Urbe performed the action. This means the antecedent of the pronoun is "Urbe." Thus, you must change the second person pronoun "you" to match the third person antecedent "Urbe."

CORRECT: Urbe surprised the teacher when **he** pulled out a harmonica in the middle of class.

Here is another example:

One should always brush your teeth before bed.

This is an example of switching pronoun case. "One" is third person singular, so it requires a singular pronoun. But, because we do not know the gender of the person, we must say "his or her," or "one's."

CORRECT: One should always brush **his or her** teeth before bed.

CORRECT: One should always brush **one's** teeth before bed.

NUMBER ERROR. This is when the pronoun does not match its antecedent in number. Just like with subject/verb agreement errors, if the antecedent is singular, the pronoun must be singular.

Urbe surprised the teacher when they pulled out a harmonica in the middle of class.

Here again, the pronoun does not match the antecedent Urbe, only this time it is not because the person shifted. "Urbe" is singular, and "they" is plural.

CORRECT: Urbe surprised the teacher when **he** pulled out a harmonica in the middle of class.

GENDER ERROR. This is when a pronoun does not match its antecedent in gender. The pronoun could be feminine while the subject it is referring to is masculine. Notice that we have slightly adjusted the sentence in the example below to include more context clues about the gender of Urbe. The SAT will always give you enough information to determine the gender of a subject, especially if the name is uncommon.

Urbe surprised the teacher when she began
playing his harmonica in the middle of class.

In this example, we can determine from the context clue "his harmonica" that "Urbe" is a masculine subject, and thus we need to change the feminine "she" to "he."

CORRECT: Urbe surprised the teacher when he began
playing **his** harmonica in the middle of class.

Blind Spot

The English language does not have a gender-neutral pronoun in the singular to refer to people, so we often use they or their. It is just easier to say than "he or she," but it is incorrect to use their as a singular pronoun on the SAT. Their is plural.

Unclear or Missing Antecedent

A pronoun must have a clear antecedent. This means that you should be able to clearly identify *one* word or phrase to which the pronoun refers. Sometimes on the SAT, it will be unclear which item the pronoun is referring to because of a lack of information in the sentence and surrounding context. Other times, the antecedent is missing entirely from the sentence and surrounding context. Take a look at these two examples:

The new and improved textbooks are now available for them to distribute.

This is an example of unclear pronoun usage. There is no antecedent in the sentence, so we do not know who "them" is referring to. Thus, we have to replace "them" with a noun that identifies who is doing the distributing.

CORRECT: The new and improved textbooks are now available for **the teachers** to distribute.

* * *

At the same time, a workers' strike for higher wages was raising awareness of the plight of the laborer. Workers associated with this began to embrace the philosophy of Karl Marx.

This is a more difficult example of unclear pronoun usage. Focus your attention on the pronoun "this," which does not have a clear antecedent. Although it might sound grammatically correct, "this" can refer to either "the workers' strike" or to "the plight of the laborer," and so it is incorrect. To correct this unclear pronoun usage, you have to qualify the pronoun by placing one of the two nouns after it. Do not worry about deciding which one to choose, either is correct, it just depends on what the answer choices provide.

> **CORRECT:** At the same time, a workers' strike for higher wages was raising awareness of the plight of the laborer. Workers associated with **this plight** began to embrace the philosophy of Karl Marx.

> **CORRECT:** At the same time, a workers' strike for higher wages was raising awareness of the plight of the laborer. Workers associated with **this strike** began to embrace the philosophy of Karl Marx.

Pronouns in the Wrong Case

Another type of pronoun error that is tested on the SAT deals with pronoun case. Pronoun case is relatively simple. There are three pronoun cases, each with its own function:

SUBJECTIVE: pronouns as subjects, doing the action of the sentence

OBJECTIVE: pronouns as objects, receiving the action of the sentence

POSSESSIVE: pronouns that express ownership

On the SAT, the only error that is tested with pronoun case deals with a confusion between subject and object pronouns. A pronoun must be in the correct form: subject or object, depending on its function in the sentence. If it is serving as the subject, doing the action, then it must be in the subjective case, and if it is serving as an object, receiving action, it must be in the objective case.

Take a look at this table, which illustrates the difference between subject and object pronouns:

Subject (Does Action)	Object (Receives Action)
I hit the ball	The ball was hit to **me**
He/she hit the ball	The ball was hit to **him/her**
They hit the ball	The ball was hit to **them**
We hit the ball	The ball was hit to **us**
Who/what hit the ball?	To **whom/what** should I hit the ball?
It hit the ball	The ball was hit to **it**

In a simple sentence, it is very easy to hear the pronoun case error. Read each of the following examples aloud:

- Me purchased a new car.

- Him has been my best friend for my entire life.

- They gave the medal to she.

Hopefully you heard the error in each of these and corrected "me" to "I," "Him" to "He," and "she" to "her." These are pretty easy, but the SAT increases the difficulty by placing the pronoun in a noun phrase. This essentially means the pronoun is connected to a noun, as in "Terry and I."

To determine if a pronoun in a noun phrase should be a subject or object, cross out the noun and conjunction to isolate the pronoun and then read the sentence. If it sounds funny, like in the sentences above, it's wrong.

Reggie, my new tutor, delivered the anatomy and
physiology books to John and I.

"I" is a subject pronoun, standing in for a noun that performs an action. The phrase "delivered the books to" needs to be followed by an object pronoun, because the pronoun is receiving an action. By crossing out "John and," you can hear the error in "Reggie delivered the books to I."

CORRECT: Reggie, my new tutor, delivered the anatomy and
physiology books to **John and me**.

Sometimes you are required to determine if the pronoun "who" or "whom" is in the correct case. To figure this out, you must check to see if "who" is doing action or receiving action. "Who" is correct when an action is being performed, because "who" is a subject pronoun. If an action is being received, it should be "whom."

Whom is coming with me to the party later?

In this example, "Whom" is serving as a subject, doing the action of coming to the party, and so it is incorrect.

CORRECT: Who is coming with me to the party later?

Hint

A quick way to determine if the pronoun should be *who* or *whom* is by plugging in *him/her* or *he/she* in place of *who* or *whom*. If *him/her* sounds normal, then *whom* is correct. If it sounds like it should be *he/she*, then *who* is correct. You can rearrange the sentence to make it easier.

"To whom should I give these books?" → "I should give these books to whom?" → "I should give these books to him?"

Thus, *whom* is correct.

Takeaway

Cross out words to isolate the pronoun and the antecedent, and draw a line from one to the other to see if they agree. Keep pronouns clear and consistent with their antecedents.

PRACTICE: PRONOUN ERRORS

1) Jane and Bertha went to the mall after school <u>and she</u> bought shoes.

A) NO CHANGE

B) and her

C) and Jane

D) and; she

2) If you find a lost ticket on the floor of the concert venue, simply return it <u>to them</u>.

A) NO CHANGE

B) to the ticket takers

C) to those

D) to it

3) Larry was driving to the market when a squirrel darted in front of one's car, causing him to swerve and crash into a tree.

A) NO CHANGE

B) of her car,

C) of his car,

D) of your car,

4) Oliver was quite depressed after the Mets lost yet again, so he decided to call Barry and I and see if we wanted to visit the aquarium, which always cheered him up.

A) NO CHANGE

B) Barry and me

C) Barry and we

D) them

5) In the future, because of robotics, surgery will no longer be limited by the dexterity of the surgeons or by its intelligence and knowledge.

A) NO CHANGE

B) it's

C) there

D) their

6) After examining the asteroid crater, scientists determined that one had discovered a new element.

A) NO CHANGE

B) he or she

C) it

D) they

7) By receiving a high number of views on her hit single on YouTube, the artist showed the record executives that our music has a wide appeal.

A) NO CHANGE

B) her

C) its

D) their

8) Each of the students dropped off their backpacks before heading to the pep rally.

A) NO CHANGE

B) whose backpacks

C) there backpacks

D) his or her backpack

9) The man, which had been traveling all day, collapsed onto his couch when he arrived home.

A) NO CHANGE

B) who had

C) he had

D) that had

Its, _which_, and _that_ are used for nonhuman items such as animals and objects. _Who_ and _whom_ are used for people.

Parallelism

So far, we've discussed three grammatical pairs that must be consistent: subjects and verbs, pronouns and antecedents, and nouns representing the same thing. There is one other form of consistency tested on the SAT: **parallelism**. The rule of parallelism states that items serving parallel functions in a sentence must be parallel in grammatical structure. Think of these linked grammatical elements like parallel lines: what one does, the other must do. The way one is, the other must be.

Parallel Verb Forms

The two most commonly tested verb forms in parallelism errors on the SAT are the infinitive and continuous, or gerund, form. As we stated on page 293, the infinitive refers to the base form of the verb, as in _to be_ or _to eat_, and the continuous form refers to the verb ending in –ing, as in _running_ or _jumping_. The only difference between continuous and gerund form is that continuous always acts like a verb, and the gerund acts like a noun or adjective.

Part of Speech

For these, parallelism is demonstrated by having a noun parallel to another noun or a verb parallel to another verb. This is commonly tested with gerunds because it is easy to confuse gerunds with verbs.

- In "My favorite activity is swimming," the verb _swimming_ is a gerund because it is acting like a noun: swimming is a thing, an activity.

- In "I was swimming in the pool," _swimming_ is acting as a verb. It is in continuous form as an action that is being performed.

Comparative Words

Comparative words are words that create comparisons between different elements in the sentence. Comparative words must be parallel.

Memorize this short list and earn easy points:

- Either…or

- Neither…nor

- Not only…but also

Each one of the phrases above must be linked to its counterpart. *Either* must continue to *or*, *neither* to *nor*, and *not only* to *but also*. Take a look at this short example:

> Neither Kishan or Kelly looked forward to writing in-class essays.

This example begins with *neither* but then continues with *or* instead of *nor*, so it is incorrect. To make this parallel, you must correct as follows:

> **CORRECT:** Neither Kishan **nor** Kelly looked forward to writing in-class essays.

How Parallelism Is Tested on the SAT

ITEMS IN A LIST. When grammatical elements are listed together, they are serving the same function so they must be parallel.

> Joe enjoys boxing, running, and to hike.

Looks at the verbs in this example. Two of them use -ing, but the last one doesn't match—it isn't parallel. If you start a list using one verb form, you must continue using that same verb form.

> **CORRECT:** Joe enjoys **boxing, running, and hiking**.

ITEMS BEING COMPARED. When grammatical elements are compared with one another, they are serving the same function because they are linked and thus must be parallel. Take a look at this example:

> Gaia enjoyed playing her French horn more than to clean it.

In this example, the verb *playing* is linked to the verb *to clean* through comparison, which is a parallel function. Therefore, both verbs must be parallel in form, which they are not. *Playing* is in the gerund form, but *clean* is in its infinitive form. In other words, they don't match.

> **CORRECT:** Gaia enjoyed playing her French horn more than **cleaning** it.

Illogical Comparison

Sometimes the reason elements of a sentence are not parallel has nothing to do with grammatical structure. The grammatical structure could be parallel and yet there might still be an error in the logic of the comparison. This is a type of parallelism error in which illogical items are compared to one another.

For example, you can compare a person to a person or an action to an action, such as Bob to Joe or swimming to bicycling, but you cannot compare swimming to Joe. The SAT will purposefully create illogical comparisons. For example, you cannot say, "Most students prefer watching movies to books." *Watching movies* is an action, but *books* is an object. The sentence must be corrected to "watching movies to reading books," which compares an action to action, not an action to an object.

An easier example might be "John likes Sarah's shirt better than Nancy." Poor Nancy, beaten out by a shirt. Clearly, this is an illogical comparison—you cannot compare Sarah's shirt to all of Nancy. You must compare Sarah's shirt to Nancy's shirt, or Sarah to Nancy.

The way to spot an illogical comparison is by examining the comparison within the context of the sentence and its intended meaning. If the comparison makes the meaning of the sentence illogical, it is incorrect and not parallel.

> Most people prefer the hamburgers at Burger Shack <u>to Burger Hut</u>.

You cannot compare the burgers at one restaurant to another entire restaurant. You must compare burgers to burgers or restaurant to restaurant

> **CORRECT:** Most people prefer the hamburgers at Burger
> Shack to **the hamburgers** at Burger Hut.

One important trick to remember with illogical comparison errors is that you can use a pronoun to stand in for the noun that is the subject of the comparison. Take a look at this example of logical comparison, phrased in two equally correct ways:

Version 1: The trees of Northern California grow much taller than the trees of southern Florida.

Version 2: The trees of Northern California grow much taller than those of southern Florida.

Notice that in the second version we replaced *the trees* with the pronoun *those*. *Those* refers to the trees and thus completes the logical parallel comparison of trees to trees. This is another grammatically correct way to demonstrate parallelism.

Takeaway

Items serving a parallel function in a sentence need to be parallel in form.

Hint

If you read the sentence in question aloud, chances are you will hear a clunk when you read over the non-parallel item. It will just sound off.

Mindset Tip

Right about now, you may be hitting a wall. You might be thinking, *"Will this grammar ever end?"* or *"How many grammar rules do I need to learn for the SAT?"* If thoughts like these are creeping into your head and you are beginning to feel exhausted and frustrated over the monotony and seemingly endless grammar section, this is perfectly normal. Every journey has a low point, and with every new skill you learn, you will trudge through an abyss.

Realize that true growth requires some pain and that even if you don't notice it right now, the litany of grammar errors and practice you are doing is not only growing your score but also building your grit. Before you continue to this next section of Parallelism and Comparison practice, do a Deep Breath Reset, and then reach down inside and find that fire. It's okay to get a little angry. Real determination is a combination of peace and fire. Breathe deeply while also getting in touch with that fire within, that unconquerable side of you that will not lie down and be beaten, and then forge onward. Sometimes the only light at the end of the tunnel is the light that shines forth from within.

PRACTICE: PARALLELISM AND COMPARISON

1) To be part of Danny's very exclusive club, you must be a senior in high school, a popular student, <u>and wrestle</u>.

A) NO CHANGE

B) and wrestling.

C) and a wrestler.

D) or wrestled.

2) Most people are more likely to be able to identify the latest reality TV star than <u>the name of a current state senator</u>.

A) NO CHANGE

B) the names of a current state senator

C) a current state senator

D) a current state senator's name

3) Cost-Rite is taking a new approach to battling poverty in America: they are preventing employees from being stuck at minimum wage by <u>provided</u> them with tuition for night school at the local community college.

A) NO CHANGE

B) providing

C) provides

D) have been providing

4) Swimming across the English Channel requires focus, stamina, and <u>being resilient</u>.

A) NO CHANGE

B) being more resilient

C) resiliently

D) resilience

5) Bobby was compassionate, helpful, and <u>being kind</u> to his family.

A) NO CHANGE

B) kindness

C) kinder

D) kind

6) America's military budget is much larger than that of any other <u>country</u>.

A) NO CHANGE

B) countries

C) military budget

D) countryman

7) Neither the New York Jets <u>or</u> the New York Giants actually play in New York.

A) NO CHANGE

B) and

C) nor

D) but

Answers

Subject/Verb Agreement (page 296)

1) Choice (B) corrects the error by changing "were" to "was" so it matches the singular subject "each." A common mistake would be to think that the subject is "actors," but in this sentence "each of the three actors" means we are dealing with them one at a time, singularly.

2) Choice (D) corrects the error by changing "were" to "was" so that it matches the singular usage of "neither/nor." Only the word "and" can create a plural subject; for example, "Jake and Larry."

3) Choice (C) makes "soar" plural to match the plural subject "golden eagles." This is slightly tricky, because the subject "golden eagles" comes after the verb "soar." Choice (D) purposely confuses "soar" with the similar-sounding word "sore."

4) "Every one of the students" is singular because "every one" refers to each individual student, one at a time. So, the singular verb "needs" is appropriate, making choice (B) correct. Choice (C) is incorrect because it introduces a new error, "picks up," which does not match with "needs."

5) Choice (D) correctly matches "Lara and Nancy," a plural subject, with the plural verb "are." Choice (C) introduces a punctuation error by using the semicolon, because "are going to rent" beings a dependent clause and should be separated with a comma.

Pronouns (page 302)

1) The use of "she" is ambiguous, because it can refer to either Jane or Bertha. Changing it to "her" is incorrect, because "her" is an object pronoun, rather than a subject pronoun. Choice (C) is correct; by changing "she" to "Jane," the ambiguity in the second clause is eliminated. Choice (D) is incorrect because it introduces a punctuation error and does not correct the ambiguity.

2) This is another error of ambiguity. Choice (B) is correct because it fixes the ambiguous pronoun usage; it identifies who the tickets should be returned to. Choices (C) and (D) are incorrect because they do not correct the ambiguity of the original sentence and because they replace "them" with pronouns that do not refer to people.

3) "One's" refers to some person, but in this sentence, the pronoun should refer to a specific person: Larry. Choice (C) is correct because the subject is Larry, and "him" refers to Larry.

4) If you cross out "Barry and" in the second clause of this sentence, you should be able to hear the error. "I" is incorrect because it is a subject pronoun, but at this point in the sentence, the singular object pronoun "me" is required. Thus, choice (B) is the correct answer.

5) "Its" is singular and used for nonhuman items, so it does not match the plural antecedent "surgeons." Choice (D), "their," correctly pluralizes the pronoun to match "surgeons." Choice (C) incorrectly suggests "there," which refers to a place, and Choice (B) incorrectly replaces the pronoun "its" with the contraction "it's."

6) "One," in the original sentence, is singular and does not match the plural word "scientists." "He or she" in choice (B), and "it" in choice (C), are also singular and do not match with "scientists." Additionally, "it" cannot be used to refer to people. Thus, choice (D), "they," is correct because it makes the pronoun plural.

7) "Our" does not match the antecedent, which is a female artist. Neither does "they," which is plural, or "its," which is possessive and cannot be used for people. Thus, choice (B), "her," is the correct answer.

8) "Their" is a plural pronoun, which does not match with the singular subject "each." Choice (C) is also incorrect, because "there" is not a pronoun, but rather a word commonly confused with "their." "Whose" is a pronoun, but it does not refer to "each of the students." Thus, answer (D), "his or her," is correct.

9) The pronoun "which" cannot refer to people, so the original sentence is incorrect. Choice (D) is incorrect for the same reason. Choice (C), "he had," is incorrect because it creates a run-on sentence. Choice (B) is the correct answer because "who" refers to people and is correct in number.

Parallelism and Comparison (page 308)

1) Choice (C) is the correct answer because it changes "wrestle," a verb, into "wrestler," a noun, to match the previous items in the list.

2) Choice (C) corrects the illogical comparison in the original sentence, which compares a person, "the latest reality TV star," to the name of a person, "the name of a current state senator."

3) Choice (B) is the correct answer because it keeps verb forms parallel throughout the sentence: they are "preventing" employees by "providing" them with tuition. Choice (D) is incorrect because it unnecessarily uses a complicated past tense form.

4) The last item in the list, "being resilient," is not parallel to the other items in the list and is unnecessarily wordy. Adding "more," in choice (B), only makes the sentence more wordy. Choice (C) is incorrect because it changes "being resilient" to an adverb, while "focus" and "stamina" are nouns. Choice (D) correctly changes "being resilient" into the noun "resilience" to match the other items on the list.

5) The words "compassionate" and "helpful" are adjectives, and the last item in the list should also be an adjective to keep the list parallel. The original sentence is incorrect because of the addition of the word "being." Choice (D) is correct because it removes the unnecessary verb and makes the list parallel. Choice (B) is incorrect because "kindness" is a noun, and choice (C) is incorrect because "kinder" is a comparative adjective, which does not make sense in this sentence.

6) This is correct as written because it states "than that of any other country." "That" signifies the military budget and so the sentence is correctly comparing a military budget to a military budget. This sentence would be incorrect if "that" were missing and instead it compared the military budget of the US to another country. Choice (B) creates a numbers agreement problem; you cannot say "that of any other countries." Choice (C) is incorrect because "that" already refers to the military budget of another country, so saying "that of any other military budget," is a redundancy and an illogical comparison. Choice (D) is incorrect because this sentence is not talking about the military budget of a person or "countryman" but rather a military budget of a country.

7) This sentence is incorrect because "neither" goes with "nor," not "or." Choice (C) is the correct answer.

Vocabulary Words 151–165

151) **altercation** (n). dispute, disagreement, argument: *The teenager was admitted to the emergency room after an altercation with his older brother.*

152) **adversary** (n). rival, enemy: *The general understood the importance of knowing the capabilities of his adversary.*

153) **dreary** (adj). a) gloomy; b) boring, lifeless: *The dreary weather contributed to the depressing mood at the funeral.*

154) **ethical** (adj). in accord with standards for morality and good conduct: *To be a priest, one must be moral and ethical.*

155) **sneer** (v). a) to smile, mock or laugh at someone: *"How can you be so cruel as to sneer at my admission of love for you?" cried the young woman;* b) (n). a look of mockery: *The man had a sneer on his face when the woman revealed her feelings for him.*

156) **apathy** (n). a) absence of emotion or feeling: *All the students had a look of apathy on their faces as they listened to the boring lecture;* b) lack of interest: *The rich man's apathy for the homeless was disappointing.*

157) **counterproductive** (adj). preventing the achievement of an intended goal; having an effect that defeat's one's purpose: *The bickering in the meeting was counterproductive to any chance of coming to an agreement.*

158) **mean** (adj). a) offensive, selfish, nasty: *He made a mean remark*; b) insignificant, small: *The poor farmer eked out a mean existence on his farm;* c) stingy d) (n). something in the middle or midway between two extremes: *The mean of 30 and 40 is 35.*

159) **dilemma** (n). a problem or predicament: *The doctor faced a real dilemma when his patient refused to take any medicine for his condition.*

160) **currency** (n). a) money b) the state of being widely accepted and circulated: *Science has given currency to the concept of survival of the fittest;* c) prevalence; popularity: *The slang term "lit" has gained currency in high schools in recent years.*

161) **recount** (adj). to tell, relate, or narrate: *Lydia derived extreme pleasure in recounting in her experience meeting Taylor Swift.*

162) **cognitive** (adj). relating to the mind, as in the processes of perception, memory, judgment, and reasoning: *The cognitive abilities of the precocious child were those of a genius.*

163) **sophisticated** (adj). a) cultured: *She showed sophisticated taste in choosing the proper wine for dinner;* b) complex, intricate: *The game of chess was too sophisticated for a four-year-old to understand and master.*

164) **plastic** (adj). capable of being molded; bendable or pliable: *The plastic quality of clay enables it to be used for many purposes.*

165) **dynamic** (adj). a) energetic, volatile: *Politicians must have dynamic personalities to be successful and win elections;* b) changing: *The US economy is a dynamic one that is constantly changing.*

Latin and Greek Roots 61–65

61) MAN: hand (emancipate, manual, manufacture, manifest)

62) MATER/MATR: mother, woman (maternity, maternal, matriarch)

63) MEM/MEMOR: memory (remembrance, memorialize, immemorial)

64) META: change (metamorphosis, metaphysical, metaphor)

65) METER: measure (metric, chronometer, thermometer)

UNTIMED COLLEGE BOARD PRACTICE

Complete the following College Board practice problems from College Board's *The Official SAT Study Guide* or online at www.collegeboard.org. Review answers after completing.

Test 1, Writing and Language, #8, 18, 19, 23, 30, 36, 40, 44

Test 2, Writing and Language, #1, 3, 5, 6, 17, 19, 29, 30, 39

Test 3, Writing and Language, #1, 5, 12, 15, 36, 38

Test 4, Writing and Language, #6, 7, 9, 12, 19, 21, 24, 28, 32, 34

Math Test: Timing and Pacing

As you probably already know, each math section of the SAT will have multiple choice questions followed by grid-in questions. The questions will get progressively more advanced as you go through each section. Question 1 on the multiple-choice portion will most likely be easier than question 10 on the multiple-choice portion. The grid-ins will follow a similar pattern. The first grid-in will be relatively easy, and the rest will get progressively more difficult.

Let's take a closer look at the two sections individually.

No Calculator Section

This section includes 15 multiple-choice questions and five grid-in questions. A helpful pacing tip is to think of this section as being divided into four 5-question blocks. Block 1 includes the first five multiple-choice questions, which are relatively easy. Block 2, which has questions 6–10, gets a little bit more difficult, and block 3, consisting of questions 11–15, can include some very difficult questions. It is important not to let those few challenging questions in block 3 demoralize and frustrate you. If you are stuck for over two minutes on one problem, simply move on to block 4, the grid-ins. Remember, since the grid-ins are essentially their own section, they revert to being easy, allowing you to regain your mojo.

Hint

Easy questions are very important! Each question is worth the same number of points. You earn the same number of points for correctly answering an easy question as you do for correctly answering the hardest question.

Mindset Tip

Remember, each mistake you make or question that you do not understand is an opportunity for growth. It is important that you take the time to learn from each of these and approach them with a growth mindset.

Calculator Section

The calculator section will include 30 multiple-choice questions and eight grid-in questions. You will have 55 minutes to complete them. Since this is a long section, it will be best to once again break the section up into four blocks. The first block, questions 1–10, is easier, and, block 2, consisting of questions 11–20, will have slightly more difficult questions. The third block, questions 21–30, will contain some of the most challenging questions on the test. Once again, you do not want to take too much time on any one question, so if you have already spent more than two minutes on a single question, move on to the next one. The fourth block, questions 31–38, will contain the grid-ins, which, just like in the No Calculator section, will start over in difficulty level.

In both sections, it is vital that you allow yourself a reasonable amount of time for the grid-ins and that you enter block 4 in a positive state of mind. You may encounter some questions that are very challenging, but don't stress. It is best not to let a few questions throw you off and take away your positive thoughts. You should not be upset when you encounter questions you do not understand. Since this is a practice test, these challenging questions will lead only to revelation mistakes.

TIMED COLLEGE BOARD PRACTICE

Complete the following College Board practice problems from College Board's *The Official SAT Study Guide* or online at www.collegeboard.org. Review answers after completing.

Complete Test 5, Section 4 (Calculator). Time yourself, but do not look at the clock until you have finished the section. This will provide you with valuable information about your pacing so you can begin to adjust as needed for future timed practice.

Chapter **12**

The Success Curve

What if, after winning the lottery, you were given a choice: you could either go home with the one million dollars you won or be given a magic penny that doubled each day for one month. Which would you choose?

Most people would naturally choose the million dollars, but would they be right to do so? Let's do a little math:

Day 1: 1 penny

Day 2: 2 pennies

Day 3: 4 pennies

Day 4: 8 pennies

Day 5: 16 pennies

Day 6: 32 pennies

Day 7: 64 pennies

We know what you're thinking. It's a week already, and you only have 64 cents. It's not even a dollar! If you chose the million dollars, you're looking pretty good right now, but let's keep it going and see what happens.

Day 8: $1.28

Day 9: $2.56

Day 10: $5.12

Day 11: $10.24

Day 12: $20.48

Day 13: $40.96

Day 14: $81.92

Day 15: $163.84

Day 16: $327.68

Day 17: $655.36

Day 18: $1,310.72

Day 19: $2,621.44

Day 20: $5,242.88

Day 21: $10,485.76

It's 21 days in and although you made 10 grand from just a penny, you're feeling a little bit nervous because you could've had a million. You have nine days left, and it seems like you will never make it to the million. What the heck? But hang in there, because you're about to witness some magic.

Day 22: $20,971.52

Day 23: $41,943.04

Day 24: $83,886.08

Day 25: $167,772.16

Day 26: $335,544.32

Day 27: $671,088.64

Now, obviously you can see what happens next…you break a million. But you're not just going to break a million, you are going shatter the million dollar mark! This is the power of exponential growth, the phenomenon that turns millionaires into billionaires, and the cornerstone of the Success Curve. Watch what happens in the next few days.

Day 28: $1,342,177.28

Day 29: $2,684,354.56

Day 30: $5,368,709.12

If you had chosen the million dollars, you would have missed out on an additional four million dollars. Now, you may be asking yourself, how is it possible for a penny to turn into five million dollars?

Simple. Exponential growth.

Exponential growth means that the rate of change does not stay the same, but rather increases as time progresses. Notice how in the penny example, you first saw an increase of 1 cent, the next day your increase was by 2 cents, the next day by 4 cents, and, by the last day, you had increased the previous day's amount by over two million dollars. Small increases in the beginning lead to big increases later, which then lead to astronomical success.

Welcome to the Success Curve

The Success Curve reflects the exponential growth associated with the growth-mindset approach to learning: building upon each newly learned skill to help build greater skills, which are then used to build even greater skills. It's the snowball effect that you just witnessed with the doubling penny.

When you learn the first SAT topic, it's hard, but once you master it, that new ability, plus your increased confidence, allows you to learn the next topic with that much more ease. That new knowledge compounds and gets added to your previous skill set and confidence level, making the next topic that much easier. This continues exponentially over time until, one day, you wake up and learning is effortless and habitual.

At this point in your practice, you are close to reaching the breakthrough point on the Success Curve. All the work you have been doing has helped you build momentum in the form of habits, skills, and confidence. The small penny steps you took in the beginning were absolutely necessary to get you to the million-dollar steps you will take soon. At some point, if you stay on course and build upon each newly learned skill, your SAT success will skyrocket.

Let's examine more closely an exponential graph to better understand the Success Curve.

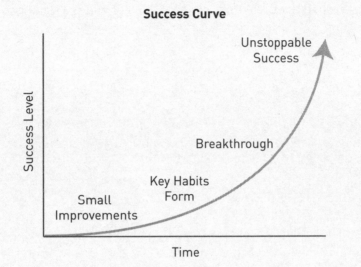

Notice that at each stage, the slope is increasing. This is the essence of exponential growth: each increment of change is larger than the last.

The above graph reflects an exponential function, meaning that the line grows at an exponential rate of change. Growth is not constant and is, in fact, almost imperceptible in the beginning of the graph. But notice how the line changes after the Breakthrough Point, curving up and growing at a much greater rate.

This is how practice toward a goal works and how success is born. People who understand this phenomenon know that they must continue to practice and work, even if they do not see much noticeable improvement at first. With this knowledge, they don't get demoralized or abandon their goals.

They also realize that once they hit that Breakthrough Point, their progress will catapult upward and additional practice will yield much greater growth. They are able to use past practice and success to learn new problems and skills, which greatly reduces the time it takes to learn new skills and find even more success. This is why it seems like successful people keep becoming more successful, while unsuccessful people keep striking out.

On the SAT, understanding the Success Curve is absolutely crucial. When you trudge through the Abyss and practice without seeing any initial improvement, just know that you are continually building skills and getting closer to the Breakthrough Point, which is when everything about the SAT will begin to click and your pace of improvement will jump by leaps and bounds.

So now, as you pass through the Breakthrough Point, hold on tight! It's going to be one hell of a ride.

Writing and Language Test: Expression of Ideas

As you delve into the second major section of the Writing and Language Test, realize that you are nearing the Breakthrough Point for grammar. Whether you know it or not, as you persevered through the Abyss of grammatical error after grammatical error, learning and applying the numerous strategies, you were building imperceptible neural pathways, reinforcing existing ones, and gradually approaching a critical mass. Different students might reach the Breakthrough Point at different times, but the result is always the same: exponential growth in perception and ability. Somewhere in the next three chapters, it will all just click. Be ready, because the growth is going to happen quickly.

"Expression of ideas" refers to how the author expresses his or her meaning and ideas. In this section you will be asked to correct errors in an author's expression. Does the writer convey his idea clearly, or is it hard to understand the point due to diction (word choice), organization, wordiness, or redundancy? As you might have noticed, these errors are different than those in the conventions of English section because they are not strictly grammar based. Rather than correcting a subject and verb that clearly do not agree (one singular, one plural) you will be asked to fix the author's style of writing so that it better communicates the point. Although this may seem subjective, there are some clear rules to follow when editing on the SAT that we have laid out for you in the next two chapters.

Diction

Diction is the author's choice of words. On the SAT, diction errors will be tested in sentences that use the wrong word for the passage context or by mismatching the formality of the language in the passage with the purpose/intent of the writer. Memorizing the vocabulary in this book (especially words with multiple meanings), reading sentences aloud, and knowing common diction traps will help you spot and correct these errors.

Commonly Misused Words and Words with Multiple Meanings

A sentence on the SAT might use the word "illusion," but based on the context the word should actually be "allusion." Notice how these two words sound alike; this is one of the devious ways the SAT tries to trick you with diction errors. Take a look at this example:

Harold was <u>effected</u> by the death of his cat.

In this example, "effect" is being confused with "affect." *E*ffect an is a noun, as in "The effects of the earthquake...." *A*ffect is a verb, as in "That movie really affected me." A good way to know the difference is to remember the two phrases "side effects" and "special effects." Both of these illustrate how "effect" is a noun.

In the example above, the word in question is an action that is happening to Harold, and thus we need the verb "affect."

CORRECT: Harold was **affected** by the death of his cat.

Another common diction trap the SAT creates is with words that have multiple meanings. The SAT will deliberately confuse one meaning of the word with another. Take a look at this example:

The criminal <u>preserved</u> his innocence in spite of the overwhelming evidence to the contrary.

A) NO CHANGE

B) kept up

C) sustained

D) maintained

"Preserved" is being used incorrectly in this context. It means to keep unspoiled or in its original state, which does not make sense in the example above. The word we are looking for should communicate that the criminal was asserting or holding the opinion that he was innocent. That word is "maintain." The problem, however is that "to assert or hold the opinion of" is a less common meaning of the word "maintain," and the common meaning is very similar to the meaning of "preserve." Look at these two sentences:

"Historical documents have been carefully *maintained* in the Library of Congress for future generations to read."

"Historical documents have been carefully *preserved* in the Library of Congress for future generations to read."

Notice how the meanings of the two words are almost identical here. "Sustained" and "kept up" similarly play off the common meaning of "maintained." This is how the SAT tries to trick you with words with multiple meanings. It will manipulate you into choosing a word that shares a meaning with the word you want but is not suitable for the context.

The criminal <u>preserved</u> his innocence in spite of the overwhelming evidence to the contrary.

A) NO CHANGE

B) kept up

C) sustained

D) maintained→ **CORRECT ANSWER**

Informal Writing

The SAT also creates diction errors by mismatching the word choice, especially when it comes to the formality of language, and the writer's intention. It might seem difficult to match diction to author intent, but on the SAT this usually means only one thing: be formal. Be formal, and don't choose answer choices that use conversational, informal English or slang. SAT passages are typically written in formal English with the intention of informing or persuading the reader. Therefore, questions that refer you to a less-than-formally written chunk of a sentence might need to be corrected. The only exception is when the diction you are asked to correct is part of an idiomatic expression (explained on the following page), which typically does not use such formal language. Take a look at this example:

The lawyer presented his case to the judge and the
jury while the defendant <u>hung out</u> in his seat.

The phrase "hung out" is conversational slang, which does not match the formality of the rest of the sentence. To correct the error, you need to elevate the language.

CORRECT: The lawyer presented his case to the judge and the
jury while the defendant **reclined** in his seat.

Idioms

An idiom, from the Greek root "id," which means "one's own," is a phrase that is essentially on its own with a meaning that is established purely by common usage. It does not follow any typical grammar rules and is unique unto itself. Although idioms include common expressions like "kicked the bucket," or "raining cats and dogs," these expressions are not the ones tested on the SAT. The idioms tested on the SAT are related to gerund/infinitive confusion and misuse of prepositions. For example, a possible idiom error might be, "I was interested on many majors in college." You should be able to hear the error: "interested on" should be "interested in." However, you probably also realize that this is not due to some grammatical rule you are recalling. The only reason you know that the correct phrase is "interested in" is because of common usage.

Let's take a closer look at the two main SAT idiom errors.

Gerund/Infinitive Confusion

Gerunds, if you remember, are verbs ending in "ing" that act as other parts of speech, like nouns or adjectives. Infinitives are verbs in their base form, like "to eat." There are some phrases in the English language that require the gerund form of a verb instead of the infinitive and other phrases that require the infinitive form instead of the gerund. Again, there is no hard and fast grammatical rule here, but confusing gerunds and infinitives in these phrases will absolutely create an error.

The businessman worried about <u>to be late</u> to his meeting.

In the example above, "to be" should sound wrong to you. In the phrase "worried about to be late," we need the gerund "being" as opposed to the infinitive "to be." Let your ear be your guide.

CORRECT: The businessman worried about **being** late to his meeting.

Hint

The confusion of "being" and "to be" is one of the common gerund/infinitive idiom errors.

Misuse of a Preposition

The other way idioms are tested on the SAT is with prepositional phrases. Certain verbs require certain prepositions, and the SAT will intentionally create errors that use the wrong preposition with the verb. Remember, a preposition is a word that modifies a noun or verb in the sentence by adding additional information about location. Here is a list of the most commonly tested prepositions on the SAT:

- about

- against

- at

- by

- for

- from

- in

- of

- on

- through

- to

- with

He listened <u>at</u> the music.

In this example, the prepositional idiom "listened at" is incorrect. The correct preposition is "to." As with gerund/infinitive confusion, your ear will help you correct this. "Listen at" should sound funny.

CORRECT: He listened **to** the music.

* * *

Most people prefer wearing contacts <u>than</u> wearing glasses.

The prepositional idiom *prefer to* is commonly tested on the SAT because most of us misspeak when we use that expression, saying things like: "I prefer this *over* that" or "I prefer this *than* that." Both of these are technically incorrect. The only preposition that *prefer* can use is *to*.

CORRECT: Most people prefer wearing contacts **to** wearing glasses.

* * *

We arrived <u>in the airport</u> with just a half hour to catch the plane.

This example is testing you on the prepositional idiom "arrived in" or "arrived at." You can arrive *at* specific places such as your friend's house, the concert venue, an airport, but you arrive *in* geographic locations, such as cities and countries. Since the example above includes a specific place to which the subject is arriving, the preposition must be "at," not "in."

CORRECT: We arrived **at** the airport with just a half hour to catch the plane.

Here is a table of common SAT prepositional idiom errors and how to correct them:

SAT Idiom Error	Correction of Error
Charles <u>serves to be</u> a mediator in his peer group.	Charles **serves as** a mediator…
Tanya read a <u>passage into the</u> prospect of living on Mars.	Tanya read a passage **on**…
<u>As a means through bartering</u> with the native people, the explorer offered his metal canteen.	**As a means of** bartering…
While <u>they await</u> for the car to pass so they could continue to play in the street, the kids chatted eagerly.	While they **waited for**…
The teacher went <u>so far to</u> hold the entire class after school for detention.	The teacher went **so far as to**…

Linguist and scholar Noam Chomsky developed a theory that we all possess an innate language ability. This is the idea that on some unconscious level, our brains have an inner sense for language; we are somehow born with an understanding of how words and sentences work.[12] Combine this with all the language you've heard since birth—the books you've read, the television you've watched, the conversations you've had—and you have quite a formidable intuition for language. This is why trusting your ear works so well.

For the following diction and idiom errors, read the sentence out loud, then plug each answer choice into the sentence and read it out loud. If you still don't have a sense of what the correct choice is, try putting the phrase or word in a new context. On some level, you might remember it. Take for example the word "stark." You might not know this word exactly, but somewhere on a deeper level, you might have a sense of its meaning. The way to access this is to read it aloud and in a familiar context, like the phrase "in stark contrast to something."

PRACTICE: DICTION AND IDIOM ERRORS

1) For whatever reason, in our culture it has been decreed that peanut butter's perfect <u>compliment</u> is jelly.

A) NO CHANGE

B) complement

C) conspirator

D) compatriot

2) The college students listened attentively to the guest lecturer, an <u>imminent</u> Cold War historian.

A) NO CHANGE

B) incident

C) eminent

D) ominous

3) Which choice best maintains the paragraph's straightforward, informative tone?

The National Geographic miniseries demonstrated the cycle of life by showing the many different animals and where they fit in the food chain. Perhaps the <u>most significant thing we got</u> from this series was how intertwined and fragile many ecosystems are.

A) NO CHANGE

B) most significant thing we gotten

C) most important item we had figured out

D) most significant lesson we learned

4) As a means <u>for appeasing</u> the taxpayers, the local government passed the Public Easement Act.

A) NO CHANGE

B) in appeasing

C) through appeasing

D) of appeasing

Mindset Tip

Diction and idiom errors are great examples of why it is important to build correct habits from the beginning. When we speak correctly and notice the correct speaking habits of others, we begin to hone an ear for grammar so that we can spot these tricky diction and idiom errors on the SAT.

5) Jon, a new lawyer, was excited to give his presentation to <u>several perspective</u> clients in an attempt to recruit them for his business.

A) NO CHANGE

C) several perceptive

B) several prospective

D) several introspective

Misplaced Modifiers: Rearranging the Parts of a Sentence

Modifiers are phrases in the sentence that describe other parts (usually nouns) of the sentence. Think of them as really long adjectives made up of multiple words. They can occur in many different forms—appositive phrases, nonrestrictive or restrictive clauses, etc.—but they all must follow one important rule: modifying phrases must be as close as possible to the word they modify in a sentence.

The SAT will test you on modifying phrases by purposely misplacing them in the sentence. In other words, they will separate the modifying phrase from what it is supposed to be modifying, which will create an illogical meaning within the sentence.

Take a look at these examples:

<u>Cooked with expired tomato sauce, Gerald</u> threw the chili out.

As the sentence is currently written, the phrase "cooked with expired tomato sauce" is modifying "Gerald," which is the noun that immediately follows. The sentence must be rearranged so that the chili is what is cooked, not Gerald.

CORRECT: Gerald threw the chili out **because it was** cooked with expired tomato sauce.

* * *

<u>Running through the woods, a branch hit Thomas</u> in the face.

In this example, the modifying phrase "running through the woods" is not next to the item it is modifying. When you ask yourself, "Who is doing the running through the woods?" the answer should be "Thomas." So, the sentence must be rearranged so that it is Thomas who is running through the woods, not the branch.

CORRECT: Running through the woods, **Thomas got hit** in the face with a branch.

Hint

If you visualize in your mind what a sentence is saying as it is written, it will help you understand the error and perhaps give you a chuckle. Imagine poor Gerald being cooked! Or imagine a branch literally running through the woods and socking Thomas in the face.

One special type of modifier error that the SAT tests is the dangling modifier. A dangling modifier is when the subject or noun that the modifying phrase is supposed to be modifying is completely absent from the sentence. You can spot these if, when you ask yourself "Who or what is being modified?," the answer is "I don't know." If this type of error sounds vaguely familiar, it is because a similar rule is applied to pronouns and antecedents. Just as a pronoun needs a clear antecedent, a modifying phrase needs something to modify.

Take a look at this example:

Traditionally punctual with <u>mortgage payments,</u>
<u>my mortgage check</u> was sent in late this month.

In this example, the modifier is describing the person who is paying the mortgage check, but that person is not mentioned in the sentence. This is a dangling modifier, because there is no subject being modified. To correct the error, you must insert a subject to be modified for the sentence to make sense.

CORRECT: Traditionally punctual with mortgage payments,
I sent in my mortgage check late this month.

Takeaway

Modifiers go next to what they modify.

PRACTICE: MODIFIER ERRORS

1) One of the largest gatherings of comic book fans, people from all over the world visit Comic Con.

A) NO CHANGE

B) Comic Con attracts visitors from all over the world, one of the largest gatherings of comic book fans.

C) One of the largest gatherings of comic book fans, Comic Con's fame attracts visitors from all over the world.

D) One of the largest gatherings of comic book fans, Comic Con attracts visitors from all over the world.

2) Because of their propensity for eating rodents, most people keep cats as house pets.

A) NO CHANGE

B) Because of their propensity for eating rodents, house pets such as cats are kept by most people.

C) Because of their propensity for eating rodents, keeping cats is a common practice among most people.

D) Because of their propensity for eating rodents, cats are commonly kept as house pets.

3) Amazon is a tech company enjoying the comforts of home that allows consumers to shop for products.

A) NO CHANGE

B) is a tech company that allows consumers to shop for products while enjoying the comforts of home.

C) are a tech company that allows consumers to shop for products while enjoying the comforts of home.

D) is a tech company that allows products to be shopped for by consumers at home who are enjoying comforts.

4) <u>Hoping to get out of school early for prom, the note was written and given to my teacher.</u>

A) NO CHANGE

B) Hoping to get out of school early for prom, my teacher was given a note.

C) Hoping to get out of school early for prom, I gave my teacher a note signed by my parents.

D) Hoping to get out of school early for prom, my parents gave my teacher a note.

Answers

Diction and Idiom Errors (page 327)

1) Choice (B) correctly replaces *compliment*, which means praise, with *complement*, which means counterpart or accompaniment. The words *conspirator* and *compatriot* are both used to refer to people.

2) The word *imminent* means "inevitably will happen." It sounds similar to the correct answer *eminent* (C), which means distinguished or scholarly. *Incident* means event. *Ominous* suggests impending doom.

3) As written, "we got" is informal and does not match the tone of the rest of the paragraph. "We gotten" is slang, and is grammatically incorrect. While choice (C), "most important item we had figured out," sounds more formal, it is unnecessarily wordy and does not capture the same meaning as the original phrase. Thus, choice (D), "most significant lesson we learned," is correct.

4) The correct idiomatic phrase is "as a means of appeasing the taxpayers…," choice (D). *Of* is the correct preposition to use in the phrase "as a means of."

5) Choice (B) uses the correct word, *prospective*, which means potential. *Perspective* means a vantage point or point of view, *perceptive* means seeing clearly or intelligent, and *introspective* means introverted, shy, and reflective.

Modifier Errors (page 330)

1) The original sentence suggests that "people" are the largest gathering of comic book fans; Choice (B) suggests that "the world" is one of the largest gatherings, and choice (C) suggests that "Comic Con's fame" is the largest gathering. Only choice (D) corrects the misplaced modifier by placing Comic Con immediately after the phrase that modifies it.

2) Choice (D) correctly places "cats" after the phrase that describes them, instead of the original sentence that suggests people eat rodents, Choice B that suggests house pets in general eat rodents, and choice (C) places a verb after the modifying phrase "eating rodents."

3) Choice (B) correctly arranges the sentence without introducing new errors. Choice (C) rearranges the sentence but introduces a plural verb, while choice (D) rearranges the sentence awkwardly and uses a passive voice.

4) Choice (C) correctly adds a subject to the sentence, fixing the dangling modifier. Choice (B) implies that the teacher was the one hoping to attend prom, while choice (D) implies that the parents wanted to attend.

Vocabulary Words 166–180

166) **sediment** (n). deposit or residue usually at the bottom of a river bed: *The sediment was churned up after the violent storm, making the river murky.*

167) **onset** (n). a beginning: *The onset of malaria is marked by a high fever and dizziness.*

168) **prolong** (v). to extend the duration of: *Hoping to avoid prolonging the already three-hour class, Jimmy refrained from asking questions.*

169) **underscore** (v). to emphasize: *The movie's graphic violence seemed to underscore the insensitivity of today's society.*

170) **ample** (adj). sufficient; abundant: *There was ample food at the buffet for the party.*

171) **sullen** (adj). bad-tempered, brooding, and irritable: *His sullen demeanor made him unpleasant to be around.*

172) **indifferent** (adj). not caring one way or another; without bias: *The teacher was indifferent to the students' complaints about the amount of homework assigned.*

173) **objective.** a) (n). goal: *The main objective of the game is to capture all your opponents' men*; b) (adj). uninfluenced by personal feelings or prejudice; unbiased; based on evidence and facts: *A newspaper journalist must remain totally objective when reporting the news.*

174) **subjective** (adj). placing a great deal of emphasis on one's attitudes or opinions; biased: *A person's evaluation of a piece of art is very subjective.*

175) **deception** (n). fraud, dishonesty, trickery: *The unscrupulous salesman used deception on the gullible man to make him buy his product.*

176) **shortcoming** (n). failure or defect; deficiency: *Tony's biggest shortcoming is his fear of public speaking.*

177) **drawback** (n). hindrance; undesirable aspect or feature: *The plan was a good one except for the drawback of not having enough people to implement it.*

178) **subdue** (v). a) to conquer or bring under one's control: *It took three policemen to subdue the violent criminal;* b) to calm or soothe: *The mother's gentle voice subdued the crying child.*

179) **dispute** (v). to argue or debate: *I disputed the speeding ticket because I was driving well within the speed limit.*

180) **acquisition** (n). a) the act of gaining possession: *The acquisition of uninhabited territories by the corrupt corporation made the environmental groups worried*; b) an addition.

Latin and Greek Roots 66–70

66) MISS/MIT: to let go, send (emit, dismiss, remiss, admit)

67) MOLL: soft (emollient, mollify)

68) MON/MONIT: to warn, scold (remonstrate, admonish, monitor)

69) MON/MONO: one (monarchy, monochromatic, monotonous)

70) MOR/MORT: death (moribund, morbid, mortify, mortuary)

UNTIMED COLLEGE BOARD PRACTICE

Complete the following College Board practice problems from College Board's *The Official SAT Study Guide* or online at www.collegeboard.org. Review answers after completing.

Test 1, Writing and Language, #1, 7, 10, 24, 25, 33

Test 2, Writing and Language, #10, 11, 21, 28, 32, 34, 36, 38, 41

Test 3, Writing and Language, #11, 16, 25, 40

Test 4, Writing and Language, #5, 13, 16, 23, 30, 42, 43

Math Test: Exponential Expressions, Equations, and Functions

Many of the same concepts and principles you learned about the Success Curve will also apply to SAT math questions. The Success Curve is an example of an exponential function, which occurs anytime a constant is raised to an unknown power, such as:

$$f(x) = b^x$$

In the function above, b represents the exponent base, which must be greater than zero, and x represents the exponent. An example of an exponential function would be $f(x) = 2^x$, with 2 being the base and x being the exponent. What makes it exponential? Simple. There is a variable in the exponent.

Let's examine the table of values and corresponding graph of $f(x) = 2^x$, which looks very much like the Success Curve shown earlier.

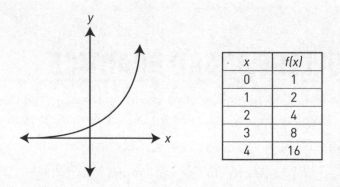

x	f(x)
0	1
1	2
2	4
3	8
4	16

In this function, the y-intercept is (0,1), because when you plug in 0 for x, you get 2^0, and anything raised to the power of 0 is equal to 1.

Looking at the table of values, notice how the x values increase by 1 each time, but the outputs increase by a different number each time. In fact, the output values are doubling, just like with the penny example from earlier.

Below are some more examples of exponential expressions, equations, and functions that you may see on the test.

$$5,000(1 + 0.01)^t$$

$$y = 1,000(0.86)^{10}$$

$$T(x) = 10(1.24)^x$$

Exponential Growth and Decay

Many SAT questions will test you on your understanding of exponential growth and decay, which are both applications of the exponential function. Exponential growth occurs when an amount increases by a fixed rate over a period of time, resulting in larger increases over time. Exponential decay occurs when an amount decreases by a fixed rate over time, resulting in smaller decreases as time goes on.

The equation for each is shown below.

GROWTH: Total = Initial amount$(1 + \text{rate})^{\text{time}}$

DECAY: Total = Initial amount$(1 - \text{rate})^{\text{time}}$

Here, *rate* means "rate of growth" or "rate of decay." The rate, which is a percent, will need to be written as a decimal. When using the equation for exponential growth, you will be adding 1 to the rate, which will make the number inside the parentheses, known as the growth factor, greater than 1. Conversely, when using the equation for exponential decay, since you are subtracting the rate from 1, the number inside the parentheses, known as the decay factor, will always be less than 1.

It is important that once you identify a function, equation, or expression as exponential, you determine if it is exponential growth or decay.

This is a very important concept, as the formulas for growth and decay are very similar, with the major difference being that exponential growth requires you to add 1 to the rate, and exponential decay requires you to subtract the rate from 1.

Here are two examples, the first being exponential growth and the second being exponential decay.

$$100(1.1)^t$$

$$100(0.9)^t$$

While they are both exponential expressions with a rate of 10%, it is easy to recognize that the expression on top represents growth, since the growth factor is greater than 1, and the expression on the bottom represents decay, since the decay factor is less than 1.

Hint

You will need to memorize the formulas for exponential growth and decay, as they will not be given to you. Knowing them will earn you at least 10 points because you will be able to answer exponential growth and decay questions.

Writing Exponentials

Writing an exponential expression, equation, or function is a skill that is quite simple to master, as long as you know and understand the formulas for growth and decay.

Let's try an example:

The population of a city grows at a rate of 2% each year. Write an expression for the total population, t, years from now if the current population is 214,892.

The key word to identify is "grow," which tells you to use the equation for exponential growth.

$$\text{Total} = \text{Initial}(1 + \text{rate})^{\text{time}}$$

Now it is just a matter of substituting the given information into that equation. The initial amount is 214,892 and the rate is 2%, which needs to be converted to 0.02.

$$214,892(1 + 0.02)^t$$

$$214,892(1.02)^t$$

This expression will give you the total number of people after t years. For example, you could figure out how big the population of the city would be after 3 years by plugging in 3 for t. Most exponential growth and decay questions will appear on the Calculator section, and you should use your calculator to determine the answer. However, it is important to remember the rules of order of operations, or PEMDAS.

Complete the math inside the parentheses first, then raise that number to the power, and then multiply that number by the initial amount in front. Here are the correct steps for finding the total population after 3 years.

$$214,892(1.02)^3 \rightarrow 214,892(1.061208) \rightarrow 228,045$$

This next example requires you to write exponential growth expressions and determine their totals.

> Rachel was planning to deposit $10,000 into a savings account that offers 4.5% interest annually. The bank manager was able to get her an increased rate of 5%. If Rachel plans on keeping the money in the account for 10 years, how much more money will she earn than if she did not receive the increased rate? Round your answer to the nearest cent.

Blind Spot

A common mistake students make is to incorrectly convert the percent to a decimal. To avoid making this mistake, move the decimal point two places to the left or divide the percent by 100 on the calculator.

To correctly answer this question, you must write two exponential growth expressions: one that uses the rate of 5% and the other that uses the rate of 4.5%, as shown below.

$$10,000(1.05)^t$$

$$10,000(1.045)^t$$

Since the number of years is 10, you can plug 10 in for t and determine the value for each.

$$10,000(1.05)^{10} = \$16,288.95$$

$$10,000(1.045)^{10} = \$15,529.69$$

The question is asking you to find the difference between the two, so you should subtract the two totals and get:

$$\$16,288.95 - \$15,529.69 = \$759.26$$

Blind Spot

One mistake that many students make is subtracting the rates and plugging the new rate into the formula for growth. That would result in an incorrect answer.

PRACTICE A

1) Miranda deposits $1,000 into a savings account that earns 1.25% per year. Write an expression for how much her account will be worth in x years.

2) The population of a town is currently 12,000 people. If it is decreasing at a rate of 8.2% each year, what will the population of the town be in 8 years? (Round to the nearest whole number.)

Interpreting Exponentials

Some SAT questions will ask you to interpret parts of exponential equations or functions, such as the initial amount or the growth rate.

As you saw earlier, the initial amount is the number in front of the parentheses.

To identify the rate, you must first determine if the given exponential expression, equation, or function is one of growth or decay. If it is growth, set the expression $1 + r$ equal to the number inside the parentheses and solve for r.

Here is an example.

What is the growth rate of the function $f(t) = a(1.2)^t$?

A) 1.2%

B) 2%

C) 20%

D) 120%

We know the function is exponential growth because the number inside the parentheses is greater than 1, and we can determine the growth rate by setting $1 + r$ equal to 1.2. Then we can solve for r.

$$1 + r = 1.2$$

By subtracting 1 from both sides to solve for r, we can see that r is equal to 0.2, which is 20% when converted to a percent, or (C). You may be able to see that 1.2 is 0.2 more than 1, and may not need to use the equation.

Now that you know how to find the rate of an exponential growth function, let's try an example with exponential decay.

What is the decay rate of the function $h(\text{x}) = 1{,}000\,(0.99)^x$?

A) 0.1%

B) 1%

C) 10%

D) 99%

We know that this is exponential decay because the growth rate is less than 1. To find the rate, set 0.99 equal to $1 - r$, and solve for r.

$$1 - r = 0.99$$

After you subtract 1 from both sides, you get:

$$-r = -0.01$$

To solve the equation above, just divide both sides by −1 to get 0.01, which would be 1%. You may not need the equation as you may see that 0.99 is 0.01 less than one.

PRACTICE B

1) What is the growth rate of the expression $200(1.6)^t$?

A) 1.6%   **C)** 60%

B) 6%   **D)** 160%

2) What is the decay rate in the equation $y = 2(0.75)^x$?

A) 25%   **C)** 2.5%

B) 75%   **D)** 7.5%

3) The exponential growth function $g(x) = 84(b)^x$ represents Julia's grade after x months. If Julia increases her grade by 6% each month, what is the value of b in the given function?

Linear Versus Exponential Functions

Linear and exponential functions have a lot in common. Exponential functions are constantly increasing or decreasing, as are most linear functions. However, the one major difference between the two is that an exponential expression, equation, or function grows or decays by a *percentage* of the current value. A linear one, on the other hand, will increase or decrease by a *constant* number, like 3. If you are not sure if the equation is linear or exponential, look to see if there is a rate being applied to the current value. Just be careful! Doubling , tripling, quadrupling, etc., are all forms of exponential functions.

Here are some examples of each:

Linear	Exponential
• Your bank account increases $10 per week	• You increase your grade 10% a week
• Your grade goes up by 2 points per month	• Your SAT score goes up 12% each month.
• You save 10% of your initial deposit each year	• Your bank account grows 8% each year.

Here's an example for you to try.

Nikki just accepted a job as a data scientist and will earn $100,000 to start. She will be given an option for her raise schedule. Which of the following would represent exponential growth?

A) Nikki's salary will increase $10,000 each year.

B) Nikki's salary will increase by 15% of her initial salary each year.

C) Nikki's salary will increase by 5% each year.

D) Nikki will receive $1,000 more per month.

Be careful! Just because there is a percent in the answer choice doesn't mean it is automatically exponential growth. The best approach to answering this question is eliminating answer choices. Choice (A) is increasing by a constant number each year, so you can eliminate it.

Choice (B) may at first look exponential because of the percent, but because it is increasing by the same amount each year, it is actually linear, and thus can be eliminated.

Choice (C) is exponential because when you increase her salary by 5%, her new salary will be larger than the previous one, meaning that the next raise of 5% will constitute a larger increase.

Choice (D) is also linear, as it increases by the same amount each time.

Hint

If a rate is doubling, then 2 will be the final number inside the parentheses. If a rate is tripling, it will be 3. Half-life is a commonly used term for exponential decay, and has a rate of 50%, so you would use 0.5 inside the parentheses.

PRACTICE C

1) The formula for yearly compounded interest can be given by the function $f(x) = a(m)^t$, with a being the initial amount and t being time in years. If John deposits $1,000 into an account that earns 8.5% interest a year, what number should he substitute in for m?

2) Riley starts a new job as a structural engineer, which pays $112,000 per year with a 10% raise each year. Which of the following equations would represent Riley's salary, y, in dollars, x years from now?

A) $y = 112,000 + 10^x$

C) $y = 112,000(110)^x$

B) $y = 112,000 + 1.10^x$

D) $y = 112,000(1.10)^x$

3) Which of following scenarios represents exponential growth?

A) Maggie's grade increases by 5 points each month.

B) Sarah's extra credit points double every month.

C) Yianni's grade point average increases 0.05 points each month

D) Grant's homework grade increases at a constant rate of 3 points per month.

4) The function $f(x)$ is shown in the table below.

x	$f(x)$
0	4
1	6
2	12
3	30

Which of the following could represent the function $f(x)$?

A) $f(x) = 2x + 4$

C) $f(x) = 3^x + 3$

B) $f(x) = 3x + 4$

D) $f(x) = 3^x - 3$

5) The graph below shows the distance Scottie traveled while riding his bike around town.

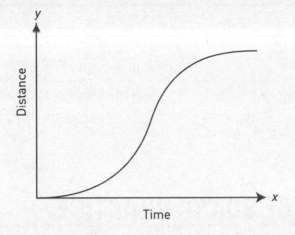

Which of the following is the most accurate description of Scottie's bike ride?

A) He started off slow, picked up speed, and then slowed down again.

B) He started off fast and then slowed down.

C) He rode at a constant speed the entire time.

D) He rode at a fast speed, slowed down, and then picked up speed again.

Answers

Practice A (page 338)
1) $1,000(1 + 0.0125)^x \rightarrow 1,000(1.0125)^x$

2) $12,000(1 - 0.082)^8 = 6,052$

Practice B (page 340)
1) C

3) 1.06

2) A

Practice C (page 342)
1) 1.085

4) C

2) D

5) A

3) B

COLLEGE BOARD QUESTIONS

Test 1, Calculator, #37, 38

Test 2, No Calculator, #14

Test 2, Calculator, #27

Test 3, Calculator, #21, 28

Test 4, Calculator, 13, 14, 15, 20, 37, 38

TIMED COLLEGE BOARD PRACTICE

Complete the following College Board practice problems from College Board's *The Official SAT Study Guide* or online at www.collegeboard.org. Review answers after completing.

Test 6, Math: No Calculator and Calculator sections

Chapter **13**

Perseverance: Moving the Rock

You've probably heard the common expression "stuck between a rock and a hard place." It means you're stuck, trapped, immobilized, with nowhere to go. This expression embodies the horrible frustration that overwhelms you when you feel like you have no options to improve your situation. While we all may have felt this way at some point in our lives, it is not the death sentence that we make it out to be. Just because you think you're stuck does not mean you have no way of getting out and breaking through the barrier that blocks you. A growth-mindset approach to learning allows you to re-vision the old expression: "When you're stuck between a rock and a hard place, *move the rock*."

Let's say you struggle with timing on the reading section of the SAT. Every time you attempt the full 65-minute section, you run out of time and do not get to an entire passage. You are, however, also not doing well at Plan B, the reading strategy that teaches you not to read the entire passage and instead work on certain questions in a specific order. It seems like you have no options, no hope. Both approaches are failing you and you're stuck. It is time to move the rock! Double your effort by increasing the number of reading sections you do in a week and shaving minutes off each time to gradually increase your reading speed. Keep at it for a month or two and watch that rock move.

This is what we call perseverance.

Perseverance is the difference between an 1100 and a 1400. It will determine if you can push beyond the limits of your potential and into the realm of excellence. Perseverance is what allows you to make it through the Abyss, pass through the Breakthrough Point of the Success Curve, and to build a new habit: or, a new self.

At some point during the test, you will inevitably come across an extraordinarily difficult question that you just can't seem to find the answer to, or an excessively wordy question that requires sifting through a great deal of extraneous information. Perhaps you are on your fifth reading passage, and it's a paired passage with two primary sources from the eighteenth century, and your attention and stamina are waning. We call these types of questions and passages "Rock Movers."

Rock Movers are the questions, passages, or moments on the test when your ability to persevere is needed to finish the question and find the correct answer. At first, you might see these types of questions as obstacles or impediments on your path to success, but these Rock Movers are vital to your score, your confidence, and your transformation. They have the power to completely change your perception of yourself. Think about what happens when you get one of the ultra-difficult questions correct. Well, maybe you think it was a fluke. But, what if you get two or three of them right? You change the way you view yourself. That is why perseverance through Rock Movers is vital to transformation and success.

But how do you develop perseverance?

Just as your brain can grow, your perseverance can grow through practice and effort. Your grit, resilience, and toughness are not something you are born with. You develop them over time. On the flip side, this perseverance muscle can also weaken over time through lack of use. If you only take the easy way out or try the simplest of problems, you will never work that muscle. You can build your perseverance muscle by working a little bit longer on tougher questions, the Rock Movers, and all while staying positive and trusting in your ability to find the answer. Each time you do this, your perseverance gets stronger and stronger.

This is one skill that takes some time to ingrain. It is, however, one of the greatest traits a person can possess. You must develop the SAT stamina and perseverance to ultimately see the changes you want. And remember, the SAT is not exactly a short exam, so your persistence will no doubt be put to the test.

We are going to start adding in more of these Rock Movers from the College Board tests. These questions are more challenging than normal and will take a complete effort to get correct.

The SAT writers are trying to separate the students that persist from the ones that give up. You know what type of individual you are. Never give up. Move that rock!

Writing and Language Test: Paragraph Editing

The following error types go beyond simply correcting the author's expression within a sentence. These errors are about rearranging and editing content within an entire paragraph or passage to better communicate the author's idea and create logical cohesion throughout the text. Let's look at the most important expression of ideas paragraph-editing errors.

Rearranging the Parts of a Passage

Errors relating to rearranging parts of the passage ask you to check whether a sentence is in the right place in the passage or if it needs to be moved. In these questions, the sentences are numbered with a bracketed number such as [1] [2] or [3].

To answer these correctly, follow these steps:

1) Read the sentence to which the question is referring so that you know what you are looking to rearrange or move. When reading it, try to determine if it is a core idea, supporting point, or introductory statement.

2) Reread the paragraph with the sentence in mind, thinking about where it may belong.

3) Reread the context surrounding the sentence. The surrounding context refers to the sentence at hand and the sentences that precede and follow it. If the sentence sounds like it fits within the surrounding context, it might need to stay where it is. If it does not sound right, try removing the sentence and then rereading the section. If it flows naturally, then the sentence should not be where it is now.

4) Plug the sentence in where you think it is most relevant, and remember to keep related ideas next to one another.

Hint

If the sentence speaks of a term or idea as if you should know about it, but it was never mentioned before, the sentence might need to be placed later in the passage, following the introduction of that term or idea. Other clues might include pronouns that have no antecedent nearby, like "their" or "this" as in "this belief." If the sentence is in the wrong place, you will not know the belief to which the author is referring when he or she says "this belief."

[1] Joshua looked around, finally taking notice of his surroundings. The carpets were covered in crumbs, the dishes lay in the kitchen sink, and the mail had begun to pile up. [2] Grandma was sick; she had been sick for a while and she was not getting better. [3] Suddenly, with all the callous inhumanity of an abrupt shove on the subway, Joshua saw it all. He saw himself coming back home, putting his education on hold. He saw himself setting roots firmly in the house until Grandma passed. [4] His book bag dropped with a loud thud. [5] Everything was in disarray; the house, without the care of his grandmother, succumbed to entropy. [6] The life that he had up till now was about to change.

To make this paragraph most logical, sentence 5 should be placed:

A) where it is now

B) after sentence 1

C) after sentence 3

D) after sentence 6

Sentence 5 explains the state of the house and thus should come in the beginning, when Joshua first enters. It also provides an appropriate transition to the discussion of the grandmother's condition.

ANSWER: B

Takeaway

Follow the above steps and put yourself in the author's shoes, asking "where is this sentence most relevant?"

Mindset Tip

Most students dread practicing rearranging the parts of a passage, combining sentences, or adding and deleting content problems. They think that these problems are tedious, require a good deal of reading, and often trick you. You, however, are not like most students. You see these Rock Movers as opportunities to build your grit muscle, bolster your confidence, and add those important points to your score. At least one fourth of the grammar section is made up of questions like these, which is great for you, because it means that you have that many more opportunities to separate yourself from the pack. If all the questions were easy, how would you distinguish yourself from little Johnny Smith, who can also answer them correctly? You need to master these Rock Movers.

Combining Sentences and Eliminating Redundancy

Sometimes the questions ask you to combine two sentences at an underlined part. With these questions, it is important to remember the rule of concision: if you can communicate the same meaning in a shorter more concise way, do so. Key points to combining sentences and eliminating redundancy are:

- Understand the relationship between two sentences or two ideas.

- Connect sentence parts to communicate the correct meaning.

- Use the correct transition or conjunction.

- Eliminate unnecessary or redundant parts.

- Follow the rules of modifiers by placing them next to what they modify.

Hint

Ask yourself: can I consolidate, condense, or eliminate certain parts of a sentence and still communicate the same meaning?

Which choice most effectively combines the two sentences at the underlined portion?

It had been a grueling three days of tryouts. The extreme spring conditioning workouts that followed made the tryouts seem like child's play.

A) of tryouts, the extreme

B) of tryouts, but the extreme

C) of tryouts, and this extreme

D) of tryouts: furthermore, the extreme

Answer: B. This correctly sets up the contrast between the two sentence parts and combines them without repeating unnecessary information.

Around football season, the hallways are decorated with Cardinals. Cardinals are the high school mascot.

A) Cardinals,

B) Cardinals; also, Cardinals are

C) Cardinals: on the other hand, Cardinals are

D) Cardinals, the mascot; which is

Answer: A. This concisely connects the two sentence parts without adding unnecessary redundancy or changing the sentence's meaning. Combining sentences is often as simple as deleting unnecessary words, adding a comma, and connecting a dependent clause, like "the high school mascot."

Transitions Between Ideas

Many questions related to the writer's expression of ideas will require you to use the correct transition. Think of transitions like tools: you need the right tool for the job, and the right transition to convey meaning. The SAT will present you with questions that purposefully misuse a transition word so that the relationship between sentences and ideas makes no sense. You will have to reread the sentence or sentences surrounding the underlined clause in order to understand the context. These are a few key points:

- When connecting clauses, make sure to determine the relationship between the parts.

- When coordinating ideas in a paragraph, make sure to reread surrounding context to determine the type of transition you will need.

- Predict in your head what type of transition you would insert in the sentence.

  Regina is an environmentalist <u>since</u> she does forget to recycle on occasion.

  A) NO CHANGE

  B) moreover

  C) whereas

  D) but

Answer: D. Because Regina is an environmentalist who forgets to recycle, we need a contrast word to connect the two sentence parts. Thus, D is our answer.

Use the table below to familiarize yourself with the different categories of transitions.

Consequence	Contrast/ Comparison	In Addition	Restating/ Summarizing	For Example	Sequence
accordingly	although/ though	additionally	all in all	for instance	meanwhile
as a result	but	also	in essence	in this case	subsequently
by which	despite	as well as	in other words	including	then
consequently	even though	furthermore	in short	such as	while
hence	however	likewise	to summarize		
so	nevertheless	moreover			
therefore	regardless	similarly			
thus	whereas				
whereby	while				
	yet				

Here are some sample sentences that use some of the transitions from each category correctly:

Consequence

- The forecast called for rain; <u>as a result/consequently/therefore/hence/thus/accordingly</u>, practice was canceled.

- Yianni devised a program <u>whereby</u> people could track their expenditures on a daily basis.

Contrast/Comparison

- Caroline claimed she was able to sneeze on command, <u>but/yet</u> no one believed her.

- Green leafy vegetables are considered an important brain food. Morgan, <u>however,</u> avoids them like the plague.

- <u>Despite/regardless of</u> his low grade point average, Terrance still got accepted into college because of his stellar SAT score.

- <u>Even though/although</u> he had a low grade point average, Terrance still got accepted into college because of his stellar SAT score.

- Terrance had a low GPA; <u>nevertheless,</u> because of his stellar SAT score, he still got into college.

- Katie prefers vacationing at the beach, <u>whereas/while</u> Parth prefers vacationing by lakes.

In Addition

- He was finally free of her. She wouldn't be able to tell him what do anymore; <u>moreover,</u> he would no longer need to pacify her when she threw tantrums.

- The lawyers called their key witness to the stand, who gave convincing testimony that appeared to exonerate the defendant. <u>Furthermore/Also/Additionally,</u> the lawyers discredited the prosecution's expert witness by proving his credentials were fraudulent.

- Jill is a good fencer. <u>Likewise/similarly,</u> she is a skilled rock climber.

Restating/Summarizing

- The brain can grow with repeated practice. New neural pathways form with targeted learning. Positive thinking increases your capacity for problem solving. <u>In short/to summarize/in other words</u>, with effort, you can get smarter!

For Example

- Technology is continuously changing, and at a rapid rate; <u>for example/for instance,</u> in the last five years alone, numerous new models of phones and tablets were introduced to consumers.

- There are many new types of technology that emerge on a yearly basis, <u>such as/including</u> tablets, phones, computers, and software programs.

Sequence

- Milosz's mistaken use of vanilla extract instead of olive oil in his croissants <u>subsequently</u> became the basis of his greatest recipe.

Blind Spot

You can start a sentence with "because" and with "however." Despite what your teachers taught you in middle school, these two words constitute appropriate sentence beginnings and may be the correct answer choice on the SAT.

Over the past 10 years, **1** <u>the use of tablets and smart phones has become a cornerstone of retail and food services</u>. Now at least one in three preteens owns and operates a smart phone. The current average use time has increased among preteens and teenagers as well. Ten years ago, before the app boom (a period of time when the number of apps available for smart devices tripled in one year), average use was around 2 hours per day. In 2017, when study X was conducted, we found that this average use time had doubled to 4 hours per day. **2** <u>Because</u> many believe this teaches independence and accelerates intellectual growth, there are actually myriad negative effects of the increased reliance on and use of smart phones in preteens and teens. Study X also found that increased use of smart phones severely stymied the development of preteens' interpersonal skills, while also contributing to a rise in social phobias. Teenagers in high school reported lower self-esteem on average and trouble sleeping on a weekly basis. Sure, smart phones can do a number of great things, like provide directions, call a ride, or look up a phrase in Italian. But, while they might have some benefits in the immediate present, their cumulative effect on the social and emotional development of our children must be examined and reflected upon. The future of our children is indeed in jeopardy.

Which choice most effectively sets up the examples that follow?

A) NO CHANGE

B) the use of tablets and smart phones has increased dramatically among preteens.

C) the use of tablets and smart phones has decreased considerably

D) the use of tablets and smart phones has yielded many profitable business opportunities

ANSWER: B. This choice, unlike the others, correctly sets up the examples concerning ownership and use of smart phones and tablets among preteens. Retail, food services, and profitable business ventures are not mentioned elsewhere in the passage, so choices (A) and (D) are incorrect, and choice (C) is the exact opposite of the what the subsequent examples list.

2

A) NO CHANGE

B) Furthermore

C) Similarly

D) Although

ANSWER: D. "Although" correctly sets up the author's change of direction in the second half of the sentence and the rest of the paragraph.

Takeaway

Determine the relationship between ideas or sentence parts, predict the correct type of transition, and plug in an answer choice.

Hint

With transition questions, sometimes you can eliminate two answer choices immediately if you determine that both of the transition words listed mean essentially the same thing.

A) NO CHANGE

B) Therefore

C) However

D) Consequently

Consequently and *therefore* have the same meaning, and because you cannot choose between them, they are both wrong.

Adding or Deleting Content

Some questions will ask you to put yourself in the author's shoes and make decisions about whether to add or delete content. Although these questions seem more difficult because they have multiple parts, if you re-vision them, you may find that they are actually easier. A two-part question that requires both parts to be correct means twice as many opportunities to eliminate wrong answers.

To answer correctly, follow these steps when adding or deleting content:

• Recall the main idea of the paragraph.

• Reread the surrounding context.

• Ask yourself, "What does this contribute to the author's point?" If the answer is "nothing," then delete.

• Check the "because!" If the reason why a sentence or phrase should be added or not added is a valid one, then that might just be your answer.

Fast food restaurants are not only popular because of convenience and expedited service, but also because most food costs considerably less. Take the 4 for 4 deal at Wendy's **1** nothing beats such prices.

1 At this point, the writer is considering adding the following information:
", which allows you to buy any four items off the dollar menu for only four dollars"

Should the writer make this addition here?

A) Yes, because it adds emotional impact to the author's writing.

B) Yes, because it explains what the 4 for 4 deal is, helping the reader understand its cost-saving features.

C) No, because it digresses from the main topic of the inexpensive nature of fast food.

D) No, because it undermines the author's main claim of the benefits of fast food.

ANSWER: B. This choice correctly states that the clause should be added and gives a logical reason that connects to the author's point.

Changing Content

Changing content is a similar type of question to adding or deleting content. These questions require you to change the existing content to better fit the style, main idea, or purpose of the passage.

Follow these steps when changing content:

- Determine what the question requires of you.

- Reread the sentence in question.

- Reread the surrounding context.

- Find the answer choice that fulfills all the parameters set in the question, without creating new grammatical errors or sounding repetitive and wordy.

Dinosaurs most likely went extinct due to climate change. **1** A sudden change in climate triggered the death of many cold-blooded dinosaurs by drastically lowering the global temperature but also the cold weather led to a decrease in the proliferation of viruses and bacteria.

1 Which choice most clearly supports the statement made in the first part of the sentence?

A) NO CHANGE

B) and also by decreasing plant life over time, an important link in the food chain of plants, herbivores, and carnivores.

C) but in some, forced the evolution of a much more advanced thermoregulation system in their bodies.

D) but the mammals, which were warm-blooded, were much more capable at adapting and surviving this mini ice age.

ANSWER: B.

Choice (B) adds a second supporting example of why climate change led to the dinosaurs extinction. (A) is incorrect because as it is written, the underlined portion of the sentence does not support the earlier idea of why the cold weather made the dinosaurs go extinct, but instead gives an unrelated positive result of the cold weather. (C) is incorrect because it describes an advantage to climate change, and (D) creates a comparison to mammals instead of adding a second example of why climate change led to dinosaur extinction.

Introductory and Transitional Content

One particular subcategory of changing content is so common that it deserves its own focus. Sometimes, instead of simply asking you to change content, the SAT asks you to add an introductory or transitional sentence to the paragraph. With these types of questions it is extremely important to reread the surrounding context; if the question asks you to add an appropriate introductory sentence, you will have to reread the entire paragraph to which it will be added. Lastly, if the question asks you to add a transitional sentence, you have to reread the context before and after to make sure you are correctly linking the ideas that come before and those that follow. If the question gives you the option to not add the introductory sentence or delete the transition sentence, do not automatically take it. Many times, the transition sentence or introductory sentence is necessary. Take a look at this example from *Saint Augustin* by Louis Bertrand:

> **1** Outside of learned or theological circles people no longer read him. Such is true renown: we admire the saints, as we do great men, on trust. Even his *Confessions* are generally spoken of only from hearsay.

1 Which choice most effectively sets up the information that follows?

A) Saint Augustin is now little more than a celebrated name.

B) Saint Augustin is perhaps the most influential saint of all time

C) Saint Augustin was most known for helping the poor

D) Saint Augustin did not deserve the title of saint

With this example, it is important to read the two sentences that follow the proposed introductory sentence. These give you an idea of what the paragraph is about—that Saint Augustin's teachings are not really read or known in detail anymore. Choices (B), (C), and (D) do not introduce this notion and thus can be eliminated. Choice (A) is our answer.

Graph-Related Content

Some questions will ask you to change content to match a graph that is connected to the passage. With these questions, it is important to remember that the content of the passage must accurately represent the content of the graph and that the graph cannot be changed, only the content of the passage.

Follow these steps when correcting graph-related content:

- Analyze the graph using the graph analysis method: read the title of the graph, check the x and y-axis labels, check any additional information or footnotes, and determine what is being measured.

- Reread the underlined sentence to determine if it correctly represents the graph.

- Find the answer choice that correctly represents the graph and does not introduce any new grammatical errors.

The company is looking for new ways to generate revenue after reviewing its quarterly data and finding that <u>sales declined progressively throughout all four quarters</u>.

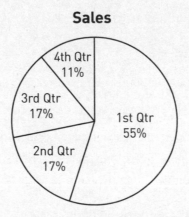

1) The writer wants the information in the passage to correspond as closely as possible with the information in the graph. Given that goal, which choice most effectively rewrites the sentence?

A) NO CHANGE

B) sales increased drastically from quarter 1 to quarter 2.

C) there was a large drop in sales from quarter 1 to quarter 4.

D) sales basically remained static from quarter 1 to quarter 4.

ANSWER: Choice (C) most accurately represents the information in the graph. Choice (A) is incorrect because the sales did not progressively decline; the sales from the second and third quarters remained the same. The sales also did not increase or remain static.

Mindset Tip

Check in with your mental state and your breath. Catch yourself if you start doing any negative forecasting (predicting that something will be unpleasant or difficult). When you say to yourself, "This is gonna be the worst," you are far more likely to have a horrible experience. Instead, bring balance and positivity back into your mind by taking a break and doing three to five minutes of Deep Breath Resets. These are a perfect complement to long, perseverance-building chapters such as this one. Intermittent deep breathing allows for greater stamina and improved focus, which will be important as you get ready to tackle the next chunk of College Board practice problems.

Redundancy

The SAT tests redundancy as a stand-alone error, which means you need to be on the lookout for unnecessary repetition. When you see pairs of similar phrases, such as "frequently/many times," or "tremendous/even overwhelming," or "annual/every year," together in the same sentence, you have a redundancy error. For these questions, "DELETE THE UNDERLINED PORTION" will usually be the correct answer. Follow these two simple steps when answering:

• Check to see if an idea or phrase is repeated unnecessarily.

- Ask yourself, "If I remove this, will the sentence still essentially say the same thing?" If the answer is yes, *delete* the redundancy.

> The new YouTube star is famous <u>and well-known</u> among people of all ages.
>
> A) NO CHANGE
>
> B) or well-known
>
> C) and commonly known
>
> D) DELETE THE UNDERLINED PORTION

ANSWER: D is the best answer because *famous* and *well-known* essentially mean the same thing.

Wordiness

The SAT requires you to correct wordiness or awkward phrasing in a passage. In these cases, it may be hard to pin down an exact grammatical rule, so it is important to remember the tenets of good writing: concise phrasing, active rather than passive voice, and getting to the point. Sometimes when we try to sound formal, we end up just being wordy and awkward.

To answer this type of question, follow these rules:

- Check to see if there is a shorter answer choice that conveys the same meaning as the underlined portion. If there is, choose it.

- Eliminate choices that are phrased in passive voice. Active voice puts the subject, the doer of action, at the beginning of the sentence. "Renee ran the marathon" is active. Passive voice puts the object at the beginning of the sentence and the subject at the end of the sentence, as in, "The marathon was run by Renee." This should sound awkward to you.

- Avoid the phrases *had been*, *has been*, and *have been*, where appropriate. These typically make sentences awkward and are often used incorrectly.

- Be wary of sentences that restate a verb or subject unnecessarily, as in, "The lawyers were excited about their new clients and they were also excited about the new contract." This sentence could be improved: "The lawyers were excited about their new clients and the new contract."

As a result of the reform, <u>many new documents are now able to be distributed by politicians.</u>

A) NO CHANGE

B) politicians can now distribute many new documents

C) many new documents are now able for distribution

D) politicians can now distributes many new documents

ANSWER: B. This corrects the passive voice by moving "politicians" to the front of the sentence as the subject. (D) is incorrect because it introduces a subject/verb agreement error with "politicians" and "distributes."

PRACTICE

1) <u>Since</u> much of the island was covered with jagged rocks and thorns, Harold decided to go exploring.

A) NO CHANGE

B) Because

C) Even though

D) Thus

2) <u>Despite being</u> an avid reader, Reggie decided to attend the sixteenth annual Readaholics Convention.

A) NO CHANGE

B) DELETE THE UNDERLINED PORTION

C) Although

D) Furthermore

3) In the sixties, the American government wanted something to eclipse the successful launch of Sputnik, <u>for</u> NASA sent a man to the moon.

A) NO CHANGE

B) however

C) so

D) but

4) Which choice most effectively combines the two sentences at the underlined portion?

Life was not always easy <u>for William. He had to</u> work two jobs, babysit his little sister when his mom worked late, and battle a severe learning disability.

A) for William, he had to

B) for William, because he had to

C) for William, but he had to

D) for William, even though he had to

5)

[1] She seemed oblivious to his curious eye. [2] He ever so slightly adjusted his perfect slouch, sitting straighter, paused, and then took out his pencil. [3] As Thomas, mohawk carefully spiked, looked on from two desks behind her, Eva took notes, and notes, and notes. [4] The sound of the pencil pressing down hard as she wrote grated on Thomas' ears. [5] But, what about all those tattoos? What about the lip ring, and the middle finger she casually rolled out for the cops who patrolled the school parking lot? [6] Thomas felt his chest tighten. [7] Had he been going about it all wrong? [8] Perhaps it was time to actually take school seriously.

To make this paragraph most logical, sentence 2 should be

A) where it is now

B) placed after sentence 8

C) placed after sentence 4

D) placed after sentence 3

6) Coca-Cola epitomizes brand name power; when a person buys a soft drink, that person is being subtly influenced by the Coca-Cola logo and brand. Similarly, when a person goes out to buy a car, <u>he or she also likes those cars with good safety features</u>.

The author would like to continue the stylistic pattern established earlier in the paragraph. Which choice most clearly accomplishes this goal?

A) NO CHANGE

B) he or she also like those cars with recognizable brand names

C) he or she is also subtly influenced by popular car brand names

D) he or she is also into cars that have the best brand names

7) Annually, the company throws a Christmas party for all the employees <u>every year.</u>

A) NO CHANGE

B) every years

C) each year

D) DELETE THE UNDERLINED PORTION

Hint

Earn an easy 10 points on the SAT by spotting those "annually/every year" redundancy errors.

Answers

1) Choice (A) is illogical because "since" implies that Harold decided to go exploring because of the jagged rocks and thorns. Choice (B) is illogical for the same reason. Choice (D), "thus," is similar to "because of," as is incorrect. Choice (C), "even though," correctly coordinates the contrast between sentence parts.

2) Choice (A) sets up a contrast between sentence parts, but this sentence is constructed as cause and effect. For the same reason, choice (C) is incorrect. Choice (D) is incorrect because "furthermore" implies that another point or item is being added. Choice (B) correctly deletes the unnecessary contrasting transition.

3) This sentence is set up to show cause and effect. The word "for" is inappropriate in this case, because it means "as a result of." Both "however" and "but" create contrast, which is not the intended meaning of this sentence. *So* means "resulting in," meaning choice (C) is the correct answer.

4) Choice (A) is incorrect because using a comma without a conjunction will create a run-on sentence. Choice (B) correctly combines the two sentences while fulfilling the cause and effect relationship. Choice (C) is incorrect because the first sentence part is a result of the second, not a contrasting statement; choice (D) is incorrect for the same reason.

5) This sentence does not make sense in its original location because the previous sentence discusses the female character. It is incorrect after sentence 4 because it interrupts Thomas's train of thought, and it is incorrect after sentence 3 because it interrupts a description of another character. It makes most sense after sentence 8, where it logically follows the statement "Perhaps it was time to take school seriously." Choice (B) is the answer.

6) Choice (A) does not follow a parallel sentence structure, so it is incorrect. Choice (C) is correct because it creates parallel structure, matching the earlier usage of "is subtly influenced by." Choice (B) is incorrect not only because it does not follow a parallel structure but because it creates a subject/verb agreement error with "he/she" and "like." Choice (D) is incorrect because it is too informal.

7) The inclusion of "annually" and "every year" creates redundancy in this sentence. Choice (D) is correct because it eliminates the redundancy without introducing any additional errors.

Vocabulary Words 181–195

181) **recollect** (v). to remember: *Bill could not recollect where he put his keys.*

182) **bleak** (adj). a) bare, desolate; b) without hope: *Cormac McCarthy's* The Road *is the story of a bleak post-apocalyptic future.*

183) **foreshadow** (v). to hint at a future event: *Authors foreshadow future events to keep the reader thinking and predicting about the ending of the story.*

184) **ominous** (adj). signifying harm to come; threatening: *Bobby looked up at the sky to see an ominous black cloud looming overhead.*

185) **possess** (v). a) to have: *Jane possessed poise and resilience in the face of adversity;* b) to occupy or control: *Ralph was possessed by a spirit of resentment toward his family.*

186) **deplorable** (adj). causing grief; very bad, wretched: *The house was in a deplorable condition, so the town decided to demolish it.*

187) **squalor** (n). the state of existing in filth or misery: *Most of the poor in the small village lived in a state of squalor.*

188) **salutary** (adj). a) good for one's health: *Jane enjoyed traveling to Greece because she believed the sun and sea had a salutary effect on her;* b) promoting or conducive to some beneficial purpose: *Opening a Roth IRA and putting money in each year will be salutary to your financial health.*

189) **respite** (n). a period of rest, a break: *After five hours of testing, Paul needed a respite.*

190) **befall** (v). to happen to: *Sara was excited to read the next chapter because she heard that something important befell the main character.*

191) **prominent** (adj). standing out, particularly evident: *The most prominent feature of the building was the giant gargoyle standing guard atop the tower.*

192) **homogeneous** (adj). alike: *Honors classes typically have homogeneous populations of students.*

193) **consensus** (n). collective agreement on the same opinion: *The jury members finally reached a consensus and were ready to deliver their verdict.*

194) **imply** (v). to suggest: *Jade might not have actually said it, but her displeasure at the way the event was handled was clearly implied.*

195) **biodiversity** (n). variety among animals and plants: *Most small islands, due to their geographical constraints, do not have a great deal of biodiversity.*

Latin and Greek Roots 71–75

71) MORPH: shape (amorphous, metamorphosis)

72) MUT: change (immutable, mutate, permutation)

73) NAT/NAI/NAS: birth (naïve, nascent, innate, native)

74) NOC/NEC/NOX: death, harm (noxious, necrosis, innocuous, innocent)

75) NOM/NYM: name (synonym, ignominy, anonymous, pseudonym)

UNTIMED COLLEGE BOARD PRACTICE

Complete the following College Board practice problems from College Board's *The Official SAT Study Guide* or online at www.collegeboard.org. Review answers after completing.

Test 1, Writing and Language, #2, 5, 6, 9, 12, 13, 14, 20–22, 28, 29, 31, 34, 37–39, 42

Test 2, Writing and Language, #2, 4, 7, 9, 11, 12, 15, 18, 22–26, 31, 37, 42, 43, 44

Test 3, Writing and Language, #2, 3, 6–9, 13, 17, 18, 22, 23, 30–33, 37, 39, 42–44

Test 4, Writing and Language, #2, 4, 8, 10, 11, 14, 15, 17, 18, 20, 25–27, 31, 33, 37–39, 41, 44

Math Test: Preparing for the Passport to Advanced Math

> *"It's not that I'm so smart, it's just that I stay with problems longer."*
> —Albert Einstein

Congratulations. You have earned your passport to the advanced math topics on the SAT. Think about what a passport represents: it is a credential that allows you to travel to foreign lands. Why would people choose to leave their homes? Adventure and growth.

This passport affords you adventure and growth in new and challenging topics in the advanced portion of the SAT. Your passport also establishes you as a worthy mathematician. It was earned when you mastered the basic skills from Heart of Algebra, such as:

- Solving linear equations

- Combining like terms and the distributive property

- Solving systems with substitution

- Function notation

- Rearranging

- Writing, interpreting, and graphing linear equations and functions

Your mastery of these topics will serve as the foundation that allows you not only to travel to unfamiliar ground, but also to thrive in the adventures that the advanced math questions have to offer.

These advanced math topics encompass:

- Simplifying advanced mathematical expressions

- Working with quadratics

- Solving advanced equations

- Graphs of polynomials

Traversing through these challenging topics and questions may seem scary at first, but the opportunity for growth is like nothing else. You will most certainly need perseverance to complete this journey, but the reward will be well worth it.

Working with Exponents

Advanced math questions will test you on your ability to correctly apply the rules of exponents. Look at the exponent rules below, which are the most common rules needed for the SAT.

Rule	Example
$a^m \times a^n = a^{m+n}$	$x^4 \times x^2 = x^6$
$(a^m)^n = a^{mn}$	$(x^4)^2 = x^8$
$(ab)^m = a^m b^m$	$(2x)^2 = 4x^2$
$\dfrac{a^m}{a^n} = a^{m-n}$	$\dfrac{x^6}{x^3} = x^3$
$\left(\dfrac{a}{b}\right)^m = \dfrac{a^m}{b^m}$	$\left(\dfrac{2}{3}\right)^2 = \dfrac{4}{9}$
$a^0 = 1$	$3^0 = 1$

Blind Spot

When you apply the exponent rules, make sure to take your time, as it is normal for students to make a small mistake. For instance, you may multiply the exponents when you should be adding them, or divide them when you should actually be subtracting them.

Here is an example of a Rock Mover that combines the properties of exponents and fractions.

$$(x^6y^9)^{\frac{1}{3}} \cdot (x^2y)^2$$

The expression above is equivalent to which of the following?

A) x^5y^6

B) x^6y^5

C) x^8y^7

D) $x^{12}y^{12}$

Start by multiplying $\frac{1}{3}$ by both x^6 and y^9 to get x^2y^3.

Then multiply 2 by both the exponents of x^2 and y to get x^4y^2, which leaves you with $x^2y^3 \times x^4y^2$.

Finally, add the exponents of the same variable and you get x^6y^5, or (B).

Here is another example that contains fractions and requires you to use the exponent rules. Remember, when adding fractions, you need a common denominator.

$$\frac{4x^4y^2}{\left(2xy^{\frac{1}{2}}\right)^3}$$

The expression above is equivalent to which of the following, given that x and y are greater than zero?

A) $2xy^{\frac{1}{2}}$

B) $\dfrac{xy^{\frac{1}{2}}}{2}$

C) $\dfrac{x^{\frac{3}{2}}}{4}$

D) $\dfrac{xy^{\frac{1}{2}}}{4}$

Mindset Tip

You will master fractions only by practicing them often. Instead of seeing fractions as a nuisance, re-vision them as score boosters.

While this is a challenging question that consists of multiple steps and some common traps, the great problem solver focuses solely on the first step, which is to simplify the denominator by cubing each of the bases inside the parentheses. Be careful when simplifying the denominator, as it is a common SAT trap! If you simplify it too fast, you may forget that you need to cube the 2.

$$\frac{4x^4y^2}{2^3x^3y^{\frac{3}{2}}} = \frac{4x^4y^2}{8x^3y^{\frac{3}{2}}}$$

We can now simplify the numbers and the individual variables. The fraction $\frac{4}{8}$ can be simplified to $\frac{1}{2}$ and $\frac{x^4}{x^3}$ can be simplified to just x.

Using the exponent rules to simplify for y will require you to find a common denominator. Since we are subtracting a whole number and a fraction, we need to change 2 to have a common denominator of 2, or

$$y^{\frac{4}{2} - \frac{3}{2}} = y^{\frac{1}{2}}$$

If you put everything together, you get $\frac{xy^{\frac{1}{2}}}{2}$, which is choice (B).

While this question did require perseverance, it was also solved using the basic exponent rules. If you know what strategy to choose and have faith in your ability, these challenging questions become simple.

PRACTICE A

1) $x^2 \times x^4$

2) $\dfrac{a^6}{a^2}$

3) $\dfrac{a^6}{a^8}$

4) $(m^2)^4$

5) $\left(\dfrac{a}{b}\right)^3$

Rational Exponents

The previous example contained $y^{\frac{1}{2}}$, which is an example of a rational exponent, and contains a fractional exponent in which the numerator is the exponent and the denominator is the root.

Let's start with the most basic example of a rational exponent, $x^{\frac{1}{2}}$, which is another way of saying the square root of x.

$$x^{\frac{1}{2}} = \sqrt{x}$$

The SAT will require you to know that a radical can also be written as a rational exponent.

Here is the basic property:

$$a^{\frac{1}{n}} = \sqrt[n]{a}$$

For instance, the cube root of x, or $\sqrt[3]{x}$, could also be written as $x^{\frac{1}{3}}$. The fourth root of x, or $\sqrt[4]{x}$, is equivalent to $x^{\frac{1}{4}}$.

A more advanced form of this property can be written like this:

$$a^{\frac{m}{n}} = \sqrt[n]{a^m}$$

Notice the root is still the denominator and the exponent is the numerator. Here is an example:

$$x^{\frac{2}{3}} = \sqrt[3]{x^2}$$

When rewriting rational exponents as radicals, remember the numerator is the exponent and the denominator is the root.

Rational exponents can be rewritten in many ways. For example, you could rewrite $x^{\frac{3}{2}}$ as $(x^{\frac{1}{2}})^3$ or $\sqrt{x^3}$.

Negative Exponents

Another advanced exponent property you will need to know deals with negative exponents. These are pretty simple once you know that a negative exponent becomes positive by using the reciprocal of the base. When you do this, negative exponents in the numerator become positive and are moved to the denominator, and negative exponents in the denominator become positive and are moved to the numerator. Here are some examples:

$$x^{-2} = \frac{1}{x^2}$$

$$\frac{1}{x^{-2}} = x^2$$

$$2^{-3} = \frac{1}{2^3} = \frac{1}{8}$$

$$\frac{x^{-2}}{y^{-2}} = \frac{y^2}{x^2}$$

Here is an example that combines negative and rational exponents.

$$\frac{a^{-\frac{1}{2}}}{b^{-3}}$$

The expression above can be rewritten as which of the following, given that $a \neq 0$ and $b \neq 0$.

A) $\dfrac{b^3}{\sqrt{a}}$

B) $\dfrac{b^{-3}}{\sqrt{a}}$

C) $b^3 \sqrt{a}$

D) $\sqrt{ab^3}$

Because both exponents in this expression are negative, this question requires you to move the numerator to the bottom and the denominator to the top, meaning the two switch places.

$$\frac{b^3}{a^{\frac{1}{2}}}$$

Since $\dfrac{b^3}{a^{\frac{1}{2}}}$ is not an answer choice, $a^{\frac{1}{2}}$ needs to be rewritten as $\sqrt{a}$, which is choice (A).

PRACTICE B

Answer the following, given that a and b are both greater than 0.

1) The expression $\sqrt[3]{a^2}$ can be rewritten as $a^{\frac{m}{n}}$. What is the value of $\dfrac{m}{n}$?

2) $a^{-\frac{1}{2}}$ is equivalent to which of the following?

A) $-2\sqrt{a}$ C) $\dfrac{1}{2a}$

B) $\dfrac{1}{a}$ D) $\dfrac{1}{\sqrt{a}}$

3) $a^{\frac{1}{2}}b^{-3}$ is equivalent to which of the following?

A) $\sqrt{a}\,b^3$ C) $\dfrac{\sqrt{a}}{b^3}$

B) $\dfrac{1}{\sqrt{a}\,b^3}$ D) $\sqrt{ab^3}$

4) $\sqrt[4]{x^2 y^3}$ can be rewritten as which of the following?

A) $x^{\frac{1}{2}} y^{\frac{4}{3}}$

C) $x^2 y^{\frac{4}{3}}$

B) $x^{\frac{1}{2}} y^{\frac{3}{4}}$

D) $x^2 y^{\frac{3}{4}}$

Simplifying Advanced Expressions

As we learned in Chapter 1, the SAT will require you to simplify expressions using various procedures, including combining like terms and the distributive property. Some Passport to Advanced Math questions may contain expressions that must be simplified using another form of the distributive property, commonly referred to as FOIL, which will be necessary to answer some challenging questions we will soon see.

Distributing using FOIL

The acronym FOIL means First-Outer-Inner-Last and is a way to remember how to multiply two binomials. For example, to multiply $(x + 1)$ and $(x + 2)$, you would multiply the first terms to get x^2, then the outer terms and get $2x$, then multiply the inner terms to get $1x$, and finally multiply the last terms and get 2. This can be written as:

$$x^2 + 2x + 1x + 2$$

Finally, combine the like terms to get $x^2 + 3x + 2$. Here is an example to try:

$$2(x + 3)(x - 4)$$

The expression above can be rewritten as which of the following?

A) $x^2 - x - 12$

B) $2x^2 - x - 12$

C) $2x^2 - 2x - 12$

D) $2x^2 - 2x - 24$

This type of question will ask you to simplify the original expression by distributing and using FOIL. You can either distribute the 2 first or FOIL the two binomials to begin. We will FOIL first and then distribute.

$$2(x^2 - 4x + 3x - 12)$$

$$2(x^2 - x - 12)$$

$$2x^2 - 2x - 24$$

or, (D)

Simplifying and Identifying Coefficients

Some questions will require you to simplify an expression and rewrite it as the given form, such as $ax^2 + bx + c$. You may need to use methods such as distributing, combining like terms, or FOIL.

After simplifying, the question will ask you to identify what a, b, or c is. The letters a and b represent coefficients, or the number in front of the variable. The letter c represents the constant, or the number that has no variable. Here is an example:

If the expression $2x(x - 1) + 3x + 12$ is rewritten in the
form $ax^2 + bx + c$, what is the value of b?

The first step to solving this problem would be to distribute the $2x$ to both the x and the -1 to get:

$$2x^2 - 2x + 3x + 12$$

After you distribute, combine the like terms to get $2x^2 + x + 12$.

By requiring you to identify b, the question is asking for the coefficient of the x term.

$$2x^2 + x + 12 = ax^2 + bx + c$$

It may help to stack the two to see what b is.

$$2x^2 + 1x + 12$$

$$ax^2 + bx + c$$

$$b = 1$$

Squaring a Binomial

There is one more type of simplifying you need to know: how to simplify an equation or expression when you raise a binomial to a power, as in the example below.

$$(x + 2)^2$$

It is very common for students in test situations to think this is $x^2 + 4$.

This would be incorrect because you are not squaring the x and then squaring the 2, but rather you are squaring the entire expression. It must be written out as $(x + 2)(x + 2)$ and then you can use FOIL to multiply. Below is a challenging example. Don't forget to follow the order of operations! Exponents first, then multiplication.

If $f(x) = x^2 + 4$, which of the following is equivalent to $f(x + 3)$?

A) $x^2 + 13$

B) $x^2 + 6x + 13$

C) $x^3 + 13$

D) $x^3 + 6x^2 + 13x$

To evaluate a function, substitute the expression $(x + 3)$ in for x, which will give you:

$$(x + 3)^2 + 4$$

The key step is to correctly square the binomial, rewriting it as $(x + 3)(x + 3)$, which, after you multiply, will result in $x^2 + 6x + 9$. The final step would be to combine the 9 and the 4 to get $x^2 + 6x + 13$, which is choice (B).

Factoring Quadratics

The SAT loves quadratics, and if you really want to excel, you should learn as much as you can about them. A quadratic expression has a degree of 2, which means the highest exponent is 2. A quadratic expression can be written in the form $ax^2 + bx + c$.

Quadratics are one of the most important concepts in the advanced math area, and factoring is integral to simplifying them. When you approach a quadratic that needs to be factored, you want to use the factoring checklist:

- Factoring out the greatest common factor

- Factoring a trinomial

- Taking the difference of two squares

- Factoring by grouping

Each of the items is explained below.

Factoring Out the Greatest Common Factor

When factoring out a greatest common factor, also known as the GCF, you are looking for the largest term that can be divided into each item. Here is an example showing how to factor out the GCF of a binomial:

$$2x^2 + 4x$$

To factor the expression above, look for what each term has in common. They both have a factor of 2, as well as an x, so you can factor out $2x$.

Once you factor out the $2x$, see what you need to multiply $2x$ by to get back to the original expression.

What do you need to multiply by to get to $2x^2$? You need another x.

What would you multiply $2x$ by to get $4x$? 2.

So, the expression above can be rewritten as:

$$2x(x + 2)$$

Notice that if you were to distribute this expression out, you would end up with the original expression.

Factoring Trinomials

A trinomial is a type of quadratic that has three terms, such as $x^2 + 7x + 12$.

While factoring trinomials can get complicated, the SAT questions involving factoring will be pretty straightforward.

The key to factoring trinomials is to find the factors of the constant that add up to the number with the x. The constant is the number without a variable.

In other words, to factor the trinomial above, ask yourself, what numbers multiply to be 12 and add up to 7? Those two numbers are 4 and 3, which means the trinomial can be rewritten as $(x + 4)(x + 3)$.

How about this next trinomial?

$$x^2 - 2x - 15$$

Now, look for factors of -15 that add up to -2. This means that one factor must be negative and the other positive, because to get a negative product, you must multiply a negative and a positive. Since the two factors must combine to be negative, the larger number should be negative and the smaller number positive. What are they?

$$(x - 5)(x + 3)$$

Here is another example of a trinomial that can be factored.

$$x^2 - 9x + 20$$

Now you are looking for two numbers that multiply to positive 20, yet add up to -9. How does that happen? Both factors must be negative. Don't forget, when you multiply two negative numbers, you get a positive.

$$(x - 4)(x - 5)$$

Factoring Out the Greatest Common Factor of a Trinomial

There may be trinomials that have a number in front of the x^2. First check if all three terms are divisible by that number so that the expression can be simplified. For instance,

$$2x^2 + 12x + 16$$

Notice how all three terms are divisible by 2, so you can factor it out.

$$2(x^2 + 6x + 8)$$

The remaining trinomial is also factorable, so look for factors of 8 that add up to 6.

$$2(x + 4)(x + 2)$$

Hint

Factoring, like any other skill, can be mastered through effort and practice. Once you are able to correctly apply the four methods of factoring, you will realize that the advanced SAT questions aren't that complicated at all.

Difference of Two Perfect Squares

This is a very important topic and will appear in a variety of questions!

Factoring the difference of two perfect squares is special. It can formally be written as

$$a^2 - b^2 = (a + b)(a - b)$$

The SAT usually has some type of question that requires you to know difference of two perfect squares. Here are some examples:

$$x^2 - 25 = (x + 5)(x - 5)$$

$$a^2 - 1 = (a + 1)(a - 1)$$

$$4x^2 - 9 = (2x - 3)(2x + 3)$$

$$x^2 - 6 = (x - \sqrt{6})(x + \sqrt{6})$$

Although it might seem complicated, you are taking the square root of both terms to factor them. Look at the first example. The square root of x^2 is x and the square root of 25 is 5.

Blind Spot

You can only use difference of two squares when it is subtraction. It will not work with addition. So, you could not factor $x^2 + 9$ using this method.

Here is a challenging example that will test your knowledge of the difference of two perfect squares:

$$x^4 - y^4$$

What is another way to write the expression above?

A) $(x^2 + y^2)(x - y)(x + y)$

B) $(x - y)^2(x + y)^2$

C) $(x - y)(x + y)^3$

D) $(x + y)^2(x - y)(x + y)$

Since the expression above is asking for the difference of two perfect squares, it can be rewritten as $(x^2 + y^2)(x^2 - y^2)$. Since the expression $(x^2 - y^2)$ is another form of difference of two squares, it can be simplified to:

$$(x^2 + y^2)(x - y)(x + y)$$

The correct answer is choice (A).

PRACTICE C

Factor each:

1) $x^2 - 6x$

2) $5x^2 + 10x$

3) $8x^2 - 32x$

4) $18x^2 - 10x$

5) $8a^2 + 2a$

6) $x^2 + 15x + 36$

7) $x^2 + 7x + 10$

8) $x^2 - 5x - 14$

9) $x^2 + x - 12$

10) $x^2 - 3x - 18$

11) $x^2 - 8x + 12$

12) $x^2 - 12x + 20$

13) $3x^2 + 9x + 6$

14) $4x^2 + 20x + 24$

15) $x^2 - 25$

16) $x^2 - 16$

17) $16x^2 - 9$

18) $9x^2 - 16$

19) $x^2 - y^2$

20) $a^4 - 16$

Factoring by Grouping

Some questions may require you to factor using a method called grouping. You may have heard this in math class, because grouping is also a way of factoring trinomials. You will know to use grouping when there are four terms, such as in the expression $x^3 + x^2 - 9x - 9$. The first step in grouping is to split the four terms into groups of two, then factor the GCF from each side by seeing what each group has in common.

$$x^3 + x^2 - 9x - 9$$

$$(x^3 + x^2) + (-9x - 9)$$

Now factor the GCF from each set of parentheses.

$$x^2(x + 1) - 9(x + 1)$$

If both expressions in parentheses are the same after factoring, you know you are on the right track. Group the outside terms together and separate out the common expression from the parentheses.

$$(x^2 - 9)(x + 1)$$

Now notice how one of the expressions, $(x^2 - 9)$, can be factored using the difference of two squares. The final answer would be:

$$(x - 3)(x + 3)(x + 1)$$

One more important thing about factoring: each set of parentheses above is what we call a factor. So $(x + 3)$ would be a factor of the original expression, $x^3 + x^2 - 9x - 9$.

Try some tougher problems in Practice D. A warning, though: these next few questions are challenging, even for the expert math student. They require perseverance!

Mindset Tip

As you practice, note that we have structured the problems to go from easy to hard, just like on the SAT. If you are struggling with a problem toward the end of a practice set, realize it could be a hard question. Do not give up on it; instead, embrace the struggle as an opportunity for growth.

PRACTICE D

1) Which of the following is equivalent to $a^2 - b^2$?

A) $(a - b)(a + b)$

C) $(a + b)(a + b)$

B) $(a - b)(a - b)$

D) $(a - b)^2$

2) Which of the following is a factor of the expression $x^2 - x - 12$?

A) $(x - 3)$

C) $(x - 4)$

B) $(x + 4)$

D) $(x - 6)$

3) Which of the following is equivalent to $4x(x + 2) - 3(3x - 2)$?

A) $4x^2 - x + 6$

C) $4x^2 - 17x + 6$

B) $4x^2 + x + 6$

D) $4x^2 + 17x - 6$

4) Which of the following is equivalent to $(x + 1)(x^2 - 2x + 4)$?

A) $x^3 + x^2 + 2x + 4$

C) $x^3 - x^2 + 2x - 4$

B) $x^3 + x^2 - 2x + 4$

D) $x^3 - x^2 + 2x + 4$

5) Which of the following is equivalent to $-(x-3)$?

A) $-x-3$

C) $x+3$

B) $x+3$

D) $3-x$

6) If $f(x) = 2x^2 - 4$, find $f(2x)$.

A) $4x^2 - 4$

C) $8x^3 - 4$

B) $8x^2 - 4$

D) $16x^2 - 4$

7) If m is equal to $x+3$ and n is equal to 9, which is equivalent to $m^2 - n$?

A) $x^2 + 6x - 9$

C) $x^2(x+6)$

B) $x(x+6)$

D) $x^2 + 9$

8) The expression $4x^2 + 12xy + 9y^2$ is equivalent to which of the following?

A) $(x+y)^2$

C) $(x+3y)^3$

B) $(2x+3y)^2$

D) $(2x+3y)^3$

9) Which of the following is equivalent to $x^3 + x^2 - 16x - 16$?

A) $(x^2+16)(x+1)$

C) $(x+4)^2(x+1)$

B) $(x^2+16)(x-1)$

D) $(x+4)(x-4)(x+1)$

10) Which of the following is equivalent to $x^2 - 3$?

A) $(x+3)(x-3)$

C) $(x-\sqrt{3})(x+\sqrt{3})$

B) $(x+1.5)(x-1.5)$

D) None of these

> **"***I have not failed 10,000 times. I have not failed once. I have succeeded in proving that those 10,000 ways will not work. When I have eliminated the ways that will not work, I will find the way that will work.***"**
>
> —Thomas Edison

While it is important to fail, the real key is to keep trying. We call this "failing your way to success." If your first attempt at an advanced math does not work, try another, and keep trying until you find the strategy that works.

Answers

Practice A (page 370)

1) $x^{2+4} = x^6$

2) $a^{6-2} = a^4$

3) $a^{6-8} = a^{-2}$

4) $m^{2(4)} = m^8$

5) $\dfrac{a^3}{b^3}$

Practice B (page 372)

1) $\dfrac{2}{3}$

2) D

3) C

4) B

Practice C (page 380)

1) $x(x-6)$

2) $5x(x+2)$

3) $8x(x-4)$

4) $2x(9x-5)$

5) $2a(4a+1)$

6) $(x+12)(x+3)$

7) $(x+5)(x+2)$

8) $(x-7)(x+2)$

9) $(x+4)(x-3)$

10) $(x-6)(x+3)$

11) $(x-6)(x-2)$

12) $(x-10)(x-2)$

13) $3(x^2+3x+2)$ which factors to
$3(x+2)(x+1)$

14) $4(x^2+5x+6)$ which factors to
$4(x+3)(x+2)$

15) $(x-5)(x+5)$

16) $(x-4)(x+4)$

17) $(4x-3)(4x+3)$

18) $(3x-4)(3x+4)$

19) $(x-y)(x+y)$

20) $(a^2+4)(a-2)(a+2)$

Practice D (page 381)

1) A

2) C

3) A

4) D

5) D

6) B

7) B

8) B

9) D

10) C

UNTIMED COLLEGE BOARD PRACTICE

Complete the following College Board practice problems from College Board's *The Official SAT Study Guide* or online at www.collegeboard.org. Review answers after completing.

Test 1, Math: No Calculator, #15

Test 2, Math: No Calculator, #4

Test 3, Math: No Calculator #3

Test 3, Math: Calculator, #33

Test 4, Math: No Calculator, #5

Chapter **14**

The Wolf Pack

One thing all successful people will tell you, no matter what they achieved, is that their journey was hard. Even after passing their Breakthrough Points and riding the Success Curve, there were times they felt like quitting, faced major setbacks, and didn't think they were capable of succeeding. But they'll also tell you that while these unpleasant experiences are to be expected, there is one thing that not only makes the journey to success easier, but also magnifies the ultimate success that is attained: your Wolf Pack.

Your Wolf Pack is a group of people who have your best interests in mind. They pick you up when you fall, boost your self-confidence, and only see the very best version of you. In short, they support you.

Right now, your Wolf Pack may consist of parents, teachers, guidance counselors, coaches, classmates, teammates, and friends. These are the people you spend the majority of your time with, and therefore the ones who have had the greatest influence on your mindset, actions, and beliefs. As entrepreneur and author Jim Rohn famously said, "You are the average of the five people you spend the most time with."

If you want to continue your quest to higher SAT scores, you have to add people to your Wolf Pack who are going to challenge you to get better. If your goal is to become a great test taker, then you need to spend more of your time with great test takers.

This is the reason even the best in the world have multiple coaches and several mentors throughout their journey. You need support from coaches and mentors when times get tough. They believe in you when others don't, and help you view challenges and obstacles in your life from a different, grander perspective.

Your Wolf Pack, though, is not limited to those adults in your life, but can also include other students who are at the level of success that you want to attain. These are the students who already have the habits of success ingrained in them. Just by spending time around them, you will be able to pick up these habits as well. Better yet, these students are a source of inspiration.

If they can do it, so can you!

But don't just settle on being around people with high test scores and grades. Rather, surround yourself with people committed to pursuing their dreams, no matter how incredible they seem: those who want more out of life and are ambitious enough to seek it out, optimistic enough to believe they can find it.

These are the ones who will push you through barriers instead of pulling you back down. Students with a strong Wolf Pack are typically more resilient and more likely to persevere through rough spots. Their self-image seems to be carved in stone, not drawn in sand. In other words, they have a strong belief in themselves that is not changed so easily.

Not only will your Wolf Pack help improve your life, but it will also give you a strong foundation to begin helping others improve theirs. Knowing you have support and guidance when you need it gives you the ability to lend that same guidance and support to others. When others in your life have adopted a fixed mindset, it's your turn to help open their eyes to what a growth mindset can do for them.

Now, go find your Wolf Pack!

Writing and Language Test: Practice

Now that you have completed your study of the most common errors on the Writing and Language Test, it is time to apply these new skills by doing a full untimed passage. The passage below contains nearly all the different types of grammar errors you will encounter on the SAT. As you progress through it, make sure to apply the method for spotting writing errors: read the title of the passage, read the passage as you work through the questions, read the questions aloud to see if you can hear the error, plug in answer choices, and remember that shorter/simpler is better.

Bad Guys Are Better

Perhaps one of the most integral parts of a **1** story, is its characters. For an author to depict a truly real character, he must first differentiate **2** between unimportant, trivial details and **3** telling details; those details that give clues to a character's nature. Most of the better characters emerge through this careful attention to telling details. For example, rather **4** than giving a long diffuse explanation, authors should provide several telling details, which will often prove to be the determining factors in how the reader views the character. [1] Some of the most **5** interesting characters is those with a disposition devoid of all **6** empathy. The evil characters who demean other characters and make it their mission **7** to submerge the goodness of others. [2] Their power and the interest they garner is not diminished by the hero's attempts to **8** destroy them; however, they eclipse the hero and take over the scene.

Bad guys are just more interesting. The readers are bored of the same mundane plotline where the hero wins. They want to see the consequences that result when the average person transforms into an evil villain. **9** This dynamic type of character fills the seats in movie theaters. It reminds viewers of the frailty and malleability of their own conditions. Take Satan from *Paradise Lost*, for instance. Much **10** to the dismay—or, some argue, delight; of John Milton, Satan became the hero of the work for many of its readers. **11** [3] Although it might seem bizarre, Milton did indeed **12** go about digressing from the plot for long sections **13** of text on the epic poem to explain **14** Satan's condition and why he became evil. [4] We are all **15** disinclined to emphasize with evil people, but when it comes to literature **16** people relish the villains. **17** However, if you ever want to become a writer, be sure to write about villains. **18**

A) NO CHANGE

B) story is its characters

C) story; is its characters

D) story is it's characters

A) NO CHANGE

B) among unimportant, trivial details

C) between unimportant and trivial details

D) between trivial details

A) NO CHANGE

B) telling details. Those details

C) telling details, those details

D) telling details and those details

A) NO CHANGE

B) then giving a long diffuse

C) than gave a long diffuse

D) then gives a long diffuse

A) NO CHANGE

B) interesting characters are

C) interesting characters were

D) interesting characters is,

A) NO CHANGE

B) empathy; the evil characters who demean other characters and make

C) empathy—the evil characters who demean other characters and make

D) empathy, and the evil characters who demean other characters and make

A) NO CHANGE

B) to submit the

C) to subvert the

D) to sublimate the

8

A) NO CHANGE

B) destroy them; however, them eclipse the

C) destroy them; nevertheless, they eclipse the

D) destroy them; rather, they eclipse the

9 Which choice most effectively combines the underlined sentences?

A) This dynamic type of character fills the seats in movie theaters furthermore reminding viewers of the frailty and malleability of their own conditions.

B) This dynamic type of character fills the seats in movie theaters and it reminds viewers of the frailty and malleability of their own conditions.

C) This dynamic type of character fills the seats in movie theaters because it reminds viewers of the frailty and malleability of their own conditions.

D) This dynamic type of character fills the seats in movie theaters while also reminding them of the frailty and malleability of their own conditions.

10

A) NO CHANGE

B) to the dismay—or, some argue, delight—

C) to the dismay—or, some argue, delight

D) to the dismay—or, some argue, delight:

11 At this point, the writer is considering adding the following sentence.
   Satan was first called Lucifer before he fell from Heaven.
   Should the writer make this addition here?

A) Yes, because it provides historical context for the character in question.

B) Yes, because it adds more telling details about Satan, illustrating the writer's earlier point.

C) No, because it makes a claim about Satan that is unsubstantiated.

D) No, because it interrupts the flow of the passage with irrelevant details.

A) NO CHANGE

B) go and digressed from the plot

C) go about digressing within the plot

D) digress from the plot

A) NO CHANGE

B) of text in the epic poem

C) of text for the epic poem

D) of text at the epic poem

A) NO CHANGE

B) Satans' condition

C) Satans condition

D) Satan's condition;

A) NO CHANGE

B) disinclined with emphasizing

C) disinclined to empathize

D) disinclined to emulate

A) NO CHANGE

B) people relishes the villains

C) you relish the villains

D) we relish the villains

The writer wants to conclude by tying together the points made in the first paragraph with the topics discussed in the second paragraph. Which change best accomplishes this goal?

A) NO CHANGE

B) So, if you ever want to become a writer, make sure you write about villains, not the good guys.

C) So, if you ever want to become a writer, remember to focus on the telling details of a character, and if you want that character to captivate your reader, make him a villain.

D) Therefore, if writing is the profession for you, avoid giving long diffuse explanations of characters and instead focus on only a few telling details.

18 The writer is considering adding the following sentence:

Surprisingly, the telling details we typically remember are those attached to villains.

Where is the most logical place to insert the sentence into the passage?

A) Before sentence 1

B) After sentence 3

C) After sentence 2

D) After sentence 4

Mindset Tip

Before reviewing the answers to this practice section, set aside some time to check in with your Wolf Pack. Periodic check-ins are vital to your mental and emotional stability. Your Wolf Pack keeps you afloat and reminds you of your intrinsic value, no matter the score, the mistakes, or the pitfalls you encounter on this SAT journey. Think about a heavy weight resting on a sheet of ice; if it is localized on one point, the ice will most likely break, but if it is divided and spread out along different parts of the ice, there will be no break. Your Wolf Pack helps you carry your burdens, and thus allows you to lift off and soar.

Answers

1) Choice (B) correctly eliminates the unnecessary comma. Choice (C) incorrectly uses a semicolon and choice (D) confuses "it's" and "its."

2) Choice (D) correctly eliminates the redundancy, since "unimportant" and "trivial" have virtually the same definition.

3) Choice (C) correctly fixes the fragment by using a comma to connect the dependent clause, "those…nature," to the rest of the sentence. (B) does not correct the semicolon error and (D) is unnecessarily wordy.

4) Choice (A) correctly leaves the sentence unchanged. "Than" is the correct comparative word and the verb "giving" is in correct tense and form. Choices (C) and (D) add a new verb error.

5) Choice (B) corrects the subject/verb agreement error. "Characters" is plural so the verb must be "are."

6) Choice (C) correctly uses a dash to connect the dependent clause "the evil…others." A semicolon would be incorrect because "the evil…others" cannot stand alone as a sentence.

7) Choice (C) correctly fixes the word choice error. "Submerge" means to dunk under water, while "subvert," in this context, means to corrupt.

8) Choice (D) correctly uses the correct transition, "rather," and does not add any new errors. Choice (B) adds a new error with the object pronoun "them."

9) Choice (C) correctly coordinates the cause and effect relationship between to the two sentence parts by using "because."

10) Choice (B) corrects the punctuation error by replacing the semicolon with a dash, which maintains the consistency of the punctuation.

11) Choice (D) is correct because the statement is irrelevant background information that does not further the point that Milton spent a great deal of time detailing the character of Satan.

12) Choice (D) eliminates wordiness and concisely uses just the action verb "digress."

13) Choice (B) corrects the preposition error, replacing "on" with "in."

14) This is correct as written, so the answer is (A). The apostrophe should be before the "s," because Satan is singular, and no semicolon is warranted.

15) Choice (C) corrects the diction error. "Emphasize" means to underscore or stress, whereas "empathize" means to identify with the feelings of another.

16) Choice (D) makes the sentence parallel by replacing "people" with first person plural "we," which is how the sentence begins.

17) Choice (C) includes both topics discussed in the passage: the idea of focusing on important details and the point that villains make better characters.

18) Choice (A) correctly places the sentence immediately before the topic shifts to a discussion of villains, and so serves as an introduction to the next point the author is making.

Vocabulary Words 196–210

181) **speculate** (v). a) to reflect or wonder; b) to make an educated guess: *It is foolish to speculate what the future holds for the world.*

182) **erratic** (adj). deviating from what is normal in behavior or beliefs; odd: *Frederick, Robert's pet turtle, had begun acting erratically, crawling in slow circles, so he decided to take him to the vet.*

183) **miser** (n). someone who hoards their money; a cheapskate: *Scrooge in* A Christmas Carol *is the classic miser.*

184) **sanction** (v). to give official authorization, consent, or permission: *The university refused to sanction the parade because it usually resulted in underage drinking.*

185) **inclination** (n). preference, liking: *Lydia has a definite inclination for fashion design.*

186) **postulate** (v). a) to make a claim as a basis for reasoning or arguing: *Many philosophers have postulated that there may be a parallel universe;* b) (n). a fundamental law or condition: *Euclid's fifth postulate of geometry was difficult to prove.*

187) **intermittent** (v). alternately occurring; sporadically beginning and then stopping repeatedly: *The weather was strange that day: it rained intermittently for a few hours. It would rain, then stop, and then rain again.*

188) **compromise** (v). a) to negotiate or reach settlement by give and take: *Sometimes one must compromise to keep peace and harmony;* b) to make vulnerable or weaken; to jeopardize: *It is not wise to compromise one's values just to fit in.*

189) **optimistic** (adj). inclined to look on the bright side and be hopeful: *Having an optimistic attitude toward life makes you live longer.*

190) **dubious** (adj). doubtful; uncertain: *I am very dubious of so-called miracle cures.*

191) **tentative** (adj). unsure; uncertain; not definite or positive; hesitant: *The United States government came to a tentative agreement with the Indian tribes over the disputed territories.*

192) **latter** (adj). the second item mentioned of two: *Since I am being forced to make a decision, I choose the latter option.*

193) **critical** (adj). a) expressing disapproval or negative judgments of: *The reviewer was highly critical of the book written by the young author;* b) serious; life-threatening, grave, or at a point of crisis: *The man was rushed to the hospital in critical condition.*

194) **unfounded** (adj). without evidence or substance; unsupported, speculative: *The lies and rumors that plagued the young woman were completely unfounded.*

195) **hypothetical** (adj). theoretical; assumed; not supported by evidence: *The scientist did not like to waste time on hypothetical theories and imaginings.*

Latin and Greek Roots 76–80

76) NOV/NEO: new (innovate, novice, novelty, neoclassical, Neolithic)

77) NUMER: number (enumerate, numeral)

78) OLOGY: the study of (psychology, biology)

79) OMNI/PAN: all (omniscient, omnivore, omnipotent, panacea, pandemic, panegyric, pandemonium)

80) OPT: choose (option, adopt, optimal)

Math Test: Solving Advanced Equations

If you spend enough time around great test takers, you realize they have certain things in common: keen math skills, perseverance, and the ability to solve a variety of complex equations. Being able to solve quadratic, rational, exponential, and radical equations will allow you to correctly answer some of the more challenging questions on the SAT, thus improving not just your score but your confidence as well.

Hint

Earn an easy 20 points by realizing that, although you will be learning the different methods for solving these advanced equations, you can still plug in answer choices for multiple-choice questions. When plugging in answer choices, make sure you follow the order of operations correctly.

Solving Quadratic Equations

Solving quadratic equations is almost as important as solving linear equations. A quadratic, as you learned in the previous chapter, is a type of equation that contains a variable that is raised to the second power, such as $y = x^2 - 2x + 1$.

The first thing to know about solving a quadratic equation is that each equation can have zero, one, or two solutions. Solutions, which can also be referred to as zeros, roots, or x-intercepts, are the points where the quadratic crosses the x-axis when graphed.

There are three strategies that you can use to solve a quadratic equation:

1) Factoring

2) The square root property

3) The quadratic formula

Solving by Factoring

Most quadratic equations on the SAT can be solved by factoring first. In the previous chapter, you simplified a quadratic from standard form to factored form. For example, a quadratic in standard form, such as $x^2 + x - 12$, can be written in factored form as $(x + 4)(x - 3)$.

The key to solving a quadratic equation that is written in factored form is to make sure the equation is equal to 0 so that you can apply what is called the **zero product property**. The zero product property allows you to set each factor equal to 0 and solve for the given variable in both equations.

Here is an example of a quadratic equation that is already factored, so you can jump right to using the zero product property:

$$(3x + 2)(x - 5) = 0$$

What is the solution set in the equation above?

A) $\{-5\}$

B) $\{5\}$

C) $\left\{\dfrac{2}{3}\right\}$

D) $\left\{-\dfrac{2}{3}, 5\right\}$

This quadratic equation is already written in factored form and is set equal to 0, so you can apply the zero product property by setting each factor equal to 0, as shown below:

$$3x + 2 = 0$$

$$x - 5 = 0$$

Once you set each factor equal to 0, solve both equations.

$$x = \frac{-2}{3}$$

$$x = 5$$

The correct answer is (D), since the solution set of $\left\{-\dfrac{2}{3}, 5\right\}$ means that $x = -\dfrac{2}{3}$ and $x = 5$. While choice (B) in this example was a solution, it did not represent the entire solution set.

Most quadratic equations will require you to factor them before applying the zero product property. Let's take a look at an example that will require you to solve a quadratic by factoring out the GCF and then applying the zero product property.

Which of the following is a solution to $5a^2 + 10a = 0$?

A) –2

B) –1

C) 1

D) 2

This quadratic equation can be solved by first factoring out the GCF, which is $5a$, from both terms. It can then be rewritten as:

$$5a(a + 2) = 0$$

Now that the quadratic is factored, set each factor equal to 0 and solve for a.

$$5a = 0 \rightarrow a = 0$$

$$a + 2 = 0 \rightarrow a = -2$$

Notice that there are two solutions to this quadratic, but only one of them is a possible answer choice.

Questions that require you to solve for quadratics may limit the solutions in various ways. Here is an example that asks you to solve a quadratic written in trinomial form. It can be solved by factoring and using the zero product property.

What positive integer is a solution to $x^2 + x - 2 = 0$?

The equation in this example can be factored to:

$$(x + 2)(x - 1) = 0$$

By using the zero product property, set both factors equal to zero and solve each of them.

$$x + 2 = 0 \rightarrow x = -2$$

$$x - 1 = 0 \rightarrow x = 1$$

Since the question wanted you to find a solution that is a positive integer, the correct answer would be 1, since the other solution is negative. This is why it is important to identify key information as you read the question to know what the question is asking you to find.

PRACTICE A

Find the solutions to each:

1) $2x^2 - 8x = 0$

2) $x^2 - x - 42 = 0$

3) $x^2 - 6x + 9 = 0$

4) $x^2 - 16 = 0$

5) $4x^2 - 9 = 0$

Rearranging Quadratics

So far, each of the quadratic equations we solved has been set equal to 0. Whenever you are solving quadratics by factoring, make sure that they are set equal to 0 before factoring or applying the zero product property. How do you get a quadratic equation equal to 0? Use the same rearranging techniques you learned from earlier chapters. Here is an example:

What is the solution to $2x^2 - 4x = -2$?

To correctly solve this quadratic equation, you must first rearrange some terms so that the equation is equal to 0 on one side. The easiest way to do this is by adding 2 to both sides, which would give you:

$$2x^2 - 4x + 2 = 0$$

Once the equation is equal to 0, you can solve by factoring. This quadratic contains a GCF of 2 and can be rewritten as $2(x^2 - 2x + 1) = 0$. The trinomial inside the parentheses can also be factored, so the entire equation can be rewritten as:

$$2(x - 1)(x - 1) = 0$$

When applying the zero product property, the 2 in front will not matter since you can divide both sides by 2 to cancel it out. To solve, set each of the factors equal to 0 and solve each for x.

$$x - 1 = 0 \rightarrow x = 1$$

$$x - 1 = 0 \rightarrow x = 1$$

Clearly, both solutions are the same. This is an example of a quadratic equation with only one solution.

Below is a more challenging example that will require you to use previously learned skills.

What is the average of the solutions to the equation $2x^2 - 3x - 20 = x^2 - 2$?

The first step is to rearrange the equation so that one side is equal to 0. The best approach would be to move all the terms to the left side of the equation so that you do not have $-x^2$, which would be much more difficult to factor.

$$2x^2 - 3x - 20 = x^2 - 2$$
$$-x^2 \qquad + 2 \quad -x^2 + 2$$

$$x^2 - 3x - 18 = 0$$

$$(x - 6)(x + 3) = 0$$

$$x = 6 \text{ and } x = -3$$

To find the average, add the two solutions and divide by 2.

$$\frac{6 + (-3)}{2} = \frac{3}{2} \text{ or } 1.5$$

PRACTICE B

Find the solutions to each equation.

1) $x^2 + 6x + 12 = 4$

2) $x^2 - 2x = 8$

3) $x^2 + 5x - 2 = 6x + 10$

Systems of Linear and Quadratic Equations

You may need to solve a system of equations that contains a quadratic equation. This can be done using the same substitution method learned in Chapter 4. Just like a system with two linear equations, the solution to the system of linear and quadratic equations represents the point at which the two equations intersect.

In the system of equations shown below, if $x > 0$, what is the value of y?

$$y = x^2$$

$$y - 4x = 12$$

This question can be solved easily by using substitution because one of the variables is by itself. You can replace y with x^2.

$$x^2 - 4x = 12$$

$$x^2 - 4x - 12 = 0$$

$$(x - 6)(x + 2) = 0$$

$$x = 6; x = -2$$

Since the question tells you that $x > 0$, you can eliminate -2, which makes the solution 6.

However, the question asks you to find the value of y, so you must plug 6 in for x into either of the equations.

$$y = (6)^2 = 36$$

Anytime you are solving a system, it is crucial that you know what the question is asking for. Here is another example that will require you to flex your problem-solving muscle.

$$x = y + 4$$

$$2x^2 - 8x = 2y$$

Which of the following is a possible x value of a solution to the system of equations above?

A) –4

B) 0

C) 2

D) 4

This challenging question will certainly test your perseverance and your problem-solving skills. There are two ways to solve this question. The first approach, substituting $(y + 4)$ in for x in the second equation, is the most common for students. This will give us:

$$2(y + 4)^2 - 8(y + 4) = 2y$$

While you can find the correct answer using this approach, it is time-consuming, as it will require you to square a binomial with FOIL, distribute, and combine like terms to solve the quadratic.

Another, much more efficient, approach requires rearranging the first equation to get y by itself, or $y = x - 4$. You can then substitute $x - 4$ for y in the second equation.

$$2x^2 - 8x = 2(x - 4)$$

This equation is much easier to solve than the equation resulting from the first approach.

$$2x^2 - 8x = 2x - 8$$

$$2x^2 - 10x + 8 = 0$$

$$2(x^2 - 5x + 4) = 0$$

$$2(x - 1)(x - 4) = 0$$

The solutions to this equation are 1 and 4, making the correct answer (D).

PRACTICE C

Find the points of intersection of each system of equations.

1) $y = 2x + 4$
$y = x^2 + 1$

2) $x^2 = 2y - 6$
$y = 3x - 1$

Solving Quadratic Equations Using the Square Root

Some quadratics can be solved by taking the square root of both sides. Taking the square root cancels out squaring a variable because they are inverse operations. For example, the equation $x^2 = 9$ can be solved by taking the square root of both sides, as shown below.

$$\sqrt{x^2} = \sqrt{9}$$

Remember that taking a square root to solve an equation will produce two answers: a positive and negative value, since plugging in 3 or –3 for x results in 9. This means the solutions to the equation are:

$$x = \pm 3$$

To truly understand the concept of inverse operations, let's explore another way of writing the square root, this time as the rational exponent of $\frac{1}{2}$. If we rewrote the term $\sqrt{x^2}$ as $(x^2)^{\frac{1}{2}}$, you can see that the 2 and the $\frac{1}{2}$ will cancel out and thus are inverse operations.

Here is another example of a quadratic that is best solved using a square root. Note that the equation is equal to a perfect square, which is a clue that we can take the square root of both sides.

$$(x - 1)^2 = 16$$

What is a solution to the equation above?

Your first step should be to take the square root of both sides.

$$\sqrt{(x-1)^2} = \sqrt{16}$$

Since you are taking the square root of both sides to solve the equation, the equation should be rewritten as:

$$x - 1 = \pm 4$$

From here, you can write two separate equations and then solve for both.

$$x - 1 = 4 \rightarrow x = 5$$

$$x - 1 = -4 \rightarrow x = -3$$

Blind Spot

Don't forget that quadratics can produce two solutions. Anytime you take the square root of both sides, the answer will include both a positive and negative number. $x = \pm 2$ means that $x = 2$ and $x = -2$.

PRACTICE D

1) $(x + 2)^2 - 9 = 7$

2) $4x^2 - 10 = 26$

Solving Quadratic Equations Using the Quadratic Formula

The third method for solving quadratic equations is the quadratic formula, which is shown below.

$$x = \frac{-b \pm \sqrt{b^2 - 4ac}}{2a}$$

The quadratic formula can be used to solve any quadratic written in the form $ax^2 + bx + c = 0$. It will be necessary to use this formula for quadratics that cannot be solved by factoring or by using a square root. The formula will not be provided to you, so you must memorize it.

Here is an example of a quadratic equation that should be solved with the quadratic formula:

Find the solutions to $x^2 + 4x - 6 = 0$.

You may try to factor first, but since there are no factors of −6 that add up to 4, you will need to use the quadratic formula.

Let's start by identifying a, b, and c: a and b are the coefficients of the variables, and c is the constant. You can substitute those values into the formula.

$$a = 1; b = 4; c = -6$$

$$\frac{-4 \pm \sqrt{4^2 - 4(1)(-6)}}{2(1)}$$

You can now simplify using order of operations. Be careful with the negative signs!

$$\frac{-4 \pm \sqrt{16 + 24}}{2}$$

$$\frac{-4 \pm \sqrt{40}}{2}$$

You may be required to simplify a radical by looking for factors that are perfect squares. In this case, $\sqrt{40}$ can be simplified to $\sqrt{4} \cdot \sqrt{10}$, or $2\sqrt{10}$.

$$\frac{-4 \pm 2\sqrt{10}}{2}$$

The next step is to rewrite the rational expression by splitting the numerator into two fractions and simplifying each of them, as shown below.

$$-\frac{4}{2} \pm \frac{2\sqrt{10}}{2} = -2 \pm \sqrt{10}$$

From here, you can rewrite the above expression as two solutions (remember that quadratics can produce two solutions).

$$x = -2 + \sqrt{10}$$

$$x = -2 - \sqrt{10}$$

For multiple-choice questions, it may be helpful to peek at the answer choices, as they may indicate that the quadratic formula is the correct strategy to solve the question. The correct answer choice may not require as much simplifying, so it will be helpful to know how far you have to go.

PRACTICE E

Solve each equation using the quadratic formula.

1) $x^2 + 6x + 7 = 3$

2) $2x^2 - 3x + 1 = 0$

Solving Radical Equations

A radical equation is any equation containing a radical, such as $\sqrt{x} = 5$.

Radical equations can be solved by isolating the radical and then raising both sides of the equation by the power that would eliminate that radical. In most cases, the radical will be a square root, like in the equation above, which can be eliminated by raising both sides of the equation by the power of 2. For the equation above, that would result in x being equal to 25.

An alternate approach to solving this equation is to rewrite $\sqrt{x}$ as $x^{\frac{1}{2}}$. This is similar to what we discussed in solving quadratic equations using the square root property. To isolate x, simply raise both sides of the equation to the second power, as shown below.

$$\sqrt{x} = 5$$

$$x = 25$$

Here is another example.

$$\text{What is the solution to } \sqrt{x+2} = 6?$$

Since the radical is already isolated, square both sides to eliminate the radical.

$$\left(\sqrt{x+2}\right)^2 = (6)^2$$

$$x + 2 = 36$$

Once you eliminate the radical, the equation can be solved by subtracting 2 from both sides, so x would equal 34.

An important note on solving radical equations: you *must* plug the answer back in to the original equation to make sure that solution works.

$$\sqrt{34+2} = \sqrt{36} = 6$$

Radical equations can create what are called extraneous solutions, which is an answer that is not a true solution to the equation. Since you have to plug in your solutions anyway, the most efficient way to solve radical equation multiple-choice questions is to plug in the answer choices.

It would also be helpful to memorize the basic square roots.

$$\sqrt{1} = 1 \qquad \sqrt{4} = 2 \qquad \sqrt{9} = 3 \qquad \sqrt{16} = 4$$

$$\sqrt{25} = 5 \qquad \sqrt{36} = 6 \qquad \sqrt{49} = 7 \qquad \sqrt{64} = 8$$

$$\sqrt{81} = 9 \qquad \sqrt{100} = 10 \qquad \sqrt{121} = 11 \qquad \sqrt{144} = 12$$

PRACTICE F

Solve for x:

1) $\sqrt{5x-4} - 3 = 1$

2) Which of the following is the solution to $\sqrt{x+2} = x$?

A) −1

C) 1

B) 0

D) 2

Solving Rational Equations

The next types of equations we will learn to solve are rational equations, which are equations that contain a variable in the denominator of a fraction.

Some rational equations can be solved by converting each side of the equation to a proportion and then using cross-multiplication. Here is an example:

What is the value of x in the equation $\dfrac{2}{x} = 7$, given that x ≠ 0?

If you solve the equation as is, you could multiply both sides by x to get $7x = 2$. Or, you could rewrite the equation as a proportion.

$$\frac{2}{x} = \frac{7}{1}$$

Multiply 2 by 1 and 7 by x to get $2 = 7x$.

Finally, divide both sides by 7.

$$x = \frac{2}{7}$$

This next example will require a few more steps but can be solved in a similar fashion.

$$\frac{x+1}{x-2} = m$$

Solve the equation above, given that m is equal to 3.

Start by substituting 3 in for m, then rewrite the equation as a proportion.

$$\frac{x+1}{x-2} = \frac{3}{1}$$

Then, cross-multiply. Be sure to distribute the 3.

$$x + 1 = 3(x - 2)$$

$$x + 1 = 3x - 6$$

$$2x = 7$$

$$x = \frac{7}{2}$$

Another approach would be to multiply both sides by $(x - 2)$, which is shown below:

$$(x-2)\frac{x+1}{x-2} = 3(x-2)$$

Notice how this step will cancel out the $(x - 2)$ on the left, putting you in the same position as would solving with a proportion.

Solving Exponential Equations

Exponential equations contain a variable in the exponent, such as $2^x = 32$. The key to solving an exponential equation is to get both sides of the equation to have the same base. This means rewriting a number as a smaller number raised to a power. Here is an example.

What is the value of x in the equation $2^{x-1} = 8$?

To solve the equation above, you would need to rewrite 8 with a base of 2, or 2^3.

$$2^{x-1} = 2^3$$

Once the bases are the same, just set the exponents equal to each other and solve.

$$x - 1 = 3$$

The solution to the equation above is 4.

Here is another example that contains an exponential equation and requires you to use the exponent rules we learned in the previous chapter.

$$2^x \cdot 4^{x+1} = 16$$

What is the solution to the equation above?

This question is without a doubt a challenging one, as you need a deep understanding of a variety of topics to solve it. A good first step would be to make the bases the same by converting each to a base of 2.

$$2^x \cdot (2^2)^{x+1} = 2^4$$

Now you can apply the exponent rules to the left side of the equation. First, you must distribute the exponent of 2 to the $(x + 1)$ to get:

$$2^x \cdot 2^{2x + 2} = 2^4$$

Second, since you are multiplying the bases, you can add the exponents to get:

$$2^{x + 2x + 2} = 2^4 \rightarrow 2^{3x + 2} = 2^4$$

To solve the rest of this equation, set the two exponents equal to each other, then solve for x.

$$3x + 2 = 4$$

$$3x = 2$$

$$x = \frac{2}{3}$$

PRACTICE G

1) What is the solution of the equation shown below, given that $x \neq 3$?

$$\frac{2}{x-3} = 5$$

2) What is the average of the y-values of the solutions to the following system of equations?

$$y = x^2 - 5x + 8$$

$$y = 4x - 12$$

3) In the system shown below, if (x, y) is a solution and $x < 0$, what is the value of y?

$$y = x^2 + 2$$

$$x + y = 4$$

4) Which of the following are the solutions to the equation $2x^2 - 6x = -2$?

A) $\frac{-3}{2} + \frac{\sqrt{5}}{2}$ and $\frac{-3}{2} - \frac{\sqrt{5}}{2}$

B) $\frac{3}{2} + \frac{\sqrt{5}}{2}$ and $\frac{3}{2} - \frac{\sqrt{5}}{2}$

C) $\frac{3}{2} + 2\sqrt{13}$ and $\frac{3}{2} - 2\sqrt{13}$

D) $\frac{-3}{2} + 2\sqrt{13}$ and $\frac{-3}{2} - 2\sqrt{13}$

5) Which of the following are the solutions to the equation $\frac{1}{2}x^2 - 6x - \frac{1}{2} = 0$?

A) $6 \pm \sqrt{37}$

B) $-6 \pm \sqrt{37}$

C) $\frac{6 \pm \sqrt{37}}{2}$

D) $\frac{-6 \pm \sqrt{37}}{2}$

6) Which of the following is a solution to the equation $\frac{2^x}{8^x} = 16$?

A) -4 **C)** 0

B) -2 **D)** 2

7) If $a^{\frac{1}{2}} = 4$, what is the value of a?

8) If $a > 0$ and $a^{-2} = 4$, what is the value of a?

9) What is the average of the solutions to the equation $2x^2 - x - 5 = 0$?

$$y = x^2 + 4x$$

$$y = -4$$

10) How many solutions does the system of equations shown above have?

A) 0   C) 2

B) 1   D) 3

Answers

Practice A (page 398)
1) $x = 0, x = 4$ **4)** $x = 4, x = -4$

2) $x = 7, x = -6$ **5)** $x = \dfrac{3}{2}, x = -\dfrac{3}{2}$

3) $x = 3$

Practice B (page 400)
1) $x = -4, x = -2$ **3)** $x = 4, x = -3$

2) $x = 4, x = -2$

Practice C (page 402)
1) $(3, 10), (-1, 2)$ **2)** $(4, 11), (2, 5)$

Practice D (page 404)
1) $x = 2, x = -6$ **2)** $x = \pm 3$

Practice E (page 405)
1) $-3 \pm \sqrt{5}$ **2)** $x = 1, x = \dfrac{1}{2}$

Practice F (page 407)
1) 4

2) D

1) $x = \dfrac{17}{5}$

2) 6

3) 6

4) B

5) A

6) B

7) 16

8) $\dfrac{1}{2}$

9) $\dfrac{1}{4}$

10) B

UNTIMED COLLEGE BOARD PRACTICE

Complete the following College Board practice problems from College Board's *The Official SAT Study Guide* or online at www.collegeboard.org. Review answers after completing.

Test 1, Math: No Calculator, #14, 16, 20

Test 1, Math: Calculator, #25

Test 2, Math: No Calculator, #7, 13

Test 3, Math: No Calculator, #10

Test 3, Math: Calculator, #26

Test 4, Math: No Calculator, #10, 13, 15, 18

Chapter **15**

Big-Picture Thinking: Discovering Your True Purpose

> **"**The two most important days in your life are the day you are born and the day you find out why.**"**
> —Mark Twain

Previously, we discussed how important setting goals is to your preparation for the SAT and how you should aim for more than just achieving an SAT score; you should also embody the habits that will help you achieve that score. Pursuing your goal SAT score is merely a catalyst to help you to become the person you truly want to be. Throughout this book, you have been building future power by adopting the habits you deem necessary for success. Now it is time for you to unleash that future power by aligning with your true purpose.

Discovering a grander purpose for your future is extraordinarily powerful. It allows you to see the big picture rather than focus on the minor details and obstacles along the way. Discovering your purpose will also allow you to relinquish any attachment to a specific score or a specific college. When you think big picture first, you realize how many paths you can take to get to your destination and how many possible destinations will fulfill your purpose.

Big-picture thinking will also drastically reduce the stress and anxiety you feel about your future, thus increasing your positivity. Do not concern yourself with the exact road map of how to get to your destination; instead, have faith that the habits you have accumulated will get you there.

Let's look at two students with similar goals and different mindsets.

Bobby decides he wants to attend *the* top physical therapy school and believes that his sole purpose is gaining acceptance into this university. He finds out that the SAT score needed for definite acceptance is a 1350, so he practices and practices and practices until he thinks he is ready.

Bobby finally takes the SAT, but due to his anxiety about getting the score he needs to be admitted to his dream school, he blanks on problems he should know. Bobby gets a 1020. He believes his life is over because he did not get accepted into the school of his dreams. Bobby is inconsolable.

Lindsay has also decided to pursue physical therapy because of her deep passion for helping others. She discovered this passion before she began searching for colleges with physical therapy programs and, as a result, she took the time to visit with physical therapists and people in similar fields. After spending a good deal of time around these people, Lindsay realizes that she could fulfill her purpose in many ways: occupational therapy, nursing, physical therapy, physical training, speech pathology, etc. She also learns from her interactions with actual physical therapists that none of them took the same path to get to where they were. Some did six-year BA and MA programs, while others started off at community college and eventually transferred. Lindsay makes it a goal to get into a top physical therapy university, but she knows that even if she does not gain acceptance, she can still find a way to fulfill her purpose of helping others in a therapy field.

Because of her big picture thinking and the knowledge that she'd find a way to achieve her goal no matter what, she is relaxed and focused during the SAT. As a result of her flexible thinking, positivity, and anxiety-free approach, she crushes the SAT and scores a 1350. Lindsay gets into a top physical therapy school, but chooses to go to a different school that better fits her.

Had her purpose only been to get into a specific school, rather than to help others through physical therapy, Lindsay may not have gotten into the school that was right for her, nor would she have recognized all the opportunities that were available to her.

So, what are the lessons here?

First, there is no one path to success. Believing that there is only one option could actually limit your ability to succeed.

Second, rigid, small-picture thinking can create anxiety. If you believe that you must follow an exact path with no deviation, and that there is only one possible college or job that will make you happy, you will become incredibly anxious. What if you make a misstep? What if you deviate? Your body tenses up and your ability to think clearly is reduced dramatically. Rather than setting a small-picture goal, discover a greater purpose.

Now, if you do not know what your true purpose is, that's okay; as with growth mindset, your true purpose will grow and develop over time. All you need do is think big.

Dream big and set grand goals but be loose about the particulars of how you achieve them. Focus on the process. Every step is a learning experience, whether or not that step sends you toward success or what appears to be a failure. Be more general in your statements about what will make you happy by using big-picture thinking, and remember you will find a way to get there.

Writing and Language Test: Timed Practice I

In this chapter, we will review the method for answering questions on the writing section. It is important for you to understand these simple strategies and ingrain them in your practice so that they eventually become habit. See the Writing and Language overview in Chapter 9 for a more in-depth explanation of these steps.

Answering Writing Questions: Review

1) Read the title of the passage.

2) Read the passage as you work through the questions.

3) Read the sentence in the question aloud.

4) Check the answer choices. Note what is different in each answer choice to learn what you need to correct.

5) Eliminate wrong answers.

6) Plug your choice into the passage.

7) When you're stuck between two seemingly similar choices, choose the shorter of the two.

8) Consistency is king.

Writing and Language Test Pacing Strategy

The timing and pacing of the Writing and Language test is very similar to that of the Reading Test. Remember that all questions are worth the same number of points, so you want to pace yourself in such a way that allows you to answer the most questions correctly. Follow one of these two timing and pacing strategies as you work through the Writing and Language Test.

Plan A

Read the passage as you work through the questions. Give yourself approximately 9 minutes for each passage and the accompanying 11 questions.

Use this strategy if, after having read all the passages, you have no trouble completing a full Writing and Language Test in the time allotted. This is the best strategy overall because it gives you the most information about the main idea of the passage. However, if you have trouble completing the Writing and Language Test in the time allotted, choose Plan B.

Plan B

STEP 1: Read the title of the passage.

STEP 2: Go right to the questions and read the sentence they direct you to, making sure to read the surrounding context as well (typically, all you need to read is one sentence before and one sentence after).

STEP 3: Whenever you see bracketed numbers that look like "[1],"read the entire paragraph in which they appear, because you will be required to rearrange the sentences.

PRACTICE WITH PLAN B

Let's apply Plan B with the condensed passage below and see how effective it can be. Do not read the passage; instead, use Plan B to answer the questions.

This excerpt has been adapted from "The Wright Brothers' Aeroplane" by Orville and Wilbur Wright. It details the brothers' early experiments in flight.

We began our active experiments at the close of this period, in October, 1900, at Kitty Hawk, North Carolina. Our machine was designed to be flown as a kite, with a man on board, in winds from 15 to 20 miles an hour. **1** Similarly, upon trial, it was found that much stronger winds were required to lift it. Suitable winds not being plentiful, we found **2** it necessary; in order to test the new balancing system, to fly the machine as a kite without a man on board, operating the levers through cords from the ground. This did not give the practice anticipated, but it inspired confidence in the new system of balance.

In the summer of 1901 we became personally acquainted with Mr. Chanute. When he learned that we were interested in flying as a sport, and not with any expectation of **3** <u>mending</u> the money we were expending on it, he gave us much encouragement. At our invitation, he spent several weeks with us at our camp at Kill Devil Hill, four miles south of Kitty Hawk, during our experiments of that and the two succeeding years. He also witnessed one flight of the power machine near Dayton, Ohio, in October, 1904.

The machine of 1901 was built with the shape of surface used by Lilienthal, curved from front to rear like the segment of a parabola, with a curvature

$1/_{12}$ the depth of **4** <u>its</u> cord; but to make doubly sure that it would have sufficient lifting capacity when flown as a kite in 15- or 20-mile winds, we increased the area from 165 square feet, used in 1900, to 308 square feet—a size much larger than Lilienthal, Pilcher, or Chanute had deemed safe. **5** <u>Although the attempted flights at 308 feet were more than twice those at 165 feet with the second trial being the closest to sustained lift,</u> the lifting capacity again fell very far short of calculation, so that the idea of securing practice while flying as a kite had to be abandoned. Mr. Chanute, who witnessed the experiments, told us that the trouble was not due to poor construction of the machine. We saw only one other explanation—that the tables of air-pressures in general use were incorrect.

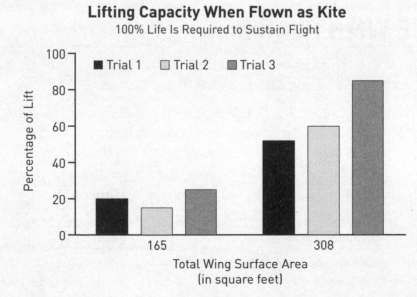

Lifting Capacity When Flown as Kite
100% Life Is Required to Sustain Flight

1

A) NO CHANGE

B) But,

C) Because,

D) Additionally,

2

A) NO CHANGE

B) it necessary: in order to

C) it necessary—in order to

D) it necessary, in order to

3

A) NO CHANGE

B) convalescing

C) recovering

D) recuperating

4

A) NO CHANGE

B) it's

C) their

D) his

5 The writer wants to include information in the passage that is consistent with the graph. Which choice most effectively accomplishes this goal?

A) NO CHANGE

B) Because the attempted flights at 308 feet were less than half those at 165 feet, with the second trial being the farthest from sustained lift,

C) Although the attempted flights at 308 feet were more than twice those at 165 feet, with the third trial being the closest to sustained lift,

D) Since the attempted flights at 308 feet were nearly identical to those at 165 feet with the second trials being the closest to one another,

Answers

1) For this question, you must reread the sentence before and the sentence with the underlined portion. After reading it with the word "similarly" in the sentence, read it without "similarly" and predict your own transition. You should be able to hear that the two sentences contrast with one another, which leaves only choice (B), "but." "Because" is a consequence transition and "Additionally" is transition that means another item, adding to the previous idea.

2) This is a punctuation consistency error. To correct this, you need only read the sentence with the underlined portion. You should notice that "in order to test the new balancing system" is an interrupting descriptive phrase and that it ends with a comma, which means you must change the semicolon at the beginning of the phrase to a comma for consistency. Thus, the answer must be (D).

3) In this diction error, you might notice that there is a theme in the answer choices. This is common for diction errors on the Writing and Language Test; these types of errors purposefully use the wrong contextual meaning of a word with multiple meanings. Although it is not correct for this context, "recovering" can mean healing from an illness, and so the answer choices purposefully use variations of this meaning in order to trick you. "Recovering the money we were expending on it," means getting it back, not healing, and so we can eliminate all choices that are synonyms to healing: (A), (B), and (D). Thus, the answer is (C).

4) This is a typical pronoun/punctuation error. "Its" is correct as written because the antecedent, "shape," is singular, so "their" would be incorrect. We also want a pronoun here, not the contraction "it is." Thus, the answer is (A).

5) In this graph question, you do not need to read any part of the passage other than the question with the underlined portion and the graph. Once you examine the graph carefully, you will realize that all the trials at 308 feet were more successful than those at 165 feet, so choices (B) and (D) can be eliminated. Choice (A) is also incorrect because the second trial was not the closest to sustained lift, the third trial was. Thus, the answer is (C).

Mindset Tip

Having a Plan B is important for pacing on both the Writing and Language Test and the Reading Test, but it is also crucial to your goal setting and mindset. Realizing that there is always a Plan B, or backup plan, takes some of the stress and anxiety off you. Your initial plan or strategy does not have to bear the weight of all your hopes and dreams, because it does not have to be the only plan. With big-picture thinking, there are countless other ways to achieve your goals and countless goals that you can achieve. Just remember, as you implement your chosen timing and pacing strategy on the Writing and Language Test, that there is always a Plan B to your path to success.

Vocabulary 211–225

211) **philanthropist** (n). someone who makes charitable donations: *The philanthropist who donated millions to help the poor wished to remain anonymous.*

212) **grievance** (n). a protest or criticism that merits retaliation: *If you have a grievance concerning your work environment, you should report it to Human Resources.*

213) **null** (adj). without value or consequence; zero: *The contract was deemed null and void after the one party violated its terms.*

214) **foe** (n). an enemy or adversary: *Lex Luther proved to be one of Superman's most formidable foes.*

215) **contemplate** (v). to think upon, to ponder and reflect: *The spa had a meditation room where one could go and contemplate life.*

216) **scope** (n). range or extent; aim or purpose: *The scope of the project was beyond the capabilities of the contractor.*

217) **manifest** (v). to reveal to the senses or mind: *It is said if you think about something long enough, you will be able to manifest it in your life.*

218) **reconcile** (v). to settle or resolve: *The husband and wife were able to reconcile their differences in lieu of divorce.*

219) **insurrection** (n). organized opposition to authority: *The insurrection at the company occurred because of poor working conditions and low salaries.*

220) **penitent** (adj). feeling or expressing remorse for wrongdoing: *The young teen was sincerely penitent for robbing the old lady.*

221) **homage** (n). respect: *The ancient Greeks paid homage to their gods by giving sacrifices.*

222) **abate** (v). to lessen or decrease in severity: *Once Wanda took an aspirin for her headache, the pain abated.*

223) **exacerbate** (v). to make worse, aggravate, or intensify: *The constant crying of the infant exacerbated an already uncomfortable situation on the airplane.*

224) **foist** (v). to force onto another: *The history professor was constantly trying to foist his radical ideas onto his students.*

225) **superfluous** (adj). serving no useful purpose; having no excuse for being: *Ernest Hemingway despised superfluous words and, as a result, had a frank, concise style of writing.*

Latin and Greek Roots 81–85

81) PAC/PEAC/PLAC: peace, to please (pact, peace, pacify, placid, placebo, implacable, complacent)

82) PAR: equal (disparate, parity, paramount, apart, apartheid)

83) PARA: beside or near (parallel, paradox, paralegal, paranormal, paramedic)

84) PAS/PATH: feeling, disease (empathy, antipathy, apathy, sympathy, dispassionate, impassive, pathogen, sociopath, psychopath)

85) PATER/PATR: father (patriarch, paternal, expatriate)

TIMED COLLEGE BOARD PRACTICE

Complete the following College Board practice problems from College Board's *The Official SAT Study Guide* or online at www.collegeboard.org. Review answers after completing.

Test 5, Writing and Language, #1–44

Math Test: Graphs of Functions

This section will cover graphs of quadratic functions and polynomial functions, as well as transformation rules that can be applied to any function you may see on the test.

As these topics get more difficult and the skills required more advanced, you might begin to feel some anxiety. For many of these problems, though, just having a general idea of what is presented is enough to find the answer. It's okay to not know it all. In fact, being comfortable with not understanding certain aspects of a given problem will allow you to tap into your inherent problem-solving capacity, which you have expanded throughout this book. Do your best to learn and master the multitude of topics in this chapter, but remember, the foundation is already set, and the skills are in place for you to solve any problem on the SAT, no matter how foreign it may look.

Graphs of Quadratic Functions

To excel on the SAT math section, you will need a deep understanding of graphs of quadratic functions. While these questions can seem complicated, knowing a few key points will greatly increase your chances of getting the question correct.

The graph of any quadratic function is a parabola, which is a symmetrical U-shaped curve that either opens up or opens down. A parabola that opens up can be thought of as decreasing, then increasing; a parabola that opens down can be thought of as increasing, then decreasing. The point where the parabola transitions from either decreasing to increasing (or increasing to decreasing) is called the vertex. The vertex is the lowest point on an upward-opening parabola and the highest point on a downward-opening parabola.

For an example, look at the graph of $f(x) = x^2$, shown on the next page, which has a vertex at $(0, 0)$ and opens upward.

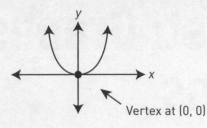

Vertex at (0, 0)

Using the Transformation Rules

The SAT will require that you know how to transform graphs of functions, which just means moving and changing the graph of the original function. It is easy to demonstrate these rules using a quadratic function, and the same rules can be applied to many functions that you will see on the test. Here is the first rule:

Transformation Rule 1: $-f(x) \rightarrow$ Reflection About the x-axis

An example of this transformation rule is $f(x) = -x^2$, which is still a parabola, but since the coefficient of the x^2 term is negative, it will result in the parabola flipping over the x-axis so that it opens downward. The graph is shown below:

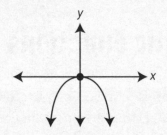

The vertex of this function is still at (0, 0), as the graph did not shift, it just "flipped" over the x-axis. There is, however, a difference between the vertex of $f(x) = x^2$ and $f(x) = -x^2$. In the first parabola, the vertex is the low point of the parabola, or the minimum. In the second parabola, the vertex is the high point of the parabola, or the maximum.

Transformation Rule 2: $f(x) + k \rightarrow$ Vertical Shift

The second transformation causes the parabola to shift up or down k units. If k is positive, you move the graph up that many units, and if k is negative, you move it down that many units. Here is an example that asks about the x-intercepts, or the points where the parabola crosses the x-axis.

Which of the following functions contains two x-intercepts?

A) $f(x) = x^2$

B) $f(x) = -x^2$

C) $f(x) = x^2 + 3$

D) $f(x) = x^2 - 3$

All you need to correctly answer this question is to know the parent graph of x^2 and the two transformation rules we just learned. The graph of choice (A) is shown at the top of page 424 and the graph of choice (B) is shown on the bottom of page 424. Both will only touch one point on the x-axis, so those choices can be eliminated, since they only contain one x-intercept. The graphs of (C) and (D) are shown below:

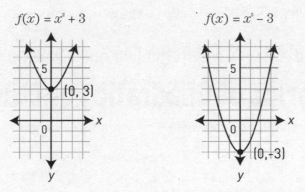

The first graph, choice (C), has no x-intercepts, while the second crosses the x-axis at two points, making choice (D) the correct answer.

Blind Spot

The test may also refer to x-intercepts as solutions, roots, or zeros.

Transformation Rule 3: $f(x - h) \rightarrow$ Horizontal Shift

The third transformation rule is a movement of the function to the right or left. Be careful with this transformation, as the graph moves opposite to the direction you would expect. For instance, the function $f(x - 2)$ would shift a graph 2 units to the right, while the function $f(x + 2)$ would shift the graph two units to the left. Here is an example that combines transformation rules 1 and 3:

If $f(x) = x^2$, which of the following is true about the graph of the function $y = -f(x - 4)$?

A) It's shifted 4 units to the left and opens down.

B) It's shifted 4 units to the left and opens up.

C) It's shifted 4 units to the right and opens down.

D) It's shifted 4 units to the right and opens up.

This question is asking you to simply describe the transformations that $-f(x - 4)$ would cause. Start with the negative sign on the outside. The negative means a vertical reflection, causing the parabola to open down and allowing us to eliminate choices (B) and (D). Since the -4 is inside the parentheses, it will cause the graph to move 4 units to the right, making the correct choice (C).

The three transformation rules we have seen so far can be used for any function. However, the next three concepts you'll learn will apply only to quadratic functions.

The Three Forms of Quadratic Functions

Quadratic functions or equations can be written in one of three forms:

1) Vertex Form

2) Standard form

3) Factored Form

Vertex Form

Some quadratic functions will be written in what is called vertex form, which, not surprisingly, shows the vertex of the parabola. These functions look like this:

$$f(x) = a(x - h)^2 + k$$

The vertex of the parabola will always be (h, k), with the x-coordinate of the vertex being h (the opposite of the number being added or subtracted inside the parentheses). The y-coordinate of the vertex, k, is the number that is added or subtracted outside the parentheses. The number in front of the parentheses, a, tells you if the parabola opens up (if it's positive) or down (if it's negative). This form is just an application of the transformation rules we just learned.

Take a look at the equation $y = (x - 1)^2 + 5$. We know the vertex of the parabola is at $(1, 5)$, and we know it opens up because a is positive. Quadratic functions written in vertex form are great because no work is needed to find the vertex. Here is an example:

Which of the following equations, when graphed, represents a parabola that opens down and has a vertex at $(1, 5)$?

A) $y = -2(x - 1)^2 + 5$

B) $y = -2(x - 1)^2 - 5$

C) $y = -(x + 1)^2 + 5$

D) $y = 2(x - 1)^2 + 5$

Since the parabola opens down, there must be a negative number in front of the parentheses, so choice (D) can be eliminated. The x-coordinate of the vertex must be written with the opposite sign, so you can also eliminate choice (C). Finally, the y-coordinate stays positive, making the correct answer choice (A).

Here is another example that also uses the vertex form of a quadratic function.

If $f(x) = (x - 1)^2 + 4$ and $g(x) = a$ intersect at exactly one point, what is the value of a if a is a constant?

Let's begin by graphing the parabola, which has a vertex at $(1, 4)$ and opens up. We can also graph the line $y = a$, which is a horizontal line. In order for the two graphs to intersect at only one point, the horizontal line must go through the vertex. If it were any higher, it would cross two points of the parabola, and if it were any lower, it would not intersect the parabola at any points.

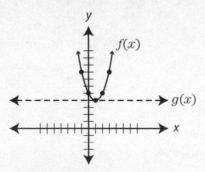

To find the value of a, just determine how far up the y-axis the vertex is, so $a = 4$.

Standard Form

The standard form of a quadratic function is $f(x) = ax^2 + bx + c$, with c being the y-intercept. If a is positive, the parabola opens up, and if a is negative, the parabola opens down. You can also find the x-coordinate of the vertex of the parabola by using the formula $\frac{-b}{2a}$.

What is the minimum value of the function $f(x) = 2x^2 - 8x + 3$?

A) –6

B) –5

C) 2

D) 3

We can identify this function as a quadratic and therefore know the graph will be a parabola that opens upward. The minimum of a parabola is the vertex, so we can use the formula $\frac{-b}{2a}$ to find the x-coordinate, which is $\frac{-(-6)}{2(2)}$, or 2. The question is asking for the "value" of the function, which refers to the y-coordinate, and can be found by plugging 2 in for x, as shown below:

$$f(x) = 2(2)^2 - 6(2) + 3 = -5$$

The correct answer is choice (B).

Completing the Square

You may also be required to rewrite a quadratic written in standard form into vertex form. This can be done using a method called completing the square. Here is an example:

The function $f(x) = x^2 + 6x + 4$, written in vertex form, is equivalent to which of the following?

A) $f(x) = (x - 3)^2 - 5$

B) $f(x) = (x + 3)^2 - 5$

C) $f(x) = (x - 3)^2 + 5$

D) $f(x) = (x + 3)^2 + 5$

The first step to completing the square is to replace $f(x)$ with 0, and move the constant (the number without a variable) over to that side, leaving you with:

$$x^2 + 6x = -4$$

The next step is to create a perfect square trinomial by dividing the coefficient in front of the x by 2 and then squaring it, which results in 9. We will add that number to both sides of the equation.

$$x^2 + 6x + 9 = 5$$

Since the left side is something called a perfect square trinomial, we can factor it to $(x + 3)(x + 3)$, or $(x + 3)^2$. We can then subtract 5 from both sides, resulting in $(x + 3)^2 - 5 = 0$. By replacing 0 with $f(x)$, the final answer will be $f(x) = (x + 3)^2 - 5$, or choice (B).

You could also have used the formula $\frac{-b}{2a}$ to identify the vertex.

Standard Form to Factored Form

Many quadratic equations and functions written in standard form can be factored to identify the x-intercepts.

For example, the equation $y = x^2 + x - 12$ can be rewritten as $y = (x + 4)(x - 3)$. You can then use the zero product property to identify the x-intercepts are at $(-4, 0)$ and $(3, 0)$. We'll talk more about factored form on the next page.

Note that not all quadratics written in standard form can be factored. However, you may need to determine how many x-intercepts are contained within a quadratic function written in standard form. To do this, you can use what is called the discriminant, or $b^2 - 4ac$. This may look familiar, as it is part of the quadratic formula.

A positive discriminant will have two x-intercepts, a discriminant of zero has one x-intercept, and a negative discriminant will have no x-intercepts.

How many solutions does the function $f(x) = 2x^2 - x + 5$ have?

A) None

B) One

C) Two

D) Three

Since you are looking for the number of solutions, which are the same as x-intercepts, just substitute the coefficients into $b^2 - 4ac$.

$$(-1)^2 - 4(2)(5) = -39$$

Don't forget order of operations when solving these problems! The discriminant is -39, which means there are no solutions, or choice (A).

Factored Form

The final form we will cover is factored form, which is also referred to as intercept form because you can quickly identify the x-intercepts. Take the equation $y = (x - 5)(x + 1)$, for example. If you set both factors equal to 0 and solve, you get $x = 5$ and $x = -1$.

This example that has a function written in factored form:

What is the x-coordinate of the vertex of the function below?

$$f(x) = (x - 6)(x + 2)$$

This is a quadratic function written in factored form, so we can identify the x-intercepts as $x = 6$ and $x = -2$. We also know the parabola will open up, since there is not a negative in front of the parentheses.

Since every parabola is symmetrical, the vertex is always located in between the x-intercepts of the parabola. It is actually the midpoint of the x-intercepts and can be found by adding the x-intercepts together and dividing by 2. To find the x-coordinate of the vertex from the function above, simply find the average of 6 and -2, as shown below:

$$\frac{6 + (-2)}{2} = \frac{4}{2} = 2$$

Here is a graph of the quadratic you just worked with.

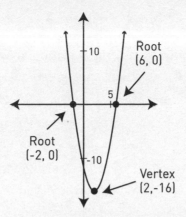

Notice how the vertex is in the middle of the two roots. The example above asked you to find the x-coordinate of the vertex, but how would you find the y-coordinate? Just plug in 2 in for x in the original function, or $(2-6)(2+2)$, and you will get -16.

Hint

Remember these key points:

- Factored form shows you the x-intercepts.

- Vertex form shows you the vertex.

- The terms "minimum" and "maximum" are ways of describing the vertex.

- The vertex is the midpoint, or the average of the two x-intercepts.

Here is one more challenging example that will require all your quadratic expertise!

$$y = 2(x + 6)(x - 4)$$

Which of the following is equivalent to the equation above and is written in vertex form?

A) $y = 2x^2 + 4x - 48$

B) $y = 2(x + 1)^2 - 50$

C) $y = 2x(x + 1) - 50$

D) $y = 2(x + 1)^2 - 48$

This is a great example of a question that can be answered using creativity and resourcefulness, as there are so many possible ways of finding the correct answer.

Since the question is asking for the answer in vertex form, or $y = a(x-h)^2 + k$, you can eliminate choice (A) because it is written in standard form, and choice (C) because it is not in the correct form.

Because you are left between choices (B) and (D), you will need to identify the correct vertex for the original equation. The best strategy for this is to find the midpoint of the two x-intercepts, which are at $x = -6$ and $x = 4$.

$$\frac{(-6) + 4}{2} = -\frac{2}{2} = -1$$

This tells you the x-coordinate of the vertex is at -1. To find the y-coordinate, you need to plug the x-coordinate into the original equation, as shown below:

$$y = 2(-1 + 6)(-1 - 4)$$

$$y = 2(5)(-5) = -50$$

Now you know the vertex is at $(-1, -50)$, which makes the correct answer choice (B).

Knowing the meaning of the words "domain" and "range" can have a positive impact on your score. The domain is the set of all possible x-values, and the range is the set of all possible y-values. In the previous example, the range is $y \geq -50$.

Graphs of Polynomials

Many of the concepts that apply to quadratic functions will also apply to polynomial functions, which are another advanced math topic. A quadratic function is a type of polynomial, as polynomial terms can be written as ax^n and polynomial expressions may contain multiple terms. Here are some examples of polynomial functions you may see:

$$f(x) = x^4 - 2x^3 + x^2 + 4x - 1$$

$$g(x) = -(x + 1)^3(x + 6)$$

While graphs of polynomials can get complicated, for the SAT there are only a few things you need to know, and you already know most of them. Polynomials can be written in factored form and, just like with quadratics, factored form will allow you to quickly find the x-intercepts.

Here is an example that contains a polynomial function.

Which of the following are the zeros of the function $h(x) = (x + 1)(x - 1)(x - 2)^2$?

A) $x = -1, x = 1, x = -2$

B) $x = -1, x = 1, x = 2$

C) $x = -1, x = 1, x = 4$

D) $x = -1, x = 1, x = -4$

To find the zeros, which are the same as the x-intercepts, just set each factor equal to 0 and solve, as shown below:

$$x + 1 = 0$$

$$x - 1 = 0$$

$$(x - 2)^2 = 0$$

Solving the first two equations is simple and gives you x-intercepts at -1 and 1. The last equation is a little bit different, but after you take the square root of both sides of the equation, $(x - 2)$ is still equal to zero, so the final x-intercept will be 2. Notice how the squaring of the factor has no effect on the value of the x-intercept.

The square, since it is an even power, will change the way the graph behaves at that x-intercept; it will "bounce" off the x-axis. This is more of an advanced topic and if you have graphed polynomials before you know what this means. Do not worry if this is confusing; just focus on finding the x-intercepts.

Here is a crazy-looking polynomial example for you to analyze:

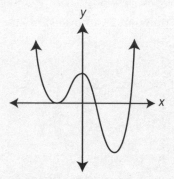

Which of the following functions could represent the graph shown above?

A) $f(x) = 2(x - 2)^4(x + 3)^3(x - 6)$

B) $f(x) = 2(x + 3)^2 (x - 2)(x - 6)$

C) $f(x) = 2(x + 2)^3(x - 3)^2(x + 6)$

D) $f(x) = 2(x + 2)^3(x - 3)^2(x + 6)$

Mindset Tip

Focus on what you know. Sometimes understanding only certain key concepts will be enough to solve the problem. For example, just being able to identify a quadratic function written in vertex form may be enough to find the correct answer.

If you were to encounter this question on test day, simply begin by identifying the x-intercepts from the graph, which are approximately $x = 2$, $x = -3$, $x = 6$. You can now use this information to eliminate answer choices. Since finding the x-intercepts requires you to set each factor equal to zero and solve, the correct factors would be $(x-2)$, $(x+3)$, and $(x-6)$, which appear in answer choices (A) and (B). So, you can eliminate choices (C) and (D).

Notice what is happening at the x-intercept of $(-3, 0)$. It is bouncing off the x-axis, which means the factor of $(x+3)$ must be raised to an even power, just like answer choice (B), which is the correct answer.

PRACTICE

1) What is the x-value of the vertex of the function $f(x) = -(x-10)(x+1)$?

2) What is the y-value of the vertex of the function $f(x) = -2(x+6)(x+2)$?

3) If the equations shown below intersect at two points and a is a constant, which of the following could be the value of a?

$$y = (x-1)^2 + 3$$

$$y = a$$

A) -1 **C)** 3

B) 2 **D)** 4

4) What is the minimum value of the function $f(x) = 2x^2 - 4x + 1$?

A) -1 **C)** 1

B) 0 **D)** 2

5) Which of the following represents the range of the equation $y = -(x+4)^2 + 2$?

A) $y \le 2$ **C)** $y \ge 2$

B) $y \le -4$ **D)** $y \ge -4$

6) Which of the following equations could represent the graph below?

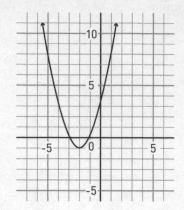

A) $y = (x + 1)(x - 3)$

B) $y = (x - 2)^2 - 1$

C) $y = x^2 + 4x - 3$

D) $y = x^2 + 4x + 3$

7) If the equation of a parabola was given as $y = a(x - 2)^2 - 3$ and passes through the point $(1, -1)$, what is the value of a?

A) −2

B) −1

C) 1

D) 2

8) The graph of $f(x)$ is shown below. What is the y-intercept of $y = f(x) - 3$?

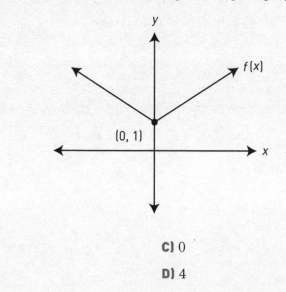

A) −3

B) −2

C) 0

D) 4

9) Which of the following is a polynomial with four roots?

A) $y = (x + 2)^2(x - 2)^2$

C) $y = (x^2 + 1)(x - 1)(x + 3)$

B) $y = (x - 1)^2(x - 3)(x + 5)$

D) $y = (x^2 - 4)(x + 1)(x - 1)$

10) What are the x-intercepts of the equation $y = x(x - 2)(x + 6)$?

A) $x = -6$ and $x = 2$

C) $x = -2$, $x = 0$, and $x = 6$

B) $x = -6$, $x = 0$, and $x = 2$

D) $x = -2$ and $x = 6$

11) If a quadratic function has x-intercepts at $(2, 0)$ and $(4, 0)$, which of the following is a factor of the function?

A) x

C) $x + 4$

B) $x + 2$

D) $x - 4$

12) What is one possible solution to the equation $x^3 + x^2 - 9x - 9 = 0$, given that $x > 0$?

Answers

1) $\frac{9}{2}$ or 4.5

2) 8

3) D

4) A

5) A

6) D

7) D

8) B

9) D

10) B

11) D

12) $x = 3$

UNTIMED COLLEGE BOARD PRACTICE

Complete the following College Board practice problems from College Board's *The Official SAT Study Guide* or online at www.collegeboard.org. Review answers after completing.

Test 1, Math: Calculator, #30

Test 2, Math: No Calculator, #10

Test 2, Math: Calculator, #7, 29

Test 3, Math: No Calculator, #12, 16

Test 3, Math: Calculator, #12, 16

Test 4, Math: No Calculator, #11

Test 4, Math: Calculator, #12, 28, 30

Chapter **16**

Thinking Dangerously

In the past few weeks, you have broken the bad habits that had previously limited your potential. You have worn a groove in your mind through consistent practice and mindset training, which will now allow you to build positive mental habits. You have set goals at the beginning of this journey that you hope to reach. These are all highly positive steps, but they are just the beginning.

Now that you have climbed with us to reach this point, it is time to look down and realize the ground you stand on is actually a springboard that can propel you into a limitless sky. Welcome to the beginning of your potential.

To harness the full power of your potential, you must begin to think differently—to think dangerously. Throughout your life, you have been mostly programmed to think safely and to set reachable goals. Parents and teachers wanted to see you succeed, to watch you revel in your successes rather than wallow in defeat after pursuing an out-of-reach goal. While this might have served you then, it does not serve you now.

Now that you have a growth mindset and see failure as opportunity, you can make one final adjustment to your thought process by avoiding "safe thinking," which is predicated upon self-limiting beliefs that tether you to mediocrity.

You might say, "Well, I know what I can do. I'm going to shoot for a 1200, that's good enough for me!" Eliminate the phrase "good enough for me;" don't fear dreaming too big! Instead, fear not dreaming big enough. If you are always afraid of being let down, you will never rise up in the first place. Remember, if we think safely, we will only ever lead safe, mediocre lives. It is time to think dangerously!

When we say "think dangerously," we are not talking about actual danger here. We don't want you driving dangerously on your way to the test. Rather, we want you to think in a way that allows your true self to be unleashed—the self that existed before you felt boxed in by artificial measures of your ability, like GPA and class rank.

When you think dangerously, you don't worry about your goals. Criticisms and warnings, like "that might be shooting too high," fall on deaf ears. You don't worry about the details of how you'll get there, because you have no doubt that you eventually will.

People who think dangerously aren't afraid to pursue crazy dreams. Dangerous thinkers push past the limits of their capabilities. There is no fear of getting a question wrong or not achieving a goal, because every step you take is a step forward.

Writing and Language Test: Special Cases and Timed Practice II

Before we begin our second timed practice, let's take a moment to review some of the more difficult questions in the Writing and Language section. This is the Danger Zone: these questions might intimidate the regular, safe-thinking student, but they are a welcome challenge to the dangerous thinker. The dangerous thinker realizes that these special cases, when mastered, yield insights that can be applied to a multitude of different grammar questions and can thus drastically increase your score.

Below is a sample passage and five questions that illustrate the most important special cases of the Writing and Language Danger Zone.

Over the past 10 years, the use of tablets and smart phones has increased dramatically among preteens. Now at least one in three preteens owns and operates a smart phone, **1** this is highly troubling unto itself. The current average use time, however, has also increased among preteens and teenagers. Ten years ago, before the app boom (a period of time when the number of apps available for smart devices tripled in **2** one year, average use was around 2 hours per day. In 2017, when study X was conducted, we found that this average use time had doubled to 4 hours per day. Teens claim that the "I" technology is an integral part of their lives and cannot be eliminated. The tablet (for streaming services) and the smart phone **3** (an expensive device) have become as basic a necessity as food or water. Many also believe these devices teach independence and accelerate intellectual growth, but there are actually myriad negative effects of the increased reliance on and use of smart phones in preteens and teens. Study X also found that increased use of smart phones severely stymied the development of preteens' interpersonal skills, while also contributing to a rise in social phobias. **4** Teenagers in high school reported lower self-esteem on average and trouble sleeping on a weekly basis. Sure, smart technology can do a number of great things, like provide directions, call a ride, or look up a phrase in Italian. **5** But, the future of our children is indeed in jeopardy.

Special Case 1: The Relative Clause

A relative clause is a dependent clause that starts with *who*, *whom*, *whose*, *that*, or *which*, and adds additional information about another part of the sentence to which it relates. These are important to understand because some questions will require you to make an independent clause dependent. On the SAT, you'll recognize these questions by a comma right outside of the underlined portion.

1

A) NO CHANGE

B) these are highly troubling unto themselves

C) who is highly troubling unto itself

D) which is highly troubling unto itself

For this question, you must perform the sentence test, even though no punctuation point is underlined. You will see that the first clause, "Now at least one in three teens owns and operates a smart phone," can stand alone as a sentence, and so can the second clause, "this is highly troubling unto itself." Usually, this would be an easy punctuation fix, but because the comma is not underlined, it cannot be changed.

Therefore, to solve this special case, you must make the underlined portion of the sentence fulfill the grammatical rules of the comma. This means you must make the underlined portion dependent. First, you must eliminate the pronoun "this," which in this case serves as a subject and makes the clause independent, and replace it with "which," a relative pronoun. A relative pronoun introduces a relative clause, which is a type of dependent clause that modifies or describes another part of the sentence.

Choice (B) is incorrect because "these" creates a pronoun error and does not make the clause dependent. Both choices (C) and (D) make the clause dependent by using relative pronouns, but "who" in choice (C) is for people and this phrase is relating to an idea, not a person. Thus, (C) is incorrect. The answer must be (D).

Look at some examples of relative clauses in action:

- The fish **that** Rob caught was humongous.

- The third experiment of the series yielded tangible results, **which** came as a surprise to many of the older scientists.

- My dad, **whom** I respect, recently retired.

- The concert, **which** lasted all day, attracted people from all over the world.

There are some other grammatical nuances to these types of clauses. But on the SAT, all you need to be able to do is replace an independent clause with a dependent clause when the context of the sentence demands it by using one of the above bolded relative pronouns. As we alluded to earlier, *that* and *which* are for non-people, and *who* and *whom* are for people.

Special Case 2: Parentheses

Parentheses are another special case on the SAT and, although they follow the same rules of consistency as dashes and commas, there are a few important distinctions. Just like a pair of dashes or commas, parentheses are used to section off a part of the sentence. Also, parentheses must come in pairs; you cannot have one without the other. On the SAT, you will primarily be required to add a missing parenthesis, but it is also important to know the distinct punctuation rules that accompany parentheses. When the parenthetical material is not a complete sentence, punctuation always goes outside of parentheses. The only time punctuation goes inside parentheses is when the parenthetical material is a complete sentence unto itself.

2

A) NO CHANGE

B) one year,)

C) one year)

D) one year),

You have a couple of options in correcting this underlined portion. Choice (A) is incorrect because you cannot just have one parenthesis. Notice how earlier in the passage, there is an opening parenthesis: "Ten years ago, before the app boom (a period of time when the number of apps available for smart devices tripled…" That means you need to add a second parenthesis to close the parenthetical statement.

Next you must determine whether the comma goes inside or outside the parentheses. Because the parenthetical material "a period…one year" is not a complete sentence, you can eliminate choice (B).

You then have to figure out if you need a comma, so you must check the preceding sentence part. "Before the app boom" is an interrupting phrase with nonessential information, otherwise known as a nonrestrictive clause, which means you must bookend it with commas. Therefore, you need a comma after the parenthetical explanation of app boom. This leaves us with choice (D).

Special Case 3: The Supporting Example

One special type of question requires you to change the underlined portion of a sentence so that it adds a parallel supporting example that matches an earlier supporting example. These are more difficult because, rather than just deciding where a sentence belongs or if it should be deleted or kept, you must meet several criteria to answer correctly, taking into account both style and content. Here, style refers to parallel construction and content refers to the preceding context.

3 Which choice provides information that is most consistent in style and content with the description of devices?

A) NO CHANGE

B) in one's spare time

C) for social media

D) for outside of school

For this type of question, you must reread the sentence and pay attention to the sentence part that the underlined portion must be made parallel to. Notice that you must correct for both style and content, which is important, because an answer choice could fix one but not the other. Let's look at choice (D) as an example of this. Choice (D) makes the underlined portion parallel to "for streaming services" by using "for," but it does not correct for content. The first example lists a *use* of the tablet (for streaming services) and so the second example must list a *use* of the smart phone. "Social media" is the use listed, and so the answer is (C).

These types of questions are more common than you may think, so it is important to practice this type of double reading: reading for both content and style.

Special Case 4: Graph Insertion

This type of question requires you to decide whether or not a graph should be inserted in the passage. Usually, you are just asked to match the content of the passage with the information in the graph, so these graph insertion questions are unique. Think of these types of questions as cousins to the add/delete content questions. All you really have to decide is if the graph is relevant to the surrounding context.

4 At this point, the writer is considering adding the following graph:

Price Change of Smart Phones

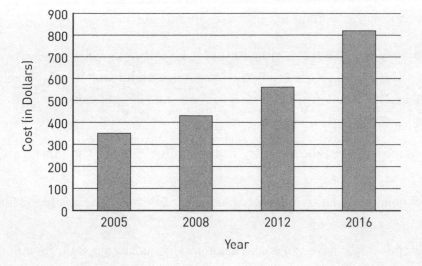

Should the writer make this addition here?

A) Yes, because it supports the claim that smart phones are expensive.

B) Yes, because it offers an important counterpoint to the author's argument.

C) No, because it presents information that is not directly related to the author's discussion of the harmful effects of smart phones.

D) No, because it does not provide information about the salaries of families with teenagers who use smart phones.

At first glance, this question may seem intimidating, and you may wonder just how you should answer it. This question, though, just like any other question about adding or deleting content, is rather straightforward. Remember that the number in the passage that corresponds to the question number is the place in the passage where you are being asked to insert this graph, so you must check that spot. In that location, the author is discussing harmful effects of smart devices related to social phobias, self-esteem, and sleeping. Nowhere in the passage, or at that location, is price discussed. Thus, you should already be leaning toward an answer of "No, do not add the content," but you should check the statements just to be sure.

There is no claim about the expensive nature of smart phones, so (A) is out, and the graph does not offer any counterpoint to the author's argument, so (B) is incorrect. Choice (D) is half right—the graph should not be added, but the reasoning is off topic. So, the answer is (C).

Special Case 5: The Concluding Sentence

Sometimes an expression of ideas question will ask you to examine and potentially revise the concluding sentence of a passage. In these situations, the simpler/shorter answer choice is usually not better. This is a very important exception to the rule of concision.

5 The writer wants a conclusion that recaps his argument about the negative impacts associated with smart phone use despite their current appeal. Which choice best accomplishes this goal?

A) NO CHANGE

B) Even though they have these amazing features, smart phones and tablets are still far too expensive.

C) Smart technology will be an inevitable part of our future, and this is highly detrimental to our children.

D) But, while they might have some benefits in the immediate present, their cumulative effect on the social and emotional development of our children must be examined and reflected upon.

Now, if you have read the entire passage (which you would need to do for a content-related question like this one), you should know exactly what the writer is trying to communicate. Choice (A) does not address the parameters of the question: recapping the negative impact while also touching upon the current appeal. Choice (B) can be eliminated because expense does not factor in to the author's argument, and (C) is off topic because it discusses smart phones as an "inevitable part of our future" and generalizes that they are "highly detrimental to our children."

This leaves you with choice (D). You may feel anxious about choosing this option due to its length and the fact that it starts with a conjunction. However, (D) does fulfill all the parameters set in the question, and it does so quite eloquently. It includes the current appeal of smart phones and recaps the main problems with smart tech as laid out by the author.

This teaches us an important point: sometimes it is necessary to choose the longer answer. "Shorter is better" is not always true, especially when the question is content-related or asks for a paragraph or passage wrap-up. (In the next chapter, we will explain why it is okay to start with the dreaded "But.")

Mindset Tip

The chapters surrounding this one require you to do a great deal of long timed practice to reinforce those neural pathways and build your grit and confidence. This chapter and the next also teach you the advanced grammar strategies and thinking that go hand in hand with great test taking. As you master these final lessons and complete the timed practice, let your mind wander out of the safe zone. Don't just think about attending "reasonable colleges," earning a "good score," or achieving "good enough." Start thinking dangerously.

You are nearing the end of this book, having built new mental habits designed to unlock your unknown potential. There is no reason to believe that the goals you set in the beginning still make sense for you. Set new goals; dangerous, grand goals; goals that might prompt others to say, "Don't get your hopes up." This is the type of dangerous thinking that should accompany this next timed practice.

Vocabulary Words 226–240

226) **yield** (v). a) to produce: *The farm yielded a bountiful harvest last year;* b) to return or produce payment in the form of profit or interest: *The investment yielded 5% a year;* c) to surrender: *The team's motto was never give up, never yield;* d) to cause: *They were unsure what new changes the revolution would yield.*

227) **endure** (v). to hold out against or withstand: *Prisoners of war often endure great suffering before they ever see freedom.*

228) **modest** (adj). humble; not egotistical or arrogant: *A modest man, Charles never looked for praise or acclaim.*

229) **versatile** (adj). a) capable of performing a variety of different tasks; resourceful and adaptable: *To be successful in Hollywood, you have to be very versatile actor who can sing, dance, and do stunts;* b) having or capable of many uses: *The Swiss Army knife is a versatile tool.*

230) **obstinate** (adj). stubborn: *Mules are known for being quite obstinate, although in reality they are excellent work animals.*

231) **reformation** (n). a rebuilding or restructuring: *The Protestant Reformation was a great restructuring of the church.*

232) **subvert** (v). to overthrow, undermine, or sabotage: *Communists try to subvert the principles of capitalism.*

233) **pious** (adj). a) showing a strong belief in God; very religious: *Jane was pious, visiting church every Sunday;* b) showing fake or hypocritical belief in religion: *Father John acted pious, but was not truly holy. He used his piety to merely increase his status.*

234) **paternal** (adj). fatherly: *Having no paternal figure in one's life can result in a difficult childhood.*

235) **subordinate** (adj). subservient or inferior: *Troy did not enjoy working in the mailroom at the giant law firm; since he was in a subordinate position, nearly everyone could boss him around.*

236) **simulate** (v). to act out, fake: *The astronauts were put into an Olympic swimming pool to simulate the conditions of the space station.*

237) **misconception** (n). fallacy, error, misunderstanding: *A commonly held misconception is that the Earth is flat.*

238) **devise** (v). to conceive of, invent, formulate: *Scientists are perpetually trying to devise a method for controlling the weather.*

239) **tranquility** (n). a state of peace and quiet: *When Faith hikes in nature, she experiences a sense of great calm and tranquility.*

240) **adhere** (v). to stick to; to abide by or obey: *Martin Luther King Jr. adhered to principles of nonviolence and refused to lash out against his enemies.*

Latin and Greek Roots 86–90

86) PEN/PUNI: punish/pay (impunity, penal, penalize, penalty, penance, penitence, penitent, penitentiary, punish, punitive, repent)

87) PHIL: love (philanthropist, philosophy, bibliophile, Philadelphia)

88) PHON/SON/TON: sound (telephone, euphony, cacophony, sonogram, sonic, monotonous, tone)

89) POLI: city (political, metropolis, cosmopolitan)

90) POV/PAU: poor (paucity, impoverished, poverty, pauper)

TIMED COLLEGE BOARD PRACTICE

Complete the following College Board practice problems from College Board's *The Official SAT Study Guide* or online at www.collegeboard.org. Review answers after completing.

Test 6, Writing and Language, #1–44

Math Test: Dangerous Math Topics

Some SAT math questions may require you to simplify a rational expression, such as $\frac{x^2-1}{x-1}$. While this may look straightforward, it is actually a dangerous task, because most students will move too quickly and cancel out the –1's, which is incorrect.

When simplifying rational expressions, you can only cancel out common factors, which the rational expression above does not have—yet. In order to simplify that expression, factor the numerator using the difference of two perfect squares method, which would give you $\frac{(x-1)(x+1)}{(x-1)}$. Now the numerator and denominator have common factors in $(x-1)$, which can cancel out, leaving you with only $(x + 1)$, which is the simplified answer.

Here is an example that is asking you to simplify a rational expression. Your first step should be to see if you can factor the numerator or denominator.

$$\frac{2x^2+6x+4}{2x+4}$$

The expression above is equivalent to which of the following?

A) $x + 6$

B) $x + 1$

C) $2x + 2$

D) $2x + 4$

The first thing to know is that you cannot cancel out the 4s. You can only cancel out factors. So, the key to solving this question is to factor. Start by factoring the numerator and then the denominator. Once factored, the expression can be rewritten as:

$$\frac{2(x+2)(x+1)}{2(x+2)}$$

Now that the expression is rewritten as factors, you can cancel out the ones that are the same. The 2s cancel out, and so do the $(x + 2)$s. This will leave you with just $x + 1$, or choice (B).

Simplifying Using Long Division

Not all rational expressions can be simplified with factoring. For example, the next question cannot be factored and will require an alternate strategy to find the correct answer. This next example will require you use what is called polynomial long division.

Mindset Tip

Polynomial long division seems like the most tedious, frustrating, complicated process in the entire math world. But appearances can be deceiving. The complicated nature of polynomial long division makes it hard for the SAT test makers to fool you with trick answers. Polynomial long division is what it is, and once you have mastered it, you have mastered it for life.

Hint

You may decide to use synthetic division, which you might have learned in class, to simplify this example. However, not all of these question types can be solved using synthetic division; therefore, it would be good to master long division.

Which of the following is equivalent to $\dfrac{x^2 + 6x + 10}{x - 1}$, given that $x \neq 1$?

A) $x - 10$

B) $7x - 10$

C) $x + 7 + \dfrac{17}{x - 1}$

D) $x + 7 + \dfrac{3}{x - 1}$

Since the numerator cannot be factored, we must use long division to simplify it.

Begin by setting up the equation in same way you would to divide two numbers:

$$x - 1 \overline{\smash{\big)}\, x^2 + 6x + 10}$$

Start by focusing only on the leading terms of each expression. In this case, x is the leading term in the expression $x - 1$, so you would ask, how many times does x go into x^2? You are looking to see what you can multiply x by to get x^2. Since it is x, put an x on top.

$$x - 1 \overline{\smash{\big)}\, x^2 + 6x + 10}^{x}$$

Now you can multiply x from the top by $(x - 1)$ to get $x^2 - 1x$, which will go underneath the $x^2 + 6x$. Now each term can be subtracted vertically.

$$
\begin{array}{r}
x \\
x-1\overline{\smash{\big)}\,x^2+6x+10} \\
x^2-1x
\end{array}
$$

Make sure to subtract each term. The first terms—in this case, the x^2s—should always cancel out.

After you've subtracted, you're left with $7x$, since $6x - (-1x)$ becomes addition. You can now bring the 10 down next to the $7x$, as shown below:

$$
\begin{array}{r}
x \\
x-1\overline{\smash{\big)}\,x^2+6x+10} \\
-\underline{(x^2-1x)} \downarrow \\
7x+10
\end{array}
$$

Now, look to see what number you can multiply the x from $(x - 1)$ by to get $7x$. That number, which is 7, will go on top, as shown below:

$$
\begin{array}{r}
x+7 \\
x-1\overline{\smash{\big)}\,x^2+6x+10} \\
-\underline{(x^2-1x)} \\
7x+10
\end{array}
$$

The same process we just used with the x can be repeated for the 7.

$$
\begin{array}{r}
x+7 \\
x-1\overline{\smash{\big)}\,x^2+6x+10} \\
-\underline{(x^2-1x)} \\
7x+10 \\
-\underline{(7x-7)} \\
17
\end{array}
$$

The next step is to subtract the two expressions, $(7x + 10)$ and $(7x - 7)$, which results in 17. This number that is left over cannot be divided into x, which represents the remainder. The remainder can be written the same way as it would if you were dividing two numbers—as the numerator in a fraction, in which the original expression is the denominator: $\dfrac{17}{x-1}$. This makes the final answer $x+7+\dfrac{17}{x-1}$, which is choice (C).

If the remainder of the previous example had been equal to zero, then the expression $x + 1$ would be a factor of $x^2 + 6x + 10$. Since there was a remainder, then $x + 1$ is not a factor.

Adding and Subtracting Rational Expressions

You may need to add or subtract fractions that contain algebraic expressions in the numerator or denominator. It is actually quite simple; just change the denominator so that both are the same. Let's try an example below:

$$\frac{1}{(x-4)} + \frac{1}{(x+2)}$$

Which of the following is equivalent to the expression above, if $x \neq 0$?

A) $\dfrac{2}{2x-2}$

B) $\dfrac{2x-2}{(x-4)(x+2)}$

C) $\dfrac{-2}{(x-4)(x+2)}$

D) $\dfrac{2}{(x-4)(x+2)}$

The common denominator is $(x - 4)(x + 2)$, which means you have to multiply the first fraction by $(x + 2)$ and the second fraction by $(x - 4)$. Remember to multiply the numerators as well. Here is the first step:

$$\frac{(x+2)}{(x-4)(x+2)} + \frac{(x-4)}{(x-4)(x+2)}$$

Now that both fractions have the same denominator, you can add the two numerators together, which requires combining like terms.

$$\frac{(x+2)+(x-4)}{(x-4)(x+2)}$$

$$\frac{2x-2}{(x-4)(x+2)}$$

The correct answer choice is (B).

Here is another example for you to try.

$$\frac{1}{(x-1)} + \frac{1}{3(x-1)}$$

Which of the following is equivalent to the expression above?

A) $\frac{4}{3x-3}$

B) $\frac{2}{3x-3}$

C) $\frac{3}{3x-1}$

D) $\frac{2}{3(x-1)}$

To get the common denominator, just multiply the first fraction by 3. You'll get:

$$\frac{3(1)}{3(x-1)} + \frac{1}{3(x-1)}$$

Now, combine the two fractions by adding the numerators.

$$\frac{3+1}{3(x-1)}$$

When you add the numerators, you get $\frac{4}{3(x-1)}$, which is not an answer choice. However, by distributing the 3 in the denominator, you get answer choice (A).

PRACTICE A

Solve questions 1–4 using long division.

1) $\frac{x^2+5x-3}{x-2}$

2) $\frac{2x^2+3x+4}{x+2}$

3) $\frac{2x^2-9x+6}{2x+3}$

4) $\frac{6x^3+2x^2-6x+9}{2x+4}$

Simplify each expression.

5) $\dfrac{1}{x+1} + \dfrac{1}{x-4}$

6) $\dfrac{2}{x-4} + \dfrac{1}{2(x-4)}$

7) $\dfrac{1}{x+1} - \dfrac{1}{x-4}$

Solving Advanced Rational Equations

There are some rational equations that you may not be able to solve simply by multiplying or setting up as a proportion. You may need to use a method called clearing the denominators, which is done by multiplying each term by the common denominator of all the fractions. Here is an example:

$$\frac{2}{x} - \frac{3}{2} = \frac{1}{4}$$

If $x \neq 0$, what is the value of x in the equation above?

This equation could be solved by adding $\dfrac{3}{2}$ to both sides, but another approach would be to multiply each term by the common denominator of all the fractions. This would look like:

$$\frac{2 \cdot (2)(4)(x)}{x} + \frac{3 \cdot (2)(4)(x)}{2} = \frac{1 \cdot (2)(4)(x)}{4}$$

The purpose of doing this is to cancel out the denominator with its matching factor in the numerator. In the first fraction, the xs will cancel; in the second, the 2s will cancel; and the 4s will cancel in the third fraction. This will leave you with the following equation:

$$2(2)(4) - 3(4)x = 1(2)(x)$$

$$16 - 12x = 2x$$

Now you are left with a simpler equation, which can easily be solved by adding $12x$ to both sides.

$$16 = 14x$$

Now, divide by 14 to get $\dfrac{16}{14}$, or $\dfrac{8}{7}$.

Blind Spot

While completing these challenging multi-step questions, it is more likely that students will make careless mistakes. Stay focused throughout and pay attention to the little details.

Here is another, more challenging example:

Which of the following is a solution to the equation $\dfrac{2}{x} = \dfrac{3}{x+1} + \dfrac{1}{2}$, if $x \neq 0$ and $x \neq -1$?

A) -5

B) -4

C) 2

D) 4

To solve this dangerously difficult equation, begin by multiplying each term by the common denominator, which is $2x(x + 1)$.

$$\frac{2 \cdot (2)(x)(x+1)}{x} = \frac{3 \cdot (2)(x)(x+1)}{(x+1)} + \frac{1 \cdot (2)(x)(x+1)}{2}$$

After you cancel out the common factors, you are left with:

$$2 \cdot 2(x + 1) = 3 \cdot 2x + 1x \cdot (x + 1)$$

You can simplify this to get:

$$4x + 4 = 6x + x^2 + 1x$$

$$4x + 4 = x^2 + 7x$$

Since this leaves you with a quadratic equation, move all the terms to the right side.

$$0 = x^2 + 3x - 4$$

The easiest way to solve this equation is by factoring, so it can be rewritten as:

$$0 = (x + 4)(x - 1)$$

This can be solved as $x = -4$ and $x = 1$, making the correct answer choice (B).

The previous two examples contained statements such as $x \neq 0$ and $x \neq -1$. When answering these questions, do not let those statements throw you off, as they are only stating the domain of the function. The reason that these two questions contained such statements is because you can never have 0 in the denominator of a fraction, since that would make the fraction undefined. If x was equal to 0 or −1, the denominator would be equal to 0.

You can also use the concept of domain to answer the following question:

Which of the following is true about the domain of the function $f(x) = \dfrac{1}{x^2 + 6x + 8}$?

A) $x \neq 0$

B) $x \neq 6$

C) $x \neq -8$

D) $x \neq -4$ and $x \neq -2$

Since we know that a fraction can never have 0 in the denominator, set the denominator equal to 0 and then solve for x, as shown below:

$$x^2 + 6x + 8 = 0$$

$$(x + 4)(x + 2) = 0$$

$$x = -4 \text{ and } x = -2$$

Plugging in either of these two values, −4 and −2, would result in the denominator of 0, which makes the correct answer choice (D).

Rearranging Rock Mover Equations

We learned about rearranging equations in earlier Heart of Algebra chapters, but we never applied this skill to advanced equations. Now that we know how to solve advanced equations, let's apply these skills to some more challenging questions. The question below is a great example.

The root mean square velocity can be found using the formula $V = \sqrt{\dfrac{3Rt}{m}}$, with V being the velocity, R being the universal gas constant of 8.314 J/K, t being the temperature in Kelvin, and m being the mass. Which of the following correctly expresses the universal gas constant?

A) $R = \dfrac{V^2 m}{3t}$

B) $R = \dfrac{V^2 mt}{3}$

C) $R = \dfrac{m\sqrt{V}}{3t}$

D) $R = \dfrac{3V^2 t}{m}$

At first glance, to the untrained eye, this looks more like a science question than a math question. But by investigating the answer choices, you can see that the question is merely asking you to rearrange the formula and isolate R, which is the universal gas constant.

Your first instinct may be to substitute 8.314 into the formula. However, the answer choices do not contain the 8.314, so you do not want to complete this step.

To get your answer, you must first get rid of the square root by squaring both sides of the equation:

$$V^2 = \frac{3Rt}{m}$$

This equation is now easier to work with. You can eliminate the fraction by multiplying both sides by m.

$$V^2 m = 3Rt$$

One last step to get R by itself is to divide both sides by $3t$, which will give you:

$$\frac{V^2 m}{3t} = R$$

The correct answer is choice (A).

This was a tough question and you may not have been able to answer it correctly—yet. Do not put a limit on your abilities saying that you will not be able to solve these Rock Movers. Often, the things we say to ourselves determine if we succeed or fail.

Advanced Interpreting

Some questions will test your understanding of how formulas or equations operate, such as the example below:

> The area of the circle is given by the equation $A = \pi r^2$, with A being the area of the circle and r being the radius. If you doubled the radius of a certain circle, what would happen to the original area?
>
> A) It would stay the same.
>
> B) It would double.
>
> C) It would triple.
>
> D) It would quadruple.

There are a few ways to find the correct answer to the question and they both require you to use the given formula.

If we know the original radius is r, then the new radius, since it is doubled, is $2r$. So, to find the new area, plug $2r$ in for r in the equation $A = \pi r^2$, resulting in:

$$A = \pi(2r)^2$$

This is the key step—don't just square r, but square 2 as well, which will give you:

$$A = \pi(4r^2) \text{ or } A = 4\pi r^2$$

If we compare the $4\pi r^2$ to the original πr^2, it is clearly four times larger, making choice (D) the correct answer.

Another strategy to answering this question is to make up a number for the radius, such as 2.

If the radius is equal to 2, then the area would be 4π. To find the new area, double the radius of 2, which is 4, and plug that into the formula to get 16π. Now to finish solving, compare 4π and 16π to find that 16π is four times larger.

Complex Numbers

A complex number contains a real part combined with an imaginary part and can be written in the form $a + bi$, with a being the real part and bi being the imaginary part. You actually worked with complex numbers in Chapter 1, when you combined like terms. The next, more advanced step on the SAT is to multiply and divide complex numbers.

When working with complex numbers, or i, one important detail to know is that $i^2 = -1$. Anytime you see i^2, you can substitute in -1. Here is an example that requires you to multiply two complex numbers.

Which of the following is equivalent to $(2 + i)(3 - 4i)$?

A) $10 - 5i$

B) $10 + 5i$

C) $15i$

D) 15

To begin, distribute the first expression using the FOIL method, as shown below.

$$2(3) + 2(-4i) + i(3) + i(-4i)$$

$$6 - 8i + 3i - 4i^2$$

You can combine the like terms of $(-8i)$ and $(3i)$, while also substituting -1 in for i^2.

$$6 - 5i - 4(-1)$$

$$6 - 5i + 4$$

$$10 - 5i$$

The correct answer is choice (A).

Here is another example that can be solved with the same technique.

What is the value of $(2 + 3i)(2 - 3i)$?

You may notice that the two factors being multiplied are the same, but with opposite signs. This is a special case—watch what happens after you multiply them together.

$$(2 + 3i)(2 - 3i)$$

$$2(2) + 2(-3i) + 3i(2) + 3i(-3i)$$

$$4 - 6i + 6i - 9i^2$$

$$4 - 9(-1)$$

$$4 + 9$$

$$13$$

You are left with a real number. The imaginary component disappeared. Remember this concept for the next example.

Blind Spot

Questions containing complex or imaginary numbers may contain the statement $i = \sqrt{-1}$, which is not usually needed to answer the question, so it should not affect your approach. It is more important to remember that $i^2 = -1$.

Dividing Complex Numbers

There is a good chance you will be asked to divide complex numbers. While the process may appear complex, it is simple to follow and will most likely appear without twists or traps on the test.

Whenever you have a complex number in the denominator, you will want to multiply the numerator and denominator by its conjugate. The conjugate is the exact same expression, just with a different sign (+ / −) in the middle. For example, the conjugate of $(2 - i)$ would be $(2 + i)$.

When writing the conjugate, change only the sign between the number and the imaginary number. The previous example contains conjugate expressions and shows why they are used when dividing complex numbers: they eliminate the imaginary part.

To divide two complex numbers, multiply the numerator and denominator by the conjugate of the denominator. It sounds difficult, like a lot of math mumbo jumbo, but just know that as long as you learn and practice the strategies, regardless of what they are called, you will one day master these problems.

Here is an example for you to try.

Which of the following is equivalent to the expression $\frac{3-4i}{2+i}$?

A) $\frac{3}{2} - 4i$

B) $\frac{2}{5} + \frac{11i}{5}$

C) $\frac{2}{5} - \frac{11i}{5}$

D) $\frac{2}{3} - \frac{11i}{3}$

This question type is risky for most students and, as a result, some students do not even bother with it. However, you now know that this question can be solved by multiplying the numerator and denominator by $(2 - i)$ and thus can grab points that other students leave on the table.

$$\frac{(3-4i)(2-i)}{(2+i)(2-i)} = \frac{3(2)+3(-i)-4i(2)-4i(-i)}{2(2)+2(-i)+i(2)+i(-i)} = \frac{6-3i-8i+4i^2}{4-2i+2i-i^2}$$

Now you can combine like terms and substitute –1 in for i^2.

$$\frac{6-11i+4(-1)}{4-(-1)} = \frac{6-11i-4}{4+1} = \frac{2-11i}{5}$$

By peeking at the answer choices, you know to rewrite this rational expression as two fractions, keeping 5 in the denominator of both. This gives you $\frac{2}{5} - \frac{11i}{5}$, or choice (C).

PRACTICE B

1) If $x \neq 4$ and $x \neq -3$, which of the following is equivalent to $\dfrac{x^2 + 6x + 8}{x^2 + x - 12}$? Please simplify.

A) $\dfrac{(x+2)}{(x-3)}$

C) $x+4$

D) $x+2$

B) $\dfrac{(x+4)(x+2)}{(x+4)(x-3)}$

2) If $A = 2x - 4$ and $B = x + 2$, what is the value of $A + B^2$?

A) $x^2 - 6x$

C) $x(x+6)$

B) $x(x+2)$

D) $(x+4)(x+2)$

3) The expression below is the same as which of the following, given that x is greater than 0?

$$\frac{2}{x+4} + \frac{3}{x+3}$$

A) $\dfrac{5}{2x+7}$

C) $\dfrac{5x+7}{(x+4)(x+3)}$

B) $\dfrac{2x+7}{(x+4)(x+3)}$

D) $\dfrac{5x+18}{(x+4)(x+3)}$

4) Which of the following is equivalent to $3(1 + i) - 2i(3 - i)$?

A) $1 + 3i$

C) $3 - i$

B) $1 - 3i$

D) 4

5) Which of the following is equivalent to the expression $\dfrac{5-i}{1+2i}$?

A) $\dfrac{3-11i}{3}$

C) $\dfrac{7+11i}{5}$

B) $\dfrac{3+11i}{3}$

D) $\dfrac{7-11i}{5}$

6) $(a+b)\left(\dfrac{a}{2b}\right)$ is equivalent to which of the following?

A) $\dfrac{a^2}{2b} + \dfrac{a}{2}$

C) $2a$

B) $\dfrac{a^2 + a}{2}$

D) $\dfrac{a^a}{2b} + ab$

7) Which of the following are the solutions of to the equation $\dfrac{3}{x+4} + \dfrac{2}{x+1} = 1$, given that x is not equal to -4 or -1?

A) $x = \sqrt{7}$ and $x = -\sqrt{7}$

D) $x = 7$ and $x = -7$

B) $x = \sqrt{4}$ and $x = \sqrt{3}$

C) $x = -4$ and $x = -1$

8) Which of the following is equivalent to $\dfrac{2x^2+x-4}{x+1}$?

A) $x-4$

C) $2x-1+\dfrac{5}{x+1}$

B) $x-1+\dfrac{3}{x+1}$

D) $2x-1+\dfrac{-3}{x+1}$

Use the following to answer questions 9 and 10.

The formula for finding the volume of a cylinder is $V=\pi r^2 h$, with V being the volume, r being the radius, and h being the height.

9) Which of the following correctly displays the given formula, in terms of r?

A) $r=\sqrt{\dfrac{V}{\pi h}}$

C) $r=\dfrac{V^2}{h\pi}$

B) $r=\sqrt{\dfrac{Vh}{\pi}}$

D) $r=\left(\dfrac{V}{h\pi}\right)^2$

10) If the radius and the height of a cylinder were both doubled, which of the following would be true?

A) The volume would double.

C) The volume would be multiplied by 8.

B) The volume would be multiplied by 4.

D) The volume would be multiplied by 12.

Answers

Practice A (page 454)

1) $x+7+\dfrac{11}{x-2}$

2) $2x-1+\dfrac{6}{x+2}$

3) $x-6+\dfrac{24}{2x+3}$

4) $3x^2-5x+7-\dfrac{19}{2x+4}$

5) $\dfrac{2x-3}{(x+1)(x-4)}$ or $\dfrac{2x-3}{x^2-3x-4}$

6) $\dfrac{5}{2(x-4)}$ or $\dfrac{5}{2x-8}$

7) $\dfrac{-5}{(x+1)(x-4)}$ or $\dfrac{-5}{x^2-3x-4}$

Practice B (page 463)

1) A

2) C

3) D

4) B

5) A

6) A

7) A

8) D

9) A

10) C

UNTIMED COLLEGE BOARD PRACTICE

Complete the following College Board practice problems from College Board's *The Official SAT Study Guide* or online at www.collegeboard.org. Review answers after completing.

Test 1, Math: No Calculator, #13

Test 1, Math: Calculator, #36

Test 2, Math: No Calculator, #11, 12, 15

Test 2, Math: Calculator, #22, 23

Test 3, Math: No Calculator, #5, 7, 13

Test 3, Math: Calculator, #13

Test 4, Math: No Calculator, #14

Test 4, Math: Calculator, #25, 35

Chapter **17**

Self-Image and Self-Confidence

"Change 'I think I can' to 'I know I can.'"

Self-image and self-confidence are two sides of the same coin.

Self-image is a tricky thing. We all have one; we all believe we have certain strengths, weaknesses, and other traits. But where does self-image come from? None of you were born thinking you are a horrible test taker, or that you are the funny kid, the kid who's bad at math, or the weirdo outcast. Somewhere along the way, you had an experience, or even a pattern of experiences, that made you determine that this was who you are. Perhaps there is a pivotal event you can remember that shaped who you are, or, more accurately, who you *think* you are.

Self-image is just that: an image of the self, but not the true self. It is not innate, and it is not fixed.

Here is a helpful analogy:

When we get up in the morning, we shower, brush our teeth, get ready for school, put on our clothes, and then *put on ourselves*. Think of your self-image as just another item of clothing you don every day. And these clothes change slightly all throughout your life.

Why does this matter for the SAT? Well, sometimes students get it into their heads that the image they created for themselves, whether consciously or subconsciously, is who they actually are. And often these images are distorted, twisted, and bent beyond all recognition. It's like looking in a funhouse mirror and seeing a warped version of yourself. These negative self-images block them at every turn on the road to SAT success. They also create a sense of helplessness, and a "why bother" attitude toward difficult questions. "Why bother even trying on this math question? I know I'm the kid who's bad at math."

Strong self-confidence, which arises from a positive self-image, is also critical to success. Why is self-confidence on the SAT so important? Perhaps to answer this, it is best to understand the effect self-doubt, or a lack of self-confidence, has on you.

Self-doubt can impede your brain's functioning. Something strange happens in our brains when we doubt ourselves: we engage in something called mental chatter, essentially talking to ourselves in our heads. *Oh, but wait, I just selected A for the last two questions, so one can't be A,* or, *I thought I knew this, huh, that should have come out to 458.* This chatter might seem harmless, but it interrupts the brain's natural functioning. Suddenly, in the middle of solving a math problem or finding a grammatical error, the speech center of our brain barges in and creates confusion. Now what would normally be a smooth-functioning brain is a chaotic, sluggish mess. All of this because self-doubt makes us start questioning ourselves.

We need to learn to trust our brains and trust ourselves. The brain is a finely tuned machine and, with the right practice, it is more than capable of arriving at the correct answer, often quite intuitively.

But so many students come to us lacking confidence in themselves, riddled with self-doubt. It is a common problem for high-schoolers, many of whom feel like they are destined never to have self-confidence.

Let's get one thing straight: strong self-image and self-confidence don't happen by accident. These are developed through the intentional and deliberate actions that you take. They come from a combination of positive thinking, hard work, and focused effort on improving your skills.

You must take these steps to change your self-image and your self-confidence. Here is how to begin:

1) CUT YOURSELF SLACK. There is not a person in the world who, at some point, did not question his or her ability.

2) TAKE BABY STEPS. The first problems you tackle should be within your sphere of proximal development, which is a fancy term for the just-right difficulty level. You do not want to jump straight to the Rock Mover ultra-difficult questions. You also don't want to just do super-easy questions forever. Take on the easier questions first and work your way to tougher and tougher questions.

3) TACKLE ROCK MOVERS. The ultimate step in improving self-image and boosting your self-confidence is to tackle those questions that you don't think you can do. Once you have a couple Rock Movers under your belt, your self-confidence will begin to grow. More importantly, when you tackle Rock Movers, you create what we like to call a self-reinforcing cycle. Here is how it works: you answer a Rock Mover correctly, your confidence grows and, due to your increased confidence, you attempt and successfully answer an even more difficult Rock Mover, and so on and so forth. In this way, your confidence feeds your testing prowess, and your testing prowess feeds your confidence.

4) USE POSITIVE LANGUAGE. Start to use positive language when referring to yourself and avoid self-limiting put downs. "God, I suck at this." "Well, you're lucky I didn't figure out the tip, because my math is terrible." These subtle phrases are detrimental to your self-image. We become the words we use.

5) CHANGE YOUR BODY LANGUAGE. Start to adopt the body language (how you sit, how you walk, how you carry yourself, how you interact with others) of someone who has self-confidence. Interestingly enough, our brains actually take cues from our bodies so that if we slouch, avoid eye contact, or roll our shoulders forward, our subconscious minds interpret that body language and reinforce a poor self-image. So, stand straight, roll your shoulders back, stick your chest out, make eye contact, and act confident. Act confident, and then become confident.

Writing and Language: Timed Practice III

Punctuation errors occur in nearly one-third of the questions on the SAT, so it is crucial to continually review the punctuation rules tested on the SAT. Memorize these rules and practice until you know them by heart. This is very similar to memorizing formulas in math: once you know them and have practiced applying them, these punctuation questions are easy points on the SAT.

For a more in-depth review, see Chapter 11.

Review Punctuation Errors

1) The sentence test: A semicolon must separate two independent clauses.

> The team lost several games in a row; therefore, the coach decided
> to change the starting lineup.

2) The colon and dash rule: A colon or dash is typically preceded by an independent clause and used to set up a reason, example, explanation, or list. The clause that follows a colon or a dash either can be an independent or dependent clause. Dashes can also be used in place of commas to separate nonessential information from the sentence.

> Veronica enjoys many different activities: hiking, swimming, jogging.

> Veronica enjoys many different activities: she enjoys hiking, swimming, and jogging.

> Some people treat their pets—the dogs, cats, birds, etc., that traipse by their side—as little versions of themselves, calling them names like Harold, Sophie, and Mr. Fluffington.

3) The comma rule: A comma must separate items in a list or a dependent clause from the rest of the sentence, or be used to section off nonessential sentence items.

> The elephant, a crowd favorite, paraded around the circus tent.

4) The apostrophe rule: An apostrophe indicates possession. The apostrophe goes before the *s* if the word is singular and after the *s* if the word is plural. *It's* is not possessive, but an abbreviated form of *it is*.

> The body's immune system is what protects it from disease and infection.

Blind Alley: The Final Checkpoint

In this final section of grammar strategy review, we will learn about and review all the major blind spots of the Writing and Language Test. Once you pass this checkpoint, you will have all the training and skills you need to become a writing and language master and be ready for the final timed Writing and Language Test.

Let's take a look at a familiar passage:

In the science fiction novel *Ender's Game*, boys selected to enter battle school train on simulators akin to video games in order to prepare to fight the **1** Buggers. The Buggers are a hostile alien threat. The simulators create an immersive virtual experience in which the battle school cadet uses a joystick and other controls to navigate outer space and take out Buggers. This simulation training is a cornerstone of the novel and eventually what saves humanity. What is important to note about *Ender's Game,* though, is not the foresight Orson Scott Card showed with his rendering of a virtual reality–type scenario, but the age he chose

to make the people tasked with this simulator training and the job of saving humanity. Adults are not chosen to fly the simulators; children are. Why? Why could it be that the very fate of the planet is handed over to kids under the age of 15? The answer is **2** simple: they are better at it. Children are adaptable, malleable, and much more prepared to engage with new, different technologies than adults are. This is why it is illogical to deny children—the ones most suited for new technology— new technology.

Children must be raised in such a way that allows them to engage with new and different technology because these technologies represent new ways of communicating and interacting with information and society. The jobs that the children of today will be applying for will be grounded in these new means of communication and interaction. The inventions of tomorrow will be born of the minds of the children today, minds that need to be plugged into the techno-socio framework of society. **3** Granted, there is, of course, reasonable limits; infants should not be handed an iPad instead of a rattle. **4** Moreover, not long after these infants develop motor skills and the ability to recognize the world around them, they should be introduced to these technologies. It may not be from a hostile alien race, but our tech-savvy children will most certainly save humanity.

Blind Spot 1: Replacement of Underlined Part

Whenever you plug in an answer choice, you must ensure that you replace the entire underlined portion with your new answer. If it is underlined, it will be replaced, and if it is not underlined, it will remain. If you are going quickly, you may make the mistake of not fully replacing the underlined part, which could make you doubt your choice, since it will sound awkward without full replacement.

Take a look at this example:

1 Which choice most effectively combines the sentences at the underlined portion?

A) Buggers, being

B) Buggers, because they are

C) Buggers,

D) DELETE THE UNDERLINED PORTION

You can eliminate choices (A) and (B) because they both make the sentence awkward or overly wordy, but take a look at (D). Sometimes, deleting the underlined portion is correct because it makes the sentence more concise, but if you did that here, the sentence part would read: "in order to prepare to fight the a hostile alien threat." Clearly, this does not make any sense because you are missing the subject, "Buggers." But if you are going too quickly and not replacing the entire underlined portion, you might miss this Blind Spot. Thus, the answer is (C).

Blind Spot 2: The NO CHANGE Dilemma

On many of the questions on the Writing and Language Test, you have the "NO CHANGE" answer choice. To most students, this is the choice that haunts them, makes them doubt themselves, and gets into their heads. But, armed with knowledge of the test and a simple mindset adjustment, this can all be avoided.

First, some useful knowledge: about one in every five questions has a choice of NO CHANGE, which does not mean that every fifth question is NO CHANGE, but that on a test consisting of 44 questions, you can expect approximately seven to nine with NO CHANGE answers.

Second, a mindset adjustment: the SAT is randomized, which means there is no rhyme or reason to when a NO CHANGE will appear. It could be at the very beginning of the section or there could be two NO CHANGE questions in a row. Changing your answer choice because of how many NO CHANGE answers (or any other answer choices) you got in a row will always lower your score in the long run. Rather than try to game the test and allow the placement of these NO CHANGE answers to mess with your head, just treat each question separately and choose the best answer based on style, content, and grammar, regardless if it is NO CHANGE or not.

With that in mind, try this one.

2

A) NO CHANGE

B) simple;

C) simple, which is

D) simple, because

Wrong mindset: Question 2 can't already be NO CHANGE; they wouldn't throw a NO CHANGE at me this early on. Maybe I read it wrong and the semicolon is the better choice?

Right mindset: Okay, well I didn't hear an error right away when I read it aloud, but let me check the choices to be sure. The semicolon in (B) could work the sentence parts before and after the punctuation pass the sentence test, but a colon could also work with two independent clauses, so I will hold off on choosing yet. (C) is overly awkward and (D) does not convey the correct relationship between sentence parts. The clause after the colon, "they are better at it," is the answer to the question posed in the clause before the colon. This perfectly fits the criteria for the usage of a colon: setting up a list, reason, or example. The answer must be (A), NO CHANGE.

Notice how in the correct mindset for the question, the notion of how early this question is or how many NO CHANGEs there have been does not even factor into the student's head. She simply follows the writing and language method and trusts the skills she has acquired.

Blind Spot 3: New Errors Added In

Many of the questions on this section will include answer choices that correct the error in the underlined portion, but add a new error that was not present in the original text. These are designed to test your attention to detail and the thoroughness with which you review the answer choices. Look at the following question:

3

A) NO CHANGE

B) Granted, there are, of course, reasonable

C) Granted; there are, of course, reasonable

D) Granted, there is, of course, reasoned

After reading the sentence, you might hear the subject/verb agreement error with *is* and *limits*, but if you do not, upon checking the answer choices, you will notice that the verb is in question. You should then follow the strategy of drawing a line from the subject to the verb to see if they match. Once you do this and realize *is* must be *are* you can eliminate choices (A) and (D). Before choosing (B) or (C), though, look closely at each answer. You should notice that (C) adds a new error by replacing the comma after *Granted* with a semicolon. This would fail the sentence test because *Granted* cannot stand alone as a sentence. Thus, the answer is (B).

Blind Spot 4: Starting a Sentence with a Conjunction

At some point during your elementary, middle, or even high school career, an overworked, exasperated English teacher might have proclaimed, "Never start a sentence with a conjunction or the word because!" (Conjunctions are *for, and, nor, but, or, yet, so*—FANBOYS.) While this might have helped your weary English teacher in the moment by reducing the number of sentence fragments students were creating, the truth of the matter is that it is absolutely, perfectly, 100% okay to start a sentence with a conjunction. Some of the most important English language guides, including The *Chicago Manual of Style*, Garner's *Modern American Usage*, Fowler's *Modern English Usage*, and, most importantly, the College Board, all agree that starting a sentence with a coordinating conjunction is acceptable, and even dates to Old English. In fact, sometimes a conjunction at the beginning of the sentence enhances the rhetorical effect of the sentence or point.

Take a look at this question.

4

A) NO CHANGE

B) But, not long

C) Furthermore, not long

D) Consequently, not long

Since this question involves a transition error, you must reread the sentence before the underlined portion as well as the sentence with the underlined portion. Having done so, you should find that the relationship between the two sentences is a contrast. You can eliminate (A) and (C) since both of these terms add on to the previous idea. You can also eliminate (D) because "consequently" is a transition of consequence. This leaves you with (B), which you might normally have been wary about choosing, but since you know the fear of starting with a conjunction is unfounded, you can choose (B) confidently.

You have reached the end of the strategy section of the Writing and Language Test and are about to embark on your final timed practice. Realize that you now have within you all the writing and language tools you will ever need to conquer this section of the SAT, and that success is that much closer.

Vocabulary Words 241–255

241) **sway** (n). influence or authority: (v). to influence or persuade; *The boy was swayed by the persuasive advertisement on television.*

242) **alleged** (adj). unproven, suspected: *Before you are formally convicted by a jury, the crime is simply alleged.*

243) **vacillate** (v). to waver back and forth; to be indecisive: *Henry vacillated between the two choices: either get up and leave, or stay and face the bully.*

244) **temperament** (n). personality; the combination of mental, physical, and emotional traits: *People often opt to get golden retrievers due to their amiable, sweet temperament.*

245) **commonplace** (adj). ordinary, everyday, common: *Barry was not fazed by the sound of sirens—they were commonplace in the city, where he'd lived for many years.*

246) **colloquial** (adj). informal, conversational, slang: *"What's up?" is a colloquial expression.*

247) **autocratic** (adj). tyrannical, oppressive, domineering: *Mussolini was known as an autocratic dictator.*

248) **render** (v). to cause to be or become; make: *The sight of his longtime crush rendered Jerry speechless and weak in the knees.*

249) **cow** (v). to intimidate, frighten: *Cowed by the sight of the dragon, the not-so-brave knight hightailed it back to his castle.*

250) **allude** (v). to refer casually or indirectly: *In his lecture, the professor frequently alluded to the Bible as a means of explaining certain stories.*

251) **tangible** (adj). concrete, physical; real: *Happiness is not tangible; you cannot go out to the store and buy it or physically share it with another. It is an abstract concept.*

252) **biased** (adj). favoring one person or side over another: *Many have come to believe that news programs are biased in their presentation of the facts.*

253) **gross** (adj). a) the total, without deductions: *Your gross pay before taxes will always be more than your net pay after all the deductions have been taken out;* b) extreme in nature or flagrant: *The politician was accused of a gross misuse of public funds;* c) unrefined or unsophisticated, crude: *Although it was gross sketch, it was enough to help the witness identify the assailant;* d) obscene or vulgar: *The remarks he made to the substitute teacher were gross and highly inappropriate.*

254) **vain** (adj). a) unproductive; ineffective or futile: *The town's attempts to stop the floodwaters were in vain because the storm was too ferocious;* b) obsessed with oneself: *A common criticism of celebrities is that they are vain and superficial.*

255) **aggregate** (n). a) the sum, total, or cumulative amount: *The aggregate of votes clearly showed that Harvey had won in a landslide;* (v). b) to collect into one sum or mass: *The results were aggregated after the experiment;* (adj). c) combined: *The aggregate survey results were used to determine the overall morale of the business.*

Latin and Greek Roots (91–95)

91) POLY: many (polytheistic, polyamorous, polygon, polynomial)

92) PORT: carry (transport, export, import, deport, importance)

93) PREHEND: grasp (apprehend, comprehend, reprehend)

94) PRO: a lot, for (prolific, profuse, prodigious, prodigal, proliferate, prodigy)

95) QUER/QUES: ask/seek (question, quest, query, querulous)

Mindset Tip

After taking the time to complete this latest 35-minute practice section and study these vocabulary words and roots, put the book aside, walk to a mirror, and look at yourself. Think of the you that you put on every morning and the you that you dream of becoming. Think of the you that you are currently transforming into through hard work, practice, and new neural pathways. Your self-image is changing, and soon enough the person you see in the mirror will be the person you've always believed would master the SAT—the person who looks a little well-worked after a long practice section, the person with some pen stains or eraser shavings on his or her clothes, sleeves rolled up, eyes focused.

TIMED COLLEGE BOARD PRACTICE

Complete the following College Board practice problems from College Board's *The Official SAT Study Guide* or online at www.collegeboard.org. Review answers after completing.

Test 7, Writing and Language, #1–44

Math Test: Timed Practice

In this chapter, you will complete a timed practice consisting of both the No Calculator and Calculator sections of practice test 7.

Let's begin by reviewing some important points to remember as you take this test.

Focus on the Approach

It is important to approach each question, especially word problems, using the same method:

1) Carefully read the question, collecting and organizing the key information.

2) Choose the correct strategy to solve with.

3) Make sure you correctly answer the question.

Here is an example that is best solved using the steps listed above.

> Sean and Jill are using a hose to fill their swimming pool for the summer. The amount of water in their pool is given by the equation $T = 24m + 100$, with m being the number of minutes the hose has been on and T being the total amount of water, in gallons, in their pool. Which of the following is true if $m = 0$?
>
> A) It takes 24 minutes to fill up the pool.
>
> B) It takes 100 minutes to fill up the pool.
>
> C) There are 24 gallons of water in the pool before the hose is turned on.
>
> D) There are 100 gallons of water in the pool before the hose is turned on.

After carefully reading the question, it is important to identify the key information, which would be the equation $T = 24m + 100$ and $m = 0$. Next, you will determine the strategy to solve, which will be interpreting a part of an equation and determining the meaning of m being equal to zero.

In the equation, the T represents the total, the 24 is the number of gallons the volume of the pool increases by each minute, and the 100 is the initial amount of water in the pool. By saying that m is 0, you are saying that no time has elapsed. You can also plug 0 in for m to get $T = 100$. So, at 0 minutes, the total is equal to 100 gallons.

You can now go through each answer choice and eliminate all incorrect choices and identify the correct one.

Choices (A) and (B) do not make sense because the pool will not be filled at 0 minutes, and choice (C) is not correct either, making the correct answer choice (D).

Knowing the Level of Difficulty of the Question

In the previous timed practice, we talked about the questions getting progressively more difficult as you go and the importance of knowing where you are in the section. For example, if you are answering question 2, you can expect it to be easy, and you most likely do not have to worry about any tricks or traps. However, if you see a similar style question later in the test, realize that you might have to avoid a trap and it may not be as easy as it appears. Let's look at an example of a question that may appear somewhere in the middle of either multiple-choice section.

If $a = \sqrt{x} + 2$ and $x \geq 0$, which of the following is equivalent to a^2?

A) $x + 2$

B) $x + 4$

C) $x + 4\sqrt{x} + 4$

D) $x + 4x + 4$

This example, while not a complex math topic, is one that should be approached carefully, as you could easily fall for the trap that this question presents.

Most students would correctly rewrite a^2 as $(\sqrt{x} + 2)^2$. However, many students, especially under testing conditions, will incorrectly say this is equivalent to $x + 4$, which is answer choice (B).

The student that understands the layout of the section realizes that this question may be moderately difficult, is on the lookout for missteps and traps, and avoids this careless mistake by rewriting $(\sqrt{x} + 2)^2$ as $(\sqrt{x} + 2)(\sqrt{x} + 2)$. That student can distribute using FOIL to get $x + 2\sqrt{x} + 2\sqrt{x} + 4$, which is the same as choice (C).

Big-Picture Math

Many questions can be solved using multiple strategies. When you are flexible in your thinking, in a positive state of mind, and have confidence in your abilities, many of these strategies will magically come to you when you need them. It does not matter the strategy you use to solve a question; all that matters is you choose one that works for you. Here is an example of a question that can be solved using many methods:

> The function $f(x) = 3x^2 - 27$, when graphed on the coordinate plane, has x-intercepts at which of the following points?
>
> A) $(-3, 0)$ and $(27, 0)$
>
> B) $(-3, 0)$ and $(3, 0)$
>
> C) $(-9, 0)$ and $(9, 0)$
>
> D) $(0, 0)$ and $(9, 0)$

Since the question is asking us to find the x-intercepts, we can set the function equal to zero and then solve for x.

$$3x^2 - 27 = 0$$

This can be solved using either factoring or by taking the square root of both sides. Both methods are shown below:

Solving with Factoring	**Solving with Square Root**
$3(x^2 - 9) = 0$	$3x^2 - 27 = 0$
	$+ 27 + 27$
Factor using difference of two perfect squares	
	$3x^2 = 27$
$3(x - 3)(x + 3) = 0$	
	$x^2 = 9$
$x = 3$ and $x = -3$	
	$x = 3$ and $x = -3$

When taking the square root of both sides, make sure to include the positive and negative solutions.

Remember that a few questions on each test can be solved by plugging in answer choices, including the previous example.

Sheep in Wolf's Clothing

Remember not to be intimidated by questions you have never seen. There are many ways to write math equations, which is why rearranging is such a useful skill. To put a different spin on the timeless fairy tale, what looks like a wolf may just a sheep masquerading in wolf's clothing. Next time you see an elaborately written new equation, take a deep breath and have faith that one of the many strategies you know will work, and you will find a starting point.

Here is a question that you have most likely never seen before, but will be capable of solving correctly. Just like in the previous example, there are multiple ways to solve it.

What is the product of the solutions to the equation $(x + 4)^2 + 6(x + 4) = -8$?

There are two ways to solve this question. The method that you would probably use is also the one that takes the most time, but will still allow you to find the correct answer. Start by squaring the binomial and distributing the 6.

$$x^2 + 8x + 16 + 6x + 24 = -8$$

Since this is a quadratic equation that can be solved by factoring, you will want to set the equation equal to 0 by adding 8 to both sides. You can then combine like terms to get:

$$x^2 + 14x + 48 = 0$$

This can be factored and solved as shown below:

$$(x + 6)(x + 8) = 0$$

$$x = -6 \text{ and } x = -8$$

Remember to always answer the question completely. In this one, since they ask for the product of the two solutions, you want to multiply −6 and −8 to get 48.

This method will obviously yield the correct answer, but there is a more efficient way to solve this question. If you add 8 to both sides, you get:

$$(x + 4)^2 + 6(x + 4) + 8 = 0$$

Notice that the first two terms of the equation both contain an $(x + 4)$. If you call that expression a, you can rewrite the equation as $a^2 + 6a + 8 = 0$, which can then be factored to $(a + 4)(a + 2) = 0$. When you solve this equation, you see that a is equal to −4 and −2. Next, you can set $x + 4$ equal to both of those and solve each for x, as shown below.

$$x + 4 = -4$$

$$x + 4 = -2$$

$$x = -8 \text{ and } x = -6$$

No matter which approach you choose, correctly answering this difficult question requires dangerous math thinking. In fact, being open to both approaches is a sign of your growing self-confidence. When you start believing that it is your abilities that are solving the problems, you are well on your way to becoming an expert mathematician.

Remember, there is no question you can't solve.

TIMED COLLEGE BOARD PRACTICE

Complete the following College Board practice problems from College Board's *The Official SAT Study Guide* or online at www.collegeboard.org. Review answers after completing.

Test 7, Math: No Calculator and Calculator Sections

Chapter **18**

Let Me Sleep on It

Are SAT questions easier to do with an unfocused, foggy mind or a focused, alert one?

The answer to this question is obvious, but what is not obvious is the simple, often overlooked means of developing a more focused mind: improving your sleep.

Sleep is perhaps one of the most underrated aspects of test prep, yet it is the most all-encompassing. Your sleep affects every aspect of your test prep, from your memory to your focus to your mood, and even how quickly you ingrain new skills. Improving the quality and quantity of sleep is, in fact, the quickest way to accelerate your progress on the Success Curve. Sleep can have a profound impact on your life, and it is something we actually enjoy doing. Who doesn't love to sleep?

Unfortunately, it is very easy to adopt poor sleep habits. Just one or two nights a week of late-night studying, Snapchatting, sports games, musical concerts, or the like is enough to throw off our sleep patterns. Overbooked schedules, excessive stress, and our love for electronics all come between us and restorative, brain-boosting sleep.

When we do not sleep enough, we have difficulty learning and concentrating, become irritable and depressed, and struggle with managing our stress. And we know from Chapter 5 that when we are in a negative state of mind, our problem-solving ability diminishes.

All in all, lack of sleep is a catastrophe for the SAT.

Why Sleep Is Awesome

A student who is well rested will be in a better mood, which will lead to a better problem-solving capacity. That student will be able to persevere through the difficult problems, focus and concentrate for longer periods of time, manage stress with ease, and, most importantly, learn new skills more quickly.

Have you practiced a new skill for weeks and weeks without seeing noticeable improvement until, one week, you take a break and then *BOOM!*, the next time you try it, you somehow get the hang of it? No genie came and granted you a wish, and no magic spell was cast, so how did you improve without even practicing? Sleep. While you sleep, not only do your brain and body heal, but your new neural pathways also solidify their connections. Picture sleep as an impossibly skilled seamstress knitting together your neural pathways so that when you wake up, you have a new mosaic of skills.

Trust us, sleep is powerful. Getting a good night's sleep is like going from a phone in need of an upgrade with battery life in the red to the newest model, fully charged.

How to Improve Your Quantity of Sleep

You should approach sleep in the same way you've approached the SAT: with a growth mindset.

Sleep is something that has a cumulative effect—it builds over time. You can't get great sleep for just one night and expect instantaneous success. The key is to create a sleep schedule that not only allows you to get a consistent amount of sleep each night, but also to consistently sleep well each night.

Adults need 7–8 hours of sleep every night, but teenagers need even more. Your goal should be to get 9–10 hours each night, with an acceptable compromise of 8 hours. While this may seem hard at first, it is quite possible, as long as you create a sleep schedule and have the discipline to stick with it. Start small by adding an additional hour of sleep and then seeing the effect it has on your well-being. Next, choose a time before 11 p.m. to go sleep each night, and a time you will wake up in the morning that will allow you to sleep for 8–10 hours, and stick to those times consistently.

Remember, the time you wake up on the days you don't go to school, like weekends, should be consistent with the time you go to sleep and wake up on weekdays. Our bodies are programmed to go to bed when the sun goes down and wake up when the sun comes up.

How to Improve Your Quality of Sleep

Sleeping more only works if you actually sleep. If you are restless, toss and turn, or get up frequently, your sleep will not benefit you as much as it should.

Here are a few things you can do to improve your quality of sleep:

- Make your room as dark as possible and, if you do need to get up in the middle of the night, avoid turning on bright lights. Light disrupts the balance of your melatonin, an important hormone for sleep.

- Adjust your room's temperature. The ideal sleeping temperature is 67 degrees.

- Avoid eating within two to three hours of falling asleep.

- Avoid drinking more than half a cup of liquid within an hour of falling asleep to avoid having to use the bathroom in the middle of the night.

- Unplug! Turn off all electronics, especially phones, televisions, and video games, an hour before going to bed.

- Try journaling. Writing down your thoughts, in the form of accomplishments of the day and goals for the next day, is a great way to decompress.

- Read a book. There is a reason why parents read bedtime stories to their children. Pleasure reading in bed puts the brain in a happily passive state and primes it for sleep.

- Meditate or do some Deep Breath Resets for 5–15 minutes before going to bed. This is a great way to detoxify yourself from all the emotional stress of the day.

Essay: Introduction to the Essay

The SAT essay is an optional timed essay, included as the final section of the SAT. You are given 50 minutes to analyze a passage and write an essay based on your analysis. Unlike the essay on past SAT iterations, this essay does not require you to choose a viewpoint and argue it. Instead, you must analyze how the author of the given passage constructs his or her argument. Common passages include speeches from Martin Luther King Jr., former president Jimmy Carter, and other famous orators. However, before we go over the method for writing the essay, let's review some frequently asked questions about the SAT essay.

How Is the SAT Essay Scored?

First, the SAT essay does not factor into your scaled score. You will get a combined score out of 1600 for the English and Math sections, and a separate essay score out of 24.

Your essay will be graded on three categories: analysis, reading, and writing. For each category, two separate graders will give you a score of 1–4. Based on their combined grading, you will receive a score of 2–8 for each category. The two scores for each category will then be added together, giving you a separate score of 2-8 for analysis, reading, and writing.

Here is a breakdown of the categories, each of which will be discussed in depth later in this chapter.

ANALYSIS. This focuses on how effectively you analyzed the author's argument. Were you able to break down the author's argument to see what makes it tick? Did you incorporate quoted evidence of the author's argumentative techniques in your essay?

READING. This focuses on how well you understood the author's argument. Does your essay make sense? Does it highlight rhetorical devices and techniques that further the correct argument? Or did you misinterpret the author's point?

WRITING. This focuses on how well you wrote the essay. Did you adhere to conventions of English syntax and usage, use elevated vocabulary, and organize your essay so that it flows seamlessly from one paragraph to the next? Do you have an introduction, conclusion, and at least two body paragraphs?

We recommend you try to write three body paragraphs, but two solid body paragraphs will suffice.

Mindset Tip

Do you not see yourself as a great writer? Change the way you view yourself and your writing ability. Instead of saying "I'm not good at writing," say, "I'm not good at writing…yet." By doing the practice in these chapters, you will begin to develop your writing ability and find that all great writing can be broken down into very simple, easy-to-learn strategies.

Should I Choose to Write the Essay?

To write or not to write: that is the question. While this may seem like a conundrum, it has a straightforward answer. The short answer is "yes, write the essay." But, if you would like further elaboration, consider three factors when deciding to write the SAT essay:

1) Is it required or recommended by the college(s) to which you are applying?

A quick search on College Board or on a school's website should tell you whether the SAT essay is required or recommended. If, after searching, you still cannot find the information you need, make a phone call to the admissions office so you can be sure you know a college's stance on the SAT essay. Needless to say, if it is required or just recommended, you should opt to write the essay.

2) Can the SAT essay set you apart from your peers?

If you are good at writing or believe, as we have taught you, that you can develop this skill with practice and effort, then it might be worthwhile to write the essay. You are looking for whatever it takes to make you stand out, and a solid essay score might just do that.

3) Do you want the colleges to which you are applying to perceive you as motivated?

This final consideration is something we tell all our students, and it trumps all other factors. We suggest you write the SAT essay. It is important to show that you are willing to put in the extra effort to succeed. If you are content with your score on the SAT essay, you can forego the essay on future SATs and focus solely on the math and English.

The SAT Essay Prompt

This is a sample SAT essay prompt that we will use to demonstrate the SAT essay-writing method.

Write an essay in which you explain how the author builds an argument to persuade his audience that our national parks should be preserved to ensure historical legacy and literacy. In your essay, analyze how the author uses one or more of the features listed in the box that precedes the passage (or features of your own choice) to strengthen the logic and persuasiveness of his argument. Be sure that your analysis focuses on the most relevant features of the passage.

As you read the passage below, consider how the author uses:

- evidence, such as facts or examples, to support claims

- reasoning to develop ideas and to connect claims to evidence

- stylistic or persuasive elements, such as word choice or appeals to emotion to add power to the ideas expressed

When writing the SAT essay, it is important to follow a proven method that outlines the writing process. This method consists of the following four steps:

- Annotating the passage (10 minutes)

- Organizing your thoughts (5 minutes)

- Writing the essay (30 minutes)

- Proofreading the essay (5 minutes)

Blind Spot

Your essay should NOT explain whether you agree with the author's claims, but rather explain how the author builds an argument to persuade his or her audience.

Annotating the Passage (10 minutes)

The first step of any SAT essay is to read the passage and determine how the author is making his or her point. How is he or she persuading the reader? To do this, it will be helpful to underline the rhetorical elements or narrative techniques and persuasive strategies that help the author make an argument. First, though, you need to identify these narrative techniques. Below are six such techniques.

Aristotle's Elements of Persuasion

Argument hasn't changed much in the last couple thousand years because human nature hasn't changed. We can still be swayed by our hearts or our minds. Around 350 BC, Aristotle set the standard for the art of persuasion by devising a system of three principles that form the basis of any argument. These consist of logos, ethos, and pathos, which are described below.

Logos

Logos, like the name implies, is the use of logical reasoning to develop an argument. Such reasoning can include the use of facts, evidence, and statistics to prove a point or the citing of certain authorities on a subject; logos can also include the use of historical and literal analogies to prove a point through comparison or contrast.

Think of a car commercial—the kind that lists the multitude of safety features, cites a number-one rank in *Consumer Reports*, gives you hard numbers for fuel economy, and then explains the rationale for making a purchase. "Why compromise? Why not get the security of an SUV and the fuel economy of a sedan? Try our SUV/sedan mid-range hybrid." This is a great example of logos because it provides the buyer with facts, statistics, and a logical reason for purchase: the idea that the buyer can get the best of both worlds in this car. You can see logos in action in these examples from the National Park Service.

> *Example One:* Its responsibilities include administering the National Historic Landmarks program, which has designated more than 2,300 nationally significant properties since 1935, and the National Register of Historic Places, which now includes more than seventy thousand sites. The Service provides matching grants to restore public and privately owned historic places through the Historic Preservation Fund.

Example Two: Of some 556 seniors surveyed at 55 of the nation's top colleges and universities, only 60 percent placed the American Civil War in the correct half of the nineteenth century. Only 34 percent identified George Washington as the American general at the Revolutionary War battle of Yorktown—37 percent thought the general was Ulysses S. Grant. At 78 percent of the institutions polled, no history whatsoever was required as part of the undergraduate program.

Example Three: "It is not surprising," states the report by the American Council of Trustees and Alumni, "that college seniors know little American history. Few students leave high school with an adequate knowledge of American history, and even the best colleges and universities do nothing to close the knowledge gap." As historian David McCullough observed in the same report, "We are raising a generation of young Americans who are historically illiterate."

Ethos

Ethos is a rhetorical technique in which the writer or speaker appeals to the reader's morals and ethics. It is the use an ethical appeal to convince an audience or reader of the author's credibility or character by using language or examples to make oneself sound fair or unbiased. It is also a way of introducing one's expertise.

To get a good idea of ethos, imagine another car commercial, only this time, instead of presenting facts and statistics, the commercial focuses on a central person. Perhaps that person is a trustworthy public figure, celebrity, or athlete. After this spokesperson convinces you of his or her credibility, that person will persuade you to buy the car based on the many ethical and moral reasons, such as clean-air technology, which helps the environment, and the fair wages payed to the workers who built the car. This all falls under the category of ethos.

> "Friends and fellow citizens: I stand before you tonight under indictment for the alleged crime of having voted at the last presidential election, without having a lawful right to vote."

In this excerpt from her 1873 speech, *On Woman's Right to Suffrage,* Susan B. Anthony establishes her credibility by demonstrating her own unwavering involvement in the cause of winning voting rights for women. She herself is "under indictment" for doing the very thing she is petitioning for.

Pathos

Pathos is a rhetorical technique that appeals to the reader's emotion by evoking sadness, fear, hope, nostalgia, or other feelings. It is meant to pull on the heart strings, so to speak.

Envision yet another car commercial, only this time, it's a scene of a teenager jumping into his first car, his dad's old Toyota 4Runner, and passing the driver's test. In the next scene, he's driving that same 4Runner to first job interview. Then, we see him saying goodbye to his trusty 4Runner, and now we see him with his pregnant wife at the Toyota dealership about to purchase his next 4Runner.

This commercial is about reliability and consistency, but it also evokes a certain amount of sentimentality and nostalgia. We all have fond memories of our first car: the car we picked up our first date in, the car we took on our first road trip, the car we drove to college. And, like it or not, those memories influence us. Embed those feelings in a car commercial, and you might just get a sale grounded more in emotion than logic. This is pathos.

> "The Park Service must ensure that the American story is told faithfully, completely, and accurately. The story is often noble, but sometimes shameful and sad. In an age of growing cultural diversity, the Service must continually ask whether the way in which it tells these stories has meaning for all our citizens."

In this example from the National Park Service, the author evokes a sentimental sense of pride with the notion of a shared story to which we all contribute. Storytelling is something with which all people can identify. Stories conjure up memories of childhood, of princes and witches, good and evil. By comparing our history to a story, the author is calling forth those feelings and inviting the reader to help shape its plot and write a happy ending.

> "Let every nation know whether it wishes us well or ill, that we shall pay any price, bear any burden, meet any hardship, support any friend, oppose any foe in order to assure the survival and the success of liberty."

President Kennedy inspired people with his 1961 inaugural address. A luminescent pride glowed in the heart of his audience as he assured them of his promise to be uncompromising in the upholding of America's democratic values.

Diction

Diction is an author's word choice, specifically words that have an emotional charge or a secondary connotation other than the literal dictionary definition.

Think of another SUV commercial that calls car trips "journeys into the great unknown," refers to the SUV as a "fortress on wheels," and names the driver a "great explorer." This commercial is manipulating its audience through diction. By choosing words associated with feats of bravery and adventure, the creators of this commercial liken the driver of this car to a hero. The words inspire the purchase of the SUV, regardless of how practical the car might be for the consumer.

> "With malice toward none, with charity for all, with firmness in the right as God gives us to see the right, let us strive on to finish the work we are in, to bind up the nation's wounds, to care for him who shall have borne the battle and for his widow and his orphan, to do all which may achieve and cherish a just and lasting peace among ourselves and with all nations."

In his second inaugural address, Lincoln makes use of powerful diction to convey his point. He uses language associated with caring for the sick and injured, such as "bind up the nation's wounds," as if it is the very nation itself that must be healed. He also makes sure to remind his listeners of the great toll of the war with words like "widow" and "orphan." By doing so, Lincoln seeks to unify his audience through both shared pain and shared responsibility: many on both the North and South in the Civil War, having lost people dear to them, can identify with his words.

> "Brother, this council fire was kindled by you; it was at your request that we came together at this time….Brother, you say you want an answer to your talk before you leave this place….Brother, listen to what we have to say. There was a time when our forefathers owned this great island….Brother, our seats were once large, and yours were very small; you have now become a great people, and we have scarcely a place left to spread our blankets….Brother, continue to listen.

In his speech, "Religion for the White Man and the Red," the Seneca chief Red Jacket repeatedly refers to the missionary Joseph Cram as "Brother," which emphasizes kinship and common ground, but he then goes on to use simple unadorned language to convey how little the Seneca have now as a result of the white man. He states, "our seats were once large and yours were very small; you have now become a great people and we have scarcely a place left to spread our blankets." Red Jacket can convey his point without anger or provocation by using everyday words to evoke lasting symbolic images.

Point of View

Point of view is the perspective from which a narrator or speaker relates events, identified through the pronouns used. Below are typical points of view used in rhetoric.

FIRST PERSON (I, ME, MY). This is immediate, candid, intimate, and can be a powerful persuasive tool, especially if the narrator wants the reader to dive into and vicariously experience a certain event. First person perspective allows for this personal engagement.

FIRST PERSON PLURAL (WE, US, OUR). This point of view is inclusive and creates a sense of togetherness. Politicians and leaders are notorious for using first person plural when they speak to evoke camaraderie. They want it to appear that they share common ground with the average Joe.

SECOND PERSON (YOU, YOUR). This point of view is rarely used for an entire work of literature or speech; rather, it is usually a quick departure from first person or third. It can add an accusatory, conspiratorial, informal, or conversational style to the narration.

THIRD PERSON (HE, SHE, THEY, THEIR). This point of view gives the reader or listener a broader view. It can be more detached and objective, free of personal bias.

> "In offering to you, my countrymen, these counsels of an old and affectionate friend…"

In this line from President Washington's farewell address, he portrays himself not as a revered leader, but as an old friend and countryman: someone on the same level as the people to whom he speaks. First and second person point of view ("you, my countrymen") creates this personal and intimate tone.

> "My friends: This is not a fireside chat on war. It is a talk on national security; because the nub of the whole purpose of your President is to keep you now, and your children later, and your grandchildren much later, out of a last ditch war for the preservation of American independence, and all of the things that American independence means to you and to me and to ours."

In response to the Axis powers' threats at the cusp of World War II, FDR gives a famous Fireside Chat titled "The Arsenal of Democracy," encouraging the American people to recognize the need to stop Axis aggression by supporting Allied war efforts. The structure, presentation, diction, and point of view of the these "chats" are designed to humanize the president and make him seem like a friend joining for tea in the living room rather than an a president in an austere out-of-reach office. FDR creates this effect most effectively with point of view by using second person "you" to address the people directly, personally. He also connects himself with the people in a shared belief by using first person and first person plural, stating "to you and to me and to ours."

Syntax

Syntax is the use of punctuation (specifically rhetorical questions and exclamations), sentence length, parallelism, antithesis, and repetition to persuade. Below are examples of common elements of syntax that authors or speakers use to persuade.

EXCLAMATIONS: Used to denote excitement, anger, and any other extreme emotion.

RHETORICAL QUESTIONS: Questions that are not intended to be answered. These have the effect of drawing attention to an obvious point or persuading the reader to acknowledge a foregone conclusion that he or she would be foolish not to agree with.

SENTENCE LENGTH: Typically, extremely long or short and abrupt sentences are noteworthy. A lengthy sentence could draw attention to the litany of advantages of the author's proposal, and an abrupt sentence could grab the reader's attention or create suspense.

PARALLELISM: Phrasing successive words, phrases, or clauses in similar/parallel grammatical structure creates cohesion and connects ideas, as well as a rhythmic, musical quality that makes the writing more memorable and persuasive.

ANTITHESIS: Putting contrasting items side by side in similar/parallel grammatical structure is effective for connecting two unlike concepts, and by doing so, draws attention to them.

REPETITION: Repeating words, phrases, or ideas. Anaphora is a specialized form of repetition in which the first couple of words of each line repeat.

"Last night Japanese forces attacked Hong Kong.

Last night Japanese forces attacked Guam.

Last night Japanese forces attacked the Philippine Islands.

Last night the Japanese attacked Wake Island.

And this morning the Japanese attacked Midway Island."

As we explained in chapter 3, in his "Request for a Declaration of War on Japan," President Franklin Roosevelt skillfully employs syntax to create rhetorical effect. The anaphora of "Last night Japanese forces attacked" creates a sense of urgency and fear. It makes it seem like the Japanese are everywhere—the repetition of the word "attack" overwhelms the listener. FDR could have easily stated, "Last night Japanese forces attacked several locations," but he chose to echo the word "attack" and lay out each of the attacks one by one to evoke this urgency.

"Each time we gather to inaugurate a President we bear witness to the enduring strength of our Constitution. We affirm the promise of our democracy. We recall that what binds this nation together is not the colors of our skin or the tenets of our faith or the origins of our names. What makes us exceptional—what makes us American—is our allegiance to an idea articulated in a declaration made more than two centuries ago…"

President Obama, in his second inaugural address, uses the phrases "we gather," "we bear witness," "we affirm," "we recall." Repeating the word "we" produces the effect of creating a sense of shared purpose. Following this, Obama uses parallelism to create a rhythmic, memorable effect and emphasize that only one thing makes us exceptional: an idea we share. He says it's "not the colors of our skin or the tenets of our faith or the origins of our names." By using the construction "not this or this or this," Obama makes it clear what defines us as a people in terms of what does not.

"And so, my fellow Americans: ask not what your country can do for you—ask what you can do for your country. My fellow citizens of the world: ask not what America will do for you, but what together we can do for the freedom of man."

JFK's famous line, "ask not what your country can do for you—ask what you can do for your country," is an example of brilliant antithesis. By phrasing these contrasting ideas side by side in parallel form, JFK underscores the paradigm shift he hopes to achieve in the American consciousness: that the American people must take an active role in making their government and country great.

Imagery and Metaphorical Language

Imagery includes any vivid image, such as visual, auditory, or olfactory (related to smell), that the reader or listener can picture in his or her mind's eye. Metaphorical language refers to any metaphor used to evoke a certain feeling in the reader or listener. Sometimes a single image or metaphorical symbol emblazoned in the listener's or reader's mind can be more effective in persuasion than a whole essay of facts and evidence.

> "The energy, the faith, the devotion which we bring to this endeavor will light our country and all who serve it — and the glow from that fire can truly light the world."

Here, JFK invites the listener to envision America as a beacon, glowing for all to see, lighting the way for the rest of the world, and conquering the darkness. This is both metaphor and vivid imagery and proclaims America's place in the world as a leader and exemplar to follow in just two simple lines.

Organization and Structure

Organization and structure refer to how the author or speaker arranges his or her ideas. Are they chronological? Does he or she include flashbacks? Is the argument set up in point/counterpoint fashion? Each of these modes of organization can have powerful persuasive effects.

> "As a man whose roots go deeply into Southern soil, I know how agonizing racial feelings are. I know how difficult it is to reshape the attitudes and the structure of our society. But a century has passed, more than a hundred years, since the Negro was freed. And he is not fully free tonight."

In this speech, Lyndon B. Johnson sets up his argument that true racial equality has not yet been attained by first claiming that he knows how difficult it is to change society. Immediately following this, Johnson gives his counterpoint, beginning with "But…" This point/counterpoint structure underscores his perseverance and determination in ending racism.

Organizing Your Thoughts (5 minutes)

Once you have annotated the passage and found the narrative and persuasive techniques used by the author, it is time to categorize them. You cannot write about them all, so you must find the top two or three narrative techniques within the passage. For example, let's say diction, facts and statistics (logos), and imagery are the most prominent techniques of a passage. Divide them up such that each of the essay's body paragraphs will utilize one of these techniques:

Body Paragraph 1: List all relevant examples of diction

Body Paragraph 2: List all relevant facts and statistics

Body Paragraph 3: List all relevant examples of imagery

Writing the Essay (30 minutes)

The next step is to write the essay. Once you have all your thoughts organized, using the above method, this is just a matter of writing clearly and cohesively. Below is a practical, user-friendly structure for the essay (note that, while three body paragraphs are recommended, two solid paragraphs will suffice):

1) INTRODUCTION PARAGRAPH

- Write an introductory sentence that summarizes the plot of the passage.

- Include a "bridge to analysis," one to two sentences that elaborate further upon the author's argument and begin to explain the ways the author builds this argument.

- State your thesis. The thesis is a concise statement that identifies the most important narrative techniques the author uses to create his argument.

2) BODY PARAGRAPH 1

- Introduce the first narrative technique and how it furthers the author's argument.

- Give examples of the first narrative technique from the passage.

- Explain how the examples build the argument.

3) BODY PARAGRAPH 2

- Introduce the second narrative technique and how it furthers the author's argument.

- Give examples of the second narrative technique from the passage.

- Explain how the examples build the argument.

4) BODY PARAGRAPH 3 (OPTIONAL, BUT PREFERRED)

- Introduce the third narrative technique and how it furthers the author's argument.

- Give examples of the third narrative technique from the passage.

- Explain how the examples build the argument.

5) CONCLUSION PARAGRAPH

- In one sentence, list all three examples that you used in your essay, explaining how they built your argument.

- Restate or reformulate the thesis, reminding the reader of your argument.

- Extend and elaborate upon the author's main point. This should be a general statement or parting insight that reinforces the rhetorical power of the author's argument and its effect.

Review and Proofread (5 minutes)

Read your essay back to yourself to check for grammatical errors, redundancies, or confusing sections. Rewrite any parts in need of revision.

Mindset Tip

These analytical skills will become the building blocks of your self-confidence as an essay writer. The quickest way to improve your belief in your essay-writing ability is to learn the tools to analyze an author's argument and then apply them through consistent practice. Whatever attitudes or past beliefs you had about yourself as a writer are irrelevant. Drop them and start practicing the SAT essay with the strategies we are providing you. Remember the tenets of growth mindset: anything can be learned and anything can be improved—even writing.

Vocabulary Words 256–270

256) **monotonous** (adj). dull, repetitive, boring: *The professor droned on and on through his monotonous lecture, listing all the major battles in the Civil War.*

257) **intolerable** (adj). unbearable: *Lucia, used to tropical weather and mild winters, found the Canadian cold intolerable.*

258) **despair** (n). hopelessness, misery: *After his beloved gerbil died, Roy fell into a state of great despair.*

259) **plight** (n). difficulty, hardship: *The Trail of Tears embodied the very worst of the plight of the Native Americans.*

260) **malicious** (adj). intentionally harmful: *Maleficent from* Sleeping Beauty *is so named due to her malicious nature.*

261) **discord** (n). disagreement, conflict: *A marriage filled with discord is a marriage destined for divorce.*

262) **evoke** (v). to call forth, produce, arouse, or elicit: *By depicting the family's hardships so vividly, the poet was able to evoke a sense of despair.*

263) **scorn** (n). open hatred: *No amount of counseling would repair the friendship between the two; Felicity felt only scorn for Jacquelyn.*

264) **indignation** (n). righteous, deeply felt anger at something offensive or insulting: *After returning to a home overrun by crude suitors, Odysseus, overcome with indignation, took his revenge.*

265) **demanding** (adj). requiring a great deal of effort; arduous and difficult: *Manual labor is a physically demanding job.*

266) **arbitrary** (adj). based on random choice; haphazard; without reason: *Lottery numbers are chosen arbitrarily.*

267) **enumerate** (v). a) to count or mention several items one by one: *It is impossible to enumerate the many benefits of being in love;* b) to tally up or determine the number of: *The king enumerated 2,300 people in his kingdom who depended on him.*

268) **aloof** (adj). distant, remote, standoffish: *The woman's aloof demeanor made her appear unfriendly.*

279) **malleable** (adj). flexible; capable of being molded: *Thomas, with his malleable mind and gullible nature, was the perfect candidate to join a cult.*

270) **ornate** (adj). elaborately adorned; excessively showy: *The house was decorated with ornate and gaudy furnishings.*

Latin and Greek Roots 96–100

96) QUI: quiet (acquiesce, quiescent, tranquil)

97) SCI: know (prescient, science, conscientious)

98) SE/DIV: apart (segregate, seclude, secede, separate, divide)

99) SENS/SENT: feel, take notice (sensate, sensuous, sensory, sentient)

100) SOL: sun (solar, solstice, solarium, parasol)

Math Test: Additional Topics in Math

The fourth area of content on the SAT Math Test is called Additional Topics in Math and pertains mostly to topics learned in geometry. The test will only contain about six questions from this area; however, these questions are a great opportunity to increase your score because they are most likely easier than the topics and questions you answered in the previous chapters.

Working with Angles

The first geometric concepts that we will work with are various angle properties. You should know the following two angle pair relationships.

COMPLEMENTARY ANGLES: Two angles are complementary if their sum is 90°. Together they form a right angle and are commonly used in right triangles.

SUPPLEMENTARY ANGLES: Two angles are supplementary if they add up to 180°. When combined, the two angles will form a straight line, as shown below.

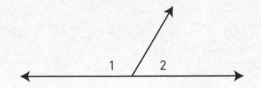

If $\angle 2 = 60°$, then to find $\angle 1$, just subtract 60 from 180. You get 120°.

Hint

Drawing diagrams is a great way to boost your score. If the question does not provide a diagram, draw one, and if it does provide a diagram, use it by adding in any information the problem may give you.

Here's an example using these important concepts:

In right triangle ABC, Angles ∠A and ∠C are complementary. If ∠A = 60°, find ∠C.

To find angle C, it will help to draw a diagram of a right triangle. Remember that the interior angles of a triangle add up to 180°.

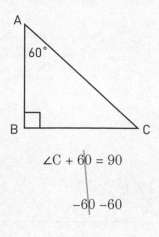

$$\angle C + 60 = 90$$

$$-60\ -60$$

$$\angle C = 30°$$

Here's another example:

Two angles are supplementary and one of those angles is 40° more than the other. What is the value of the smaller angle?

In this question, you will have to use your knowledge of supplementary angles while also implementing the strategy of converting words to math.

Begin by calling one angle x, and since the other angle is 40° more, you can call that angle $(x + 40)$. We also know that the two angles added together is 180°, so you can set up the equation $x + (x + 40) = 180$. This equation can be solved by combining like terms to get:

$$2x + 40 = 180$$

Solve by subtracting 40 and then dividing by 2 to get 70°. To find the other angle, just add 40 to 70 to get 110°. Remember to be aware of what the question is asking. This question requires you to find the smaller angle, which is 70°.

PRACTICE A

Find x for each.

1)

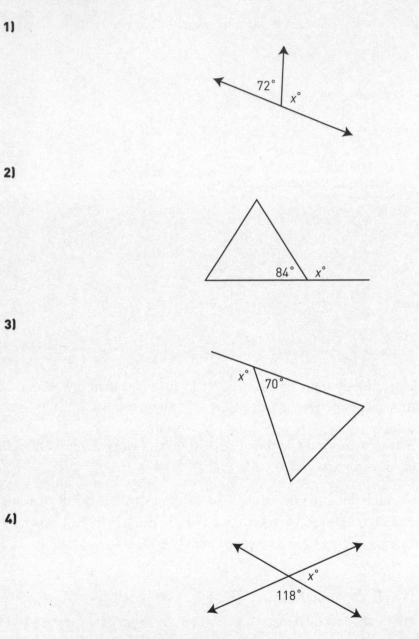

2)

3)

4)

5) Two angles are complementary and one of the angles is two times larger than the other. What is the measure of the larger angle?

Vertical Angles

Another angle pair relationship to know is that of vertical angles, which are created when two lines intersect in what usually looks like an X. In the diagram shown below, angles 1 and 2 would be vertical angles. Notice how they are opposite each other.

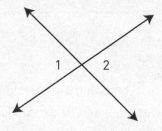

Vertical angles are equal to each other. You can find the other pair of angles by subtracting from 180.

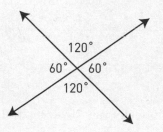

A fundamental concept to know is that angles around a point, as shown above, will always add up to 360°. Below are two examples that will require you to use this information and the vertical angles concept.

Find the missing variables.

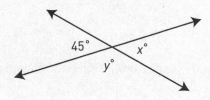

Since this problem deals with vertical angles, x will be 45°.

To find y, realize that the two angles, 45° and y, are supplementary since they are adjacent and form a straight line. So, subtract 45° from 180° to get 135°.

What are the values of x and y if line m is parallel to line n?

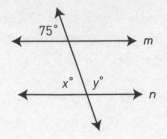

This example contains a transversal that intersects two parallel lines. This will create eight angles, with four of them equal to 75°. You can see where those angles would be below:

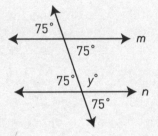

To find the other missing angles, just subtract 75° from 180° to get 105°, which is what all the remaining angles will be.

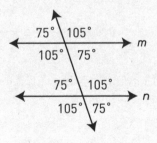

Notice the pattern to the angles: they alternate. This pattern will appear whenever a transversal intersects parallel lines.

$$x = 75°$$

$$y = 105°$$

The Triangle Fundamentals

Understanding a few simple concepts involving triangles and the different types of triangles will certainly increase your score. The most fundamental rule is that all three angles of any triangle will add up to 180°. Here is an example.

In triangle ABC, $\angle A$ is 55° and $\angle B$ is 58°. Find the measure of $\angle C$.

Begin by drawing and labeling a diagram.

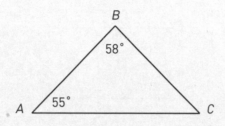

Since all three angles of a triangle add up to 180°, you can write an equation to solve for the missing angle.

$$c + 55° + 58° = 180°$$

$$c + 113° = 180°$$

$$c = 67°$$

HINT

In a quadrilateral, or four-sided shape, the four angles add up to 360°. The formula for finding the sum of the interior angles of a polygon is $(n - 2) \times 180$, with n being the number of sides. The sum of the exterior angles of all polygons is 360°.

Isosceles Triangles

An isosceles triangle is special because it has two congruent, or equal, sides. It also has two equal angles that are located opposite the congruent sides, as shown in the triangle below. Since side AB is equal to side BC, then $\angle A$ is the same as $\angle C$.

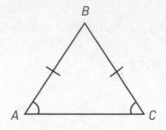

Let's try an example.

> The triangle shown below is isosceles, with side AB congruent to AC. What is the measure of $\angle 1$ if $\angle A$ is 80°?

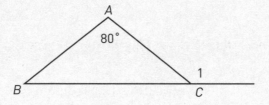

The key to working with an isosceles triangle is to determine which angles are equal.

$\angle B$ and $\angle C$ are both equal to 50° because $180° - 80° = \dfrac{100°}{2} = 50°$. $\angle C$ and $\angle 1$ are supplementary, so $\angle 1$ can be found by subtracting 180 and 50, which is 130°.

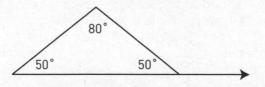

You can also apply the remote interior angle concept, which states that $\angle 1$ will always be equal to the sum of its two remote interior angles, which, as shown below, are $\angle 2$ and $\angle 4$. The previous example could have been solved by adding 80 and 50, which results in 130.

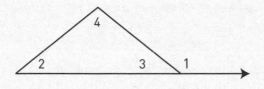

Right Triangles

A right triangle is a triangle that contains one right angle. The side opposite the right angle is called the hypotenuse and is the longest side of the triangle. The remaining two sides are called legs. Since one of the angles is equal to 90°, the remaining two angles will always be complementary.

The Pythagorean theorem allows you to find a missing side of a right triangle when you are already given two of its sides. It is written as $a^2 + b^2 = c^2$, with a and b being the legs and c being the hypotenuse.

Here is an example that demonstrates how to find the hypotenuse.

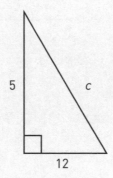

Make sure c is always the hypotenuse. Be sure to identify the hypotenuse right away.

$$5^2 + 12^2 = c^2$$

$$25 + 144 = c^2$$

$$169 = c^2$$

Take the square root of both sides.

$$c = 13$$

If you are given one of the legs and the hypotenuse of a right triangle, use the same formula but subtract first instead of adding. Here is an example:

A 10-foot ladder is leaned up against a wall. If the base of the ladder is 6 feet from the wall, how high up the wall, in feet, will the ladder reach?

The best approach to solving this question is to draw and label a diagram.

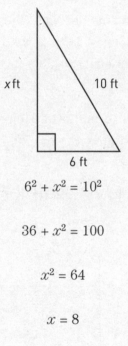

$$6^2 + x^2 = 10^2$$

$$36 + x^2 = 100$$

$$x^2 = 64$$

$$x = 8$$

Pythagorean Triples

The most commonly used right triangle is the 3-4-5, where 3 is a, 4 is b, and 5 is c. Having this memorized will save you the time of plugging sides into $a^2 + b^2 = c^2$.

Let's say you were given a right triangle that has a leg with the length of 4 and the hypotenuse is a length of 5. You do not need to do any work. You can figure out that this is a 3-4-5 right triangle, so the missing side would have to be 3.

Another Pythagorean triple to remember is 5-12-13. Not only can you use the triples 3-4-5 and 5-12-13, but also the multiples of these, including 6-8-10, 9-12-15, and 10-24-16.

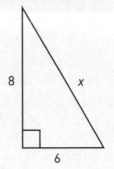

In this triangle above, the 6 and the 8 should make you think of 6-8-10, which comes from the 3-4-5. This will allow you to quickly find that the hypotenuse, or x, is equal to 10.

With all these, you can use the Pythagorean theorem. However, knowing the Pythagorean triples will save you time and energy.

Special Right Triangles

You may be required to use the properties of the special right triangles, which are given to you on the formula sheet at the beginning of each section. Let's begin with a 45-45-90 triangle.

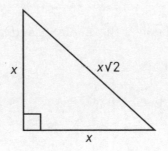

This special right triangle is also an isosceles, since it contains two congruent sides (meaning they are equal length) and two equal angles. To find the hypotenuse, just multiply the leg by $\sqrt{2}$.

Here is an example that uses the concept shown above.

If a square has an area of 16 ft², what is the length of the diagonal?

A) 4

B) $2\sqrt{2}$

C) $2\sqrt{3}$

D) $4\sqrt{2}$

To solve this question, begin by drawing a diagram of the square and diagonal.

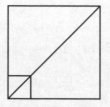

The diagonal will create two right triangles and, since each side of a square is the same length, the opposite angles will also be equal. Thus, each triangle will be a 45-45-90 right triangle. The question also states that the area is $16ft^2$, and by using the formula of $A = lw$, we can determine that the length of each side of the square is equal to 4. To find the length of the diagonal, just multiply 4 by $\sqrt{2}$ to get choice (D).

The other special right triangle to know is the 30-60-90, and is shown below:

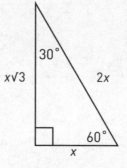

Here is an example that uses the triangle property shown above.

$\triangle ABC$ is equilateral and has a side length of 10. What is the area of the triangle?

A) 25

B) 50

C) $25\sqrt{3}$

D) $50\sqrt{3}$

This question is certainly a Rock Mover, as there are multiple steps to correctly execute, and a few properties to know. To solve, begin once again with a diagram and add in any information you are given.

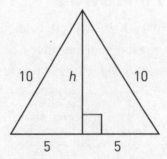

Start with what you know. Equilateral triangles have three equal sides, and in this case all the sides have a length of 10. They also have equal angles of 60°.

To find the area of a triangle, which is given by the formula $A = \frac{1}{2}bh$, you need the base, which is 10, and the height.

Finding the height is the challenging part, but since each angle in an equilateral triangle is 60°, we use the 30-60-90 property. Let's draw the right triangle located on the right, as shown below:

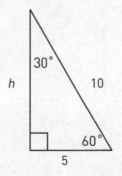

To find the height, first realize that the short leg is equal to half the hypotenuse, which is 5. The long leg, or h from the right triangle above, is equal to $5\sqrt{3}$. This is the height.

To find the area, substitute the numbers 10 and $5\sqrt{3}$ in for base and height:

$$A = \frac{1}{2}\,(10)\,5\sqrt{3}$$

This is equal to $25\sqrt{3}$, which is choice (C).

Using Trigonometry Ratios

You will most likely remember the term SOHCAHTOA from geometry class—it's a mnemonic for remembering how to find the sine, cosine, and tangent. Understanding it is vital for SAT math success. Here are the trigonometry ratios that you will need to know:

$$\sin A = \frac{\text{opposite}}{\text{hypotenuse}}$$

$$\cos A = \frac{\text{adjacent}}{\text{hypotenuse}}$$

$$\tan A = \frac{\text{opposite}}{\text{adjacent}}$$

The A next to the sin, cos, and tan represents the angle the question is referring to. Just like the Pythagorean theorem, these ratios can be applied only to right triangles.

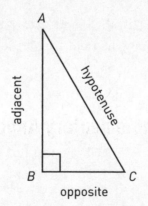

To find $\sin A$, determine which side is opposite $\angle A$, which is side BC as shown in the diagram above. Now locate the hypotenuse, or AC. The correct ratio is $\frac{BC}{AC}$.

Cos A is $\frac{AB}{AC}$ because AB is adjacent, or next to, $\angle A$.

Tan A is $\frac{BC}{AB}$.

Let's try an example using these ratios.

In triangle ABC, angle B is a right angle, AB is equal to 5, and BC is equal to 12. What is cos A equal to?

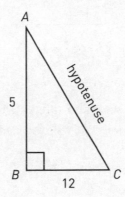

Start by drawing a diagram, as shown here. To find cos A, which is the ratio of the adjacent side to the hypotenuse, you need to find the hypotenuse, or side AC, using the Pythagorean theorem.

$$5^2 + 12^2 = x^2$$

$$x = 13$$

You may have also recognized that this was a 5-12-13 Pythagorean triple, which would have saved you a step.

Now, set up the ratio to get $\frac{5}{13}$ as cos A.

The Sine and Cosine of Complementary Angles

There is a special property that can be applied to questions that combine the ratios of both sine and cosine of the same right triangle:

In the triangle below, what is the ratio of the sin C to cos A?

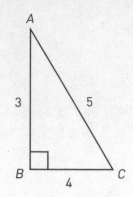

Let's begin by finding each ratio, as shown below:

$$\text{Sin } C = \frac{3}{5}$$

$$\text{Cos } A = \frac{3}{5}$$

Notice how the two ratios are equal, which means the ratio of sin C to cos A is equal to one.

This is the property to know:

If sin x = cos y, then $x + y = 90$. Or,

If ∠A and ∠B are complementary angles in a right triangle, then sin A = cos B

Simply put, in a right triangle, the sine of one non-right angle will always be equal to the cosine of the other non-right angle.

Similar Triangles

Some questions may contain two triangles that have the same shape but are different sizes. When these triangles are **similar**, their corresponding angles are equal, and their corresponding sides have equal ratios. The triangles shown below, △ABC and △DEF, are similar to each other.

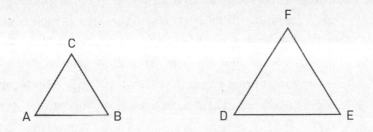

Since the two triangles above are similar, their corresponding angles are equal.

$$\angle A = \angle D$$

$$\angle B = \angle E$$

$$\angle C = \angle F$$

Another key feature of similar triangles is that the corresponding sides will have equal ratios, as shown below:

$$\frac{AC}{DF} = \frac{BC}{EF} = \frac{AB}{DE}$$

In the first ratio, side *AC* is a side of the smaller triangle and *DF* is a side on the larger triangle. You must set up each ratio in the same way. In other words, the side that you chose as the numerator and the side that you chose for the denominator must match the corresponding sides of the other ratios.

The key to solving questions about similarity is to correctly match the corresponding sides of the similar triangles and form ratios, thus creating a proportion that can be solved using cross-multiplication.

If the two triangles shown below are similar, what is the value of *x*?

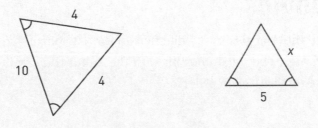

This question can be answered by correctly setting up ratios of corresponding sides. Since the triangles do not contain any letters, it will be best to use the arcs, which represent congruent angles, as a means of identification. In the right triangle, the 5 is located between the arcs, and in the left triangle, the 10 is located between the arcs. This allows you to write a ratio of $\frac{5}{10}$ and a second ratio of $\frac{x}{4}$. These two ratios create a proportion, or $\frac{5}{10} = \frac{x}{4}$, which can be solved using cross-multiplication to get $x = 2$. You could also have used the proportion $\frac{10}{5} = \frac{4}{x}$ to correctly solve for x.

Hint

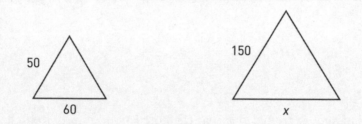

Some similarity questions can be solved without a proportion. In these triangles, the bigger triangle is three times larger, because 150 is 3 times 50.

To find x, simply multiply 60 by 3 to get 180.

Two Special Similar Triangles

Let's examine two common similar triangles that you may see on the test.

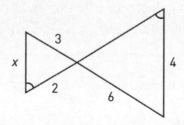

The first type looks like the triangles in the diagram above. The parts that match up are opposite and across from each other. The x matches up with the 4, but the key is to match up the 3 and the 6. See how they are opposite each other?

You may be able to figure this one out in your head, but feel free to use a proportion.

$$\frac{x}{4} = \frac{3}{6}$$

$$6x = 12$$

$$x = 2$$

The second type of similar triangles looks like those in the diagram below, where the top triangle, $\triangle ABC$, is similar to the larger triangle, $\triangle ADE$.

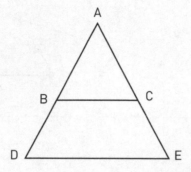

The key is to identify the corresponding sides, so BC will match up with DE, AB will match up with AD, and AC will match with AE.

$$\frac{BC}{DE} = \frac{AB}{AD} = \frac{AC}{AE}$$

Hint

In the diagram of the triangle, $\angle B$ is equal to $\angle D$ and $\angle C$ is equal to $\angle E$.

PRACTICE B

1) Two angles are supplementary. If one angle is two times the measure of the other, what is the measure of the larger angle?

2) A quadrilateral has angle measures of 36°, 84°, and 142°. Which of the following is the measure of the fourth angle?

A) 80

C) 180

B) 98

D) 262

3) In the figure below, line m and line n are parallel. What is the value, in degrees, of x?

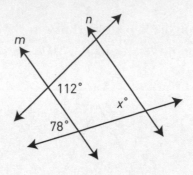

A) 68

C) 102

B) 78

D) 112

4) The triangle shown below is a right triangle. Find the area of the triangle. (The formula for finding area of a triangle is $A = \frac{1}{2}bh$).

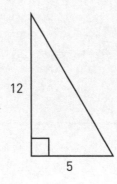

5) The two triangles below are similar. What is the value of x?

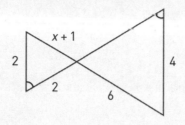

6) On line segment AC, point B is the midpoint. What is the length of segment BC?

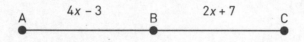

7) In the figure below, line m is perpendicular to line l. What is the value of x?

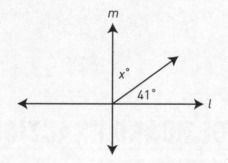

8) In triangle ABC, angle B is a right angle and $\sin A$ is equal to $\dfrac{4}{5}$. What is the value of $\tan A$?

A) $\dfrac{3}{5}$

B) $\dfrac{4}{5}$

C) $\dfrac{3}{4}$

D) $\dfrac{4}{3}$

9) In triangle ABC, angle B is a right angle and $\cos A$ is equal to $\dfrac{3}{5}$. What is the measure of $\sin C$?

10) Triangle ABC is a right triangle with AB being the hypotenuse. If $\sin A$ is $\dfrac{3}{5}$ and $\cos B$ is $\dfrac{3}{5}$, what is the sum of the measures of angles A and B?

Answers

Practice A (page 502)

1) $180 - 72 = 108°$

2) $180 - 84 = 96°$

3) $180 - 70 = 110°$

4) $180 - 118 = 62°$

5) $60°$

Practice B (page 517)

1) $120°$

2) B

3) B

4) 30

5) 2

6) 17

7) $49°$

8) D

9) $\frac{3}{5}$

10) $90°$

UNTIMED COLLEGE BOARD PRACTICE

Complete the following College Board practice problems from the College Board's *The Official SAT Study Guide* or online at www.collegeboard.org. Review answers after completing.

Test 1, Math: No Calculator, #17

Test 1, Math: Calculator, #3

Test 2, Math: No Calculator, #18

Test 3, Math: No Calculator, #11, 18, 20

Test 3, Math: Calculator, #23

Test 4, Math: No Calculator #16, 17

Chapter **19**

Food for Thought

"*Binging on soda and sweets for as little as six weeks may make you stupid.*[13]**"**

You've probably heard the expression "You are what you eat," which is the idea that what you put into your body you become, in terms of appearance, weight, and overall health. Food, however, does much more than just affect your health and your appearance: it has the power to increase or decrease your focus, cognitive ability, memory, and overall intelligence. When it comes to the SAT, the saying would be better phrased as "You think what you eat." Therefore, if you want to think better on the SAT and feel better about yourself, make better choices about the food you eat.

Have you ever eaten a greasy cheeseburger or several chocolate chip cookies and then attempted to study for a test or concentrate in a class? Chances are you felt lethargic and sleepy and had trouble concentrating. This is the food wreaking havoc on your body, dulling your senses, and clouding your judgment. To succeed in life, and on the SAT, avoid the dreaded food coma at all costs and begin to build a positive, healthy diet routine designed to boost intelligence and improve concentration. You need *brain food*.

In this chapter, we will break down the basics of healthy eating for the brain, the best brain food out there, why it works, and how to go about creating a great diet routine that will help you unlock your brain's true potential. First, though, let's discuss the foods you eat that literally make you dumber: Brain Drainers.

Just like a computer bogged down with viruses, the brain is slowed down by certain brain-draining foods. Avoid these at all costs! Unfortunately, the majority of easily accessible foods—chicken fingers, French fries, pizza, soda—are not the meals you should be eating to maximize your brain power. Although it may be difficult to eliminate these brain-draining foods entirely, there are small swaps you can make that can lead to big boosts in brain power.

Take a look at this table of healthy food swaps and replace the food or drink on the left with the one on the right.

Brain Drainer	Brain Booster
soda or other sugary drinks	water
chicken fingers	grilled chicken
candy	fruit (especially berries)
milk chocolate	dark chocolate
French fries	sweet potato
nachos	guacamole with blue corn or pita chips
sugar	raw honey
potato chips	vegetables and hummus
pretzels	walnuts, almonds, pistachios

If you notice a pattern, we are simply replacing sugary foods, processed foods, and fried foods with whole, natural foods.

What swaps can you make in your daily diet?

Just by making three to four swaps from the table above, you will be eliminating foods that hinder your brain performance and, as result, you'll be priming yourself for success on the SAT. You are on the right track for developing a healthier, more powerful brain. Now that you have the general idea of brain food, let's go a bit further and spotlight a couple of powerhouse additions to the brain boosting family.

1) Hydration: Believe it or not, one of the best things you can do for your brain is drink water. Mild dehydration can actually impede brain function. In one study, "subjects exhibited progressive impairment in mathematical ability, short-term memory and visuomotor function once 2% body fluid deficit was achieved."[14] Avoid that coffee or energy drink—these drinks might give you a quick boost of energy, but they also end up dehydrating your muscles, which constricts them and impedes blood flow to the brain…and makes you dumber!

2) Omega-3 fatty acids: These fatty acids are crucial to optimizing the brain for many reasons. They also protect against the damaging effects of sugar and high-fructose corn syrup, so if you go out and eat a candy bar, as long as you have those omega-3s, you will have some shield against that Brain Drainer's negative effects.[15] Consumption of omega-3 fatty acids can also increase gray matter. They make your brain grow! In addition, omega-3 fatty acids improve mood and boost learning and memory function.[16]

Possible sources: wild Alaskan salmon, mackerel, walnuts, eggs, flaxseed, chia seeds

3) Antioxidants: Toxic free radicals damage the brain, creating inflammation and impairing memory, concentration, and overall cognition. To beat them, consume antioxidants. Antioxidants neutralize free radicals in the brain and thus enhance brain function. Berries improve cognitive function, including memory, focus, and concentration, by drastically reducing inflammation and oxidative stress in the brain.[17] Blueberries in particular can also improve overall cognitive performance, especially in relation to completing complex tasks.[18]

Possible sources: wild blueberries, strawberries, cranberries, blackberries, apples, cherries, pinto beans, dark chocolate, ginger, cinnamon, pecans, cherries, cilantro

4) Curcumin: Curcumin can cross the blood–brain barrier for immediate absorption and has many significant benefits. It is an antioxidant that neutralizes free radicals and reduces inflammation in the body and brain. It improves memory and concentration. Most importantly though, it stimulates neurogenesis (the creation of neurons), not only of regular brain cells, but also of neural stem cells.[19]

Possible sources: turmeric, curry powder

As you begin to build your brain-food diet, remember that learning to eat for brain power is just like learning anything else with growth mindset: it takes time. It's not necessary or helpful to jump all in and completely reinvent your diet in one day. Instead, begin swapping healthier foods into your diet little by little, seeing how your body reacts to these changes. As time progresses and your body acclimates to these new foods, you can introduce more and more of them into your diet.

Essay: Timed Practice

Now that you have an understanding of the rhetorical devices authors use to build arguments and the structure of the SAT essay, it is time to review a sample essay prompt, passage, and response to understand how the method is put into action.

Sample Essay Prompt and Passage

Read the following essay prompt, as well as the passage to which it refers.

Write an essay in which you explain how the author builds an argument to persuade his audience that our national parks should be preserved to ensure historical legacy and literacy. In your essay, analyze how the author uses one or more of the features listed in the box that precedes the passage (or features of your own choice) to strengthen the logic and persuasiveness of his or her argument. Be sure that your analysis focuses on the most relevant features of the passage.

As you read the passage below, consider how the author uses:

- evidence, such as facts or examples, to support claims

- reasoning to develop ideas and to connect claims to evidence

- stylistic or persuasive elements, such as word choice or appeals to emotion to add power to the ideas expressed

---

1   While many Americans associate the Park Service with the preservation of pristine natural places, few realize that almost two-thirds of the national

5   parks—Gettysburg, San Antonio Missions, Valley Forge, the Frederick Douglass House, and Little Bighorn, to name a few—were designated specifically to preserve an important

10 aspect or moment in our nation's history.

Moreover, the Service is directed by law to assist with historic preservation beyond park boundaries—on all federal

15 lands, on tribal reservations, and in the public and private sectors. Its responsibilities include administering

the National Historic Landmarks program, which has designated more than 2,300 nationally significant properties since 1935, and the National Register of Historic Places, which now includes more than seventy thousand sites. The Service provides matching grants to restore public and privately owned historics places through the Historic Preservation Fund. The NPS-administered Historic Preservation Tax Incentives program, which encourages the preservation of historic places in town and city centers, has accounted for more than $23 billion in private investment nationwide since 1976. In many ways, the National Park Service is our nation's Department of Heritage.

Our historical heritage, however, faces important challenges in the twenty-first century. Many sites and structures have been degraded by neglect and vandalism; others are at risk because of inadequate budgetary support or insensitive national, state, and local policies. Development encroaches upon our battlefields. Historic neighborhood schools are abandoned. Prehistoric archaeological resources are looted or vandalized. Suburban sprawl consumes historic farmsteads and rural landscapes. Acid rain eats at cemetery stones, memorials, and monuments.

America may be losing something else—its historic literacy. Of some 556 seniors surveyed at 55 of the nation's top colleges and universities, only 60 percent placed the American Civil War in the correct half of the nineteenth century. Only 34 percent identified George Washington as the American general at the Revolutionary War battle of Yorktown—37 percent thought the general was Ulysses S. Grant. At 78 percent of the institutions polled, no history whatsoever was required as part of the undergraduate program.

"It is not surprising," states the report by the American Council of Trustees and Alumni, "that college seniors know little American history. Few students leave high school with an adequate knowledge of American history, and even the best colleges and universities do nothing to close the knowledge gap." As historian David McCullough observed in the same report, "We are raising a generation of young Americans who are historically illiterate."

At the same time, another study found that many Americans not only feel a strong connection to their past but hold historic sites and museums to be their most trustworthy sources of historical information, above movies, television, college professors, and even personal accounts from relatives.

The study of our nation's history, formal and informal, is an essential part of our civic education. In a democratic society such as ours, it is important to understand the journey of liberty and justice, together with the economic, social, religious, and other forces that barred or opened the ways for our ancestors, and the distances yet to be covered. Visits to historic places,

95　whether managed by the Park Service or by others, allow us to take the measure of our history in immediate ways. Parks should be not just recrea-tional destinations but springboards

100　for personal journeys of intellectual and cultural enrichment.

The Park Service must ensure that the American story is told faithfully, completely, and accurately. The story

105　is often noble, but sometimes shameful and sad. In an age of growing cultural

diversity, the Service must continually ask whether the way in which it tells these stories has meaning for all our

110　citizens. The Service must look anew at the process and make improvements. For example, the relationship between environmental and human history should be seamlessly presented as

115　inseparable chapters of our life on this planet.

To the National Park Service, the challenge is critical. Our nation's history is our civic glue. Without it, our national

120　character is diminished.

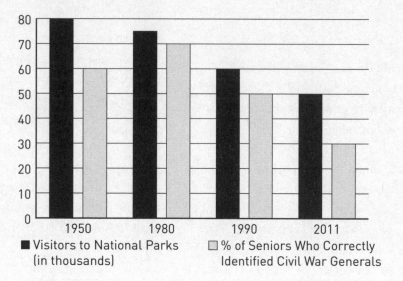

■ Visitors to National Parks (in thousands)　　□ % of Seniors Who Correctly Identified Civil War Generals

Mindset Tip

As you read the sample essay that follows, take note of your mental chatter. What do you say to yourself about writing and analysis as you examine this essay? What are your beliefs about writing? Becoming aware of this mental chatter is the first step to building your self-confidence and giving your brain the freedom to grow. Quiet that mental chatter by cutting yourself some slack. Realize that you might not be at the level of the writing below but that you will get there with practice, and with each challenging Rock Mover essay prompt, you stretch and expand your brain.

Sample Essay Response

Read the following planning table that summarizes the narrative techniques for each body paragraph, as well as the subsequent sample essay response, noting the structural components listed earlier. We have bolded the thesis.

Body Paragraph 1: Facts and Statistics	• "assist with historic preservation beyond park boundaries" • "designated more than 2,300 nationally significant properties since 1935" • "Of some 556 seniors surveyed at 55 of the nation's top colleges and universities, only 60% placed the American Civil War in the correct half of the nineteenth Century."
Body Paragraph 2: Syntax and Parallelism	• "Development encroaches upon our battlefields. Historic neighborhood schools are abandoned. Prehistoric archaeological resources are looted or vandalized."
Body Paragraph 3: Diction	• "our nation's history" • "our historical heritage" • "our national character" • "Parks should be not just recreational destinations but springboards for personal journeys of intellectual and cultural enrichment."

* We chose to categorize "our" as diction to better fit the paragraph, but it can also be categorized as point of view (first person plural)

Essay

In the passage excerpted from "Rethinking the National Parks for the twenty-first century," the author details the many important functions of the National Park Service while also stressing the decline in historic literacy and the problems the program faces in ensuring the preservation of America's historic legacy. He provides a cogent argument as to why the National Park Service is both necessary in our country and facing a critical challenge. **To build this <u>argument</u>, the author uses concrete evidence and statistics and stylistic elements such as parallel syntax, first person plural point of view, and emotionally charged diction.**

The foundation of the author's argument to improve our National Parks Service is in facts and statistics. In paragraph two, he delineates the many services that the NPS provides to the nation, from "[assisting] with historic preservation beyond park boundaries" to "[designating] more than 2,300 nationally significant properties since 1935" under its National Historic Landmarks program branch. These facts make the reader aware of the many responsibilities of the NPS. The author also emphasizes extremely troubling statistics, which serve to impress upon the reader the current need for the NPS. For example, he states that "Of some 556 seniors surveyed at 55 of the nation's top colleges and universities, only 60% placed the American Civil War in the correct half of the nineteenth century." Including both sets of statistics underscores the author's argument that the NPS is a crucial, multifaceted fixture in America and that it has a critical challenge ahead of it.

The author adds to his argument of the degradation of America's historical heritage by using parallel syntax to create the effect of an overwhelming litany of problems. In the entire third paragraph the author lists problem after problem in short, rapid-fire bursts: "Development encroaches upon our battlefields. Historic neighborhood schools are abandoned. Prehistoric archaeological resources are looted or vandalized." Phrased in this way, the situation in America seems dire indeed.

Perhaps, though, the most persuasive tactic the author uses to convey his argument is his use of poignant diction. This stylistic device, although subtle, evokes a significant emotional response from the reader. Throughout the essay the author repeatedly uses phrases such as "our nation's history," "our historical heritage," and "our national character." The use of "our" in each of these statements creates a sense of shared purpose and camaraderie. To the author, the task of maintaining and rebuilding our historical literacy and heritage belongs to all of us. The author also skillfully incorporates evocative diction toward the end of the essay. He states that the "Parks should be not just recreational destinations but springboards for personal journeys of intellectual and cultural enrichment." This diction is both personal and inspirational; it reinforces the idea that we all have something to gain from the NPS, and that it has the potential to enrich every one of our lives. The author continues by discussing the "American story," and how it must be faithfully told. Everyone can connect with the idea of the American story—stories are universal and touchstones to family and community. The author's argument is strongly enhanced by using this type of language to refer to our country's heritage.

Evocative, camaraderie-building diction, parallel syntax, and hard evidence are all important components to the argument in this essay. **Through these devices the author persuasively demonstrates both the historical importance of and current necessity of the National Park Service.** It is perhaps because of essays like these that many tax-funded government programs can continue to function and serve the American people.

* * *

It is now time to put your new skills to the test in this full practice essay. As you write, make sure to follow the method provided for analysis, annotation, outlining, and writing while also incorporating some of vocabulary we have listed below.

Mindset Tip

Did you get enough sleep last night? As you prepare to write this essay, do you find yourself yawning, daydreaming, or feeling groggy and unfocused? If so, stop. Any writing you do, or for that matter, any SAT prep that you attempt in a sleep-deprived state, will be counterproductive and have a detrimental effect on both your score and your progress. We're going to tell you to do something you probably never hear: PROCRASTINATE. It is far more effective to postpone the essay writing until you are well-rested. A well-rested writer will not only write better but also capitalize on all the learning and growth from the process.

Essay Vocabulary

Use these words when writing an essay to elevate your argument. Each of the definitions provided are aligned with usage in essay writing.

1) **illustrate** (v). to demonstrate, explain, clarify: *The author illustrates the need for tax reductions by including several alarming statistics.*

2) **depict** (v). to show: *Through his use of vivid imagery, the author depicts a vibrant community center.*

3) **portray** (v). to describe or show: *The way the author portrayed the Native Americans in his speech conveyed his respect and admiration for them.*

4) **underscore** (v). to emphasize or accentuate: *The author underscores several key points in his argument.*

5) **contend** (v). to assert or maintain earnestly: *The speaker contends that much more needs to be done to alleviate the racial tension in society.*

6) **advocate** (v). to speak or write in favor of; to support or urge by argument; to recommend publicly: *The author advocates using several different methods to combat erosion of the Jersey shoreline.*

7) **refute** (v). to counter, argue against, or dispute: *The author refuted the sitting president's tax policy.*

8) **serve** (v). to function; to work to do a certain thing: *The author's use of metaphorical language in the first paragraph serves to illuminate his point that fiscal prudence is crucial in our current economy.*

9) **convey** (v). to express; to communicate: *The author conveys his disdain for a disposable culture by quoting several experts in the field of planned obsolescence.*

10) **facilitate** (v). to enable; to assist or aid: *The author explains how a simple tweak to the current zoning plan for the city would greatly alleviate traffic and facilitate easy transportation from one borough to the next.*

Vocabulary Words 271–285

271) **nostalgic** (adj). homesick, sentimental, longing for home: *The old man was nostalgic for the carefree days of his youth.*

272) **exploit** (v). a) to use selfishly for one's own profit: *Thomas exploited Meredith's good nature by convincing her to do his homework for him;* (n). b) a notable feat or impressive act: *Achilles' exploits are well known by most scholars of antiquity and Greek mythology.*

273) **attribute** (v). a) to regard as resulting from a specified cause: *The high crime rate in the city was attributed to the drug problem;* (n). b) belonging to a person, thing or group; a quality or characteristic: *One of Gjula's best attributes is her perseverance.*

274) **civil disobedience** (n). the refusal to obey certain laws in the attempt to change legislation through nonviolent techniques such as boycotting, picketing, and nonpayment of taxes: *Civil disobedience is one expected result of an oppressive government restricting people's rights.*

275) **suffrage** (n). the right to vote, especially in a political election: *The women protested and fought for suffrage, the right to vote.*

276) **endeavor** (v). to attempt by effort: *Drew endeavored to break the record for consecutive wins in high school wrestling.*

277) **integrity** (n). honesty, moral uprightness: *The candidate won the election because many perceived him as having integrity and always doing the right thing.*

278) **alacrity** (n). cheerful eagerness: *Jillian leapt up with alacrity and accepted some celery sticks, her favorite brain-food snack.*

279) **credible** (adj). believable; trustworthy: *After deciding that the threat was credible, the FBI suspended all travel in and out of the tunnel.*

280) **cultivate** (v). to foster the growth of: *Alli cultivates an inner strength and self-love in her yoga students.*

281) **unscrupulous** (adj). without principles; immoral: *The unscrupulous practice of the mortgage companies led to the financial collapse in the banking industry.*

282) **florid** (adj). fancy and elaborate; flowery: *The castles in Sintra, Portugal are decorated in beautiful, florid tiling.*

283) **sovereign** (adj). free; not controlled by outside forces: *The emperor of the land had sovereign rule over all the inhabitants of the empire.*

284) **allegiance** (n). loyalty, commitment, fidelity: *The slaves swore their allegiance to the rebels who vowed to set them free.*

285) **naïve** (adj). ignorant due to lack of experience or youth: *The naïve little boy was easily convinced by his older brother that gremlins lived in the basement.*

Latin and Greek Roots 101–105

101) SPEC/SPIC: look, see (specious, perspective, aspect, speculate, auspicious, perspicacious)

102) STA/SED: to be in one place/unmoving (stationary, sediment, stagnant, stalwart, homeostasis, constant, sedentary)

103) SUA: smooth (assuage, suave, casual, persuade)

104) SUB/SUP: below (subdue, subordinate, subjugate, submissive, suppress, support)

105) SUPER/SUR: above (superfluous, supercilious, surpass, surmount)

TIMED COLLEGE BOARD PRACTICE

Complete the following College Board practice problems from College Board's *The Official SAT Study Guide* or online at www.collegeboard.org. Review answers after completing.

Test 1, Essay Section. Write a full essay in response to the essay prompt.

Math Test: Advanced Geometry Topics

In this chapter we will continue with advanced geometry topics including circles, volume, and a few other advanced topics.

Parts of a Circle

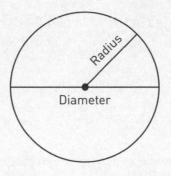

Let's start with the fundamental parts of a circle.

The **diameter** is a straight line across the circle that goes through the center. A diameter will cut a circle in half, thus creating a 180° arc.

The **radius** of a circle goes from the circle's center to any point on the circle. Each radius of a circle is equal in size.

The **circumference** of a circle is the distance around the outside of the circle. The formula for finding the circumference of a circle is $C = 2\pi r$.

The **area** of a circle is the measure of space inside the circle. The formula for area is $A = \pi r^2$.

Both formulas are on the formula sheet at the front of each SAT section.

Here are some examples pertaining to the parts of the circle.

If the diameter of a circle is equal to 8, what is the circumference of that circle?

Since the circumference can be found using the formula $C = 2\pi r$, just plug in 4 for r to get 8π, which can also be expressed as approximately 25.13.

Hint

Some questions that require a calculation using π may leave π in the answer, and others may require you to multiply it out. If you must multiply, it's best to use the π button on the calculator and pay careful attention to what decimal place the question is asking you to round to.

If the radius of a circle is equal to $\frac{2}{3}$, what is the area?

This question will just require you to plug directly into the area formula, as shown below. Do not be fooled by the fraction, as you just square the numerator and denominator.

$$\left(\frac{2}{3}\right)^2 \pi = \frac{4}{9}\pi \text{, or } 1.40$$

Let's try a more difficult example.

If the circumference of a circle is equal to 8π, which of the following best approximates the area of that circle?

A) 40

B) 50

C) 55

D) 60

This question will require some serious problem-solving skills, and since we know the circumference is equal to 8π, we can substitute that for C and solve for r, which is shown below.

$$8\pi = 2\pi r$$

$$\frac{8\pi}{2\pi} = \frac{2\pi r}{2\pi}$$

$$r = 4$$

To find the area, plug 4 in for the radius in the formula $A = \pi r^2$, or $A = 4^2\pi$, which is 16π, or approximately 50.26, making choice (B) the correct answer.

Angles of a Circle

There are two different types of angles of a circle that the SAT will require you to know: central angles and inscribed angles. A central angle has its vertex at the center of the circle and an inscribed angle's vertex is on the circle. An example of each is shown below:

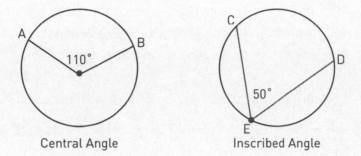

The sides of each of these angles create what is called the intercepted arc. The central angle creates arc AB, or $\overset{\frown}{AB}$. The inscribed angle will intercept $\overset{\frown}{CD}$. An arc of a circle can be measured in degrees, and the central angle is always equal to its intercepted arc, so in the circle above $\overset{\frown}{AB}$ is equal to 110°.

The intercepted arc of an inscribed angle will always be double the angle. In the circle above, the measure of $\overset{\frown}{CD}$ is equal to 100°. Since all the way around the circle is 360°, you can also find the measure of $\overset{\frown}{CED}$ by subtracting 100° from 360° to get 260°.

Length of an Arc

Arc length can also be measured by the actual distance traveled around the curve. Circumference measures the distance all the way around the circle, and arc length is the measure of the portion of the circumference around the circle.

To find arc length, use the following formula:

$$\text{Arc Length} = \frac{n^\circ}{360} \times 2\pi r$$

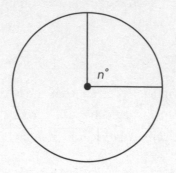

Notice the $2\pi r$, which is the formula to find the circumference. When you find the arc length, you are just multiplying the angle by the circumference and then dividing by 360°.

Try this example:

What is the length of arc AB if the radius of the circle is 5 feet? Round your answer to the nearest foot.

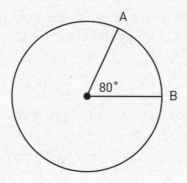

As mentioned above, arc length can be found by multiplying the ratio of the central angle over 360° by the circumference of the circle:

$$\frac{80}{360} \times 2\pi(5) = 6.98$$

The correct answer is 7 feet.

Here is another example that involves arc length.

If a circle has a circumference of 20 meters and segment AC is the diameter, find the length of arc ABC.

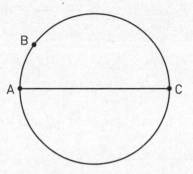

A) 5 meters

B) 10 meters

C) 15 meters

D) 20 meters

A diameter splits the circle in half, so the intercepted arc is equal to half the circumference.

Since all the way around is 20 and a diameter cuts the circle in half, then arc ABC must be equal to 10 meters, or choice (B).

The question could have also been solved using a proportion, as shown below:

$$\frac{180°}{360°} = \frac{x \text{ meters}}{20 \text{ meters}}$$

This proportion contains a ratio of the measure of the arc over 360° and another ratio that contains the arc length over the circumference. This idea will be useful for the next example.

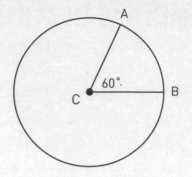

Arc AB, as shown above, has an arc length of 4π. What is the circumference of circle C?

A) 24π

B) 48π

C) 60

D) 60π

The best approach to correctly answering this question is to set up a proportion, as shown below:

$$\frac{60}{360} = \frac{4\pi}{C}$$

Since this question type could appear on the No Calculator section, the fraction $\frac{60}{360}$ can be simplified to $\frac{6}{36}$ which can then be simplified to $\frac{1}{6}$ and is now much easier to solve using cross-multiplication. The correct answer 24π, or choice (A).

Hint

You may also be asked to work with the area of a sector. A sector would be a shaded region of a circle. The formula is the same, except instead of multiplying by circumference, you will multiply by the area of the circle.

$$\text{Area of a sector} = \frac{n^\circ}{360} \times \pi r^2$$

If you are asked to find the ratio, proportion, or fraction, use only the $\frac{n^\circ}{360}$ part.

Converting Radians and Degrees

Advanced math will use radians, which is another way of measuring the central angle of a circle. All the way around the circle is equal to 2π radians, and halfway around the circle is equal to π radians. This means that 2π radians is the same as 360° and π is the same as 180°.

Some SAT questions may require you to convert from degrees to radians or radians to degrees and here is how to do so:

- To convert radians to degrees, multiply by $\frac{180}{\pi}$.

- To convert from degrees to radians, multiply by $\frac{\pi}{180}$.

Here are a few examples that require you to use these two rules.

$$60° \text{ is equal to } a\pi \text{ radians. What is the value of } a?$$

This question is asking you to convert 60° degrees to radians, so you want to multiply 60 by $\frac{\pi}{180}$ to get $\frac{60\pi}{180}$, which can be simplified to $\frac{1}{3}\pi$. This means that a is equal to $\frac{1}{3}$.

$$\frac{3\pi}{2} \text{ radians is equal to how many degrees?}$$

To convert from radians to degrees, multiply $\frac{3\pi}{2}$ by $\frac{180}{\pi}$, as shown below:

$$\frac{3\pi \cdot 180}{2\pi}$$

The first step is to cancel out the π from the numerator and denominator, which leaves you with:

$$\frac{3 \times 180}{2}$$

This expression can be easily simplified with a calculator, but can be found without a calculator by simplifying $\frac{180}{2}$ to 90 and multiplying 90 by 3 to get 270°.

Equations of Circles on Graphs

Writing equations of circles is easy, provided you know the equation $(x - h)^2 + (y - k)^2 = r^2$, in which (h, k) is the center of the circle and r is the radius.

You'll notice that h and k appear in the equation of the circle. In that equation, they are subtracted from the variables, which means that to find the center, you simply need to reverse each of their signs.

> Which of the following equations represents the circle with a diameter of 10 units and a center at $(2, -3)$?
>
> A) $(x + 2)^2 + (y - 3)^2 = 25$
>
> B) $(x + 2)^2 + (y - 3)^2 = 100$
>
> C) $(x - 2)^2 + (y + 3)^2 = 25$
>
> D) $(x - 2)^2 + (y + 3)^2 = 100$

Start by identifying the answer choices with the correct center. To write the equation of a circle, plug the values into the equation $(x - h)^2 + (y - k)^2 = r^2$. You'll get $(x - 2)^2 + (y + 3)^2$, allowing you to eliminate choices (A) and (B).

Be careful with this question! The diameter is 10, but it is the radius that is needed to correctly write an equation of a circle, thus the correct answer is choice (C).

Blind Spot

Don't forget, if you are given the diameter of the circle you must divide by 2. If the diameter is 12, the radius is 6.

Advanced Equations of Circles

This next topic is a Rock Mover and will require you to embrace challenge and perseverance. Not all equations of circles will be written as shown above and instead might appear in this form, also known as the general form:

$$ax^2 + by^2 + cx + dy + e = 0$$

This form looks intimidating and the key is to rewrite it in standard form using the same method we learned in Chapter 15 called completing the square.

Here is an example using the general form, and although it is a difficult question, with some practice you can master it.

What is the radius of the circle with the equation $x^2 + y^2 + 14x - 12y + 4 = 0$?

Start by moving the constant, or the number without a variable, over to the right.

$$x^2 + y^2 + 14x - 12y = -4$$

Before you can complete the square, group the x terms together and the y terms together.

$$x^2 + 14x + y^2 - 12y = -4$$

You will be completing the square twice, so add two blank spaces to each side. These spaces represent a number that will be added to both sides of the equation.

$$x^2 + 14x + \underline{\quad} + y^2 - 12y + \underline{\quad} = -4 + \underline{\quad} + \underline{\quad}$$

Now, determine the numbers that will fill in the spaces by dividing the coefficient of the x term by 2, and then square that number. Then complete the same process with the y term.

$$\frac{14}{2} = 7^2 = 49$$

$$-\frac{12}{2} = (-6)^2 = 36$$

$$x^2 + 14x + 49 + y^2 - 12y + 36 = -4 + 49 + 36$$

Notice that two trinomials remain, one that contains xs and another that contains ys, which can both be factored individually. You can also add the numbers on the right to get:

$$(x + 7)^2 + (y - 6)^2 = 81$$

Now that the equation is written in this form, you can identify the center and radius. Remember to adjust the signs to find the center and take the square root of the number on the right to find the radius.

The center would be (–7, 6) and the radius is 9.

Volume of Shapes

You may be asked to find the volume of a cylinder, cone, or other shapes.

The formulas will always be given to you. The key is to write the formula down, substitute in the given information, and use order of operations correctly. Here is an example to practice:

> What is the volume of a cylinder with a radius of 4 and a height of 10? Round to the nearest whole number.

Start by writing down the formula, $V = \pi r^2 h$, which can be found on the formula sheet. Now substitute the given information into the formula and simplify using order of operations.

$$V = \pi(4)^2(10)$$

$$V = 160\pi = 160(3.14) = 502.4$$

The correct answer is 502.

Some questions may give you the volume and ask you to solve for the radius or the height, which will require the same skills you learned from solving equations. Here is an example:

> If the volume of a cylinder is 100π and the radius is 5, what is the height?

Once again, begin by writing the formula down and substituting in key information.

$$V = \pi r^2 h$$

$$100\pi = \pi(5)^2 h$$

$$100\pi = 25\pi h$$

To solve for h, divide both sides by 25π to get:

$$\frac{100\pi}{25\pi} = \frac{25\pi h}{25\pi}$$

$$h = 4$$

Here is another example to try.

A cylinder has a base with an area of 16π and a height of 10. What is the volume of the cylinder?

This question requires you to use the formula for area of a cylinder, which is $V = \pi r^2 h$, but if you notice, the base of a cylinder is a circle, which uses the area formula πr^2. Really, when you are finding the volume of any shape, all you need do is multiply the area of the base by the height.

You can substitute 16π in for πr^2 and the 10 in for h to get:

$$V = 16\pi(10) = 160\pi$$

PRACTICE

1) The base of a rectangular prism has an area of 24 in^2 and a height of $\frac{1}{4}$ inch. What is the volume of the rectangular prism?

2) What is the radius of the circle with equation $(x + 3)^2 + (y - 1)^2 = 16$?

3) Which of the following is an equation of a circle with the center at the origin and a diameter of 8?

A) $x^2 + y^2 = 4$ **C)** $x^2 + y^2 = 16$

B) $x^2 + y^2 = 8$ **D)** $x^2 - y^2 = 16$

4) The volume of a cylinder is 48π and the area of its base is equal to 16π. What is the height of the cylinder?

5) What is the center and radius of $x^2 + y^2 + 6x - 10y = 2$?

A) Center at $(0, 0)$ and a radius of 2   **C)** Center at $(-3, 5)$ and a radius of 6

B) Center at $(6, -10)$ and radius of $\sqrt{2}$ **D)** Center at $(2, 4)$ and a radius of 12

Answers

1) 6

2) 4

3) C

4) 3

5) C

UNTIMED COLLEGE BOARD PRACTICE

Complete the following College Board practice problems from College Board's *The Official SAT Study Guide* or online at www.collegeboard.org. Review answers after completing.

Test 1, Math: Calculator, #24, 35

Test 2, Math: No Calculator, #19

Test 2, Math: Calculator, #24, 30, 36

Test 3, Math: Calculator, #25, 34

Test 4, Math: Calculator, #18, 24, 36

Chapter **20**

Preparation for the Test

> **"***Success comes from knowing that you did your best to become the best that you are capable of being.***"** —John Wooden

It's the night before your state championship game.

It's the morning of your first college interview at one of your top schools.

It's the day before the opening night of the school play in which you have your first leading role.

It's the day before the test that will help determine your future.

Each of these moments has the potential to bring up a lot of emotions; after all, these events can and should mean a lot to you. The typical belief is that the nervous excitement that accompanies "the night before" can often do more harm than good by sabotaging even the most poised competitors and students. Although this can happen to some kids, with the right preparation, these emotions can become the fuel for your perseverance and positivity. So, don't worry about these feelings. Realize they are normal and capitalize on the rush of energy that they will bring you.

What is on the other side of the test for you? What if you improve your score by 200 points? You could emerge from the test an entirely different person. You could use all the mindset and testing strategies correctly and realize their power. And even if you only improve by 40 points, you'll be able to recognize several areas that you can now focus on and practice, more information to guide your training moving forward. Perhaps you make several revelation mistakes and discover gaps in your knowledge that you can now fill. No matter what, this test will benefit you.

Before we continue to the final phase of your training, a full SAT, let's take a moment to reflect on the person you have become and the strategies you have learned.

- You are the person who understands the brain's ability to grow and change.

- You are the person who practices consistently to strengthen neural pathways.

- You are the person who thinks positively and increases your problem-solving ability.

- You are the person who re-visions failures and mistakes and sees them as opportunities for growth.

- You are the calm, focused person who breathes deeply to overcome stress and anxiety.

- You are the person who sets meaningful goals and possesses the self-confidence to achieve them.

- You are the person who emerges from the Abyss.

- You are person who moves the rock.

- You are the dangerous thinker who welcomes challenge.

- You are the doubling penny that, at any moment, will break through to become a million dollars.

In this chapter, you will take your first full practice SAT, which is designed to challenge you, test your stamina, and give you the opportunity to put all you've learned into action. This test is a chance for you to use your skills to prove to yourself one final time how far you've come. As with all the training that you have done before, approach this test as if it were the actual SAT. This means you should take this full SAT at 8:00 in the morning, in one full sitting, with only a few bathroom breaks.

We are including a simple protocol for you to follow to simulate the actual night before and morning of the test:

1) The night before, review English and math strategies.

- Reading Test

  » Read for the main purpose of the passage, underlining as you read to create a passage map.

  » Be wary of wrong-answer traps.

  » Go back to the passage and reread.

  » Predict the answers in your head.

- Writing Test

  » Read sentences aloud to hear errors on the Writing and Language Test.

  » Abide by the golden rule of grammar: when all things are equal, shorter is better.

  » Plug the answer choice back into the sentence to hear if it sounds correct.

- Essay

  » Read and annotate the passage noting logos, ethos, pathos, and stylistic devices.

  » Create an outline dividing your essay by device or narrative technique.

  » Make sure to have an introduction, at least two body paragraphs, and conclusion.

- Math

  » Find a starting point in longer word problems.

  » Know what the question is asking of you.

  » Realize you will not need to know every piece of information to solve for the correct answer.

  » Pick a strategy that works for you and go with it.

  » Plug in answer choices and eliminate wrong answers.

2) Get to bed early, making sure you get 8–10 hours of sleep.

3) Eat a good dinner consisting of healthy brain foods and no junk food.

4) Create a checklist of things you need for the test and have them ready before you go to bed.

5) Have the address, directions, and trip to the testing site mapped out.

6) Wake up at least an hour before you have to leave for the test.

7) Eat a good breakfast consisting of healthy foods, such as eggs, berries, and toast.

8) Go through your morning routine and then sit quietly for five minutes doing Deep Breath Resets while visualizing yourself taking the test and successfully answering problems.

9) Just before the test, remember that you have done everything that you could have done to prepare, and you are now ready.

SAT: Full Timed Practice

Congratulations. You've made it to Chapter 20 equipped with a new growth mindset and a veritable utility belt of new skills and strategies for crushing the test. Take a moment and feel proud of this accomplishment—it is no easy feat to make it through this gauntlet of SAT prep, challenges, and personal growth. The final step you must take is the biggest. You have prepared in chunks, built up your stamina with short, targeted instruction and eventual full timed sections, and now it is time to put it all together.

For this chapter, you will be provided with some vocabulary and then prompted to complete a full SAT. You will complete the Reading Test, the Writing and Language Test, the Math Test, and finally the SAT essay. To solidify your confidence in your own test-taking ability, you have to complete one full SAT just as you will on test day.

Mindset Tip

You've almost made it. With this full SAT practice test, you will have completed enough practice, mindset training, and strategy learning to fully transform as a learner, thinker, and student. Before you embark on this final leg, reflect on your journey. How have you changed? Where did you begin and where are you now? In what ways have you expanded your goals?

Vocabulary Words 286–300

286) **disenfranchise** (v). to deprive a person of the right to vote or other rights of citizenship: *The unscrupulous election committee did all they could to disenfranchise minorities.*

287) **exalt** (v). to raise up; to elevate; to praise: *The priest encouraged the congregation to pray and exalt the glory of God.*

288) **abolition** (n). the legal ending of slavery; elimination, ending: *The abolition of slavery was a major triumph for African Americans.*

289) **quell** (v). suppress, subdue, defeat: *The mother tried to quell her daughter's fear of the dark by singing her a lullaby.*

290) **zealot** (n). an overly enthusiastic person; a fanatic: *The musical zealot devoted his whole life to completing his symphonic masterpiece.*

291) **incite** (v). to stimulate, to cause: *Political activists were trying to incite a riot against the unfair government.*

292) **authoritative** (adj). a) self-confident, influential, and commanding: *The sea captain led his men with such an authoritative air that no one ever thought to question his decisions;* b) accurate, trustworthy, and reliable: *The experiment yielded authoritative information.*

293) **patriarchal** (adj). dominated, ruled by men: *Patriarchal societies deny women many rights.*

294) **ratify** (v). to approve or endorse: *It was expected that Congress would ratify the new minimum wage proposal.*

295) **doctrine** (n). a principle or policy that is taught or followed; something that is taught; teachings, collectively: *A major doctrine of Christianity is the belief in Heaven and Hell.*

296) **volition** (n). a) the act of willing, choosing; b) made by one's will: *Of his own volition, the man confessed the crime.*

297) **inalienable** (adj). something that cannot be taken away: *Freedom is an inalienable right that any enlightened society must grant its citizens.*

298) **innovative** (adj). new and original; state of the art; groundbreaking: *The light bulb was an innovative invention that revolutionized all aspects of society.*

299) **remuneration** (n). the act of paying for goods/services: *The remuneration offered by the sports organization for Tanya's time and effort in promoting their games was more than adequate.*

300) **detrimental** (adj). harmful; damaging: *Smoking is detrimental to your health.*

Latin and Greek Roots 106–110

106) THE/THEO: god (theory, atheist, polytheistic, apotheosis)

107) TRACT: drag, control (intractable, tractable, tractor, retract, attract, detract)

108) TRANS: across (transient, transitory, transcendent, transgress)

109) VAC/VACU: empty (vacancy, vacation, vacuous, vacuum, evacuation)

110) VOC/VOK/VOL: call, wish (voluntary, evoke, invoke, irrevocable, volition)

TIMED COLLEGE BOARD PRACTICE

Complete the following College Board practice from College Board's *The Official SAT Study Guide* or online at www.collegeboard.org. Review answers after completing.

Complete all of Test 8

Final Thoughts

The true purpose of this book is to help you unleash your potential so that you become a person who is capable of achieving any goal you desire. When you walk into that test site, feel the unshakable confidence that the growth mindset approach has instilled within you. Crushing the SAT is only the beginning, though. As your new mindset becomes permanent, you will realize that you already have within you all you need to overcome whatever obstacles stand in the way of you and your dreams. The SAT is a stepping stone on the path to those dreams, and the way that you have approached the test is the same way you should approach other aspects of your life. As you study for your first college exam, answer questions about yourself during your first real interview, or prepare to give that big presentation to your first prospective client, recall the lessons you learned in this book and the mental habits you've formed. They will serve as your guides as you continue to your next adventure or challenge—and continue on you should.

Do not let the SAT be your pinnacle. After you crush this test, don't stop. Growth mindset is about accomplishing present goals to achieve future goals that are more ambitious; it is about always striving to move the needle a little bit more. With this approach to life and learning, success itself is no longer a destination, but a way of life, a state of being, a mindset. Stay within this vibration of success. Capitalize on this success-bearing mindset by always saying yes to new opportunities for growth and never being content with the safe and the average. Then, get ready for the awesome future that opens up before you. You are much more than you think you are, and capable of much more than you believe. In the words of Carol Dweck: "Test scores and measures of achievement tell you where a student is but they don't tell you where a student can end up." Where you end up is entirely up to you.

Latin and Greek Roots

A: without
AB: off, away from, apart
AC/ACR: sharp, bitter
AD: toward, near
AL/ALI/ALTER: other, another
AM/EM: love
AMB: both, more than one
ANIM: life, mind, soul, spirit
ANTHRO: man, human
ANTI: against
APT/EPT: skill, ability
ARCH/CRACY: governing body, leader, chief
AUTO: self
BELL: war
BEN: good
BI: two, twice
COGN: to know
COSM: world
CARD/CORD/COUR: heart
CAST/CHAST: cut
CENTR: center
CERN/CERT/CRET/CRIT/CRIM: to judge, separate, distinguish, decide
CHRON/TEMPOR: time
CIRCU: around, on all sides
CLA/CLO/CLU: closed off from
CO/COM/CON: together
CRED: belief or trust
CULP: blame, guilt
DIA/TRANS: across, through
DIS: not, away from
DIC/DICT: speak, proclaim
DEMOS/DEM: people
DOC/DIDA: to teach
DOL: pain
DUPL: double
DUR: hard, stubborn

EQU: even, equal
ERR: to wander
EX: not, out, outside
EXTRA: beyond
EU: good, positive
FIN: end
FORT: strong, advantageous
FRAG/FRACT: to break
FRATER: brother
GRAPHY: to write
GREG: herd, group
HER/HES: to stick
GRAND: big
ID: one's own
IN/IM: inside/not
JUS/JUD: law
LEV: light, rise
LIBER/LIVER: free
LITERA: letter
LONG: long
LU/PHOS/PHOT: light
LOC/LOG/LOQU: word, speech
MAG/MAJ/MAX: big
MAL: bad, ill, evil
MAN: hand
MATER/MATR: mother, woman
MEM/MEMOR: memory
META: change
METER: measure
MISS/MIT: to let go, send
MOLL: soft
MON/MONIT: to warn, scold
MON/MONO: one
MOR/MORT: death
MORPH: shape
MUT: change
NAT/NAI/NAS: birth
NOC/NEC/NOX: death, harm

NOM/NYM: name
NOV/NEO: new
NUMER: number
OLOGY: the study of
OMNI/PAN: all
OPT: choose
PAC/PEAC/PLAC: peace, to please
PAR: equal
PARA: beside or near
PAS/PATH: feeling, disease
PATER/PATR: father
PEN/PUNI: punish/pay
PHIL: love
PHON/SON/TON: sound
POLI: city
POV/PAU: poor
POLY: many
PORT: carry
PREHEND: grasp
PRO: a lot, for
QUER/QUES: ask/seek
QUI: quiet
SCI: know
SE/DIV: apart
SENS/SENT: feel, take notice
SOL: sun
SPEC/SPIC: look, see
STA/SED: to be in one place/ unmoving
SUA: smooth
SUB/SUP: below
SUPER/SUR: above
THE/THEO: god
TRACT: drag, control
TRANS: across
VAC/VACU: empty
VOC/VOK/VOL: call, wish

Index of Vocabulary Words

Useful Math Equations

Order of Operations

Parentheses → Exponents → Multiplication/
Division → Addition/Subtraction

Translating Words into Math

+   Sum, plus, together, more than, total, combined, added to
−   Difference, minus, less than, fewer than
×   Product, times, twice, double, of
÷   Quotient, divided by, per, out of, ratio
=   Equals, is, same as

Distributive Property

$a(b+c) = ab + ac$

Slope

Slope = m = Rate of Change = $\dfrac{y_2 - y_1}{x_2 - x_1}$ or $\dfrac{y_1 - y_2}{x_1 - x_2}$

Slope Intercept Form

$y = mx + b$

The m is the slope and is always multiplied by a variable.

The b is the y-intercept, also called the constant, and has no variable.

Slope on a Graph

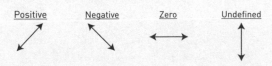

Positive   Negative   Zero   Undefined

Definition of Proportions

$$\frac{a}{b} = \frac{c}{d}$$

Percent Increase/Decrease

$$\frac{\text{Amount of Increase/Decrease}}{\text{Original Amount}} \times 100$$

Mean/Average

$$\frac{\text{sum of items}}{\text{number of items}}$$

Coordinate Plane

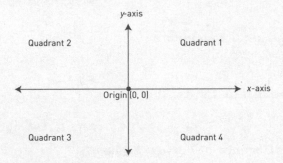

Common Conversion Factors

1 foot = 12 inches

1 meter = 100 centimeters

1 kilometer = 1,000 meters

1 hour = 60 minutes

1 day = 24 hours

1 year = 365 days

Probability

$$\frac{\text{Number of items you want}}{\text{Total number selecting from}}$$

Exponential Growth and Decay

Growth: Total = Initial$(1 + \text{rate})^{\text{time}}$

Decay: Total = Initial$(1 - \text{rate})^{\text{time}}$

Exponent Rules

Rule	Example
$a^m \times a^n = a^{m+n}$	$x^4 \times x^2 = x^6$
$(a^m)^n = a^{mn}$	$(x^4)^2 = x^8$
$(ab)^m = a^m b^m$	$(2x)^2 = 4x^2$
$\dfrac{a^m}{a^n} = a^{m-n}$	$\dfrac{x^6}{x^3} = x^3$
$\left(\dfrac{a}{b}\right)^m = \dfrac{a^m}{b^m}$	$\left(\dfrac{2}{3}\right)^2 = \dfrac{4}{9}$
$a^0 = 1$	$3^0 = 1$

Rational Exponents

$a^{\frac{1}{n}} = \sqrt[n]{a}$

Quadratic Expression

$ax^2 + bx + c.$

Difference of Perfect Squares

$a^2 - b^2 = (a+b)(a-b)$

Quadratic Formula

$x = \dfrac{-b \pm \sqrt{b^2 - 4ac}}{2a}$

Basic Square Roots

$\sqrt{1} = 1$	$\sqrt{4} = 2$
$\sqrt{25} = 5$	$\sqrt{36} = 6$
$\sqrt{81} = 9$	$\sqrt{100} = 10$
$\sqrt{9} = 3$	$\sqrt{16} = 4$
$\sqrt{49} = 7$	$\sqrt{64} = 8$
$\sqrt{121} = 11$	$\sqrt{144} = 12$

Parabola Transformation Rules

$-f(x) \rightarrow$ Reflection About the x-axis

$f(x) + k \rightarrow$ Vertical Shift

$f(x) + k \rightarrow$ Vertical Shift

Quadratic Function: Vertex Form

$f(x) = a(x - h)^2 + k$

Quadratic Function: Standard Form

$f(x) = ax^2 + bx + c$

Quadratic Function: Factored Form

$f(x) = (x - r^1)(x + r^2)$

Identify Vertex

$\dfrac{-b}{2a}$

Discriminant

$b^2 - 4ac$

Pythagorean Theorem

$a^2 + b^2 = c^2$

45-45-90 Triangle

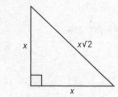

30-60-90 Triangle

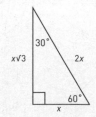

Similar Triangles

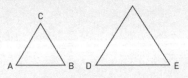

Since the two triangles above are similar, their corresponding angles are equal.

$$\angle A = \angle D$$

$$\angle B = \angle E$$

$$\angle C = \angle F$$

$$\frac{AC}{DF} = \frac{BC}{EF} = \frac{AB}{DE}$$

Parts of a Circle

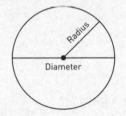

Circumference

$C = 2\pi r$

Area of a Circle

$A = \pi r^2$

Angles of a Circle

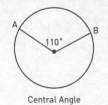 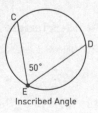

Central Angle   Inscribed Angle

Angle Definitions

Complementary angles: Two angles are complementary if their sum is 90°. Together they form a right angle and are commonly used in right triangles.

Supplementary angles: Two angles are supplementary if they add up to 180°. When combined, the two angles will form a straight line, as shown below.

Arc Length

$$\text{Arc Length} = \frac{n°}{360} \times 2\pi r$$

Equation of a Circle

$(x - h)^2 + (y - k)^2 = r^2$

Equation of a Circle in General Form

$ax^2 + by^2 + cx + dy + e = 0$

Trig Ratios

$$\sin A = \frac{\text{opposite}}{\text{hypotenuse}}$$

$$\cos A = \frac{\text{adjacent}}{\text{hypotenuse}}$$

$$\tan A = \frac{\text{opposite}}{\text{adjacent}}$$

Trig Ratios example

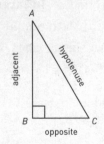

Volume of a Cylinder

$V = \pi r^2 h$

Notes

1 Blackwell, L. S., K. H. Trzesniewski, and C. S. Dweck. "Implicit Theories of Intelligence Predict Achievement Across an Adolescent Transition: A Longitudinal Study and an Intervention." *Child Development* 78, no. 1 (January/February 2007): 246–263. doi:10.1111/j.1467-8624.2007.00995.x.

2 Maguire, E. A., D. G. Gadian, I. S. Johnsrude, C. D. Good, J. Ashburner, R. S. J. Frackowiak, and C. D. Frith. "Navigation-Related Structural Change in the Hippocampi of Taxi Drivers." *Proceedings of the National Academy of Sciences of the United States of America* 97, no. 8 (April 14, 2000): 4398–4403. doi:10.1073/pnas.070039597.

3 Restak, R. M. *Mozart's Brain and the Fighter Pilot: Unleashing Your Brain's Potential.* New York: Harmony Books, 2001.

4 Ibid.

5 Ibid.

6 Fredrickson, B. L., and C. Branigan. "Positive Emotions Broaden the Scope of Attention and Thought-Action Repertoires." *Cognition & Emotion* 19, no. 3 (May 1, 2005): 313–332. doi:10.1080/02699930441000238.

7 Chen, L., S. R. Bae, C. Battista, S. Qin, T. Chen, T. M. Evans, and V. Menon. "Positive Attitude Toward Math Supports Early Academic Success: Behavioral Evidence and Neurocognitive Mechanisms." *Psychological Science* 29, no. 3 (March 2018): 390–402. doi:10.1177/0956797617735528.

8 Frank, R. "Billionaire Sara Blakely Says Secret to Success Is Failure." *CNBC.* October 16, 2013. https://www.cnbc.com/2013/10/16/billionaire-sara-blakely-says-secret-to-success-is-failure.html.

9 Moser, J. S., H. S. Schroder, C. Heeter, T. P. Moran, and Y. H. Lee. "Mind Your Errors." *Psychological Science* 22, no. 12 (December 2011): 1484–1489. doi:10.1177/0956797611419520.

10 Vogel, S., and L. Schwabe. "Learning and Memory Under Stress: Implications for the Classroom." *npj Science of Learning* 1, no. 16011 (June 29, 2016). doi:10.1038/npjscilearn.2016.11.

11 Bhajan, Y. *The Aquarian Teacher: International Kundalini Yoga Teacher Training, Level 1 Instructor*. Santa Cruz: Kundalini Research Institute, 2013.

12 Chomsky, Noam. *Knowledge of Language: Its Nature, Origin, and Use*. New York: Praeger, 1986.

13 Schmidt, E. "This Is Your Brain on Sugar: UCLA Study Shows High-Fructose Diet Sabotages Learning, Memory." *UCLA Newsroom*. May 15, 2012. http://newsroom.ucla.edu/releases/this-is-your-brain-on-sugar-ucla-233992.

14 Wilson, M. M., and J. E. Morley. "Impaired Cognitive Function and Mental Performance in Mild Dehydration." *European Journal of Clinical Nutrition* 57, no. S2 (December 2003): S24–S29. doi:10.1038/sj.ejcn.1601898.

15 Schmidt, E. "This Is Your Brain on Sugar: UCLA Study Shows High-Fructose Diet Sabotages Learning, Memory." *UCLA Newsroom*. May 15, 2012. http://newsroom.ucla.edu/releases/this-is-your-brain-on-sugar-ucla-233992.

16 Muldoon, M. F., C. M. Ryan, J. K. Yao, S. M. Conklin, and S. B. Manuck. "Long-Chain Omega-3 Fatty Acids and Optimization of Cognitive Performance." *Military Medicine* 179, no. 11S (November 2014): 95-105. doi:10.7205/milmed-d-14-00168.

17 Subash, S., M. M. Essa, S. Al-Adawi, M. A. Memon, T. Manivasagam, and M. Akbar. "Neuroprotective Effects of Berry Fruits on Neurodegenerative Diseases." *Neural Regeneration Research* 9, no. 16 (August 15, 2014): 1557–1566. doi:10.4103/1673-5374.139483.

18 Whyte, A. R., G. Schafer, and C. M. Williams. "The Effect of Cognitive Demand on Performance of an Executive Function Task Following Wild Blueberry Supplementation in 7 to 10 Years Old Children." *Food & Function* 8, no. 11 (November 15, 2017): 4129–4138. doi:10.1039/c7fo00832e.

19 Mercola, J. "Turmeric Compound Boosts Regeneration of Brain Stem Cells, and More." Mercola. October 13, 2014. https://articles.mercola.com/sites/articles/archive/2014/10/13/turmeric-curcumin.aspx.

Acknowledgments

This book would not have been possible without the help of our families, friends, colleagues, and students. Stephen would like to thank his parents Alfred and Denise for their editing, keen judgment, and unwavering support, and his sister Alexandra for her encouragement and guidance. Paul would like to thank his parents, Paul and Terry, and his sister Rachel, for all their support and guidance throughout the years. Special thanks goes to Paul's wife Katie and his children Riley and Bryce—without their encouragement and inspiration, he could never have written this book.

We would also like to thank all of the Pompton Lakes students who served as our focus group, giving invaluable suggestions throughout the writing process. These students include Lauren Sanford, Miranda Smith, Adem Nadzak, Samantha Lorenc, Steven Sanders, Kyle Shafer, Drew Flynn, Alie Capobianco, and Jessica Kellenbach. Lastly, we would like to thank the teachers and administration of Pompton Lakes High School for their support and friendship. Special thanks to Vincent Przybylinski, Anthony Mattera, and Mike Riordan for their encouragement and support over the years, and Mike Yuhas and Mike Cemelli for reviewing the math content.

About the Authors

Stephen Tarsitano is a high school English teacher, tutor, and supervisor who specializes in helping students and teachers develop a positive self-image and realize their true potential. He graduated from Muhlenberg College with a bachelor's degree in English and received his Master's of Educational Leadership from The College of New Jersey. He later earned his administrative certifications from Caldwell College. Stephen started his teaching career with Kaplan Test Prep, eventually transitioning to public education at Pompton Lakes High School. At PLHS, he teaches AP Literature and Composition as well as SAT Prep, and serves as the Supervisor of English and World Languages. Outside of school, Stephen is the cofounder of Zen Test Prep, a tutoring company devoted to expanding students' minds and fostering a love of learning within them. He is also a musician, writing original music for an indie rock band, and a Kundalini yoga teacher, leading yoga and meditation workshops. Stephen continually seeks to infuse his teaching with the mindfulness training he practices, while also cultivating within his students an approach to life that will help them achieve both happiness and success. He currently resides in Morristown, New Jersey.

Paul Koontz is a high school math teacher and football coach who specializes in motivating and helping students achieve their goals. Having studied the habits and practices of successful people in all fields, he has applied this knowledge to helping kids of all ages and ability levels find success. From winning state championships to gaining acceptance to top universities, students reap many rewards from Paul's guidance. A graduate of Fairleigh Dickinson University in Madison, New Jersey, Paul holds a bachelor's degree in mathematics and a master's degree in education. At Pompton Lakes High School, he has taught all topics in math, ranging from Algebra I and Basic Skills Prep to Honors Calculus. As a high school football coach, Paul has been the leader of one of the best defensive units in North Jersey for the past eight years. Outside of school, Paul is the cofounder of Zen Test Prep, a tutoring company that works with students of all ages, from elementary school to college. A resident of Madison, New Jersey, Paul is married to Katie; they have two small children together, Riley and Bryce. While not helping others chase their dreams, Paul likes to chase a small white ball on the golf course.

For additional tips, strategies, and inspiration, check us out at ZenTestPrep.org and GrowthMindsetU.com.